THE D.L.I. AT WAR

FOREWORD

By FIELD-MARSHAL VISCOUNT MONTGOMERY OF ALAMEIN, K.G.,
G.C.B., D.S.O.

THIS book tells the story of the part played by the Durham Light Infantry in the Second World War. Of all the infantry Regiments in the British Army, it was the one most closely associated with myself during the war. The D.L.I. Brigade fought under my command from Alamein to Germany; it was only away from me during the time I spent in Italy from September to December 1943, and that was because it had gone back to England to take part in the invasion of Normandy.

It is therefore easy to realise why I have such a great affection for the battalions of the Regiment. It is a magnificent Regiment, steady as a rock in battle, and absolutely reliable on all occasions. The fighting men of Durham are splendid soldiers; they excel in the hard fought battle and they always " stick it out to the end "; they have gained their objectives and held their positions even when all their officers have been killed and conditions were almost unendurable.

When I think back on their battles during the war I would name two occasions which stand out as worthy examples of the determination and bravery which are typical of the Durham man.

The first one is the action of the D.L.I. Brigade at the WADI ZIGZAOU during the MARETH Battle in March 1943.

The second is the action of the Brigade at the PRIMOSOLE BRIDGE in Sicily in July 1943.

The Durham Light Infantry have many fine achievements to their credit, but from my own personal knowledge I would select these two as being outstanding; both are fully described in the book.

I hope this story will be read by thousands in the north of England. Those who read it will learn with pride what the men of the Durham Light Infantry did in the fight for freedom during the years from 1940 to 1945, and they must not fail to tell the story to their children.

Montgomery of Alamein.

Field-Marshal.

INTRODUCTION

By THE COLONEL OF THE REGIMENT, LIEUT-GENERAL SIR TERENCE AIREY, K.C.M.G., C.B., C.B.E.

The end of a great war brings with it the pressing need to set down an historical record before memories grow dim and inaccurate with the passage of time and before the leading figures disappear, as inevitably they must, from the scene. We shall all be grateful to Brigadier J. A. Churchill, then Colonel of the Durham Light Infantry, whose foresight and enthusiasm set on foot the project for a history of our Regiment in the Second World War.

Major Rissik is well qualified to write this history and he has given us a vivid account of the vicissitudes of the Regiment throughout six years of war and in every theatre of it. For two centuries the Durham Light Infantry has gone about its task of settling accounts with the enemies of Britain, quietly, efficiently and always with examples of great individual gallantry. This new story cannot but stir the hearts of all of us.

There can never have been a Regiment with a closer and more affectionate connection with its home county than ours, nor a county which has backed up its Regiment more faithfully, or given more soldiers to the army, than has Durham. The names of some 12,000 men of the Durham Light Infantry, killed in the two great wars of our time, bear witness to this in the memorial books in Durham Cathedral. The history which has now been written will therefore be of poignant interest particularly to the people of Durham. But the Regiment does not recruit only from Durham, nor do all Durham men serve with us, so the book will also meet a wider interest.

It is indeed time that these events were recorded for they are now slipping back into the realms of military history and we have already had a battalion fighting a new war in Korea for nearly a year. The story of the Durham Light Infantry in the Second World War is one that must inspire us all to maintain in the future that high standard of professional efficiency and individual quality which our Regiment has always demanded.

Terence Airey

Lieut.-General.

AUTHOR'S PREFACE

It has been a privilege to write the story of the Durham Light Infantry during the arduous years of the late war; and considerable research has been necessary among files, War Diaries, letters and many other documents in order to complete it. Many members of the Regiment, too, have provided me with their own recollections of what occurred on specific occasions and without their help the tale could not in many cases have been adequately told.

Nevertheless, this story deals not only with the eight battalions of the Regiment who were in contact with the enemy but also with those others who served at home and did not go abroad. It is now more than six years, in some cases ten, since many of the deeds recounted took place; and it is perhaps natural that in some instances memories should now be blurred and that there should be gaps in the story which are difficult to fill. Some parts of this chronicle, therefore, are inevitably not as comprehensive as others: where in one case there is plenty to embellish the purely military narrative, in another there is little but the bare bones of the story. The greatest care has, however, been taken to ensure the accuracy of the narrative; and whenever a particular battalion has been mentioned the manuscript has been submitted for checking either to the Commanding Officer at the time or to another member of long standing in that battalion.

Space does not allow me to mention individually all who have made a contribution to this book. I thank them all warmly none the less for that. But I owe a special debt of gratitude to the following members of the Regiment whose care and patience have either provided material or produced invaluable suggestions and criticism, and without whose help this book could not have been completed: Lieutenant-General Sir Terence Airey K.C.M.G., C.B., C.B.E., (Colonel of the Regiment) Brigadier J. A. Churchill, C.B.E., D.S.O., M.C., Brigadier F. W. Sandars, D.S.O., Brigadier C. D. Marley, D.S.O., T.D., Brigadier P. Kirkup, D.S.O., O.B.E., M.C., T.D.,

Colonel W. I. Watson, T.D., Lieutenant-Colonel R. B. Y. Simpson, D.S.O., Lieutenant-Colonel H. McBain, O.B.E., M.C., Lieutenant-Colonel C. R. Battiscombe, Lieutenant-Colonel P. H. M. May, D.S.O., M.C., Lieutenant-Colonel W. H. Lowe, O.B.E., Lieutenant-Colonel C. D. Hamilton, D.S.O., Lieutenant-Colonel W. M. F. Vane, T.D., M.P., Major J. R. Cousens, M.B.E., Major C. Fanning Evans, Major E. Browne, M.B.E., Major J. W. Kelly, Captain J. G. McKenzie and Captain Wilfred Miles, one of the official historians of the First World War.

I am further indebted to Major-General Sir Howard Kippenberger, K.B.E., C.B., D.S.O., E.D., for details of the war record of the Canterbury Regiment and the Nelson-Marlborough-West Coast Regiment of New Zealand; to Major J. W. Houlden of the Winnipeg Light Infantry of Canada for particulars of service of that Regiment; and to the Imperial War Museum for permission to reproduce certain official photographs.

I also wish to offer my most grateful thanks to my cousin, Miss Bernys Rissik, who drew the maps; to all those who have kindly lent photographs for reproduction; and to Mrs. S. M. Liddall and Miss D. A. Robertson who have so patiently undertaken the arduous task of typing and re-typing the manuscript.

D.R.

Birchens Spring
Beaconsfield.
December, 1952

CONTENTS

Page

FOREWORD by Field-Marshal Viscount Montgomery of Alamein, K.G., G.C.B., D.S.O. ... v - vi

Introduction ... ... vii - viii

Author's Preface ... ... ix - x

CHAPTER ONE
FRANCE 1939-1940

1. 1939 1
2. The 2nd Battalion in Flanders 9
3. 151 Brigade in Northern France 21
4. The 10th and 11th Battalions in the retreat to Dunkirk 35

CHAPTER TWO
THE FIRST BATTALION IN THE MIDDLE EAST 1940-1943

1. The Western Desert and Syria 46
2. Tobruk 60
3. Malta 70

CHAPTER THREE
THE TENTH AND ELEVENTH BATTALIONS IN ICELAND 1940-1941   75

CHAPTER FOUR
151 BRIGADE IN THE MIDDLE EAST AND SICILY 1941-1943

1. Cyprus and Iraq 82
2. Gazala 84
3. Alamein to Mareth 98
4. Sicily 118

CHAPTER FIVE

THE SIXTEENTH BATTALION IN NORTH AFRICA, ITALY AND GREECE 1942-1945

		Page
1.	Tunisia	133
2.	Italy	142
3.	Greece	156

CHAPTER SIX

THE SECOND BATTALION IN INDIA AND BURMA 1942-1945

1.	India	161
2.	The Arakan	168
3.	Kohima	182
4.	From the Chindwin to Rangoon	199

CHAPTER SEVEN

THE FIRST BATTALION IN THE MEDITERRANEAN 1943-1945

1.	Cos	209
2.	Italy	218

CHAPTER EIGHT

THE DURHAM LIGHT INFANTRY IN NORTH-WEST EUROPE 1944-1945

1.	151 Brigade in France	237
2.	The 10th and 11th Battalions in Normandy	255
3.	151 Brigade in the Low Countries	269
4.	The 9th Battalion from the Waal to the Elbe	286

CHAPTER NINE

THE FIFTH AND SEVENTH BATTALIONS

1.	The 112th Light Anti-Aircraft Regiment	301
2.	The 54th Searchlight Regiment	305
3.	The 113th Light Anti-Aircraft Regiment	307

CONTENTS

Chapter Ten
THE DURHAM LIGHT INFANTRY IN HOME FORCES

		Page
1.	The 14th, 15th and 17th Battalions	313
2.	The Home Defence Battalions	320
3.	The 70th (Young Soldier) Battalion	324
4.	The Depot	329
	Postscript	335
	Appendix: The Allied Regiments	336
	Index	343

MAPS

Fig.		Page
1.	The 2nd Battalion on the River Dyle, May 1940	11
2.	North-west France (Arras inset)	facing 44
3.	Tobruk	63
4.	North Africa (Mareth inset)	facing 118
5.	Sicily	121
6.	Primosole Bridge	126
7.	Tunisia	136
8.	Italy (Gemmano and Upper Garigliano inset)	facing 154
9.	Greece—The Piraeus	158
10.	Burma	164
11.	The Arakan	166
12.	The Donbaik Front	170
13.	The Chaung north of Donbaik	172
14.	Kohima	187
15.	Cos	210
16.	North-east Italy	facing 236
17.	Normandy	240
18.	The Battle of Gheel	272
19.	The Low Countries	281
20.	North-west Germany (Sittard-Maesyck-Roermond inset)	facing 300

LIST OF ILLUSTRATIONS

Facing Page

1. Battalion Headquarters 2 D.L.I. Berçu, France, March 1940 .. .. } 32
2. Sergeants' Mess 2 D.L.I. Berçu, France, March 1940

3. 'B' Company 2 D.L.I. working on fortifications, France 1940 .. .. } 33
4. Lieut. R. W. Annand V.C. .. .. ..

5. Battalion Headquarters 1 D.L.I. Mersa Matruh, November 1940.. .. ..
6. 1 D.L.I. preparing positions in 'C' Sector, Mersa Matruh, November 1940 .. .. .. } 48

7. The Prime Minister, Mr. Winston Churchill, inspects 10 D.L.I. in Iceland .. .. } 49
8. Men of 11 D.L.I. on cliff-scaling exercises in Iceland

9. The grave of Private Adam Wakenshaw V.C. after the battle, and the gun he manned .. .. } 112
10. Private Adam Wakenshaw V.C. .. .. ..

11. Men of 151 Bde. re-enact the crossing of the anti-tank ditch, Mareth .. ..
12. Men of 6 D.L.I. on board H.M.T. "Winchester Castle" en route for Sicily .. .. .. } 113

13. The Commander of the Napoli Division after capture by 6 D.L.I. in Sicily .. .. } 128
14. Primosole Bridge .. .. -

15. 9 D.L.I. enter Catania .. ..
16. Men of 16 D.L.I. crossing the Volturno .. } 129

xv

LIST OF ILLUSTRATIONS

Facing Page

17. Men of 16 D.L.I. after crossing the Cosina River, Italy .. .. } 192
18. The Arakan foot-hills near Maungdaw looking towards the Mayu Range .. .. ..

19. Kohima, April 1944.. .. .. } 193
20. "Kuki's Piquet" from "Garrison Hill".. ..

21. 'A' Company 2 D.L.I. link up with troops of 5 Ind. Div. on the Kohima-Imphal Road .. } 208
22. Men of 2 D.L.I. on Pagoda Hill, Yzagyo ..

23. A patrol of 1 D.L.I. near Citta di Castillo, Italy .. } 209
24. Mortars of 1 D.L.I. in action, July 1944 ..

25. A patrol of 'B' Company 1 D.L.I. moves off, July 1944 .. .. } 256
26. Little Spaduro .. ..

27. A Regimental Aid Post during the battle for Lingèvres .. .. } 257
28. Dead cattle in the fields near Fontenay-le-Pesnel ..

29. Men of 11 D.L.I. coming out of the line near Fontenay-le-Pesnel .. .. } 272
30. 9 D.L.I. before the attack on St. Joost .. ..

31. Lt.-Col. John Mogg arranging safe passage for General Wolz's surrender party near Hamburg } 273
32. The Durham Light Infantry Memorial Garden, Durham City .. ..

CHAPTER ONE

France 1939-1940

I

1939

SIR John Moore may justly be called the Father of the Light Infantry. The humanised and liberalised philosophy of military training which he instituted into the British Army produced the soldiers who, in his own time, defeated all Napoleon's Marshals sent against them and, in the end, defeated Napoleon himself. "John Moore's tradition," wrote Mr. Arthur Bryant,[1] "though often neglected and obscured, survived in two great branches of the Army—the Rifles and the Light Infantry. Widely applied in 1914 and still more in the great years after 1940, it enabled men untrained to war to become superb soldiers and to defeat the finest veterans of the Continent. Their victories are now as much part of history as Waterloo and Agincourt. Though wars pass, the British soldier remains. His weapons and uniform may be changed, his tactics superseded, his body threatened with death and mutilation by new, though not more fearful weapons, but the factor of his spirit is constant."

This is the story of how one Regiment of Light Infantry inherited that tradition and maintained that spirit in the grim and glorious years of the Second World War. There was hardly a campaign in which they did not fight, hardly a theatre of operations in which at least one battalion of the Regiment was not represented. Wherever the battle raged hottest there they would be found, faithful to a fighting tradition of nigh on two hundred years.

The Faithful Durhams, to give them their nickname—a nickname won as a result of their services in the Caribbean in

[1] "The History of Light Infantry"—*Illustrated London News*, 20th Nov. 1948, p. 562.

1764—were raised in 1756 as a second battalion to the 23rd Royal Welch Fusiliers, becoming a separate Regiment two years later as the 68th Foot. Their first Colonel was John Lambton, grandfather of the first Earl of Durham. In 1783 they were described in the Army List as Durham for the first time, as most of their men were recruited from that County; but it was not till 1808, some fifty years after their birth, that they became Light Infantry as the 68th Light Infantry; and Light Infantry they have been ever since.

In 1881 the organisation of the Army was changed and the old regimental numbers of the infantry of the line were abolished. The 68th Light Infantry became the 1st Battalion, The Durham Light Infantry, and the 2nd was formed by the 106th Bombay European Light Infantry, originally raised for service in India by the British East India Company, but linked with the 68th since 1873 for recruiting purposes by their Depot at Sunderland. Both Battalions had given distinguished service before their union in one Regiment, the one in the Peninsular and Crimean wars, the other in India and Persia, of which the present Regiment's battle honours provide striking testimony.

The territorial basis of the Regiment has always been strong. Indeed the old Durham Militia can be traced back to a date earlier than the foundation of the Regular Regiment itself. In 1685 records show " 885 foot soldiers commanded by Sir Ralph Cole Bart. of Brancepeth Castle," and in 1759 " Earl of Darlington Colonel with Headquarters at Barnard Castle." In 1853 there were two Regiments of Militia and a few years later the 1st became the 1st Durham Fusiliers, losing this title in 1881 when the two Battalions were renumbered the 3rd and 4th Durham Light Infantry. Both subsequently fought in the South African war of 1899-1902; then in 1908 the 3rd became the 4th and the 4th the 3rd and, as Special Reserve Battalions, both were more closely linked with the Regular Battalions; but during the 1914 war each became a training battalion and after it went into suspended animation.

It is, however, upon the foundation of the old Volunteer Companies that the modern Territorial Battalions came to be built. With the Napoleonic Wars came the birth of many Volunteer legions; indeed their formation at that time was fairly general. 1794 saw the foundation of the loyal Sunderland

Volunteers when "several young gentlemen of Sunderland, with the spirit becoming that true loyalty so amiable in every British subject, engaged a regular sergeant to teach them the use of arms." By 1798 there were, amongst others, a Gateshead and a Darlington Volunteer Company; but after 1815 the Volunteers were disbanded when the danger of invasion passed away. It was not till 1859, after the Crimean War, that there was a general revival of the Volunteer movement, and this it is which marks the real foundation of the Territorial Army of to-day. By 1861 there were nine companies of Durham Rifle Volunteers; and in 1863 rifle green was adopted for uniform. This was later changed to scarlet with green facings, the colours of the County Regiment, save in the 6th Battalion which retains the green to this very day.

In 1908 four Durham battalions of the newly constituted Territorial Force—the 6th, 7th, 8th and 9th Durham Light Infantry—were brigaded together as 151 Brigade of the 50th Northumbrian Division, and a famous Brigade it has remained throughout two world wars. At the same time the 5th Battalion joined the York and Durham Brigade which formed part of that same Division. But Battalions have not always remained the same; the old Militia battalions have ceased to exist; and some of the Territorial battalions of former days have been converted into Artillery Regiments. It is not, therefore, possible within the compass of this chronicle to trace the histories nor recount the deeds of the many battalions raised by the Regiment in days gone by. Suffice it to say that thirty-seven Regular, Territorial and Service battalions saw service in the First World War and fourteen in the Second.[1] Not all were fighting battalions, but

[1] This does not include one battalion, particulars of which should perhaps be given here. This was the 18th Battalion, the Durham Light Infantry, which was formed at Geneifa in Egypt in the spring of 1943. It should not be confused with the 18th (Home Defence) Battalion referred to later in these pages.

The Battalion was formed as the basic battalion for a Beach Brick. A Beach Brick was a group of units with the operational task of landing and maintaining a force on enemy occupied territory until the normal base installations and the lines of communication organisation could take over. The Battalion was employed in this role both at Salerno, in Italy, and in the landings in Normandy. In the latter case, after landing stores in the early stages at a rate of approximately 3,000 tons a day, the Battalion ultimately moved to Boulogne where it assumed responsibility for the opening and working of the Port. It then moved to Calais, where it

those that were not provided, by drafts of reinforcements, the life blood of those actually in combat with the enemy. A large number of infantry battalions was the proud boast of many great Regiments in the war against the Kaiser, but as many as six battalions of the Durham Light Infantry fought together in France in 1940; in 1944 five stood side by side in the line at one stage of the fighting in Normandy; and the Regiment as a whole suffered over 3,000 killed throughout the course of the struggle against Germany, Italy and Japan.

The outbreak of war in September 1939 found the 1st Battalion in China and the 2nd at Woking. In Durham County itself the 6th, 8th and 9th Battalions comprised 151 Brigade of the 50th Northumbrian Division, later to become the most battle-hardened division in the British Army. The 5th and 7th Battalions, once infantry, had become Searchlight Regiments in 1936, while the 10th, 11th and 12th Battalions were in the process of formation.

The order to mobilise the Territorial Army was received during the afternoon of the 1st of September and, shortly afterwards, the order for its embodiment in the Regular Army. The rest of that day was spent in absorbing the men who were the peace-time backbone of what were destined to be some great fighting battalions. On the 2nd of September the 6th Battalion (Lieutenant-Colonel Harry Miller), 8th Battalion (Lieutenant-Colonel Angus Leybourne) and 9th Battalion (Lieutenant-Colonel W. F. Simpson), all of which were well over strength, were each divided into two battalions, their second lines becoming respectively the 10th, 11th and 12th Battalions and comprising together 70 Infantry Brigade of the 23rd Division. When the 12th Battalion—who were recruited mainly from Scotsmen on Tyneside—later became the 1st Tyneside Scottish, the responsibility for their administration and for providing reinforcements

---

operated transit camps handling 20,000 men a day; but one company, in February 1945, moved out to the defences of the Dunkirk perimeter and there helped to hold a vigorous German attack, capturing a considerable number of prisoners.

The Battalion was disbanded in August 1945 at Calais. Although it bore the Regiment's name, only two officers of the Regiment served with it and not very many N.C.Os and men. Nevertheless, it constituted a battalion of the Regiment and it is therefore right that it should be mentioned here.

passed to the Black Watch; but the original battalion was a Durham battalion and it continued to serve in the same brigade alongside its Durham brothers throughout the whole of the war.

These early days were hectic for all the Territorial Battalions. There was much to do, particularly on the administrative side, and not so very much time in which to do it. Trenches had to be dug and sandbags filled as part of air defence schemes; Quartermasters' troubles multiplied; and medical officers spent their days inspecting, inoculating and vaccinating tough-skinned miners. The Administrative Staff of one battalion had to form a National Defence Unit from veterans of the 1914 war and also an A.T.S. Company. As there was little difference between the attestation forms of men and women, at least one veteran was issued with an A.T.S. skirt.

Early in October the 50th Division concentrated in the Cotswolds. The D.L.I. Brigade, commanded by Brigadier Jackie Churchill—himself of the Regiment—was billeted in the area of Charlbury, Chipping Norton and Shipston-on-Stour. The 23rd Division remained in the north and 70 Brigade, also commanded by an officer of the Regiment, Brigadier Philip Kirkup, who was himself a Territorial, was stationed in the county itself. Thus all the Territorial Battalions remained in England for the first winter of the war: but all of them went to France in the first part of the New Year.

The 2nd Battalion was the first battalion of the Regiment to cross the Channel. Complete with Reservists, it sailed on the 25th of September as part of 6 Brigade of the 2nd Division. Together with the 1st Royal Welch Fusiliers and the 1st Royal Berkshire Regiment it served with this Brigade until the latter's break-up in Malaya in 1945. Before leaving Woking, officers and men were lectured by the Brigadier on Trench Warfare and the conducting of reliefs; this was supplemented by other lectures on the same subject by other officers who had had experience of the previous war. The Battalion landed at Cherbourg on the 26th, where it had a day hanging about waiting for a train. It then moved to Chauteney, near Sable, where it was billeted for a very pleasant week. Everyone got on very well with the French who, it was clear, had an almost pathetic belief in the invulnerability of the Maginot Line which most of them were convinced extended along the Belgian frontier to the sea. The next stop was at Arras from which the Battalion marched some twelve miles to billets near Bloiry. The country round about still showed traces of the last war and was bleak and open. ' B ' Company was billeted in a huge sugar beet farm and Major Hubert McBain, its commander, had a room in a palatial residence which was the envy of all. Water actually flowed when the plug was pulled, and though the highly polished chromium taps produced neither hot water nor cold they looked very nice.

The Battalion only spent a week here before moving up to its final concentration area on the Belgian frontier, where it was to remain until the move into Belgium the following spring. Most of the time during this extremely cold winter was spent in improving the frontier defences which were almost non-existent except for a few French pillboxes built in 1937. It was no easy task, as wet clay takes a lot of moving and cement cannot be poured with the temperature below freezing point. There were the usual visits from on high, including the French President and a number of imposing Field-Marshals; and on one occasion the C.I.G.S., the C.-in-C., the Corps, Divisional and Brigade Commanders were found walking up to one of the blockhouses in single file in order of seniority.

There were a number of changes in the Battalion itself. Major Tim Beart, the second in command, left in December to command the 8th Battalion who were just about to leave for France. Hubert McBain went to Division as D.A.Q.M.G., and early in March Major Bobby Simpson took over command of the Battalion from Lieutenant-Colonel Victor Yate, who had to return home for reasons of health. Everyone went about their routine duties as winter gave way to spring; periodic trips to the " fleshpots " of Lille helped to alleviate the monotony; and leave to England was allowed for those who had spent three months in France. The Battalion was ready for anything if anything were to happen. As it turned out, it had not long to wait.

*   *   *   *   *   *

The 50th Division began to arrive in France at the end of January and with it the D.L.I. Brigade. The Division was one of the few motorised divisions in the British Army and trained as such right up till the German attack. The route taken by the 6th, 8th and 9th Battalions followed closely that of the 2nd some six months before. Their experience of the French was mixed. The weeks of waiting were leaving their mark on French morale and British soldiers, who often in history have found the French attitude in war hard to understand because it was different from their own, began to notice a diversion of interest from the main task—defeat of the Germans—to more private affairs. At the village of St. Remy, for instance, where the 8th Battalion was billeted for a short while, fantastic claims were made by the locals for any loss or misfortune which could be blamed on the British troops. " The buxom French-woman who ran the village estaminet was disgusted with the behaviour of the Battalion, for nothing she could say or do would persuade the troops to raid her wine cellar. The previous battalion billeted in St. Remy—a hard drinking Scottish unit—carried out a lightning raid one night and lifted some hundreds of bottles which the messing officer paid for at retail prices. Madame quickly stocked her wine cellars again when the arrival of Captain Dixon and Lieutenant Pitt made it evident that another battalion was going to be billeted in St. Remy, but the opportunity of selling her stock wholesale at retail prices did not occur again, in spite of her frantic unofficial appeals to the troops to help themselves."[1]

The Brigade concentrated during February near Amiens and spent a hectic month in hard, exacting training. Brigadier Churchill was a tower of energy and enthusiasm and demanded a similar standard from all his subordinates. Battalion, Brigade and Divisional exercises followed in quick succession until, at the end of March, the Brigade moved up to the Belgian frontier near Lille to dig defences in the IInd Corps reserve line. The days of April passed uneventfully—save for a false alarm on the 11th for the move into Belgium—and April passed into May. On the 9th of May the 6th Battalion spent the day firing on the ranges, there was a Divisional Intelligence Exercise and in the evening a Divisional Boxing Tournament. General Sir Giffard Martel, himself a boxer, made a speech to a large audience after distributing the prizes. As Divisional Commander he enjoyed

[1] "The 8th Battalion The Durham Light Infantry 1939-45" by P. J. Lewis and I. R. English, p. 9.

great personal popularity with the troops. He spoke of the fine fighting spirit in the Division and said he was sure it would soon be tested on the field of battle. Of course he had no idea that the German attack was already being launched, but when the news came through the following morning the men were convinced he had known all the time.

*   *   *   *   *   *

70 Brigade was the last formation in which the Regiment was represented to arrive in France. Its position was somewhat different from those which had preceded it. The 23rd Division, of which it formed part, was the second line of the 50th, just as the 10th and 11th Battalions and the 1st Tyneside Scottish were the second line of the 6th, 8th and 9th Battalions. As such it had not received either the training or equipment to bring it up to the full standard required for an active service division. There were only two Brigades in the Division instead of three as this was the establishment for a motor division which, like the 50th, the 23rd was; battalions had only reached the stage of platoon training; there were no 3-inch mortars; there was a general shortage of training equipment; all transport was hired from civilian sources; and battalions were under strength.

The Division received its orders to move to France on the 23rd of March; and battalion advance parties were to start on the 10th of April. Its role was to help in the construction of aerodromes behind the front for a period of three to five months, during which normal training would continue; it would then return to England to complete this training and then be fully ready for active service operations. That was the plan, but it was soon to be blown sky-high by Hitler's offensive. Nevertheless, in order to carry it out, it had been decided that only the infantry battalions should go to France for these duties, together with the Sappers and certain parts of the R.A.S.C. No artillery was to accompany them.

Battalions were made up to strength towards the middle of April and moved to France through Le Havre on the 24th. After a few days in a camp near the port they moved to Nuncq, near St. Pol, and went into tented camps in orchards near the village. Of the 2,000 men in 70 Brigade, 1,400 had not yet fired a Bren gun and four hundred had not completed the war course with the rifle. Despite this lack of training they were to give a good account of themselves in the fateful days that lay ahead.

Work at the aerodrome began at once. It was organised carefully in shifts, the 10th Battalion doing the first shift and the 11th the second shift each day. Rifle companies worked for four days, then had two days' training and a day of rest, whilst the specialists, like signallers, worked for two days on the airfield and had four days at their specialist training. The equipment of the troops was little better than it had been in England, but it was adequate for the limited role that was envisaged. Each battalion had a limited amount of transport— though sufficient only for administrative requirements. Every man was armed with a rifle, but the battalions had each only fourteen Bren guns, about eight anti-tank rifles, no 3-inch and only a few 2-inch mortars. Their signal equipment did not include any wireless sets. No battalion had any Bren gun carriers. They were therefore not very well equipped to face the ordeal which was to be theirs within a fortnight of their arrival.

2

THE 2ND BATTALION IN FLANDERS

The German invasion of the Low Countries began on the 9th of May. The first indication that something was afoot was the sound of considerable air activity during the night of the 9th and early hours of the 10th. At about 11 o'clock on the night of the 9th Brigade Headquarters informed the Battalion that parachutists were reported to have landed in its area: but although patrols were sent out in all directions, nothing was discovered. During the night the bombing of Douai could clearly be heard, and the sound of a very heavy anti-aircraft barrage over Arras. By 4 o'clock in the morning the drone of aircraft had greatly increased and it was just light enough to see enemy bombers flying in formation west from Belgium. Several flew low and one in particular roared down the main road to Orchies and Douai just above the tree tops.

By breakfast time news of the invasion had been received officially and a warning order given for the move into Belgium.

This plan had been overhauled several times on the occasion of previous false alarms and so the C.O.'s conference to discuss final arrangements lasted barely half an hour.

Although the bombing of back areas could be heard, the next night was comparatively peaceful. The Battalion was not due to leave until the evening of the 11th and so preparations for the journey were unhurried and, apart from the dropping of one of the German screaming bombs nearby, uneventful.

At dusk on the 11th the Battalion moved off in troop-carrying transport into Belgium to take up positions on the River Dyle. The move was without incident; there was no bombing; the Belgians waved joyfully at the stream of vehicles; and the only casualties were a carrier and a platoon truck which fell by the wayside only to rejoin the Battalion a few days later. By the evening the whole Battalion was in position on the River Dyle with Battalion Headquarters in the village of La Tombe.

It was by no means an ideal position which the Battalion occupied. There was a frontage of about 2,000 yards to hold in front of which, along its whole length, ran the river and a railway line. Beyond the river several hundred yards of flat, open plain gave way to steeply rising hills, thickly wooded. Here the reserve company took up outpost positions, with instructions to withdraw into reserve on first contact. On the left of the battalion position the river formed a U-shaped loop and at the same place was crossed by the railway. To the right of the loop the ground was flat and open for some two hundred yards on the nearside of the railway. Thereafter it began to rise again into wooded slopes. To the left of the loop there was a secondary road which crossed both railway and river by bridges and ran straight through the position, dividing the area into approximately two equal parts. That part nearest the loop was flat and open, but on the extreme left the wooded slopes came down almost to the river bank.

The Battalion had three companies forward: 'A' on the right, 'B' guarding the area of the loop and 'D' on the left covering the bridges over the railway and river. Thus the main position was for the most part in a valley between wooded hills, and such little natural cover as existed was supplemented by a number of pillboxes and weapon pits which had already been constructed by the Belgians.

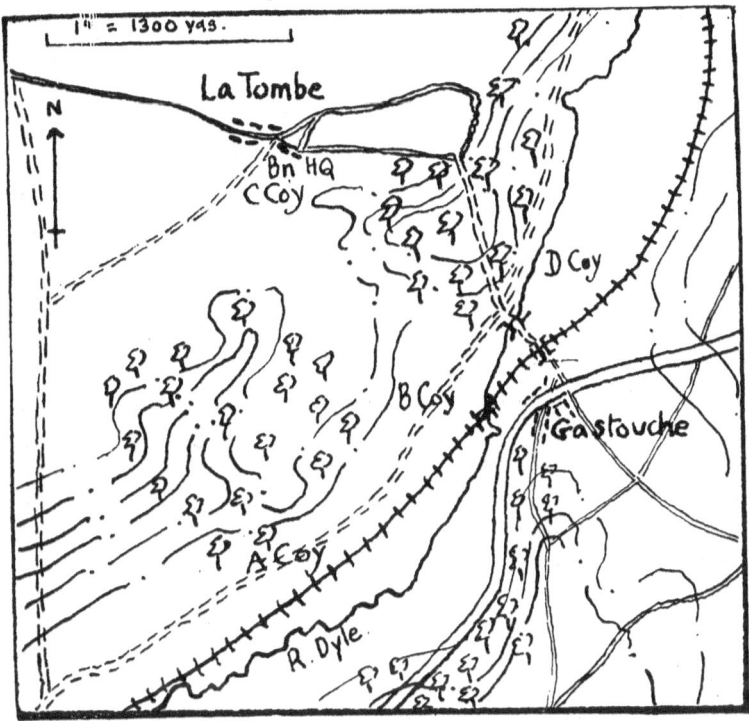

1. *The 2nd Battalion on the River Dyle, May* 1940

The rest of the 12th and the whole of the 13th were spent in improving the existing defences which it was then expected to hold indefinitely; though it is an indication of the pre-blitzkrieg mentality of the British Army at that time that when company commanders were shown their various sectors on the 12th, it was suggested that there would probably be ten to fourteen days to prepare the area before attack was likely!

However, such illusions were soon dispelled as it became increasingly clear, from the reports of refugees, that the Germans were across the Meuse and were pushing ahead fast. The number of these refugees increased, pouring down the Louvain-Namur road towards Wavre, though some crossed the bridge over the Dyle in 'D' Company's area. These refugees were a bit of a problem and their state was pitiable. The Battalion had received a somewhat strange and unexplained warning that any carrying red blankets were likely to be fifth columnists, but as well over half of them were doing so it was quite impossible to prove whether this was true or not. All one could do was to push everyone westwards and allow no loitering.

The bridges over the Dyle were blown on the 14th and first contact with the Germans—armoured cars and motor cyclists—was made about 4 o'clock in the afternoon by 'C' Company, commanded by Captain Rupert Blackett and acting as outpost company. They had put up a road block of carts and fired their anti-tank rifle, inflicting some casualties, before withdrawing as ordered with no loss. The same evening all civilians in La Tombe were ordered to evacuate their houses. In the small house where was Battalion Headquarters the occupants left at only a few minutes' notice; they took almost no belongings and the evening meal was still cooking on the fire after they and their small children had tearfully left their little home.

Meanwhile the Germans advanced into the forward slopes of the high ground facing the Battalion across the river and there remained until darkness, taking little offensive action beyond sporadic machine gun fire. Once it was dark they tried to infiltrate round the left flank, but were seen off by accurate fire from machine guns.

It was not until dawn that trouble really began. At about 6 o'clock a platoon of 'B' Company, which was holding a position near the blown bridge with the object of preventing an enemy crossing at what was reckoned to be a weak spot, was heavily attacked and overrun. The enemy had rushed them from the cover of some buildings on the far river bank, crossing the river by means of a small weir which could not be destroyed without lowering the level of the river above. Although the Platoon resisted vigorously for some hours, at the end of that time everyone was either killed or wounded save the commander, Second-Lieutenant John Hyde-Thompson. But when the Germans called upon him to surrender, he shot their leader, dispersed the rest of them with a grenade, and then escaped to the platoon on his right flank from where he organised a counter-attack on the position. This, unfortunately, was not successful; whereupon Hyde-Thompson, with a few men from the neighbouring platoon, occupied what had been his own platoon's alternative position and was able to check the enemy break-through sufficiently to stabilise the position for the present.

In order to prevent any further break-through in 'B' Company's area, the C.O. ordered 'C' Company to counter-attack the enemy there so as to restore the situation; and this attack went in at 11 o'clock in the morning with a limited amount of success. Although the left-hand platoon was almost wiped out to a man, one of the other two, under Platoon Sergeant Major George Pinkney, managed to reach the line of the railway where they held on for some time and forced the enemy back across the river. The German reaction to this was to intensify their machine-gun and mortar fire on every bit of cover they could see. Captain Frank Tubbs, commanding 'B' Company, got part of a mortar bomb in his knee and had to be evacuated. 'C' Company were unable to hold their newly won position indefinitely and, owing to the heavy casualties both they and 'B' Company had suffered, both Companies were amalgamated to hold the centre of the battalion position. P.S.M. Pinkney's platoon was withdrawn during the day, save for one section pinned down on the north of the railway: but P.S.M. Frank Walker managed to throw them food and water bottles and they withdrew once it was dark.

While all this was going on, a determined effort had been made by the enemy to break through on the Battalion's left flank, held by 'D' Company. Right at the start Captain Bill Hutton, its commander, received a mortar wound in his knee and followed Tubbs to hospital. Then a section holding one of the pillboxes down by the river ran out of ammunition and it was impossible to reach them with any more. Corporal Thompson, commanding it, tried to get his men back to the rest of the platoon, but every one of them was killed. When this news reached Company Headquarters, Company Sergeant Major Norman Metcalfe, in the absence of Lieutenant Charles Bonham who had taken over from Bill Hutton and was visiting his platoons, ordered a counter-attack by his reserve platoon which was, fortunately, completely successful: and that put a stop to any enemy infiltration from that quarter. But the Battalion was now without any reserve, had suffered considerable casualties and was spread pretty wide and with little depth. When a company of the 1st Royal Welch Fusiliers was sent to their aid from the Brigade's reserve battalion things became a little easier. It was now noon and the enemy was still held along the line of the river: and that was how the situation remained until night-fall, though mortar and shell fire kept everyone under cover and snipers were a perfect nuisance!

At night the enemy returned to the attack. He plastered every inch of the front with mortars and machine-guns. The noise was terrific, and just to add to the display he fired masses of red, green and white tracer. But there were few casualties and in no place did he break through. A determined effort was made once more to cross the bridge in front of 'D' Company's position, but, thanks very largely to Second-Lieutenant Dickie Annand, commanding the platoon defending it, the attempt was doomed to failure. " In they came with a vengeance," wrote Sergeant-Major Metcalfe to Bill Hutton afterwards, " and weren't they socked with a vengeance. They were bumped off like ninepins in bundles of ten. They seemed determined to get that bridge and therefore reinforcements were simply piled up with casualties. There must have been thousands of them: the position we had couldn't have been better. Jerry couldn't move old 'D'! We had casualties, especially 16 Platoon, but they were wonderful. Mr. Annand, Batty, Wood, Surtees—they just went mad. Jerry got up to the other side of the bridge to their sorrow; they must have thought they had demons in front of them. Mr. Annand and Co. just belted them and they even got on to the parapet to be able to pitch grenades. For two hours it was hell let loose, then Jerry gave it up and withdrew. I could hardly believe it when we checked up; we'd only about 16 casualties. We fired well over 20,000 rounds and over 100 grenades had been used . . ."

But the lull did not last long; within a short time the enemy mounted another attack with still greater force. He put down a further mortar barrage and made one more desperate attempt to bridge the river so as to get his tanks across. But, thanks very largely to the personal bravery of Dickie Annand, he made no headway. Annand's command of the platoon holding this vital position had been outstanding throughout. Twice the Germans tried to cross the demolished bridge. Twice he personally repulsed them. During the previous morning they got a bridging party into the sunken bottom of the river and when the ammunition had run out, he himself ran forward across the open, oblivious of mortar and machine-gun fire, and dispersed the German party with grenades which he carried in a sandbag. He killed some twenty Germans before he was wounded; but after rejoining the platoon he had his wounds dressed and remained in command.

When the second attack was made that night, Annand again went forward, stood on the parapet and tossed grenades on to the advancing enemy. Later, when the Battalion had been ordered to withdraw from its positions, and when he had brought his platoon safely out, it was learnt that his batman had been wounded and left behind. He then returned at once to the Platoon's original position and brought him back in a wheelbarrow before losing consciousness as a result of his wounds. For this most conspicuous gallantry Annand was awarded the Victoria Cross—the first to be won by the Regiment during this war, and one of the first to be awarded in the land fighting against the King's enemies.

The Battalion had now been fighting for just over twenty-four hours and had so far held all the attacks made against it. Nevertheless, it was quite clear to Colonel Simpson that, however gallantly they fought, persistent attacks must penetrate the line eventually. The ground between 'B' and 'D' Companies was difficult to defend, the battalion frontage was wide and depth almost non-existent. Without doubt there were snipers in the nearby woods, though whether they were soldiers or civilians was never known. Major Johnny Cousens reported that his company truck had been deliberately put out of action by some person or persons unknown; and the machine-gun platoon commander was fired on as he made his way through some woods to his platoon.

By 1 a.m. on the 16th the Dyle Valley was like an inferno. The atmosphere was tense and electric. But already the news had been received that all was not well on the rest of the front; and the C.O. had been to Brigade and received orders for the Battalion to withdraw at 1.30 a.m. This came as a complete surprise to everyone: as one of them said, " Then came the rotten order to withdraw. We were dumbfounded. We had Jerry beat to a frazzle." But the French Division on the right of the B.E.F. had fallen back on the 14th and made it necessary for the British Army to establish a defensive flank facing south; while elsewhere, of course, the Germans had punched a gap fifty miles wide in the French defences and by the evening of the 13th were already sixty miles behind the original front.

The orders for withdrawal had gone out at 11 p.m. and, as there was no time to send back for transport, everything that could not be manhandled had to be abandoned. Companies began marching out at 1.30 a.m.; passed through Ottenburg—formerly Brigade Headquarters—and made for fresh positions six miles back on the high ground west of the Terlaenen-Tombeek road. Everyone was pretty tired: three company commanders—Hutton, Tubbs and Blackett—had been wounded; and Hyde-Thompson was found to be missing. It turned out afterwards that he had been captured. The road back was full of troops, lorries and guns. Fires had started in Ottenburg where a fine old chateau was burning fiercely; and two carriers got caught up in telephone wires lying across the road and had to be abandoned. The Battalion numbered about four hundred and fifty, but 'B' and 'C' Companies had suffered worst and needed reorganising: apart from 1,800 rounds of rifle ammunition and eight boxes of grenades, there was no ammunition save what individuals had on them; there were no digging tools or wire, and very little drinking water.

The Battalion was from now on split into four groups regardless of the original companies, and signallers, pioneers and mortarmen took their places as riflemen, as all their heavy equipment had had to be left behind. They were given a 3,000 yard front to hold, but, fortunately, the enemy did not attack during the day; and though there was considerable and accurate mortar fire as the day wore on, there had been few casualties by nightfall when a further order to withdraw was given at 10.30 p.m.

The route back through Overyssche, Hoeylaert and Terblock to the Forest of Soignies was some twelve miles. Captain Oswald Pearson, the Quartermaster, had a splendid meal ready in the Forest. Although the day had been comparatively quiet, a number of strange individuals, whose identity it was difficult to determine, had been seen not far from the Battalion's positions. Two of these had been hailed but they had disappeared into a field of corn; they reappeared again in the growing darkness as Colonel Simpson was waiting with his driver for the last two companies to march out. For reasons unknown to the C.O., these two companies had been delayed; but when, as he waited, the two strangers began slowly moving towards him the Colonel decided it was time to move on, presuming that the two companies yet to report in had either been overrun or had withdrawn by some other route. Thus it was that the companies under Bonham and Cousens did not reach Overyssche until after the Battalion had left—and when they did so had no idea exactly which way it had gone. Cousens' company had been delayed in their withdrawal by a heavy German mortar bombardment; and they had to make their way across country on a compass bearing. The going was heavy and they did not reach Overyssche till 1 a.m. They then made their way to Brussels, discovered the Brigade's location and, after a march of over fifty miles, rejoined the Battalion a few days later after being given up for lost.

Meanwhile the rest of the Battalion had left the Forest of Soignies at 4 a.m. on the 17th and marched for sixteen miles through the southern outskirts of Brussels to a village near Elinghen, where they spent the day resting. Troop-carrying lorries were supposed to pick them up there but never arrived; so they marched another sixteen miles through the hours of darkness—a total in forty-eight hours of almost as many miles. As luck would have it, the lorries then turned up and the withdrawal continued by this means towards Tournai. As they passed over the Brussels-Charleroi Canal, parties of sappers could be seen preparing demolitions, while the columns of transport were subject to frequent long halts, the majority of which were due to drivers falling asleep during a check and then failing to wake up when the truck ahead moved on. At times the road for miles either way was packed head to tail with vehicles of every kind; but providence was kind and no German aircraft appeared to take advantage of this most vulnerable of targets.

By breakfast time on the 19th the Battalion reached Tournai which was still burning from a very recent air attack. It was practically deserted and the central square was a shambles; and to add to the confusion the inmates of the local lunatic asylum had been let loose. Those who could be rounded up were locked up in the museum. The Battalion's task was to occupy the line of the Escaut Canal which, it was understood, was to be held for some while. It was—for four days; but during that time there was no direct contact by the Battalion with the Germans, save for some shelling, but there was the usual spate of rumours and numerous scares—one of which resulted in the Sappers blowing the bridges before it was necessary, so cutting off a number of tanks and other vehicles which had to be destroyed. By the evening of the 22nd the whole Brigade had been ordered to continue the withdrawal and the Battalion found itself, in the early hours of the 23rd, passing through the self same village which it had left with such high hopes some ten days before. As it did so, French troops were moving up to occupy the so-called Gort line on which many weeks' work had been spent the previous winter. It was of little use now; the Germans were nearing La Bassée and by the 24th had occupied Béthune; no one knew very clearly what units were on their flanks or exactly where they were; the fog of war was beginning to descend.

On the morning of the 25th the Battalion reached Calonnes-sur-Lys. The inhabitants said the Germans had been there before them; and there were road blocks at almost every corner. All that was known, in fact, was that the Germans were moving about not so very far away. Brigade Headquarters said that scattered enemy tanks, which had been cut off, were trying to find their way back to their own lines! No indication of their line of advance or withdrawal was given, but a company of the Royal Welch Fusiliers, who were in position on the line of the Canal about a mile and a half south of St. Venant, was reported to be in contact with the enemy. St. Venant lay due west of Calonnes-sur-Lys, where Brigade Headquarters had established itself and where the Battalion now concentrated in reserve. Though, apparently, the overall situation was not clear to the Battalion, the 2nd Division was by now in position holding part of the southern flank of a corridor running between Lens and Dunkirk, through which other British Divisions and part of the First French Army round Douai were withdrawing to the sea.

The Battalion was ordered to occupy St. Venant during the night of the 25th. This it did with three companies in line, covering the approaches, and with another set back in reserve. The Germans appeared to be advancing from the south-west. The following day the Brigadier visited the Battalion and ordered the left hand company—' D ' Company—to be moved to cover a gap on the right flank which now existed between them and the 1st Royal Berkshire Regiment. The route lay over open country and the move was not an easy one to carry out. The Company was mortared and machine gunned all the way and, as a result, Lieutenant John Gregson, the commander, received the wound from which he later died. It was during the Brigadier's visit that it was learnt of the move of Brigade Headquarters from Calonnes to a position due north of St. Venant. This news was disturbing. It meant that the front now appeared to face due south and the left flank was completely exposed. It was even more disturbing when German tanks were seen later in the evening moving towards St. Floris, a mile or so to the east. Although no direct attack was made on the Battalion and the enemy's strength was not yet fully ascertained, from the amount of fire of various kinds throughout the day it became clear that the Germans had crossed the Canal to the south and had captured the forward positions of the Royal Welch Fusiliers. During the night the Germans lit a large number of fires and these appeared to encircle the Battalion's whole position.

If there had been any doubts that the Germans were preparing to attack, they were dispelled by the morning of the 27th. While it was still half light ' A ' Company, which was on the left once ' D ' Company had moved, was engaged with a strong German patrol on which it inflicted heavy casualties, but, unfortunately, with heavy loss to itself. Then, as it got lighter, tanks and armoured cars could be seen approaching from the left flank, and shortly afterwards they attacked the two left-hand companies and caused a large number of casualties. The few anti-tank guns available did their best, but they were soon put out of action and the Battalion was left with only its own anti-tank rifles. At the same time the Headquarters of the Royal Welch Fusiliers moved into the Battalion area and their C.O. confirmed that a strong force of German tanks was driving against the village of St. Venant.

Measures were now taken to strengthen Battalion Headquarters. This was situated in and around a barn on the road running through St. Venant and was just south of the St. Venant Canal which ran parallel and alongside the road. Road blocks were hurriedly put in position and defences manned and the gunner battery commander was told to engage the tanks over open sites whenever he could. But it was not long before more tanks appeared from a number of directions and began closing in on the Headquarters position. Two of them shelled it from the left flank and killed or wounded a considerable number of men lining the Canal bank, while more were seen passing through what had been ' A ' Company's position to the south. The anti-tank gun here was knocked out, though one section managed to kill a tank crew with an anti-tank rifle before they were overrun. Then the tanks closed in, some of them getting astride the slit trenches where the occupants were powerless to move yet unharmed underneath. ' D ' Company on the right was also heavily engaged and their effectives dwindled to some forty-five all told. Sergeant-Major Metcalfe was now in command as all the officers were killed or wounded, and he ordered Platoon Sergeant-Major Pearson to counter-attack the enemy who were working through the gap between the Company and the rest of the Battalion. Neither he nor his platoon were ever seen again.

Meanwhile orders to withdraw had been given by Brigade. The Royal Berkshire received them and passed them on to ' D ' Company, of whom some twenty-five men—the sole survivors—and the Sergeant-Major managed to extricate themselves, ferry themselves across the Canal and withdraw north-eastwards. But the rest of the Battalion had no such opportunity. The fire of the enemy closing in on the village was too intense to enable anyone to get up and run for it over the St. Venant bridge. The motor transport and lorries had already managed to cross the bridge and in due course withdrew with what was left of the Brigade, chiefly the Royal Berkshires. So the rest of the Battalion stood their ground and prepared to fight it out to the bitter end. There was little they could do. Their only defensive weapon left, apart from rifles, was an anti-tank rifle and that was soon put out of action. Five German medium tanks lumbered into the village. The first crossed the bridge and wiped out most of the men holding it with its machine guns and blew up the houses in which some were sheltering with its gun. Though it was brought to an abrupt halt by a direct hit from an 18-pounder gun, the end was very near.

The last stand was made in the barn beside Battalion Headquarters. The bales of fodder and hay were burning furiously. Colonel Simpson, whose leadership throughout the operations had been an inspiration to everyone and who had been suffering from a painful shoulder injury, himself set to with his revolver as infantry followed the tanks. He was an Army pistol shot as at least one German had cause to regret. No one had been more adaptable in meeting the changing circumstances of the past three weeks than he, and the Battalion had had cause on numerous occasions to be grateful for his foresight. To the very end he had forcibly pointed out to Brigade the danger that was developing from the left flank and had advocated withdrawing part of the Battalion north of the St. Venant Canal. Now the end had come; two tanks turned into the barn, German infantry poured in and the struggle was over.

All that remained of the Battalion—the survivors of 'D' Company, the transport, carriers and the men of 'B' Echelon, together with odd stragglers—came together in due course under the Quartermaster on the Hazebrouck side of the canal running behind St. Venant. They were joined by what was left of 6 Brigade to continue the retreat and embark from Dunkirk some two days later. So the Battalion came home. They had fought a great fight, and as they assembled in England once again they were joined by small parties who had got separated, by a few who had been on leave when the battle began, and by others who had been in hospital. Together this hard core of the old Battalion formed the nucleus of a new one which, some three years later, was to earn further laurels for the Regiment in the war against Japan amid the hills and jungles of Burma.

3

151 BRIGADE IN NORTHERN FRANCE

To all who took part in the advance into Belgium and the sudden and subsequent withdrawal and evacuation, the three crowded weeks will always remain a series of the strangest scenes and contrasts.

The early feeling of exhilaration, which no one could fail to feel as the B.E.F. advanced into Belgium, was transformed into dogged determination as it became plain that the French Army on the right was not holding the German attack.

Perhaps the strangest scene of all was the sudden way in which the Belgian economy broke under the strain. In forty-eight hours the Belgian countryside changed its face from the placid agricultural land known to so many tourists and soldiers in previous wars to a land of bewilderment, where half the population seemed on the move, where money had little value, and where a bicycle was much more prized than an expensive car with an empty petrol tank.

Meanwhile, and throughout the following days, the sun shone almost without interruption and spring flowers, particularly lilacs, were bursting into bloom in every farm and cottage garden. At first it seemed impossible that disaster could be so close. Yet it came swiftly; and in its midst the most static factor beyond any doubt was the British Army, together with many French units and formations which fought back with them to the coast. The local authorities in both Belgium and France lost control of a problem beyond their powers, but here and there a stalwart Mayor or Priest could be found trying to organise accommodation and relief works within their negligible resources.

To most men the refugees who blocked the roads will never be forgotten. They drifted back and forth without any clear idea of where they were going, except to avoid the battles. On one day the main drift would be to the west, and on the next back east. What would have happened if the battles had continued long beyond the three weeks is too awful to contemplate. Disease would have broken out and would have spread to the Armies. Luckily they were spared this, even though there was the unpleasant job of burying dead men, women and horses, most of them the victims of bombing.

For the Army there was the vital task of keeping the main roads clear for troops and transport. It was a formidable task and one made worse by French and Belgian horse transport, both military and civil; but the Military Police, with help from units, were largely successful in mastering it and the 50th Division, with its special training as a Motor Division, was at an advantage since every man had developed a sense of M.T. movement.

Like the 2nd Battalion, the D.L.I. Brigade received the news of the German attack early in the morning of the 10th of May. The 50th Division was not required to move forward at once into Belgium as it was in reserve, and so for the next week the main body remained where it was, carrying on with routine duties such as firing on the ranges, and hunting every now and again for reported parachutists. It was not until the 16th of May that it moved forward in the vehicles of the Troop Carrying Company of the R.A.S.C. with whom it had trained until the sections were almost part of the infantry battalions.

It was first thought that the Brigade was to move to the west side of Brussels, and in fact the advance parties had reconnoitred positions in this area. But counter orders were to follow orders, and after hectic reconnaissances, all of the type with which the advance parties were to become only too familiar, it was on the River Dendre, near Grammont and far to the west of Brussels, that they met their main bodies. These long moves were routine to units of the D.L.I. Brigade who had trained and practised them until they presented little difficulty. It was a less familiar experience, however, when on this 16th of May, the very first day in Belgium, the advance was felt to halt and the slow withdrawal to begin. The B.E.F. was already falling back from the River Dyle and the 2nd Battalion was among those who passed through 151 Brigade's positions on the Dendre. On the 18th 151 Brigade began to fall back in its turn—a move which was harassed by refugees rather than by the enemy. Nor will the men who took part in it ever forget the long march on the crowded, cobbled roads. Thirty miles on a warm day is a long march at any time, but under these conditions it was particularly trying.

On the 19th of May 151 Brigade found itself again in the familiar area of the La Bassée Canal. To date, the operations seemed not unlike the legend of the famous Duke of York, only the march had been there and back rather than up and down. But there was one new factor. The enemy was now in strength to the south as well as to the west. Everyone could see how the situation had deteriorated. The B.E.F. was extending a defensive flank facing south and occupying points along the whole

line from Douai to Péronne in an attempt to cover Arras.
By the evening of the 18th the Germans had reached Cambrai, passed St. Quentin, and brushed the forward Allied elements out of Péronne. This was the day when General Weygand took over from General Gamelin as Supreme Commander. Meanwhile the Northern Group of French Armies, under whose command the B.E.F. was, seemed stunned into ineffectiveness. The French Ninth Army, under the command of General Corap, had broken under the general assault, and it never recovered. The gap which yawned in the Allied line showed up the false strategy of attempting to defend the long land frontier by troops extended along the whole line. From now on it was apparent that the French reserves were either wrongly placed or too weak to counter-attack successfully. In fact many French reserve formations, including some armoured units, never made active contact with the enemy throughout the whole campaign.

The German armoured columns were sweeping like scythes through the communications of the forces in the north. By the 20th of May the British Cabinet began to make tentative preparations for " the emergency evacuation across the Channel of very large forces " as a last resort. Meanwhile efforts were still being made by the French in the north and the B.E.F. to march southwards towards the Somme in order to join forces with the French Armies already there. As part of this move it was resolved to attack southwards from Arras with such troops as were available. These were not a great number, and on the British side consisted only of the 5th and 50th Divisions and the 1st Army Tank Brigade. The French, on their side, were ready to co-operate with two Divisions on the right of the British. One of these, an Armoured Division, had already been in action in Holland and like the British Army Tank Brigade was far from up to strength in tanks. The plan was to launch this force on the right flank of the German corridor, so effecting a junction with the Allied troops further south, and at the same time to disrupt the supply and maintenance of the German advanced formations.

At this time Arras was held by a temporary force known as ' Petreforce ' after its commander, General Petre. In the original plan for the attack 151 Brigade was to hold a defensive position on the La Bassée Canal: but this was soon changed, and all three battalions assembled on the north side of historic Vimy Ridge in the early hours of the 21st of May in preparation for the attack to the south later in the day. Brigade Headquarters was in the hamlet of Petit Vimy, which soon became a kind of metropolis, as at least one French Headquarters established itself in farms nearby: and such vehicles of the 1st Army Tank Brigade as could still be called runners dispersed among any available buildings or cover.

In brief the plan of attack was to advance in two columns to the line of the Arras-Doullens road and then, using this line as a start line, to attack the enemy south and south-east of Arras and penetrate as far as the River Sensée. On the right the 8th Battalion was to move through Maroeuil, Warlus and Vailly to Boisleux-au-Mont; on the left the 6th Battalion's route lay through Ecurie, Achicourt and Beaurains to Henin. Each Battalion had under its command a battalion of the 1st Army Tank Brigade with its remaining battleworthy tanks. The 9th Battalion was in reserve and was to move behind the 8th.

Speed was the vital factor now. The orders for the attack were not given to battalions until 9.45 a.m., as it had been considered that the physical condition of the troops required a night's rest and if orders had been given on their arrival no one would get any. But they had eight miles to march before reaching the Arras-Doullens road, which had to be crossed at 2 p.m. This meant that the battalions had to start moving almost as soon as they received their orders and that the arrangements for co-operation with the tanks—of which no one had had any previous experience—had also to be made as they moved forward. Moreover, very little was known about the exact positions of the Germans and there was no further time for reconnaissance.

Both the 6th and 8th Battalions started off at 11.30 a.m. but neither reached the Arras-Doullens road at the appointed time for the very simple reason that the Germans were in fact in positions to the north of it. The 4th Royal Tank Regiment, who preceded the 6th Battalion, met the enemy almost at once to the west of Dainville. They shot up his transport and killed many men, and the 6th Battalion was able to clear up the area round Dainville and take several hundred dejected prisoners. This initial success put new heart into everyone and offset the fatigue of the last days' marching. But it caused a delay and the Battalion did not reach its start-line till 3.30 p.m.—an hour and a half late. By 5.0 p.m. it had occupied Beaurains.

The 8th Battalion was less fortunate, and in fact never reached the start-line at all. The 7th Royal Tank Regiment, supporting it, moved off too soon and disappeared in the distance. That was the last the Battalion saw of it. But when the leading troops reached the Arras-St. Pol road they saw striking evidence that the tanks had passed that way. German vehicles, burnt out and damaged, were strewn all over the road. Enemy dead lay where they had fallen. Some French tanks held some German prisoners, while 'B' Company, in clearing up a wood round Duisans, captured some more. The Battalion then split into two, leaving 'B' and 'C' Companies under Major Ross McLaren, the second in command, to occupy Duisans while the rest pushed on under Colonel Beart to Warlus. 'C' Company, in company with some French tanks, then attacked a cemetery near Duisans where some hundred Germans had taken refuge from the Royal Tank Regiment. When they occupied it, they found only eighteen left alive and the French stripped them to the skin and made them lie face down on the road until it was time to take them away.

By 5.15 p.m. the Battalion held both Duisans and Warlus.

It was clear by now, however, that despite the success of the operation so far as it had gone, the Division's original objective, the River Sensée, could not be reached. It was equally clear that the Germans, somewhat shaken by the 50th Division's thrust, would retaliate; this they could easily do as they had larger forces and complete superiority in the air. At about 5.45 p.m. very heavy dive-bombing attacks were made on the 8th Battalion in Warlus. They went on for twenty minutes, intermingled with low flying machine gun attacks. At about the same time the Germans launched a counter-attack with infantry and tanks. Despite the effect on morale which resulted from this first experience of the Stukas, there were only ten casualties—all wounded—and the enemy was repelled. The anti-tank gunners were quickly in action and some twenty German tanks were knocked out and left burning on the ground.

However, this was only the beginning and as soon as it was dark the Germans launched a further attack which forced Colonel Beart to withdraw his troops into a closer position in the village. Very soon this part of the Battalion was completely surrounded as German armoured patrols moved round the flanks and cut the Warlus-Duisans road and, later, further parties of Germans succeeded in cutting off the force in Duisans from Maroeuil where the 9th Battalion and Brigade Headquarters were now established.

Meanwhile, at 6.50 p.m., a similar series of attacks had been launched on the 6th Battalion in Beaurains: over a hundred planes were used in this attack and that part of the Battalion in Beaurains was forced to withdraw to Achicourt. As they did so they were attacked by a large force of tanks in the open, and though they managed to reach Achicourt their casualties were not light.

The 9th Battalion, on the other hand, had a comparatively uneventful day. First of all they moved up to Neuville St. Vaast. They found the village well looted and destroyed, with few inhabitants remaining; but wine and food were plentiful and the cows were wandering about unmilked. So most companies were able to supply themselves with as much milk as they wanted. The Battalion was bombed, but not as badly as the 6th and 8th Battalions; and it could only stand helplessly by and watch the three hundred planes attack its comrades of the 6th for over an hour unhindered.

At 4 p.m. the Battalion moved forward to Maroeuil where it tried to form a defensive area round the village. As the move began a German plane came overhead and dropped a bomb not far from the second in command, Major Sammy Battiscombe's, truck. Private Green, his driver, actually saw the bomb leave the plane; so both were able to jump for safety in time. Crippled British tanks were also coming through the village. On the whole they had only been moderately successful; for although their armour was good enough—one had stood up to seven direct hits—they had only one machine gun and once that was knocked out they were without armament. The Battalion was ordered to stay in Maroeuil for the night and in fact did so until the Brigade withdrew later on.

The Germans were now quite clearly in greatly superior

strength and during the night, while the battle raged fiercely, particularly in Warlus, orders were given for the Brigade to withdraw to Vimy Ridge. The Brigadier had already ordered the 8th Battalion to withdraw through the 9th to Maroeuil, and soon after midnight the force in Warlus, whose ammunition was running low and whose casualties were mounting, managed to fight their way through the Germans surrounding them. With the aid of some French tanks and two armoured troop carriers, which had fought their way through to the village, and with every carrier and vehicle that had not been hit, Colonel Beart managed to extricate all survivors of the force which had held Warlus so gallantly. With the French tanks covering them, they ran the gauntlet of the German fire and rejoined the rest of the Battalion, who had withdrawn earlier, in the village of Petit Vimy. The C.O. was, unfortunately, sufficiently badly wounded to have to be evacuated and his place was taken by Ross McLaren, the second in command.

Although the ultimate object of the day's operations had not been achieved, the attack had not been without an effect upon the enemy. Heavy casualties had been inflicted on him, over four hundred prisoners had been taken, and more than twenty tanks had been destroyed. The 6th Battalion's advance of ten miles into enemy territory had shown remarkable powers of endurance after the previous days' marching and lack of sleep, while the 8th Battalion's stubborn resistance in Warlus had shown they could give as good as they got. This limited counter-attack probably delayed the German advance to Calais by some two days, with a corresponding effect on the successful evacuation at Dunkirk. It certainly gave the Germans a nasty jar. Said von Runstedt afterwards: " A critical moment in the drive came just as my forces had reached the Channel. It was caused by a British counter-stroke southward from Arras towards Cambrai on May the 21st. For a short time it was feared that our armoured divisions would be cut off before the infantry divisions could come up to support them. None of the French counter-attacks carried any serious threat such as this one did."[1] It is interesting to note, too, that in this, the Brigade's first encounter with the Germans, the enemy commander's name was

[1] " The Other Side of the Hill " by B. H. Liddell Hart (1st Edn.), pp. 137/138.

Erwin Rommel. Both were to renew their acquaintance later.

After their withdrawal everybody dug themselves in along the line of Vimy Ridge with the role of holding their positions to the end as a sort of southern buttress to the whole B.E.F. But late the same night there was a further change of plan and a further withdrawal was ordered. Again there was little time for detailed planning. There was only a narrow corridor still open, as the enemy was working round both flanks of the position held by the 50th Division and the depleted French formations. However, all units of the 50th Division withdrew successfully the same night and the greater part of the French the following morning. The enemy had not followed up their success. Had they done so they would have found British transport moving nose to tail, a risk which had to be taken. Nor would it have been possible for Captain Harry Sell, the Brigade Transport officer, whose 'B' Echelon had been isolated from the rest of the Brigade by a mass of fleeing refugees and withdrawing French troops, to drive on to Vimy Ridge at 5 a.m. the following morning to check that all had retired. There was no sign of the enemy on the ridge but he picked up two men of the 9th Battalion who were sleeping peacefully by the side of the road. He then drove forward to the village of Givenchy, which was deserted and in flames, only to find as he entered at one end of the square that a German armoured column was entering it at the other! He beat a hasty retreat but on the way back found several 30 cwt. lorries parked by the roadside and apparently abandoned. As he passed he blew his horn and to his astonishment a bleary morning face appeared over the tailboard. They were the 8th Battalion's cooks' lorries with the cooks asleep in them. However, the magic words "Boche tanks" produced instant activity and this merry little convoy competed for international racing honours with the enemy down the Givenchy-Lens road!

The Brigade, meanwhile, was safely back once more on the north side of the La Bassée Canal and, save for intermittent attack from the air, was allowed a day to rest and get some sleep.

Meanwhile, the situation of the B.E.F. continued to deteriorate. Great efforts had been made to put into force the so-called Weygand plan, which involved a combined British-French attack southwards simultaneously with a strong French offensive northwards from the Somme. Indeed, on the 25th, the D.L.I. Brigade received orders for their part in this attack. But, as is well known, this operation never took place. The Belgians had begun to crumble, and as they fell back from the Lys Canal a gap began to develop between them and the British left flank. It was late on the 25th that Lord Gort decided to abandon the Weygand plan, to plug the gap left by the Belgians and march to the sea as the only hope of saving something from destruction or surrender. He therefore ordered the 5th and 50th Divisions, who were to have taken part in the attack southwards, to move north to fill the impending Belgian gap.

For the D.L.I. Brigade this was more easily said than done. In the early part of the night of the 25th the 9th Battalion, in Provin, reported considerably increased German activity south of the La Bassée Canal, and a request for aid from the French, who were holding the canal line, to whose support the Battalion's carriers had been sent. Early on the morning of the 26th the 8th Battalion had a similar experience. There had been a lot of shelling during the night, and when it became light the Battalion found that, although not actually engaged, it appeared to be in the midst of a fierce battle. Very heavy shelling was going on behind it, and a report was soon received from a French Algerian Division in the neighbourhood of Carvin that the Germans had crossed the canal and that assistance was badly needed. To this request the 8th too sent its carriers, but they had been gone only an hour when orders were received to move north with the rest of the Division towards Ypres. As the Battalion moved off it was very heavily bombed from the air—its first experience of saturation bombing—and it was somewhat disorganised as it collected in Camphin to meet the troop carrying transport.

The position of both the 8th and 9th Battalions was now somewhat precarious. The Germans were attacking fiercely and by mid-day the town of Carvin had been captured. So instead of withdrawing as planned, the 8th Battalion was ordered to counter-attack Carvin as soon as possible in order to restore a somewhat delicate situation. Meanwhile, the 9th Battalion were sufficiently heavily engaged to be unable to break off their action and comply with the rest of the Brigade's withdrawal. So only the 6th Battalion and Brigade Headquarters—except

Brigadier Churchill and a skeleton staff—moved off with the rest of the Division.

Within fifty minutes of receiving orders to recapture Carvin the 8th Battalion launched a counter-attack in conjunction with some French tanks. Despite heavy German shelling and bombing, it was completely successful in restoring the situation. But later in the day the 9th Battalion, who had suffered heavy casualties from shelling and bombing, was forced to withdraw from the line of the canal because the number of barges moored in it made it utterly valueless as an obstacle to infantry. Just before dark the same evening it was heavily dive-bombed again and suffered further severe losses. But the day's fighting for both Battalions had not been in vain. They had held their own, the 8th's attack had been completely successful, and together they had prevented an unpleasant situation from getting worse while other troops were moving up to relieve them. In the early hours of the 27th both Battalions were withdrawn and moved off in trucks to join the 6th Battalion near Ypres, where the whole Brigade took up new defensive positions.

The morning of the 28th brought the first news that evacuation was to take place from Dunkirk. General Martel himself gave the Brigade this information. Soon afterwards came the depressing news of the Belgian capitulation, which meant to the tired and exhausted troops that their left flank had collapsed and that encirclement and destruction might well befall them. Fortunately, this eventualtity had been foreseen some days previously and the gaps were plugged in one fashion or another. The Brigade withdrew that night without difficulty and again the Germans did not follow it up. The following night a further withdrawal into the Dunkirk perimeter was more fiercely contested. Air activity and accurate shelling did not diminish the difficulties, nor did the fact that the withdrawal had to be carried out whilst it was still light. Maps of the area, too, were few and in the 9th Battalion only the C.O. had one. At a critical moment of the 8th Battalion's move back the Germans launched an attack on 'C' Company; with characteristic tactical skill it was directed at the junction between that company and the battalion of another division on their flank. The attack surged round the Company and cut off its retreat; and for the rest of the night it fought a losing battle against greatly superior forces. Outgunned, outnumbered and isolated, the Company was finally overrun. Only two men escaped to tell the tale; the rest were either killed or marched away into captivity.

As the Brigade moved north towards Dunkirk conditions changed. Except for the upstanding Mont des Cats, near Cassel, the country became flatter and duller. The refugees became fewer: somehow they had surged away from the main routes. But there were other difficulties. Enemy bombing from the air became more frequent. The whole B.E.F. was moving on very few roads and could not avoid offering tempting targets. Smashed up trucks in the roadside ditches became more frequent and the slow horsed transport of so many French units caused countless hold ups.

Meanwhile the sad destruction of the B.E.F.'s own vehicles was beginning. There were detailed orders setting out the scale of transport which should be taken into the perimeter. The remainder were being destroyed by the Sappers in great parks alongside the main withdrawal roads, and at night the flames lit up the sky. It was a sad moment, but no other course was possible. As it was, movement inside the perimeter was difficult enough, with the few permitted vehicles and innumerable loose horses. Many cross roads were under observed artillery fire and any movement was likely to attract attention. It was safer to keep off the roads, but the wide dykes made movement there all but impossible as they were too wide to jump.

By the early morning of the 30th the 6th and 9th Battalions were in position on the Bergues Canal with the 8th in reserve along the Ringsloot Canal behind them. This time the enemy were less slow to follow up the withdrawal and were soon probing along the line of the canal to discover any weak spot in the defence. All the bridges on the Bergues Canal were blown, and orders given to blow those along the Ringsloot if in danger of imminent capture. The Germans had followed up so rapidly that the 9th Battalion was being shot at before companies could get properly dug in. During the day the German Air Force dropped some leaflets. On the leaflets was printed a map of the British Army holding a small area round Dunkirk surrounded by a sea of Germans. In bold English lettering were the words, " The game is up, the innings is over! There is no alternative but to surrender." The troops just laughed at this

Battalion Headquarters of the 2nd Battalion at Berçu, France, March 1940
Lt.-Col. V. A. C. Yate   Capt. C. M. Townsend   Maj. R. B. Y. Simpson

The Sergeants' Mess of the 2nd Battalion at Berçu in March 1940

'B' Company of the 2nd Battalion working on fortifications, France 1940

Universal Pictorial Press
and Agency

Lieut. R. W. Annand, V.C.

and did not believe it. Little did they know that for once the enemy was telling the truth. However, no major attack was launched that day by the Germans, though it was a day of much air action on both sides. Shelling was heavy and the stretcher bearers overworked, but the strain of days and nights with little sleep was beginning to tell, and though when darkness fell some Sappers came up to the forward troops to help with digging and wiring, little was done, as many men were so exhausted that they fell asleep where they stood.

The 50th Division was to begin embarking on the night of the 31st. This was the original plan, but, as so often before, it was soon altered. This was due to the increasing pressure by the Germans which involved 151 Brigade, particularly the 9th Battalion, in some hard fighting. Early in the day a welcome batch of reinforcements was received from 70 Brigade, the 8th Battalion receiving a number from the 11th Battalion, their second line. Casualties began to mount as the day wore on. Some ground was given on the left of the Brigade's front by the 9th Battalion during the morning. This was due to a misunderstanding by the company commander concerned as the unit on his flank had been forced back. It was later learnt that the latter was to counter-attack to regain the line of the canal and the Battalion was told to try to conform with it. Sammy Battiscombe, the second in command, collected two platoons of 'A' Company and the remains of 'D' Company and, under Captain George Wood, ordered them to attack the area of Bulscamp bridge over the canal. They were to be supported by an artillery barrage.

Down came the barrage at 12 p.m. and off went the two companies in great style. So quick off the mark were they that they got behind the enemy's defensive fire and captured the bridge and some nearby buildings without difficulty. They were very gallantly led by Wood and his Sergeant-Major, James Kemp, and Private Houle did some very good work among the wounded. By 12.30 p.m. the Battalion was re-established in its original positions on the canal.

During the afternoon Brigadier Churchill ordered a withdrawal in the centre to the Ringsloot Canal and sent two companies of Northumberland Fusiliers, which had been placed under his command, to the help of the 6th Battalion: and later a Battalion of Grenadier Guards, who had been put under command for counter-attack purposes, moved up to fill a gap in the 9th Battalion's area which had resulted from the withdrawal to the Ringsloot position. By evening, despite a hard day's fighting, the Brigade still held the canal line: and as darkness fell the Brigadier reorganised the mixture of units now under his command into three sectors under Colonel Percy, who had replaced Colonel Simpson in command of the 9th Battalion, Colonel McLaren of the 8th, and Major Adair of the Grenadiers. Colonel Peter Jeffreys, of the Regiment, had also by this time succeeded Colonel Miller in command of the 6th Battalion. At 8 p.m. orders were given for the withdrawal during the night to the beaches to the east of Dunkirk in preparation for embarkation the following day: and when this finally took place in the early hours of the 1st of June, it was perhaps significant that there was little interference from the German troops who had tried so persistently to break the canal defences, although the mole was coming under German artillery fire.

The long, continuous fighting of the last ten days was now almost over. As the weary troops reached the sand dunes around Dunkirk, there seemed little for them to do save wait for the final order to embark. Those not too tired to watch saw the epic of Dunkirk played out before their eyes. Ships small and great plied their way to and fro, picking up their human cargoes and, with gunwales awash, setting course for England. Despite the mass of troops and equipment stretched along the shore, the German Air Force was comparatively ineffective. Every now and then a British plane—in most cases the first seen by these men for the whole of the campaign—flew in to join battle with a German bomber. But, as it turned out, it was thanks to the R.A.F. that the evacuation was so little interrupted by the enemy's aircraft.

It was during these last hours, when after so many days of depressing retreat the prospect of reaching home once more must have been in every mind, that the news came that the Brigade might not be evacuated, but must be ready, if need be, to carry out a diversionary attack. Two columns were to be formed, one mobile and one marching, whose task was to break out from Dunkirk and to attack the Germans so as to cover the embarkation of the rest of the Army. The survivors were then to fight their way back to Dunkirk where they would be taken off if it was not too late.

To everyone's relief this suicidal operation was never carried out. It never, in fact, became necessary. By 2.30 p.m. it was cancelled, and the final move to the Dunkirk beach began. No weapons that could be carried were abandoned. Indeed, Sergeant Joseph Malone of the 8th carried a heavy old Lewis gun which he had picked up in the early stages of the fighting and which he said he preferred as " something solid rather than them new fangled Brens!"; while Lance-Corporal Edward Wilson, the canteen steward, had an alarm clock round his neck and a sandbag full of £40 in French currency.

Shortly after midnight the D.L.I. Brigade had embarked. The 50th Division was the last to leave France: and it was perhaps fitting that four years later, with the D.L.I. Brigade still with it, it was one of the first to set foot on it again.

4

THE 10TH AND 11TH BATTALIONS IN THE RETREAT TO DUNKIRK

Like all other troops in France, 70 Brigade learnt of the German invasion early on the 10th of May. On the 13th the 10th Battalion was moved south to guard certain temporary airfields near Abbeville, the bulk of which were actually south of the Somme. In order to get there, all other units of the Division had to lend the Battalion their transport and the move, which was made by night, was completed by 6 a.m. on the 14th. Their stay was, however, only a short one—three days, to be exact; and little of moment took place beyond parachutist scares, the local French Headquarters in Abbeville having apparently got parachutists on the brain.

Meanwhile, the 11th Battalion had remained in the Nuncq area; and it was there on the 17th that it received orders for the first of many moves to take up defensive positions which were shortly to be abandoned. At the same time the 10th Battalion handed over its airfields to troops of the 12th Division and moved back to join the Brigade in its new task. The Germans, after their initial break-through, were fast approaching Arras in their drive for the Channel ports and 70 Brigade was ordered to hold a position along the line of the Canal du Nord, approximately six miles west of Cambrai. The Brigade occupied these new positions by the following day, having fought their way through a hopeless jumble of French transport going both ways, as well as civilians, refugees on bicycles and stray cattle. The 11th Battalion and the Tyneside Scottish were the two forward Battalions, the 10th was in reserve. The Brigade front was very extended, some four or five miles astride the Arras-Cambrai road, and as the Canal du Nord had practically no water in it, its value as an obstacle was severely limited. Feverish efforts were made to put the positions into a state of defence, but the Battalions had no picks, shovels or wire to do it. At all events they had barely settled in for twenty-four hours before orders were received for the Brigade's withdrawal. Although, so far, there had been no direct clash with the enemy, some casualties had been suffered from German air attacks. Bombing and machine gunning were frequent over the whole area and not least upon the roads crowded with refugees. The Battalions now had to make their way back to Arras where the Brigade was to hold a position covering the south-east part of the town; and they did this in the early part of the morning, after blowing the bridges over the canal before they went.

Both Battalions had scarcely got into their new positions when another order came to move. Apparently the Brigade was in too isolated a position and the German armoured columns threatened its security. The withdrawal was to be carried out at half past 8 that night and Battalions were to go back through Wancourt to Thélus near Vimy. The withdrawal began as planned, but while it was still in progress orders were changed again. Apparently the situation had improved round Arras and the Brigade was to be diverted to the area of Saulty and Beaumetz and Lattre, south-west of Arras. This meant a march of between sixteen and twenty miles for the Battalions and everyone was very exhausted. They had been marching since 7 p.m. the previous evening and many junior officers and N.C.Os had not had a complete night's rest for almost ten days. Brigadier Kirkup therefore ordered the marching columns to move to the new area by stages and each battalion to use its limited transport to ferry the men during the night instead of making a forced march the whole way. So the 10th Battalion decided to lie up for a few hours at Mercatel, the Tyneside Scottish at Neuville Vitasse and the 11th Battalion at Wancourt while such transport as was available began to move at once to the Beaumetz-Saulty area, there to dump its loads and return to help ferry the infantry columns. In the early hours of the 20th companies began arriving one by one in their respective villages and everyone settled down for a few hours of badly needed sleep; though the 11th Battalion managed to get two companies and part of another ferried into Beaumetz by 5 in the morning.

Soon after it became light things began to happen. German aircraft were very much in evidence. The 10th Battalion's transport was attacked and Neuville Vitasse, where the Tyneside Scottish were, was reconnoitred from a very low altitude. The congestion on the road from Wancourt to Ficheux was considerable, but despite it the transport managed to continue its ferrying operations. The 10th Battalion, in due course, got the bulk of the Battalion into Lattre, leaving behind one company still under command of the Tyneside Scottish. The greater part of the Tyneside Scottish began marching in company columns towards Beaumetz. Part of the 11th Battalion was already in Beaumetz under the Adjutant, but one company had not received the change of orders the previous night and was presumably at Thélus, its original rendezvous; and two more had spent the night at Ficheux, a village where the road from Wancourt meets the Arras-Beaumetz road.

It was soon after the troops had got under way after their few hours' rest that the disaster overtook them which disrupted 70 Brigade for the rest of the campaign. Most of the 10th Battalion, almost in Lattre, were largely unaware of what was happening to their comrades marching along behind when a German armoured column, which had broken through south of Arras, descended upon them. Information about the enemy ever since the campaign began had been somewhat sketchy, not least during the previous twenty-four hours. Now the attack upon the marching troops was sudden and seemed to come from all sides. Those members of the 11th Battalion still in Wancourt, awaiting transport, were attacked about 8.30 a.m. by German tanks and, after a short engagement in which they could only reply with rifle fire, were either killed or captured. The C.O.,

Colonel John Bramwell, who had done so much to make the Battalion an efficient unit and who was in Wancourt at the time, was captured with them after hand-to-hand fighting with the Germans. Meanwhile, further up the road between Neuville Vitasse and the village of Ficheux, more fighting had broken out. Colonel Swinburne of the Tyneside Scottish, ahead of his Battalion in a truck on the way to Brigade Headquarters, was fired on from the outskirts of Ficheux itself. The truck was put out of action but the Colonel escaped unhurt and tried to get back to the Battalion. Before he could do so, he ran into some enemy tanks and infantry and was captured. At the same time, the two leading companies—' B ' and ' C ' Companies of the 10th Battalion, the former the last troops in the Battalion's column, the latter still under Tyneside Scottish command—were engaged by more Germans from the western outskirts of Ficheux. They were caught very much in the open and there was thus not very much they could do about it. Captain George Robinson, commanding ' B ' Company, and Captain John Kipling, commanding ' C ', had a hurried conference with the company commander of the Tyneside Scottish and then both companies deployed to the left of the road. Kipling was killed shortly afterwards; but though both companies fought gallantly they could make little headway against three successive enemy attacks from different directions in which, in the end, some twenty-two tanks were involved. However, two tanks were stopped and a number of casualties were inflicted on crews who put their heads out of the turrets, but with only rifles and bayonets the men of the two companies were gradually overwhelmed. Few escaped to tell the tale and of ' C ' Company there was not a single survivor.

In the general confusion the fighting resolved itself into a series of individual company actions and, finally, after a battle which caused the Germans some five hours' delay, the survivors extricated themselves in small parties and tried to rejoin what remained of their original units. George Robinson collected about eight men together in a spot out of sight, having feigned death to get the chance. Later in the day he lost touch with all except Privates George Walton and Percy Chapman and together the three of them set off to try to regain the Allied lines. Chapman, however, was lost on the second night after they had walked into a German tank park in the dark; so Robinson and Walton went on alone. They reached the coast on the 2nd of June, having got hold of civilian clothes for most of the journey. At first they travelled only by night but once in civilian clothes by day and night. They were among the forward German troops most of the time, often near the Allied forces but never near enough. Once they were stopped and searched by the Germans, several times they were fired at, and twice they had to inflict fatal injuries in order to get away. They were finally picked up at about 9.30 p.m. on the 4th of June just as they were preparing to push a small boat out to sea.

Back in Lattre, Colonel David Marley with the 10th Battalion of course knew nothing of what had happened. Heavy firing had been heard and he now did his best to try to gain some contact with Brigade Headquarters and the other Battalions. A wounded sergeant of the 11th Battalion first brought some news of what had happened to the rest of the Brigade column and said that the 11th were withdrawing to Hauteville. Colonel Marley then set off to look for them, but was fortunately held up by a flock of sheep just as an officer from Divisional Headquarters appeared to say that Hauteville was occupied by Germans. He also said that the Division would probably occupy a position on the St. Pol-Arras road in the area of Aubigny and Etrun and that he understood the rest of 70 Brigade had been very roughly handled. The Colonel returned to the Battalion, directing any stragglers he met from the 10th and 11th Battalions to Lattre, where he took them under his command. His battalion now comprised Headquarter Company, two rifle companies and those survivors of 'B' Company—about a platoon—who had managed to escape from Ficheux: and, though it was not known to the Colonel, the 11th Battalion in fact consisted of two companies and part of a third which had reached Beaumetz the previous night, with Headquarter Company in Thélus, the original rendezvous, and various members of Battalion Headquarters, loading parties and truck drivers having been overrun in Wancourt.

The 10th Battalion remained unmolested in Lattre although heavy firing was heard all round them. All transport was moved out of the village and given a rendezvous at Hermaville, a village some miles further north. Thither the Colonel resolved to withdraw his men that night, but, as further information came in and it became clear that the Arras-Doullens road was in German hands, he ordered the Battalion out of Lattre by 6 p.m. It was later learned that the Germans arrived a quarter of an hour afterwards.

In the meantime, the Quartermaster, Lieutenant Oldham, had arrived and laid on a meal for what remained of the Battalion. He had some further news of the situation. German armoured columns had cut the Arras-St. Pol road, and he himself had joined on to the tail of a German column, all unknown to them, for a short time along this same road. It was clearly time to move, and Colonel Marley ordered the Battalion across the St. Pol-Arras road and they reached the village of Cambligneul, a further six or seven miles to the north, very exhausted at about 6 o'clock in the morning of the 21st of May.

The Battalion was by now completely out of touch with both its Brigade and Division. It had no wireless sets. Contact had never been re-established with what remained of the 11th Battalion and the Tyneside Scottish had virtually ceased to exist. It was clear that any prospect of the 23rd Division forming a defensive flank near Aubigny was nothing more than wishful thinking. Colonel Marley therefore resolved to get in touch with the 12th Lancers, who were known to be somewhere nearby, and establish contact through their wireless sets. In due course he found them and they warned him of the peril of the Battalion's position. By this time the German armoured columns were pouring through the gap between Arras and the Somme and were well on their way to Boulogne and the coast. It will be remembered that it was on the 21st that the 5th and 50th Divisions were to make their attack south of Arras on the flank of these columns, but, apart from them, the rest of the B.E.F. was further north. The 12th Lancers and some French cavalry were the only Allied troops on the western flank of this attack, so the Battalion was out in the blue in an area occupied only by Allied reconnaissance units.

Colonel Marley then decided to report to Arras to the headquarters of "Petreforce" who were holding the town. They undertook to inform the 23rd Division of his position and it was agreed that the Battalion should remain where it was that day and move off to Lens that night. Towards evening, six R.A.S.C. lorries arrived at Cambligneul with orders to take the

Battalion to Seclin where the rest of the Division was concentrated. So the 10th Battalion, together with some forty stragglers from the 11th Battalion, crammed themselves into the lorries and, with a man on each mudguard, set forth for Seclin. Apart from a brush with some unknown but hostile riflemen on housetops in the square at Lens, the drive was uneventful; and, after reporting to Divisional Headquarters, the Battalion was directed to Gondecourt where it arrived at 3 a.m. on the 22nd of May, having covered some sixty miles in the past forty-eight hours.

It was at Gondecourt that the Battalion linked up with some more of the 11th Battalion. A number of men under Captain Alan Shipley, the Adjutant, arrived later in the day and were ordered to come under Colonel Marley's command. Later still another fifty, together with the Padre and Quartermaster, turned up and joined what was becoming in effect a composite Battalion. The bulk of these remnants of the Battalion consisted of the company which had gone to Thélus, the original battalion rendezvous, on the night of the 20th before the cancellation of these orders could reach them. There they had linked up with a battalion of the Green Howards with whom they operated until Shipley's arrival. Shipley himself had taken command of those companies of the Battalion which had reached Beaumetz on the 20th. Part of the two companies who had stopped the night at Ficheux had been involved in the general melée which engulfed the Tyneside Scottish, but the rest of them had got through. The Battalion, such as it was, was then ordered to withdraw to Berles, but, with enemy tanks roaming around, they split into company columns and moved off across country. One, after dodging some German tanks and being bombed from the air, eventually arrived at the Battalion's old camp at Nuncq. Here they fought a spirited action against some more tanks and then, in transport, managed to make for Abbeville which by this time, of course, was occupied by the Germans. So it was not long before they ran into the middle of a German column and were put in the bag. Of the rest, most of 'A' Company got through with Shipley, but, of the others, some did not join up till much later, others not at all. Many fought and died; some were taken prisoner. Each had his own adventures which cannot be recorded here.

Meanwhile, the complete absence of any signallers or signal equipment, both in the Battalions and at Brigade Headquarters, prevented Brigadier Kirkup from maintaining any effective communication with his command. Apart from two companies of the 11th Battalion at Beaumetz, no contact could be established. At 11.30 a.m. on the 20th Brigade Headquarters established itself at Berles, set up a control post and did its best to collect those members of the Brigade who came its way. By that evening these numbered some fourteen officers and over two hundred men. Contact was established with Divisional Headquarters, when the Brigadier was ordered to concentrate all those whom he had been able to collect in the woods round Souchez. But before this could be done, the Germans had intercepted any move in that direction; Brigade Headquarters was cut off from Division; and contact was never effectively re-established again in France. Thereafter more stragglers began to arrive and the Brigadier's command steadily increased till he had approximately eight hundred officers and men with him. They never succeeded in rejoining the 23rd Division or the rest of the 10th and 11th Battalions. For the remainder of the campaign they were organised into four rifle companies under Brigade Headquarters, and joined the composite command of General Curtis, the commander of the 46th Division. They then equipped themselves with every conceivable type of vehicle and became a mobile force having, as such, a number of clashes with the enemy. From time to time stragglers from the 10th and 11th Battalions joined up with them. One was Private Thomas Dabner whose adventures are worth recording. He was a truck driver of the 11th Battalion and on the 21st of May he had been ambushed and captured near Beaumetz. After disarming him the Germans told him to load his truck with wounded and follow a tank into action. It was a moonlight night when they set off, and after a while Dabner managed to escape with his truck at a road junction. Then, driving at high speed and with considerable skill, he succeeded in finding and depositing his wounded at a British Field Ambulance.

This force in due course reached Dunkirk where they embarked for England on the 28th of May.

The officers and men who gathered together under Colonel Marley were organised into a Headquarters and six rifle companies, as it was thought that the unit was less likely to be used as a single unit than as reinforcements for other Divisions. As well as Durham Light Infantrymen it comprised about a hundred survivors of the Tyneside Scottish, a few stragglers from Brigade and some from other units. But within only a few hours of formation orders were given for a move in transport to Watten near St. Omer, where the Battalion, together with 69 Brigade, was to hold the line of the Canal de l'Aa—the canal which links St. Omer with the North Sea—to help counter a threat which was apparently developing after the fall of Calais. The convoy left Gondecourt at 10 p.m. on the 22nd with an escort of armoured cars and light tanks, only to be stopped by the Divisional Commander at 4 a.m. and turned back. No one knew the reason, but that was nothing new. Once back in Gondecourt, however, the Battalion had little to do for two days, but it was during these two days that it received its nickname of " Marley Force " by which it was known for the rest of the campaign. Thereafter the Divisional Commander dealt with Colonel Marley just as he did with the Brigadier of 69 Brigade, and Marley Force took the place of what was once 70 Brigade.

Early on the morning of the 26th of May orders were received to move once more. The route was north through Beaucamps to Meteren over the Belgian border. By this time the decision had been reached that the British and French forces must march to the sea if they were to be saved from complete destruction; and it was clear to the Higher Command that all control by the French Supreme Command had completely broken down. Apart from a whole French Army, there were four British Divisions south of Lille and the Germans were trying their utmost, by two encircling movements, to close the pincers upon them. While the rest of the British Army was hotly engaged on either side of the corridor guarding the path to the sea, the 5th and 50th Divisions, as has been related, moved north to close the gap between the crumbling Belgian Army and the left flank of the B.E.F. Meanwhile, the organisation of a perimeter round Dunkirk was rapidly proceeding and, as various groups and parties of all arms arrived from every direction, they were skilfully fitted into it. It was towards the bridgehead position that Marley Force and the rest of the 23rd Division now withdrew. The Battalion made its way along

crowded roads and under constant threat of air raids—in one
of which they were attacked by six bombers—towards Meteren.
One party of about a hundred men under Lieutenant King was
left behind for special duty guarding bridges over the La Bassée
Canal. They came in for some very hard fighting and none
of them got back to England.

As they neared Meteren the Battalion was diverted, since
a heavy attack from the Hazebrouck area was apparently in
progress and it was not intended that they should become
involved. At one stage it looked as if they would be, but the
column got through and, partly marching and partly ferrying
the marching columns in such transport as they could muster,
they reached Stavele, some ten miles south of Furnes, on the
28th. The following day they took up a bridgehead position
over one of the canals, but within a few hours handed it over
to troops of another Division and moved back to Killem Linde
where the rest of the 23rd Division was concentrating. Here
the Battalion found a stray French cavalry horse, fully equipped,
which must have been but recently abandoned. The Adjutant
duly mounted it and for twenty-four hours it provided a useful,
if archaic, rallying point.

At Killem Linde all transport and unnecessary baggage was
destroyed. Sergeant Metherington, the 10th Battalion's transport sergeant, had done a fine job of work by his handling of it.
He was tireless in his determination to get the vehicles through,
despite air attacks, and his resourcefulness in making the
maximum use of it undoubtedly saved many men. On the 30th
the Battalion moved into the Dunkirk beachhead and occupied
a defensive position in rear of the 50th Division; and during the
day Alan Shipley of the 11th Battalion and some hundred men
were sent forward as reinforcements to 151 Brigade, many of
them going to the 8th Battalion. All Marley Force's Bren guns
went with them and what was left of the Force prepared to
embark the following day from the beaches at La Panne. Some
days previously when embarkation was obviously the order of the
day, Colonel Marley had jokingly promised his company
commanders the finest champagne dinner man ever saw once
they got home to England; and in order to kill time in the march
along the beaches he, the leading company commander and the
Quartermaster decided to settle the menu. They argued and

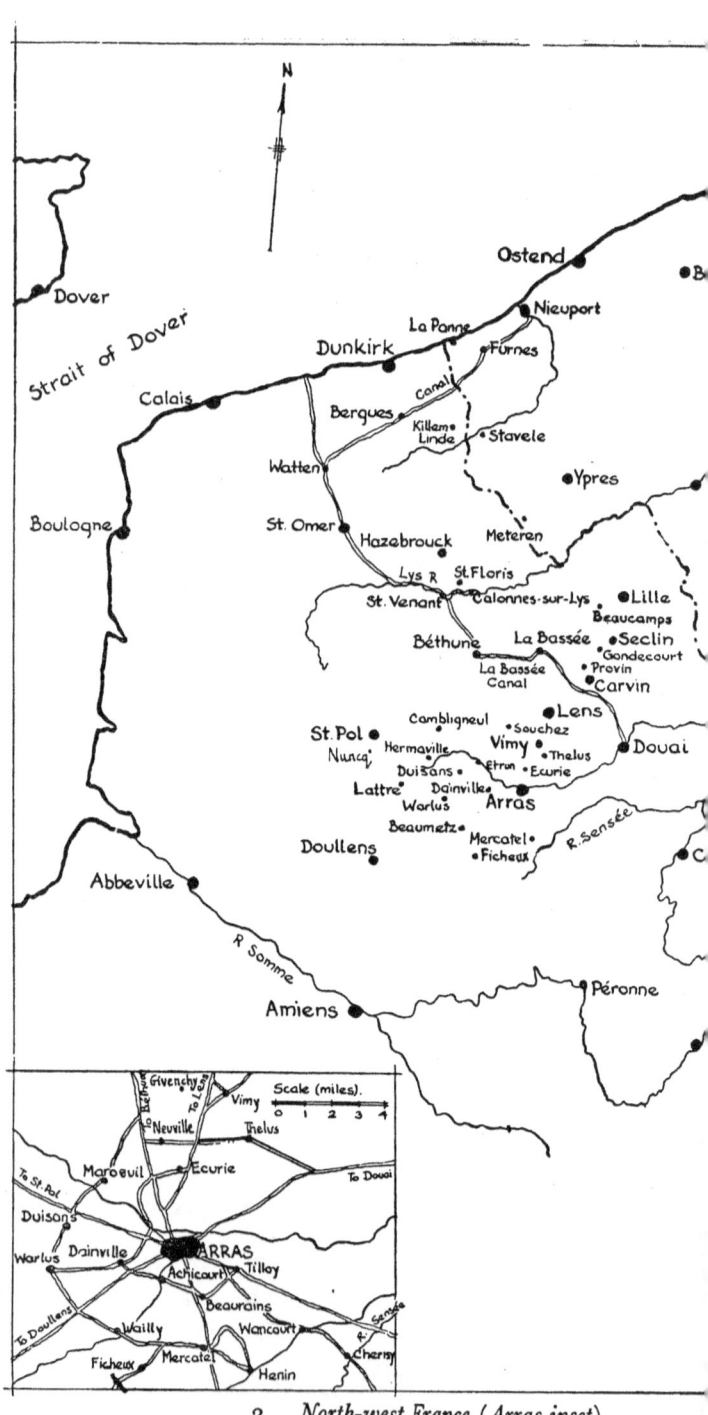

2. *North-west France (Arras inset)*

fought out the respective merits of hors d'oeuvres and smoked salmon, sole mornay and lobster cardinal, and when they had finished the dinner started on the drinks. Once back in England the Colonel's joke was transformed into a reality, and after a heavy period of coast defence work the surprised company commanders arrived one evening for a conference to find that the dinner had been arranged.

The Battalion did not in the end embark from the beaches as the sea was too rough. One platoon was taken off in rowing boats but, after suffering some casualties from shelling and bombing, the rest were ordered to Dunkirk mole where they embarked in craft of various descriptions during the latter part of the 31st of May.

CHAPTER TWO

The 1st Battalion in the Middle East 1940-1943

I

THE WESTERN DESERT AND SYRIA

WHEN war broke out the 1st Battalion was stationed at Tientsin in North China with one company on detachment at Peking as British Embassy guard, and another in camp at Shanhaikwan at the end of the Great Wall. It was commanded by Lieutenant-Colonel E. H. L. Lysaght Griffin and it had been abroad since 1937. The news of the declaration of hostilities was received, however, in somewhat unusual circumstances because since the 20th of August Tientsin and the country for many miles around it had been flooded, in some places to a considerable depth. The water in the barrack area was four or five feet deep; and the troops had been evacuated by a mixture of marching and swimming to one of Jardine Matheson's large go-downs on the Bund. The officers' mess, having two storeys, did not move; but it had to be approached by sampans which were tied up to the banisters. Some officers, therefore, heard the news that war had broken out from a passing sampan whilst playing deck tennis on the mess roof.

The Battalion's reaction to the news of war was of necessity limited. A great deal of kit had been lost in the floods, mobilisation stores—much of them for horse transport—were under water, so the Battalion contented itself with nothing more offensive than sampan patrols round the British Concession.

In December the Battalion moved to Hong Kong. The families of those who were married had gone there in October. They were followed, early in December, by the battalion advance party, composed strangely enough almost entirely of bachelors, and by the main body on Christmas Eve. Christmas Day Church Parade was conducted by the Dean of Hong Kong, who had himself served in the Regiment in the first world war. The stay in the island was, however, a very short one; and on the 6th of January 1940 the whole Battalion set sail in the S.S. " Talma," a converted coolie ship, for Suez, which was reached on the 30th. Thence it moved to Moascar into barracks which, save for a short period in 1942, were the last the Battalion was to occupy until well after the war was over; and after a further two months into tents around the quay and waterworks at Port Said. During that time—in April to be precise—Colonel Lysaght Griffin was appointed to Headquarters, British Troops in Egypt in Cairo and handed over command to Colonel G. T. Goldschmidt; and, shortly afterwards, Colonel Harry Lowe, who had been Quartermaster since 1919, was translated, at General Wavell's request, to G.H.Q. Middle East to be Quartermaster there. His place was taken by John Bush, hitherto Regimental Sergeant-Major, and Sergeant-Major George Flanagan became the new R.S.M. In June came the news of Italy's entry into the war; and the Battalion had the pleasure of incarcerating some 5,000 Italians residing in the town as well as boarding an Italian ship bound for Eritrea with a cargo of motor transport, anti-aircraft guns and valuable medical stores. Six weeks later the Battalion turned its back on civilisation, so called, and set out to relieve the Welch Regiment at Mersa Matruh, some three hundred miles westwards and then the favourite target for Italian bombers. By so doing they took their place for the first time in the Western Desert which was destined to be the main battleground of the British Army for nigh on three years, and one in which not only they but three more battalions of the Regiment were to play an active and distinguished part.

The northern desert of Africa is bigger than India. In the north it extends 1,200 miles westwards from Cairo to the hills of Tunisia and southwards for 1,000 miles to French Equatorial Africa and the Sudan. The landscape is one of sharp contrasts and is composed by no means entirely of sand. Grey plateaux of broken stones and boulders the size of footballs are followed by endless plains of brown pebbles dotted here and there with flat topped hills of black or white rock. For miles the surface is flat and firm; then suddenly, almost without warning, it gives way to soft sand and choking white dust. The African desert is one of the driest areas in the world, but along the coastal strip there is just sufficient rainfall to support a thin sporadic vegetation. In Egypt this coastal strip is backed by an escarpment which runs parallel to it. From the top of the escarpment a plateau extends south and the desert falls away in a series of terraces to a vast depression of shimmering sand dunes stretching as far as the eye can see. There are a number of such escarpments throughout the length of the desert, often stretching for several hundred miles at a time. They and the rolling dunes were the only barriers to the free movement of opposing armies.

Just east of the Egyptian frontier the escarpment turns north and puts a barrier across the coastal plain, forming a natural frontier in addition to that which the Italians wired with a broad entanglement prior to the war. Up this barrier, at Sollum, winds the coastal road and a little to the south-east a secondary track—for it is little more—climbs to the top of the now famous Halfaya pass.

The desert is a land of contrasts no less in climate than in terrain. The prevailing wind is northerly and is mild enough. Even summer nights are cool. But in winter when it rises to a storm it is bitterly cold. In summer the southerly winds, heated by the sands of the south, often whip across the desert driving dust and sand before them like hot blasts from a fiery furnace.

Communications in this largely deserted waste are few and simple. Only the coastal strip sports a proper road; otherwise there are merely the centuries old caravan routes on the flat, open desert. There are no towns worthy of the name south of the coastal route and few on it. Landmarks are scarce. They consist mainly of rock cisterns, of Roman origin, known as " Bir " in Arabic. And the names on the maps represent either these or the tomb of some desert personage. In practice they usually mean a pile of stones, a disused fort or an empty oil drum marking a caravan route.

The war in the desert was thus not merely a war against the Italians or the Germans but a war against the elements. The fierce winds, and the sandstorms they brought with them, often made movement impossible; navigation in the rolling wastes was more like that at sea than on land and much depended on accurate use of the sun compass; and to guard against the dangers of getting lost or breaking down miles from anywhere

Battalion Headquarters of the 1st Battalion at Mersa Matruh, November 1940
2/Lieut. K. Kershaw   Capt. A. St. George   Lt.-Col. E. A. Arderne

The 1st Battalion preparing positions in ' C ' Sector at Mersa Matruh, November 1940

The Prime Minister, Mr. Winston Churchill, inspects the 10th Battalion in Iceland

Men of the 11th Battalion on cliff-scaling exercises in Iceland

THE 1ST BATTALION IN THE MIDDLE EAST

every vehicle had to be self-contained with petrol, food and water. Some who fought in the desert will dwell upon its discomforts and its hostility to all forms of life, of the flies—the most faithful of camp followers—and of the sand and dust which penetrated everything; but others will talk of its strange attraction, its glorious sunsets, the welcome cool of summer evenings, and of the wild flowers which could be found near the coast in spring. " The attraction of the desert is that of woman for man. It is when she is silent that she is most attractive, most elusive, most seductive. It is when she is boisterous that one hates her most. Life with her is one continual dream of romance, for she has the power of making the traveller feel he is her sole admirer, her lonely visitor. She attracts with a magnetism which is irresistible, never assumes familiarity, never permits a liberty, gives freely of her charms which never fail to please, and one leaves her wishing for more . . . Cruel and merciless to those who play with her, generous and even gracious to those who love her and dwell with her. To ignore her is to court disaster. Her fancies and follies are various and numerous, her surprises never failing. One cannot linger or loiter in her arms. She demands efficiency and energy, characters she respects and repays. To lassitude and carelessness she metes out death in its most hideous form."[1]

The Battalion set off for Mersa Matruh under the command of Lieutenant-Colonel Goldschmidt. It reached its new location at a time when a considerable Italian Army was stationed along the Egyptian frontier. The enemy frontier forces comprised approximately four divisions, but if all the administrative troops and those guarding the great series of supply dumps between Tobruk and Sollum were included, there must have been about 300,000 men. The British forces opposing them, of which the Battalion formed part, comprised in all barely a division and its component parts consisted to a large degree of unbrigaded units. As time went by, however, the position improved. Nevertheless, the forward elements of the Desert Army now forming had by their early initiative made themselves masters of the no-man's land which stretched between the opposing forces; and their persistent raids upon the enemy

---

[1] Nicholl's " Birds of Egypt," Vol. I, p. 4.

inflicted losses out of all proportion to those they received themselves.

In these early days it was the Commander-in-Chief's policy to await the onslaught of the Italian forces near the fortifications of Mersa Matruh. From the time of its arrival in mid-July the Battalion devoted itself to performing its share in their preparation. On the 22nd of July, just as its motor transport was arriving, the Battalion experienced its first heavy daylight air raid; and it was lucky to escape with only three wounded. Raids, however, were soon quite commonplace. Between July and October there were over one hundred in strengths of up to sixty S.79 bombers. The only defence consisted of three obsolete anti-aircraft guns, manned by the Egyptian Army, and Royal Air Force Gladiators which were 20 m.p.h. slower than the bombers. So the Battalion started a Spitfire fund which had reached £200 when the first Hurricanes appeared.

In the middle of September the long awaited Italian advance began. It comprised six infantry divisions and eight battalions of tanks and before it the scanty British covering forces, consisting of three battalions of infantry and one of tanks, together with some guns and armoured cars, slowly withdrew. The Battalion took no part in these operations but continued to improve its positions round Matruh. On the 17th the Italian Army reached Sidi Barrani; and here it settled down to spend the next three months, a period of time which could not, of course, be anticipated by its opponents but which, as it turned out, was to be its undoing.

For the Battalion the period from September to December was comparatively uneventful. It was occupied with the everyday routine of digging and laying mines. In October, Colonel Goldschmidt had to leave the Battalion owing to ill health and his second in command, Eustace Arderne, succeeded to the command which he was to hold with distinction for the next two years. But though the days passed quietly enough, in the conclaves of the Higher Command was being worked out a daring offensive operation timed to begin early in December. The Italian Army which had crossed the frontier was spread over a fifty mile front in a series of fortified but widely separated camps. It was planned to strike between two of these camps—those at Sofafi and Nibeiwa—and then, turning towards the sea, to attack those at Nibeiwa and Tummar from the rear. Only a small circle of officers was let into the secret and practically nothing was put on paper; so that it was not till the very eve of the attack that those taking part knew that it was other than an exercise.

So it was with the Battalion. Early in December a composite company was formed under Colonel Arderne for an unknown task. It moved out to a wadi west of Matruh and there spent several days secretly erecting dummy tanks and vehicles of wood and hessian. Then, the day before the advance was due to begin, C.O.s were called to the Matruh Fortress commander's dug-out. Sentries were posted everywhere, one even standing at the ventilator poking up through the sand. "When we finally got inside," wrote Colonel Arderne, "and every possible security had been taken we were told a pack of lies. Only the next day, far out in the desert and on the eve of the attack, were we told the truth; the Desert Army for the first time was advancing." This bold stroke, conceived by General Wavell and executed by General Maitland Wilson, was to bring a spectacular victory which lightened the hearts of the British people during otherwise stern and sombre days.

The bulk of the Battalion was to remain in Matruh at the outset. Only the Colonel's column was to form part of the so-called "Arthur Force" which was to advance along the coast road and to try to draw off the enemy armour from the main attack at Sidi Barrani. The column's task was to erect its "tanks" in the desert so as to deceive the Italians as to the strength and content of the advance. This it proceeded to do on the night of the 9th of December. The "tanks" were erected during the dark, slit trenches were dug and as, for the sake of realism, the column was to remain with the dummies, everybody sat, feeling rather naked and defenceless, waiting for the inevitable bombing attack the following morning.

Dawn came, however, and the sun rose high in the sky without any enemy aircraft appearing. Either the Italians had not seen the dummies or they were not deceived. By nightfall not a single plane had been seen and the whole column was delighted to hear that it was to scrap its toys and join General Selby's Force Headquarters just east of Meiktila. This it proceeded to do and was then told to move next morning to a position on the coast, west of Meiktila, and await further orders.

That evening after dark the orders were received. " I wish I had kept them for the Regimental Museum," wrote Colonel Arderne: " ' Enemy strength about two brigades are holding position covering the coast. Stop. You will advance at dawn on Sidi Barrani.' Our strength was four officers, seventy other ranks and six machine-guns of the Cheshire Regiment. We had no guns, no wireless communications and no one had the least idea where Force H.Q. was. We laughed a bit too heartily when those orders came, but no one slept very peacefully."

The advance began at first light on the 12th. The machine gunners took up a position on a sandy ridge to the south. The enemy positions, or forts, could be seen quite plainly about three or four thousand yards away and there appeared to be a mass of transport and men offering themselves as ideal targets. The machine-guns opened fire and the column's three platoons moved forward over scattered desert scrub on the seaward flank. Before long the Italian artillery opened fire and for a while the advance was halted; but the shelling was so inaccurate that the column was soon on the move again. Suddenly, however, the machine gun officer shouted to the Colonel " There's a white flag, sir." " Nonsense," the latter replied; but, true enough, there was one and before long there was a host of them followed by a small car, draped in a white sheet, which careered towards the advancing platoons at great speed.

Colonel Arderne immediately jumped into his own truck and went out to meet what turned out to be an Italian officer with a formal surrender; and then, before the Italians should change their minds, he dashed on to the fort followed closely by the remainder of the column. There he found the entire Italian staff solemnly drawn up on their positions and the Brigadier or Divisional Commander—nobody ever discovered which—stepped forward, saluted and, standing in front of a vast pile of ammunition, said gravely, " Monsieur, nous avons tiré la dernière cartouche." By this time the column had caught up with the Colonel and was standing in open mouthed amazement as hundreds of fully armed Blackshirts rose from all sides where they had been dug in. It was all very sudden, totally unexpected and, indeed, rather a shock at first, but the Italians seemed only too pleased to dump their weapons as ordered and sit down. A section with a broken down Bren gun was left to guard some five hundred prisoners and the column moved on again.

They had not gone far when a new enemy position was encountered, this time at somewhat closer range. It was engaged by a platoon commanded by Second-Lieutenant " Beagle " Birchenough who himself went into action with a Bren gun. One good burst and again a white flag appeared. This time an Italian officer rushed towards the platoon and seeing Birchenough at the gun shouted, " Sir, you have killed a man." This was not a bad start for it was the latter's first shot in anger, but apologies were duly offered; prisoners were duly taken; and this incredible comic opera war continued.

Meanwhile the overall picture was exceedingly favourable. The Italians had been completely surprised. Sidi Barrani had fallen like a ripe plum and the enemy was in full retreat everywhere. The Colonel's column was not alone in its experiences of Italian surrender; for on all sides the prisoners were in fact too numerous to count. The Battalion had quite a bit to do in sorting them out; for within a day or so the rest of it moved forward from Mersa Matruh to Sidi Barrani, there to take over the evacuation of prisoners to Alexandria. This, despite their very large numbers and the shortage of both food and water, proved comparatively easy as the captives appeared only too willing to co-operate; there were no attempts to escape; and, indeed, they drove themselves away to Alexandria in their own trucks!

While the bulk of the Battalion busied itself with prisoners the original company column was reorganised and, under Major Robin Johnston, the second in command, continued to operate with the 7th Hussars in the operations resulting in the capture first of Bardia and then of Tobruk. In the battle for the latter Robin Johnston was mortally wounded while out on patrol, and the Regiment lost not only its second in command but a very gallant officer.

Bardia had fallen, with 40,000 prisoners, on the 5th of January 1941, and Tobruk, with 30,000, on the 22nd. Soon afterwards the Battalion was concentrated at Mersa Matruh and then moved back to Qassassin, near Suez, to join 2 (later 22 and still later 201) Guards Brigade. For the next two months or so, therefore, it busied itself in combined operational training in the Bitter Lakes in preparation for what was intended to be an attack on the island of Scarpanto in the Dodecanese. But this operation was not to be—in view of its hazards some thought fortunately—for before it was due to take place the Battalion, with the rest of the Brigade, was required to meet a new threat from the west in the guise of General Rommel's first offensive. The Battalion hastened off to the desert once more, arrived in Mersa Matruh early in April and then drove on to Sollum to meet numbers of vehicles streaming back in retreat.

    The events of early April had resulted in a train of misfortune for the Desert Army. Rommel's attack had begun at Agheila on the 31st of March; it had disorganised the armoured forces there; and a withdrawal had begun which did not end until the Egyptian frontier. Benghazi was evacuated on the 4th of April and by the 12th the enemy had surged round and past Tobruk—which resisted all attacks—and had taken Bardia, nearly a hundred miles beyond. By this time the Battalion, less 'A' Company under Captain "Crackers" May, was positioned around the barracks in Sollum, while 'A' Company had been sent off on that afternoon with orders to hold Bardia with one troop of light tanks, one section of carriers and an anti-tank gun which was actually pulled off the column before it even reached the town. "Crackers" May had protested that when Bardia was captured from the Italians the latter had over 30,000 men there—but in vain! Off the Company went to do what it could to protect the two large pumping stations with good water which were Bardia's main claim to fame. During the early part of the night of the 11th firing grew nearer and louder and the sound of traffic by-passing the town increased. About 10 p.m. the telephone went dead. There was no wireless in those days; but not long afterwards a dispatch rider turned up with a message saying, "Believe you are surrounded. Blow everything. Good luck." Fortunately the Sappers who were there had the pumping stations and port prepared for demolition, and about two hours later, after a series of shattering explosions, the Company was able to pull out and drive post haste in the bright moonlight back to Sollum.

    Next day the Battalion withdrew with the rest of the Guards Brigade to the area of Halfaya Pass where it occupied positions at the top and bottom of the Pass, protected away to its left flank by Brigadier Jock Campbell's much reduced Support Group. For a short while there was a period of stalemate. The enemy occupied Sollum, Fort Capuzzo and Fort Maddalena, but for the moment came no further beyond moving up to the top of the escarpment round Sollum. The Battalion set about organising a series of vigorous patrols. The most popular was one to an abandoned supply dump at Musaid where it was possible to recoup many of the comforts destroyed in the semi-panic prevailing in Sidi Barrani on the way up. The most successful was carried out by Major Harley Fox-Davies who, with thirty men, raided a German platoon post on the top of the escarpment. All but five of the enemy were killed for the loss by the patrol of one man wounded. The five, who included the first German officer to be captured in the desert and a warrant officer, were taken prisoner.

On the 23rd of April the enemy again began to advance; and it was some comfort to the Battalion to find that the leading German motor cyclists and a half track vehicle had run on to a minefield which they had carefully laid in a wadi between Sollum and Halfaya, of which the enemy had previously made over-conspicuous use. The Germans, however, never pressed home their attack at the top of Halfaya; they merely shelled it and then by-passed it, pushing on down the escarpment towards Sofafi. As a result the Brigade was forced to withdraw that night to avoid being surrounded, and the Battalion moved back to positions around Kilo 90 on the Matruh-Sidi Barrani road. Soon afterwards the whole Brigade was withdrawn still further, but for another purpose. They were to prepare for an attack upon the German positions in and around Sollum which was timed to take place early in May.

The Battalion moved up to Sofafi on the 13th of May. The actual attack was timed for dawn on the 15th, and it was to be supported by the 4th Battalion, Royal Tank Regiment, the same Regiment which had supported the 6th Battalion at Arras in 1940. The Battalion's objective was from and including Fort Capuzzo to the frontier wire on the Sollum road; and once the Fort was taken the reserve company was to move through and occupy the airfield a mile down the road to Bardia. The Scots Guards were to attack Halfaya and then move on to occupy Sollum.

On the night of the 14th the Battalion moved off in the dark along a track on top of the escarpment, preceded by the Scots Guards. At dawn the latter swung north on to Halfaya which they captured later in the morning. As soon as they were clear the Battalion, in trucks, deployed into desert formation and with thirteen tanks in the lead moved off towards Fort Capuzzo. "Our methods were very primitive," wrote Colonel Arderne, "compared with later days. There were no wireless communications and standing in my truck in the centre of the line I waved different coloured flags to represent "Advance," "Halt," "Attack." To keep in touch with the tanks usually meant halting the column, going forward in my own car to the Tank Commander's tank and then returning. Though primitive it was simple and worked well till the tanks passed over the final ridge which hid our objective from view. Intense firing was heard and then all was quiet. I went ahead to the ridge to reconnoitre. On the enemy position tanks were patrolling and firing had ceased. Our orders were to reach the objective on the heels of the tanks and we appeared to be late. I waved my "Advance" flag frantically and our convoy in M.T., covering a front of eight hundred yards, stepped on the gas and raced forward, a very thrilling sight. At the frontier wire they converged to the gaps, then spread out again and moved towards the objective. Then it suddenly dawned on me that the tanks on the objective were enemy and not our own. We watched in horror as our trucks rushed on in full view. By good fortune the enemy had made the same mistake as we had done. They had taken our convoy to be their own troops withdrawing from Halfaya and not before they got within several hundred yards did they open fire."

In the face of this opposition the three leading companies tumbled out of their trucks, opened out in perfect order and went straight into the assault. A number of casualties were suffered as they left the trucks but, strangely enough, very few more until the enemy positions were finally reached. On the left 'C' Company (Adrian Keith) occupied Capuzzo, 'B' Company ("Whistle" Crosthwaite) successfully reached its objective in the centre and 'A' Company ("Crackers" May) occupied a small feature near the frontier wire which was their objective. By this time the firing was intense and the enemy's reaction vigorous. 'A' Company found themselves within a hundred yards of an enemy gun battery but their casualties were mounting and they were unable to reach it. Furthermore, despite German armour, no anti-tank guns had yet come forward. Being without wireless sets communications depended on runners. Two were killed trying to get a message to Battalion Headquarters asking for tank support. A third message was finally carried back by Private Harry Metforth under very heavy fire.

Meanwhile 'D' Company, in reserve under Major Fox-Davies, moved forward as originally planned to occupy the airfield. As it did so the Germans launched a strong counter-attack with a large number of tanks and infantry. The Company was engulfed in this attack and few of its members were ever seen again. Those who were not killed were captured and only one man returned. But there was worse to come; for it soon transpired that the tanks of the Royal Tank Regiment had been ambushed by a group of the new German 88 millimetre anti-tank guns with the result that their strength had been reduced to three; and the German tanks which had attacked Fox-Davies' Company now began moving slowly down the objective.

The Battalion had nothing but anti-tank rifles with which to deal with the enemy armour; and they, of course, were quite useless. Their positions were therefore fairly quickly overrun. Slowly Keith from Capuzzo, Crosthwaite in the centre and May on the right were compelled to pull back, aided by a certain amount of dust which blew up, as luck would have it, at the right moment. As evening drew on the German tanks drew back too, about a mile or so; and this enabled the Battalion to extricate some more men and to rescue a number of wounded. When darkness fell the Battalion had moved into a small isolated square, with the guns in the middle. Losses had been heavy and perhaps one of the saddest was the death of Jack and Robert Meikle, twin brothers and the first two non-regular officers to join the Battalion since the outbreak of war. The medical officer, Captain Robin Lees, had been wounded in the foot but had continued to tend the wounded throughout the operation out in the open with only slight cover provided by a knocked out carrier. At all events the Battalion was now reduced to three rifle companies each of which numbered just under half its full strength and none of which had many officers left: 'A' Company had lost all its platoon commanders killed or mortally wounded.

Next morning the Battalion was withdrawn to Buq Buq. "At first light" wrote the Colonel, "the expected orders to withdraw arrived and we moved off in full view without a shot being fired. I have never discovered what lucky act of providence stopped the enemy from following up his initial success."

At Buq Buq a welcome draft of some two hundred and fifty reinforcements was received, mainly from the Essex Regiment, and the Battalion began to reorganise itself; while doing so it was moved further back still to help in the protection of airfields and there it remained for nearly a month in comparative peace until, in the middle of June, came sudden orders to concentrate and move once again to Qassassin. The Battalion was bundled into cattle trucks—most of which had not been cleaned since occupied by their previous four-footed owners!—and on reaching its destination learnt that it was to move without delay to Syria, there to join a newly formed Brigade in which its comrades in arms were to be a Czechoslovak battalion and the 4th Battalion, The Border Regiment.

Syria was one of the many overseas territories of the French Empire which at the time of the fall of France had considered themselves bound by the surrender of the Vichy Government. If the Germans had ever controlled it the effect on the position in the Middle East might well have been disastrous; so when Rashid Ali revolted in Iraq in May 1941 and called on Hitler to give him armed support something had to be done. The Germans demanded of Vichy facilities in Syria for the passage of military equipment and aeroplanes; and Admiral Darlan, early in May, negotiated a preliminary agreement with them. As a result General Wavell, although hard pressed in the desert and in Crete, was ordered to collect what forces he could and with the Free French to overcome the Vichy administration. This he did and a mixed force of British and French crossed the frontier from Palestine on the 8th of June. The force was not strong and although it made considerable progress it was clear, after a week's fighting, that reinforcements would be needed. The Battalion formed part of these reinforcements and after a rapid journey arrived at Tulkarm in Palestine at the end of the month to meet for the first time the other members of the newly formed Brigade. Though the Vichy French soon evacuated Damascus they were immovable in strong positions in the Lebanon some miles south of Beirut and in a high pass north of Mount Hermon.

On the 1st of July the Battalion took over from an Australian battalion in and around the village of Merdjayoun; and there it remained for some days in not very close contact with troops of the French Foreign Legion and some Senegalese. Apart from patrolling there was little activity; but Battalion Headquarters, which was shelled regularly each day, was besieged by local informers with information about enemy gun positions little of which could be relied on. Soon rumour began to get busy that the French were withdrawing, and early on the 10th patrols confirmed that this was in fact the case. The Battalion moved forward preceded by a mobile column consisting of 'A' and 'D' Companies together with carriers and guns. Its route lay along a narrow winding road with many hairpin bends but a fair surface. There were few passing places and nowhere wide enough to turn a vehicle round. By nightfall on the 11th the Battalion had reached Youhmour and had sent forward patrols, one of which—a fighting patrol—was to cross the river Litani and secure an observation post at Aintine. In fact, however, this little war was over. Soon after midnight orders were received that fighting was to cease and all forward troops were to stand fast for forty-eight hours. The news was not unwelcome, for at first light the Battalion would otherwise have had the unenviable task of advancing across a French artillery range in the face of French 75 millimetre guns whose crews had practised there in peace.

After a short rest the Battalion moved forward again and ultimately arrived at Ain el Assal on the 21st of July, there to build itself a camp. This village was 4,000 feet up in the hills with a wonderful view of the valley below. The journey was marred by a fatal accident when a carrier overturned and killed Second-Lieutenant Ben Liddell; he and five men wounded were the total battalion casualties of the campaign. Thereafter the Battalion settled down to building a camp and the whole place resounded to the clang of pick and shovel. Even a swimming pool was begun. Nearby Mount Hermon offered a challenge to a party of some eighty officers and men who, led by the C.O., began to climb its 9,000 feet early on the 23rd. Only thirty-eight finally reached the top, the Colonel being beaten for first place by a few yards by Private John Symes of ' D ' Company.

The next three months were uneventful. They were spent in comparatively peaceful occupation duties in various parts of Syria and Palestine, ending up in Aleppo. The days and weeks slipped pleasantly by and the lull was not unwelcome. But all lulls come to an end before long, usually suddenly; and this was no exception. On the 2nd of October the Battalion was given fourteen days' notice to move; the only equipment to be taken was that which could be carried; and officers were told they could take valises but they must be prepared to carry them a mile! On the 3rd an advance party of an Australian battalion arrived from Tobruk as a relief, and most people—in the face of this dark hint as to destination—mentally repacked their kit and decided to have one more night in Aleppo.

2

TOBRUK

A reconnaissance party under Colonel Arderne had already departed before the Battalion received its orders to move. That was at the end of September. But the arrival of the Australians made it reasonably certain that the fortress of Tobruk was the ultimate destination. Tobruk had been invested for some five months, since the 4th of April. It had withstood the onrush of the Axis forces in the previous spring and summer and had steadfastly remained an important thorn in Rommel's side. All the while its garrison had been the 9th Australian Division who had borne the heat of the day and whom the Australian Government now not unreasonably insisted should be relieved. All stores had now to be handed over to the Australians; which made the Quartermaster pull a wry face as he had just made up all deficiencies resulting from the campaign in Syria and was wondering what he would subsequently get in return.

The journey to Egypt began on the 6th of October from Aleppo station. It was pretty frightful; the train consisted of cattle trucks; and everybody was glad to reach the Suez Canal area by the 9th. Three days afterwards, at 5 in the morning,

THE 1ST BATTALION IN THE MIDDLE EAST

the Battalion climbed into trucks and left for Alexandria to embark on the last lap of the journey to Tobruk. Embarkation took place at 6.30 a.m.—just an hour and a half later. The Battalion was accommodated in two destroyers and a fast minelayer. Once beyond the harbour bar the ships made a steady thirty knots for Tobruk, arriving without incident at about 9.30 p.m. the same night. Once there, everybody was hustled out of the ships by the Navy who had to be away and out of aircraft range by daylight. The Battalion disembarked on to a sunken hulk by means of planks from the ships' sides. The sailors pushed them down the planks, then threw their kits after them and were off—all in the space of barely half an hour.

Arrived on shore companies were picked up by Australian transport, which from the bumps and noise they made had seen better days, and dumped in a wadi used as a transit area. There they remained for two days while the C.O. and company commanders were conducted round the sector to be occupied which was several days later taken over from the 2nd/48th Australians. It was known as the Figtree Sector from one solitary tree at Battalion Headquarters. No one got a sight of the town of Tobruk—or what was left of it—and indeed many members of the Battalion have probably never seen it to this day.

The Tobruk perimeter stretched for twenty-five miles from sea to sea; but there was no natural defence line. At about every hundred and fifty yards there were concrete defences which took the form of very deeply dug pillboxes, the lower stories of which comprised galleries each capable of taking a platoon. The latter were dim, dark and dank and their only light had to be provided by candles or hurricane lamps. Behind this string of concrete emplacements comprising the perimeter, and sited in depth, was a series of shallow dug-outs; and to complete the defences there was a series of extensive minefields, so many indeed that their ubiquity was confusing and the paths through them few and intricate. However, it was to them that Tobruk largely owed its virtual impregnability. The ground around the perimeter defences was flat and open, intersected here and there by an occasional wadi, but with visibility stretching many miles, which made movement in forward posts impracticable in daylight.

There was little that was attractive about Tobruk. It was

dirty and dusty and both sides sat glaring at each other much in the style of the 1914-1918 war. Routine was dull; there was plenty of patrolling; and shelling of positions and of the harbour was regular. Almost every night there was an air raid which was usually over by about 10 p.m. and after which the ships of the Navy would slip into the harbour with men or stores or both.

After about a week in the line the Battalion moved back into divisional reserve. It occupied an area which seemed to get most of the shrapnel from the harbour as well as more than its fair share of sand and dust. While there it acted as one-day host to the 2nd/13th Australians who ought to have left Tobruk but had not sailed because the Navy had been prevented from entering the Harbour. Companies of both Regiments doubled up and the Battalion's cooks surpassed themselves in producing two lots of meals. The next day the Battalion moved again— this time into the southern sector of the Tobruk fortress—and there it remained for the rest of October.

The early days of November saw little change. Patrols were as active as ever; and so were enemy bombers. In one raid an N.C.O. firing a Bren gun from a gun pit was lucky to escape unharmed when a bomb splinter cut his Bren tripod extension in two. On the 9th a large scale raid was carried out by 'D' Company on an enemy position known as "Plonk." "Plonk" was an enemy post some 1,500 yards beyond the perimeter defences. It had originally been in British hands, but had, a short time previously, been overrun by German tanks in an attack which appeared to be part of a policy by the enemy to capture a number of such small isolated posts as a means of pushing his own line forward. "Plonk" had been the object of a number of Battalion patrols from which it appeared that the enemy was trying to complete his wire from "Plonk" to the El Adem road. On the 6th a fighting patrol under Lieutenant John Craig crawled to within a hundred yards of the wire and then opened fire on a group of enemy. The enemy brought down defensive fire immediately and continued to fire with machine guns and mortars for over half an hour; but the patrol successfully withdrew having lost one man killed.

At about 6.45 p.m. on the 9th 'D' Company, under Major Hugh Vaux, assembled about a mile behind the forward Battalion positions. It was joined by a platoon of 'A' Company,

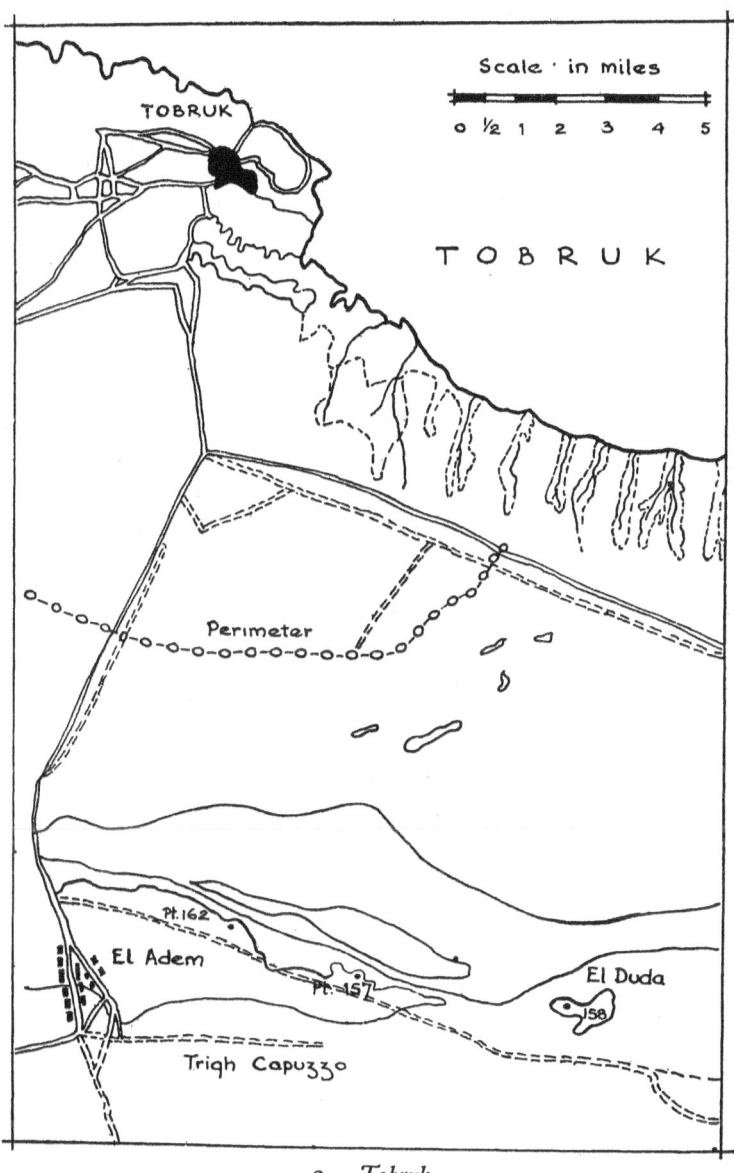

3. *Tobruk*

under Captain Jack Stafford, and some Sappers, both of whom were to take part also. Support was to be given by artillery and two platoons of heavy machine guns from the Fifth Fusiliers.

The Company crossed the start-line for the attack—which was seven hundred yards out into no man's land—at about 10 p.m. in the light of a half moon. The supporting machine gunners opened up a little before zero and appeared to be hitting the target. Then the bark of the guns broke the stillness of the night exactly on time, but only to send their shells flying well above the heads of the attackers whom it was soon apparent would get little help from them that night. Nevertheless, all went well to begin with until the leading platoon reached the enemy's front wire. This was a network on wooden pickets three feet high by about four yards in depth. The enemy mortars were ranged on this as well as his machine-guns, and as the leading platoons crossed it the first burst of fire caused a number of casualties. Then up went Very lights and parachute flares and the enemy " sangers " could be seen just a hundred yards ahead but, alas, behind another line of wire in the form of a proper apron fence.

The wire and the enemy's fixed line fire proved a major stumbling block to any further advance. Although two platoons and part of the third got through the first line of wire they ran into fixed line fire, casualties began to mount and after a further fifty yards they ran into more wire and more fixed line fire. There were still more casualties.

It thus became apparent that the final objective could only be reached at the best with very heavy casualties; the artillery fire plan had failed; and there was no alternative but to withdraw, bringing out as many wounded as possible. This the Company proceeded to do, not without difficulty, because it meant crawling for at least three hundred yards to keep under the fixed line fire. But some very gallant work was done in rescuing wounded. Private Oswald Temple, Headquarters stretcher bearer, toiled valiantly ministering to wounded within the enemy wire; and Sergeant Obadiah Stewart and Private Crawley brought two badly wounded men back, taking over three hours to do it.

All in all, though the raid had not achieved all it had set out to achieve, there is little doubt that it kept the Battalion's opponents guessing for some days to come; which was as well, for something was brewing in the desert requiring the diversion of the enemy's attention. A plan was about to be put into operation under which the newly formed British Eighth Army should leap forward from the Egyptian frontier and the Tobruk garrison should make a heavy and violent sortie towards them.

The attack by the Eighth Army was timed for the 18th of November. The sortie from Tobruk was to take place on the receipt of the codeword " Pop," and it was to be directed towards El Duda where the link-up with the Eighth Army was to take place. The Battalion's part was to be a comparatively small one consisting of a diversion with the carrier platoon while the 4th Border Regiment made a raid on Carmusa. The main sortie was to be carried out by another Brigade further eastwards.

The days between the raid on " Plonk " and the receipt of the anxiously awaited codeword were spent comparatively uneventfully. There were the usual air raids, periods of shelling by both sides and the never ending patrolling. One night a fighting patrol, under Second-Lieutenant Harry Towns, reached the wire on the east of " Plonk " only to meet heavy defensive fire on which they withdrew. One of the members of the patrol —Lance-Corporal Wright—reported in some while after the rest, having lost his direction on the way back. He had wandered into an enemy position where he was made prisoner and taken into a dug-out to be interrogated by what he thought was a German officer. After refusing to give his regiment he was made to kneel down and then revolver shots were fired over his head. Thinking his last hour had come, Wright made a bolt out of the door and managed to get away in the darkness. After a short distance he fell into a slit trench covered by a ground sheet. Several startled men scrambled out from underneath, but Wright jumped out quickly, did not wait to see who they were, and reached the perimeter defences unscathed. " It is pretty certain from this," says the War Diary, " that ' Plonk ' is garrisoned by Italians supported by Germans."

For the next fortnight a bitter battle raged to the east, south and south-east of Tobruk; but throughout it news within the fortress was at a premium. From its positions the Battalion could hear what was going on and could see the Royal Air Force bombing and strafing enemy positions and convoys; but little information reached them as to how the battle was going, save that the initial sortie had achieved considerable success. On the 26th it was rumoured that the New Zealand Division was approaching El Duda. Patrols to "Plonk" and El Adem reported that they were still strongly held by the enemy and by the end of the month a company was still standing by to occupy "Plonk" should the enemy withdraw. Throughout the 30th a very heavy battle could be heard in progress in the area of Sidi Rezegh.

In fact the New Zealanders succeeded on the 26th in joining hands with part of the Tobruk garrison in the eastern sector and shortly afterwards other troops of the Eighth Army entered the perimeter. But a German counter-attack recaptured Sidi Rezegh and forced part of the New Zealand Division to withdraw south-eastwards with heavy casualties. For a moment the Tobruk garrison was isolated once more, though it managed to maintain all the ground so far gained in its sortie. Even so the enemy still held his positions along the escarpment covering the El Adem road and before the final relief could be effected this hold had to be broken. On the 3rd of December the Battalion learnt that an attack was to be made by the Brigade on Point 157 and Point 162 on top of the escarpment due east of El Adem. The Battalion was to support the 4th Border Regiment in an attack on Point 157 and then pass through them on to Point 162. However, because the Border Regiment, who moved to El Duda on the 4th, had to put in a counter-attack on the morning of the 5th, the plan was changed and the Battalion was to attack Point 157 on its own. Late in the evening it moved off in trucks to laager for the night just inside the perimeter in the eastern sector. It remained there for two days and, while waiting, received a welcome batch of reinforcements comprising some eighty officers and men.

After some uncertainty as to whether the attack was to take place or not, the operation was finally fixed for the night of the 7th. There was this slight modification—namely that after consolidation on Point 157 the Border Regiment were to move up and exploit to Point 162. This, the reverse of the original plan, was because the Battalion had spent two days observing Point 157 and had a better idea of the ground.

At 5 p.m. the Battalion got into trucks once more and set

off for El Duda which was now occupied by a battalion of the Essex Regiment. The distance from the start line near El Duda to Point 157 was about 6,000 yards on a compass bearing of 275 degrees. The route kept the Battalion between the road just south of the escarpment and the escarpment itself, and the plan of attack was to strike the line of "sangars" held by the enemy between the road and the escarpment, rush them and then turn right handed towards the escarpment. In the event of a counter-attack by tanks cover would be available in the wadis below the escarpment, which were effective tank obstacles.

Arriving at the start line at 7.20 p.m., companies, led by guides from the Essex Regiment, moved off to the forming up areas to wait for zero hour at 8.30 p.m. It was a clear, starry night, and the moon, in its third quarter, was due to rise about twenty minutes after the advance had begun.

At 8.30 p.m. the Battalion moved forward. 'A' Company was on the left and 'C' on the right, each in line of platoons at fifty yard intervals, with 'B' and 'D' Companies behind in column of threes and Battalion Headquarters at the head of 'B'. They advanced over the desert in perfect formation with no noise save for the swish of boots brushing dry sand. "Just like our usual night training," remarked Captain "Topper" Browne, the Adjutant, to the C.O. and the words were barely out of his mouth when the crack of a rifle shot broke the silence. Someone had not applied his safety catch and off into the dark went Regimental Sergeant-Major Flannigan. A few minutes later he returned with the assurance "All right, sir, I've got that man's name." Browne was right; it was just like training!

After about two hours' marching things began to happen and the resemblance to training was thereafter purely coincidental. First some Italians could be heard singing; they always sang at night. Then there was silence and then with a crash the desert awoke and every form of tracer shell and bullet seemed to be flying in the Battalion's direction. 'B' Company and Battalion Headquarters managed to find some cover in some unoccupied "sangars". 'A' Company, who had run into the main line of enemy defences, was held up by heavy machine gun fire on fixed lines. But 'C' Company, unbeknown to the C.O. at the time, managed to make some progress; got into the sangars on the edge of the escarpment; and began mopping them up.

Generally, however, the Battalion had come to a halt and the situation was not made any easier by the fact that all the wireless sets were out of action. A platoon of 'B' Company under Second-Lieutenant Bruce Ballantyne was sent round the left flank to help 'A' Company; but despite a very gallant charge, in which Ballantyne himself was killed, the platoon was unable to make much headway.

As there seemed little prospect of making further progress without very heavy casualties, and as the enemy fire was getting heavier and the position on the right flank was obscure, the C.O. sent Captain Jim Gray, the Intelligence Officer, back to bring up some tanks. This took time, but after a long wait up they came, waddling blindly along in the dark until they fell into the holes occupied by 'B' Company and Battalion Headquarters. In due course they sorted themselves out and opened up with their machine guns on the enemy posts holding up 'A' Company. Colonel Arderne then decided to move 'B' and 'D' Companies over the escarpment in a bayonet charge behind the advancing tanks; and with himself in the lead dashed off at top speed followed by 'B' Company and Battalion Headquarters like a pack of hounds in full cry. At the first wadi they halted to reorganise; then pushed on a further two hundred yards to find the successful 'C' Company was holding the "sangars" on the edge of the escarpment with fifty prisoners in the bag; but Adrian Keith, its commander, had been killed by a grenade while rounding up prisoners, a tragic loss the Battalion could ill afford.

The tanks pushed on further still and rounded up a battery of Italian gunners, the latter, unlike their infantry, holding out to the last. While they did so the C.O.'s party moved south and came upon a dug-out which, by the noise, could only contain Italians. "Sergeant Blenkinsop was with me," wrote Colonel Arderne afterwards, "he had just seen his company commander killed and was out for blood. Down he went and after a good deal of noise there was silence and out came Blenkinsop. 'Well?' I said expectantly. Blenkinsop looked a bit sheepish and then said 'They offered me chocolates, sir, and I hadn't the heart to kill them!' I shall always remember the incident. It seemed to show so clearly the make-up of the British soldier who can never hate for long."

The action was over by 2.30 a.m. It was not possible to pursue the retreating Italians as the Border Regiment were due to pass through; so the Battalion consolidated its position, formed a short perimeter and laid wire and mines. Casualties amounted to three officers and eight men killed and one officer and twenty-six men wounded. Four 75 millimetre guns, some anti-tank guns and a number of automatics were captured together with five officers and a hundred and twenty-five men. One officer was taken complete with a motor-cycle on which was strapped a large suitcase! The next week there was a very flattering article in the Desert Army magazine about the action. It was headed " A classic night operation " and made much mention of perfect night formations and night drill. Much of the credit for the night's success belonged to Keith's Company— just another example of a victory gained by a very gallant company commander and a handful of subalterns and men.

Dawn on the 8th found the Battalion well consolidated. The Border Regiment had reached Point 162 without opposition. Rumours of a German counter-attack did not materialise and by the 10th the enemy was in full retreat to the west. El Adem was taken. Elsewhere Indian and South African troops had joined hands with the garrison from Tobruk. The siege of the town had been raised. " The tide of battle has passed us by," says the War Diary of the 11th, " and we are back to salvaging, rather like the experience at Sidi Barrani nearly twelve months ago." On the 12th the Battalion moved to a reserve area inside the old perimeter; and on the 19th, in fulfilment of a spate of rumours, found itself on the way back to the Delta for a rest, a refit and some well-earned leave. Less fortunate, however, were some members of 'B' Company who had taken over the prisoner of war cage at Tobruk. When the rest of the Battalion left for the Delta the Company was sent by sea to Alexandria together with a number of sick and wounded from Tobruk hospital. They were accommodated in various naval craft. One of these was torpedoed soon after it had started out, but those aboard were picked up by a corvette which turned back to Tobruk only to be torpedoed in turn. The Battalion lost some forty of its number in this calamity. Among the officers were John Roper who had been sick with jaundice and Ronald Dufton who was wounded in the raid on "Plonk"; and among the N.C.O.s was Sergeant John Metcalf who had been officers' mess Sergeant for many years. A miserable end to a successful period of operations.

3

MALTA

The Battalion began the first stage of its journey back to the Delta in a sandstorm. The main topic of conversation was whether Qassassin would be reached in time for Christmas. It was—after a ghastly journey in box trucks from railhead—at 10 p.m. on the 25th; and after an hour or so searching for tents everybody settled down for the night and went thankfully to sleep. Altogether a memorable Christmas Day!

With the New Year of 1942 came leave and a move into barracks at Moascar, though 'A' and 'B' Companies were detached for a while on internal security duties. It seemed almost too good to be true living in barracks, worrying about kit, fixing up games, trying to get sports gear and generally leading almost a peacetime existence. And so indeed it proved. On the 16th of January orders were received to concentrate and move by 5 p.m. the following day. This resulted in indescribable bustle and not a little confusion, for over a hundred and twenty men were still on leave and many officers and N.C.O.s on courses. Telegrams were despatched to all and sundry and the Battalion moved, in bits and pieces, back to the camp at Tahag where it had been before moving to Moascar. On the 20th it was placed at twelve hours' notice to move which was reduced to six at 4 a.m. the next morning. Later in the day orders were given to leave Qassassin station at 10 p.m. ready for embarkation. And the climax was reached when, on arrival at the station, the Battalion was met by a staff officer from G.H.Q. to say that only five hundred men and a portion of their baggage could in fact be embarked. As the whole Battalion was on the train and all their kit in trucks nothing could be done for the moment; but when Almyria Transit Camp was reached the following day a hasty conference, followed

THE 1ST BATTALION IN THE MIDDLE EAST

by feverish unpacking and repacking, resulted in a reduction to the required numbers. 'A' Company, the carriers and some members of the Battalion transport were left behind to follow when opportunity offered.

The Battalion embarked for Malta on the 24th. 'B' Company under Major John Kirby was in H.M.S. "Kingston", a destroyer, while everybody else went aboard the "Breconshire", a naval storeship. The Battalion reached the quayside at 2.30 p.m. to be told by the Captain of the "Breconshire" that he was leaving at 3.30 p.m. whether they were aboard or not. The ship was discharging a cargo of grain from the hold to make way for the Battalion's kit, which did not make things easier; and when she finally sailed kit had been manhandled aboard up till the very last moment.

The convoy was escorted by five cruisers and twelve destroyers and for the first two days the sea was reasonably calm and the journey comparatively uneventful. On the 26th the weather deteriorated and air attacks increased. The worse it became the greater grew the prospects of evading the Luftwaffe; but by late afternoon the ship's roll was so great that many cared little what happened! Torpedo bombers which appeared about 6 p.m. tried to hit one of the escorting destroyers but without success. The convoy steamed ahead for Valetta and sailed into the Grand Harbour at 10 a.m. on the 27th. The Battalion disembarked to the accompaniment of an enemy air raid on the dockyard—a taste of things to come.

'A' Company and the rest of those left behind in Egypt were not so fortunate. Their journey to the island was indeed hazardous. It began in February in the merchantman "Clan Campbell" which was hit in a heavy air attack and had to put into Tobruk before limping back to Alexandria. The ship carrying the Battalion's equipment was sunk. Another attempt was made in March, when the men of the Battalion were distributed among four vessels—the "Breconshire", "Clan Campbell", "Pampas" and another. They were escorted by four cruisers and fifteen destroyers; and there was a naval officer in each merchantman. As before, all went well for the first two days after which the convoy was attacked with increasing tempo. The climax was reached when it was reported that the Italian fleet had been sighted. Destroyers immediately laid a smoke screen, the cruisers steamed flat out straight through the convoy and the naval officers took over in their respective ships. As Malta drew nearer the attacks increased in intensity until it was clear that only Providence could save the convoy. " Clan Campbell " was sunk, though most of those in her were picked up. A destroyer raced up to pick up survivors, only to be badly holed herself. The crew, undaunted, lined the decks, raised their caps, gave three cheers for the King and all jumped together, an example of morale and discipline that none who saw it will ever forget. In a few minutes they too were picked up by another destroyer. " Pampas " was hit by two bombs which fortunately were deflected by her superstructure into the sea. As she was carrying a thousand tons of octane spirit as well as a cargo of ammunition those aboard her were more than relieved. " Breconshire " and the remaining vessel were both damaged and could not reach the harbour; and the former was ultimately beached at the southern tip of the island.

Through all these hazards, and indeed despite them, 'A' Company and the rest of the rear party in due course rejoined their comrades. They considered themselves fortunate, for the convoy was the last to reach the island for many months to come.

By the time that it was reunited the Battalion had settled into its new role and was becoming accustomed to its new routine. The island was rocky with many walls and terraces, but from its positions in the Verdalla-Rabat-Dingli area the Battalion commanded a magnificent view of the whole island. Its task was to act as the fortress's mobile reserve and for this purpose it was provided with four hundred bicycles. Its routine consisted of normal tactical exercises and the construction of anti-blast pens for aircraft on the Ta Kali and Luqa aerodromes. The latter comprised sandbags to start with, then earth-filled petrol tins and finally, when all other materials were exhausted, stone from local quarries—hard work, in the latter case, for men who were inevitably on short rations.

The tempo of the air raids steadily increased. They averaged about three a day, fortunately at regular hours which allowed one to eat, work and travel in between whiles; and there was intermittent activity at night. Battle positions were organised, counter-attack tasks laid on and rehearsals carried out for any eventuality. An extensive Radar system enabled everybody to obtain an accurate and early warning of impending raids. So effective was it that Colonel Arderne would await a " plot " of over a hundred aircraft before mounting his bicycle and freewheeling down to the airfield where the Battalion was working. There he would stand, completely imperturbable, awaiting the enemy's arrival; and he would be deeply disappointed if he were forced to take cover or—as frequently happened—the " plot " wheeled suddenly and made for another airfield.

The Battalion suffered few casualties from air raids and apart from the raids lived a normal routine existence with its full share of sporting as well as military activities. There was entertainment of a sort to be had in the towns and a local wine, aptly named " Stuka juice ", was drinkable. Nevertheless, Malta was in every way a besieged island and at the height of the raids supplies were short of both food and ammunition, each of which was strictly rationed. Soon after the Battalion arrived in the island the G.O.C.—General Beak—came to watch a demonstration of how to load motor transport. As a result it was selected as the best of the brigade and had to repeat the demonstration several days later for the benefit of others. The G.O.C. paid a second visit of inspection but on this occasion was not asked by the Regimental policeman on duty for his identity card. When he asked why not, he was informed that he was recognised. " And who am I? " said the General; only to be met by the solemn, and indeed accurate, reply " Major-General D. M. W. Beak, V.C., D.S.O., M.C."—then after a short pause, " and bar!"

The months passed by the Battalion in Malta were, by and large, uneventful and provide little of moment for the historian. But it was something of an event, albeit a sad one, when, at the end of the summer of 1942, Colonel Arderne left the Battalion to assume command of a brigade in the 10th Indian Division. For more than two years he had held command and by his personality and bravery enjoyed the esteem and unbounded confidence of all who served under him. He was a magnificent athlete with great powers of endurance and he asked of others the same physical exertion which he himself displayed. Often in Tobruk he would appear at Headquarters with a Bren gun, look round for the odd volunteer and then set off to draw the enemy defensive fire at some particular spot in order, as he would put it, " to check the usual contradictory reports of night patrols! " On one occasion with " Topper " Browne, then his Adjutant, he visited a forward company in the Tobruk perimeter. To Browne the area was not very familiar and in due course he asked the C.O. if there were any mines about. " Oh yes," said the Colonel, scraping away the sand with his boot and disclosing a German Teller mine beneath, " there's one," and he walked on as unconcernedly as if it had been a stone. On his departure command passed to John Kirby who hitherto had been second in command, and it was under him that in June 1943 the Battalion packed its bags and set sail once more for Alexandria.

CHAPTER THREE

The 10th and 11th Battalions in Iceland 1940-1941

TOWARDS the middle of 1940 troops from the United Kingdom occupied Iceland for the first time in history. Men of the Royal Marines landed on the 10th of May and were followed by first one, and then another brigade of a British Division and then by a Canadian brigade soon after the fall of France. It was an historic occasion and one in which two battalions of the Regiment ultimately played a part.

It is perhaps not always realised how important was a base in Iceland for the protection of the North Atlantic trade routes once the Germans had occupied the northern European ports. British trade routes to America had of necessity to be directed on a more northerly course and the prompt occupation of the island as a preventive measure was something which could not be allowed to go by default. The British Division chosen for the task was the 49th Division and, as remarked above, it was already there. To it 70 Brigade, newly evacuated from France, was sent when, after a short period on the Devon coast, the erstwhile 23rd Division was broken up. The Brigade remained a part of 49th Division for the rest of the war.

It was on the 28th of August that the 10th Battalion received orders that it was to go overseas as the advance party of the Brigade. Up till then all three battalions of the Brigade had been reforming after their return from Dunkirk as well as constructing and manning beach defences on the Devon coast. What remained of the battalions which had returned from France had, it is true, some battle experience; but they were not fully trained when they first crossed the Channel and much of the experience gained there was the sort which would have to be unlearnt. Between June and August drafts of officers and men from a number of Regiments arrived to make them up to strength; but most of the men had received little training; and it was left to the survivors of the original nucleus of each battalion to knock the newcomers into shape, and especially to the few Territorials to provide the Regimental connection on which to rebuild. Colonel Marley still commanded the 10th Battalion and shortly after Dunkirk Colonel Richard Ware, of the Regiment, took over the 11th. To these two officers fell the task of reorganisation.

The 10th Battalion embarked on the 11th of September and, after a rough passage in cramped conditions, reached Reykjavik five days later. Thence it deployed in the north-west of the island with its companies in varied scattered localities, often many miles apart. In fact the distance between the most southern company at Akranes and the most northern detachment—a coast watching party at Skagastrond in the extreme north—was roughly the distance between King's Cross and Northallerton.

The rest of the Brigade reached Iceland a month later after a calm crossing in—for troopships—considerable comfort.

Akranes is some fifteen miles north of Reykjavik and, although the 10th Battalion's most northerly post was in the extreme north, the northernmost company was at Blondous. It was impossible to occupy the many miles of coast line throughout its length, nor was it necessary. Most of it is quite unsuitable for the landing of troops and thus only important harbours were garrisoned. However, coast watching posts were established in between and were manned by the Navy who had direct telephone communication with their own Headquarters. They carried six months reserve rations in case—as some were—they should be cut off from the remainder of the British forces for several months during the winter.

On its arrival the 10th Battalion had been quartered under canvas in a transit camp near Reykjavik and been nearly washed away in a terrific rainstorm. Even when it moved north and, by the end of November, had fully established itself in Nissen huts, its troubles were by no means at an end, and each company depended on its own ingenuity for even the bare necessities of life Borganes, where Battalion Headquarters and one company were situated, is only thirty miles by sea from Reykjavik; but it is twice that distance by road and the road was only passable in favourable weather. So all supplies from Reykjavik had to be shipped by sea and various kinds of stores, such as N.A.A.F.I. supplies, had a way of vanishing into thin air!

The 11th Battalion occupied a camp in the area of Reykjavik itself, which it took over from the Royal Regiment of Canada. It was incomplete and consisted of a mixture of wooden and Nissen huts. The camp lay between two streams of water from hot springs, which could be used for washing. On cold days clouds of steam rose up from them and almost enveloped the camp. From this camp the Battalion maintained a number of coast watching posts and a platoon twenty miles away on the Thingvettlar Lake to watch for possible seaplane landings. It also prepared defences against a possible German landing—always a contingency treated by authority with all seriousness—at Hafnafjordur, a fishing port five miles away. Later, transport and working parties were provided to help build an aerodrome just outside the capital.

The first impressions of a newcomer to Iceland are not exactly favourable. The complete absence of trees and hedgerows gives it a forbidding appearance and long stretches of rocks, stones and lava dust, devoid of even the scantiest vegetation, lend added force to a general impression of austerity. Once accustomed to this, however, there is a rugged grandeur about the mountains—snowcapped for most of the year—and the lakes and fjords which abound throughout the island. There are no trees and all timber has to be imported. How to get it occupied much of the thoughts of the British troops during their first few weeks. They had to start from scratch and any unit with an ingenious carpenter was indeed lucky. But the Battalions soon settled in and examples of improvised ingenuity soon became apparent. Army blankets filled with wood shavings made excellent upholstery for chairs; iron brackets in the Nissen huts were found to serve a variety of uses from curtain rods to fenders; and pictures from illustrated magazines, framed with coloured or silver paper, added colour to the walls of barrack rooms and messes.

The Icelanders are stubbornly proud of their independence. Their attitude to the British troops was not at first altogether friendly. Firmly convinced that the war against Hitler would not be won, they determined to show no hospitality in case it should reach Hitler's ears and react unfavourably when Germany was at length victorious. It was impossible at first to convince them that their country had been occupied only as a precautionary measure and that a German occupation would be infinitely less pleasant. Slowly but surely this natural reserve melted away and a more friendly attitude was adopted; and this was particularly in evidence in country districts where a number of troops were shown the greatest kindness when stranded during the winter in bad weather. On one occasion a supply column of the 11th Battalion was snowed up and sought refuge in a farm where they were fed and cared for by the family for several days. The farmer refused to take any compensation, but asked instead that something should be given on his behalf to the Spitfire fund. At Skagastrond, the tiny village where the 10th Battalion had a coast watching post, Corporal Lowe—the N.C.O. in charge—was the object of the hundred inhabitants' respect and admiration. When Colonel Marley arrived on a visit of inspection he was particularly struck by the great friendliness of the population and the touching of hats and marks of respect shown to him as the Corporal escorted him round. But he soon discovered that it was not he, as C.O., who was the object of their respect, but Corporal Lowe who enjoyed what was virtually the position of uncrowned Mayor of the village!

The sun had been shining brightly the day that the 11th Battalion had disembarked and they were warned to make the most of that strange phenomenon. No sooner had the Brigade settled in than they were subjected to an infinite variety of climatic conditions; mild days, snowy days, frosty days and windy days followed one another in rapid succession. The high winds were perhaps the greatest trial and on one occasion an 11th Battalion post had to be evacuated when the roof was carried away and a stove overturned, setting the post on fire. The occupants had considerable difficulty in the accompanying blizzard in reaching a nearby farm.

The weather really began to deteriorate during the first week of November; by the 10th skating was in full swing; and on the 24th skis arrived. Each battalion had to train a ski platoon. The weather did not, however, interrupt the general routine of training, for the principle observed was to ignore the difficulties of a hostile climate so far as possible and to see that everyone should turn out at least once a week and be made thoroughly uncomfortable as part of the " keep fit " programme.

Early in the New Year of 1941 the weather turned especially cold and up to fifty degrees of frost was not unusual. There were only about four hours of daylight, so battalions staggered their meals to make the most of it. Night operations were easy; it merely meant starting at 7 a.m., as dawn was not till 10.30 a.m. In the middle of February there was heavy snow in the northern part of the island with drifts up to six or seven feet in the camps. It was not unusual for the occupants to have to dig themselves out of their huts. On one occasion during a blizzard the 10th Battalion lost a man for three hours inside the camp perimeter; he could not find his way from the perimeter to his hut and just went round in circles. But despite the weather, illness was practically unknown and morale extremely high. When off duty, time was passed with battalion concert parties, mock Parliaments, spelling bees, mock trials and such other activities as the ingenuity of officers could devise. On one occasion an E.N.S.A. concert party arrived; and the story has it that the 10th Battalion company commander at Blondous, together with four senior N.C.O.s, took over guard duties for the evening so that the rest of the company could visit it.

As spring approached the weather improved and it was easier to get out and about. Field firing exercises were frequent, as the Icelandic countryside was ideal for letting off live ammunition without restrictions. One company of the 10th Battalion was authorised to try to shoot seals which were causing a great deal of damage at the mouth of one of the rivers. The seals used to lie on the sand and the company used them as targets for section stalks with live ammunition. Battalion exercises in due course gave way to Brigade and ultimately Divisional and Force exercises; and in the intervening periods each battalion was urged to use its wireless sets more frequently between its company stations to give the signallers additional training. One night Force Signals in Reykjavik picked up some mysterious signal messages and quite a scare was started until it was discovered that it was the 10th Battalion's detachment at Blondous playing the company at Reykoskoli at darts.

In the middle of June the 10th Battalion left the north and moved south to join the 11th near Reykjavik. In July the United States Marines arrived and they and the Regiment soon became firm friends. In fact one of the first combined exercises of the war between British and American troops took place later in the year when the Marines and a company of the 10th Battalion carried out a dawn attack on Reykjavik aerodrome. In August Iceland was visited by the Prime Minister, Mr. Winston Churchill, who received a rousing welcome from both troops and Icelanders. Indeed, his visit was a turning point in the relations between the British Army and the inhabitants, who cast aside their habitual reserve to cheer the by now legendary figure with cigar, V-sign and bulldog grin. From that day the British felt that they were at last accepted.

70 Brigade spent only a few months longer in Iceland after the Prime Minister's visit. Plans had apparently been made for the island to become an American responsibility. Towards the end of the year preparations were made for the move back to the United Kingdom and, in the middle of December, the ships arrived to carry the 49th Division home. The 11th Battalion actually sailed in December, the 10th early in the New Year. Their stay had been a worth while one and when the troopships left there were many among the Icelanders who, despite their early reserve, were sorry to see them go. The Battalions had much to be grateful for; when they arrived they had barely recovered from the upheaval of Dunkirk; they had yet to settle down with their new reinforcements; and they could not yet boast that they were fully trained or really fit for war. When they left, eighteen months of hard, tough training in a harsh, tough climate had welded them together into fighting units which could face the future with confidence. By the time they left for home once more the two C.O.s upon whom the brunt of reforming and retraining had fallen had been transferred to other appointments. Both were sadly missed. Richard Ware was the first to leave when, in November, he was appointed G.S.O. 1 Northern Command. The following month David Marley was chosen to command a Brigade in England and with a heavy heart left his much loved

10th Battalion. They left behind them two battalions which, after a further spell of training in England, were to fight with distinction in Normandy two years later.

CHAPTER FOUR

151 Brigade in the Middle East and Sicily 1941-1943

I

CYPRUS AND IRAQ

WHEN the 50th Division reached England from Dunkirk it moved to the south-west and later the west of England to reorganise and resist the invasion which everyone expected Hitler would launch before the summer was out. Morale was high as it was felt that the Division had proved itself in battle and, as an all-Territorial Division drawing help from few regulars, had shown itself ready for war. As early as September, however, the Division was warned that it was earmarked as the first Territorial formation to go to North Africa when the time came; but it was not till the following spring that the date was fixed for its final departure. In the intervening months there were a number of changes consequent on the reorganisation after Dunkirk. Not least was this so in 151 Brigade. Brigadier Churchill relinquished his command of the Brigade on taking up a new appointment; his leadership during the Dunkirk campaign and his vigorous personality had endeared him to officers and men alike. The 6th Battalion was now commanded by Victor Yate who had had to leave the 2nd Battalion in March 1940 on account of ill health but was now fit again; he succeeded Peter Jeffreys on the latter's departure for the Staff College. Tim Beart still commanded the 8th and Jos Percy, formerly the Brigade Major, the 9th, which he had taken over during the campaign in France. All Battalions had experienced a turnover of both officers and men—and now the not so fit and the older had to be left behind—but they were highly trained and there was a substantial number of seasoned survivors from France in each of them.

The journey south and round the Cape was uneventful, save for the fact that the convoy sailed perilously close to the track of the "Bismarck" as that vessel raced for the shelter of Brest. Indeed, the escorting destroyers actually left to take part in the chase. Fortunately, however, she was too occupied with her pursuers to bother about anything else. As the troopships crossed the equator the time-honoured ceremony of "crossing the line" was performed. The 8th Battalion thought this boisterous ritual a fine opportunity to have some fun at the expense of their Regimental Sergeant-Major, "Spike" Jennings, who it was anticipated would be one of the star turns of the day. But these hopes were to be frustrated, for the R.S.M. vigorously maintained that he had already crossed the line as a member of the 1st Battalion when voyaging from China to Singapore. There were no ex-members of the 1st Battalion to confirm or disprove this story, and many doubted whether the China troopers sailed so far south on their way to Singapore. "But," said "Spike" Jennings, "that's my story and I'm sticking to it"; and he managed to get through the day unmolested.

The convoy arrived off Suez early in July and the Brigade was decanted into Qassassin Camp. It began arriving at Qassassin station early one morning just as the village was waking up; and this introduction to the ways of the East showed the troops what they and others were to learn very rapidly, that Egypt is—apart from Cairo, Alexandria and a few other large towns—a land of dirty native villages inhabited by a disease-ridden population, plagued by flies and smelling to high heaven. But the Brigade was not to remain in Egypt very long. It was barely two months since the German airborne invasion of Crete and troops were badly needed for the defence of Cyprus which could not be permitted to fall into German hands under similar circumstances. So to Cyprus it went at the end of the month, only a week or so after setting foot in Egypt. The journey required some rapid staff work; for the Royal Navy, whose losses had been heavy during the evacuations from Greece and Crete, were only reinforcing Cyprus by night so that their ships could be clear of the island by daylight and out of range of Axis bombers. This meant that a strict time-table had to be adhered to and battalions only had an hour to embark themselves and their baggage. It also involved a rapid if rough and ready method of unloading equipment and stores at Famagusta harbour where the naval ratings rolled everything down a gangway on to the quayside. Inevitably something ended up in the water; but this was put right by a certain fat Cypriot who appeared every morning at daybreak and for a suitable fee dived into the harbour to retrieve anything from ammunition boxes to anti-tank rifles. He did this whenever troops disembarked and had every reason to be grateful to the Senior Service for a comparatively lucrative pastime.

The Brigade remained in Cyprus till November. It was a period of intensive hard work in the preparation of the island's defences, and at the end of that time it was estimated to have completed in three months what had been expected of it in six. Moreover, the troops were able to become acclimatised to the East in surroundings less hostile to man than the desert. Their stay was not an unpleasant one, but when the time came to leave they went as quickly as they had come, with three days' notice, not back to Egypt as might have been expected, but to Palestine and Iraq with a view to fighting alongside the Russians in the Caucasus, should the Germans succeed in their drive upon Rostov and break through into Persia.

The Brigade moved by road to Kirkuk in the Iraq oilfields and then beyond it to Eski Kellek on the Great Zab river where it spent the winter. This was uneventful, extremely cold and occupied largely with routine training and the digging of defences on the crossings of the Great Zab and Kazir rivers. Towards the middle of February came the news that the 50th Division was to relieve the 4th Indian Division in the desert, and the transport convoys set off once again, this time to join the newly formed Eighth Army on the Egyptian-Cyrenaican frontier. By the end of February 1942 the Brigade was in position in the Gazala line, ready to take part in its first action for nearly two years.

2

GAZALA

The arrival of 151 Brigade in the Eighth Army coincided with a lull in operations which had begun as far back as November 1941. Then General Auchinleck had launched his offensive with the object of engaging and destroying the Axis armour, isolating the enemy positions along the Egyptian border at Sollum and Bardia, relieving Tobruk and finally sweeping the enemy right out of Cyrenaica. After some very bitter fighting Tobruk was in due course relieved, and Rommel —the D.L.I. Brigade's opponent before Arras in 1940—withdrew his forces to El Agheila. Most of the British armoured units were then withdrawn to refit and rest, and supply difficulties prevented more than the equivalent of one armoured and one infantry brigade being maintained in the area. Thus it was that when Rommel, considerably reinforced, attacked towards the end of January, he achieved immediate success and the Eighth Army found itself forced to yield up Benghazi and withdraw to Gazala. Here both sides reached the practicable limit of their communications, the British at Gazala and the Germans at Tmimi, and a stretch of some twenty miles or more separated the two armies while each made vigorous preparations for the next move.

The British lines stretched from the sea to Bir Hacheim, which was fifty miles inland and held by the Free French Brigade. The line was only continuous in the sense that a belt of mines had been laid from Gazala to Bir Hacheim with infantry divisions disposed along it in brigade localities surrounded by mine-fields. These localities were known as boxes. The 50th Division took its place in the centre of the line with the 1st South African Division to the north and the Free French to the south. It had a frontage of twenty-five miles to cover.

To the east of the main Gazala line was a series of strong points surrounded by deep minefields. The most important of these was around a junction of tracks known as Knightsbridge which was held by the Guards Brigade; while to the south-east of them, between El Adem and El Gobi, lay the 1st Armoured Division ready for any penetration through the gap between the left flank of the 50th Division and the French to the south.

The miles of no-man's land between the British and German armies were the scene of vigorous patrolling, at all events by the British, during the months of March and April. On the whole the Germans were not very active; but the Battalions had the chance to find their feet and generally to make their way about the desert. On one such patrol Captain Maurice Kirby, of the 6th Battalion, took out a mortar detachment on a truck to within 1,000 yards of the enemy with the object of dropping some forty bombs into a mass of transport and enemy positions. After twelve rounds the whole horizon was ablaze, though the enemy reacted quickly and Kirby's party had to beat a retreat. Next day a New Zealand Maori, who had been a German prisoner at the time and was hiding under a truck waiting to escape, testified to the effectiveness of the mortar detachment's aim. Apart from normal patrolling, battalions took it in turns to provide detachments—usually a company at a time—for small columns of all arms to carry out long-range patrols and to attack specific objectives; and so by the time operations on a larger scale began in earnest most people had a grounding in the ways of desert warfare.

The Germans woke up during April, and their patrols were much more in evidence. Quite clearly something was about to happen. Towards the middle of May warning was given that an attack by Rommel's forces was likely within a week; and in the moonlight of the 26th of May Rommel struck and the battle of Gazala began. The opening of the battle found a change in command of both the 6th and 8th Battalions. Some time earlier—in Cyprus to be exact—Lieutenant-Colonel Sammy Battiscombe, of the Regiment, had succeeded Victor Yate as C.O. of the 6th and on the 13th of May Colonel Beart left the 8th to take command of an East African brigade; his place was taken by Lieutenant-Colonel "Jake" Jackson, of the Green Howards, until recently second in command of the 6th and underneath an extremely blunt exterior destined to become a much admired and respected commanding officer.

Rommel's plan was to turn the open flank of the Gazala line south of Bir Hacheim, to engage the British armoured forces east of the line and defeat them, and then to combine an infantry attack upon it from the west with a tank attack from the east. Then Tobruk was to be assaulted by all the Axis forces and was expected to fall by the 30th of May. The Germans swept forward as planned but met stubborn resistance from the British armour and all the forces positioned to counter this kind of manoeuvre. After several days of bitter fighting they had made little headway and were seriously hampered by having to bring up supplies by a wide detour round Bir Hacheim.

The troops in the line proper had strict orders that they must not move out of their boxes to attack the enemy. The garrisons must hold their ground while the armour met the enemy and destroyed him. 150 Brigade occupied a rather isolated position between the Free French and the rest of the Division. This meant that if the Brigade and the French were attacked 69 and 151 Brigades had to stand fast and watch the struggle. The main contribution that the troops in the line had to make in the early stages of the battle was to withstand such attacks as were made upon them by the Italians—which they successfully did—and to launch a series of intensive daylight patrols on the Axis supply columns which were moving up to the German forces east of the line. These operations were known as commerce raiding and extremely successful they were. In one of them Captain Freddie Cole of the 6th Battalion, with two sections of carriers, wrought havoc with one column of trucks. Together with Lieutenant Philip Hampson and a patrol from the 8th Battalion, he attacked the convoy, captured three trucks and made thirty prisoners. The next day he went back for more. This time he had one section of carriers, four anti-tank guns and some machine guns and he descended upon seventeen armoured vehicles protecting a similar convoy. Both sides fought hard, but in the end Cole's party had to withdraw though not before he himself was severely wounded and his driver killed. In his weakened condition he was unable to move the body from the driving seat, so he held the dead man's leg on the accelerator and steered the carrier to safety. Such actions, though abortive, did much to maintain the offensive spirit of forces on the defensive.

Meanwhile a fierce armoured battle was raging to the east. Losses on both sides were heavy; and Rommel, to shorten his line of communications, ordered two gaps to be cleared in the British minefields. These passages, which were gradually broadened, lay on each side of 150 Brigade's box. To bring supplies through, it was vital for Rommel to destroy the Brigade which as a consequence came under intense attack. All through the 30th 150 Brigade fought to plug holes punched by an enemy who had encircled its entire position. On the 31st the enemy broke into the north-east of the box. Ammunition was running out and despite vigorous attempts from outside to get convoys through, the enemy's cordon was too strong. The rest of the 50th Division was forbidden to go to the rescue because to do so would have broken up the whole pattern on which the Army Commander wished to fight the battle. So on the 1st of June, after thirty-six hours of bitter struggle, what remained of 150 Brigade, its ammunition and supplies exhausted, was overrun platoon by platoon and those who survived were taken prisoner. It was a tragic loss and meant that the Germans and their Italian allies were firmly established in the centre of the British line.

The loss of 150 Brigade was followed by a short period of stalemate. But for 151 Brigade vigorous patrolling was still the order of the day. Commerce raiding was intensified and many supply lorries and troops were picked off like ripe plums from a tree. The few enemy trucks which tried to run for it were usually brought to a standstill in approved naval fashion by a burst of tracer across their bows. On one occasion three carriers chased an Italian tank which they peppered with Bren gun fire until it stopped and the crew surrendered. A few days later another patrol tried the same tactics on another Italian tank. Again the tank stopped and to everyone's delight and merriment out popped an Italian and said "No make me prisoner; me only on patrol." So from the point of view of the D.L.I. Brigade the first stage of the battle had gone well. It had held its positions against all comers and had hit back vigorously against its assailants. But elsewhere the progress of the battle had taken a turn for the worse. On the night of the 10th of June the Free French, after a fortnight's resistance which has since become an epic, were ordered to withdraw from Bir Hacheim. On the 13th a crucial tank battle south-west of Tobruk resulted in crippling losses to the British tank forces. The plan on which the Eighth Army Commander, General Ritchie, had been working now broke down. The 50th Division and the South African Division to the north were isolated. To the south the desert was in undisputed possession of the Germans and the two divisions could no longer act as a firm base round which the British armour could manoeuvre as there was precious little armour left. Withdrawal was therefore inevitable, and orders were given for it to be carried out on the night of the 14th.

This was to be no ordinary withdrawal. Both the South African Division and the 50th Division had to be extricated and the coast road and desert immediately south of it were only adequate for the South Africans. For the 50th Division a withdrawal eastwards would have brought them into the midst of the German armour, so for them it was to be a fighting withdrawal straight through the enemy's own positions. It was to begin with an attack westwards, to bludgeon a way through the German and Italian forward positions; then a wheel south right across their lines of communication; and finally an eastwards drive to the south of Bir Hacheim to a rallying point at Fort Maddalena on the Egyptian frontier.

The first stage of the operation required the establishment of two bridgeheads, one by 69 Brigade, the other by the D.L.I. Brigade, through which the remainder of the Division was to pass. In the latter case the task was allotted to the 8th Battalion. The Battalion was formed into three columns, each column containing a detachment of all arms. Their objective was a ridge several miles west of the main Gazala position. Two of the columns were to secure flanking positions and the third, together with the rest of the Brigade, was to pass through them. Preparations went rapidly ahead throughout the day of the 14th, aided by a dust storm which concealed much of the divisional activity from the enemy. The columns started forward about 9 p.m.

The left hand column, under Major Andrew Clarke, was heavily shelled as it moved off, but it reached its objective with only a few casualties. It passed over two Italian positions on the way; but not a soul could be seen though there were arms and anti-tank guns everywhere which had been left loaded on the parapets. There may have been Italians at the bottom of the trenches but if there were they stayed there. The column established a close laager on its objective and sent out a number of fighting and listening patrols. One of them found a deserted signal exchange and an officers' mess from which were removed a few of the spoils of war; a glass of cool vino was always acceptable even in the middle of the night.

The right hand column was commanded by Major Harry Sell and encountered stiffer opposition. Its objective was held by three companies of Italians who put down defensive crossfire from their machine and anti-tank guns. But the column surged into the attack. Carriers and armoured cars dashed on to the positions and weaved in among the trenches shooting at everything they could see in the half light. The infantry left their trucks, fixed their bayonets and proceeded to use them in no uncertain fashion. Harry Sell himself had a miraculous escape when an anti-tank shell hit his truck and stopped it dead. But he and Private Etherington, his batman, jumped out and wielding rifle and bayonet with deadly skill joined in the thick of the fighting. It was all over in a few minutes; grenades were tossed into the dug-outs and Brens and Tommy guns peppered the slit trenches. The Italians had soon had enough and those who were left came out with hands above their heads.

By the time it was fully dark the bridgehead was firmly established and the two columns had to endure an anxious period of waiting while the rest of the Brigade moved through. The Germans and Italians were by now fully alive to what was happening and the mixture of automatic and gun fire and burning vehicles was eloquent testimony to the hard struggle the rest of the Division was having. However, the bridgehead troops were not attacked further; the enemy was too occupied elsewhere, the Germans in trying to stop the mobile columns, the Italians in trying to get out of the way. Some Italians in giving themselves up asked for a lift to Alexandria and one party obligingly informed their captors that if they waited a few moments longer they could have an Italian General as well.

Into the bridgehead now came the 6th Battalion and Brigade Headquarters; and by 2.30 a.m. the bulk of them had passed through and beyond. All, that is, except for a small rear party under Major Mike Ferens and the whole of the 9th Battalion, both of whom, for special reasons, had taken the coast road to Tobruk. The rest of the Brigade, by now split up into independent columns, made hot foot for the south-west and from there due east towards the frontier. Each column had its own adventures, but the account of Major Bill Watson, second in command of the 6th Battalion, whose own truck was hit by small arms fire without the occupants being injured, is probably typical. " Of course trucks got mislaid " he wrote afterwards, " but everyone knew the compass bearings and by now most of us had became experts at moving in the desert. I never stopped that night; we passed Italian positions, trucks, and gun emplacements in the first few miles. Under cover of darkness we travelled forty odd miles. As daylight came I found most of my column had left me, but we travelled on for another hundred miles and halted for the night. I had picked up many other stragglers. It was a night when we could sleep in peace, and we all slept as we lay, near our trucks, with sentries prowling round the whole time . . . Next morning we started early to get the benefit of the cool morning. Over the first rise I found, to my joy, most of the rest of my column just making breakfast. So, joining forces, we travelled on, under a scorching sun, for another hundred odd miles, and late in the evening I joined the Colonel with his party at the pre-arranged meeting place. Next day stragglers came in, but as the day wore on it was quite apparent that our casualties were very, very few."

Once the Brigade had passed through them the 8th Battalion, too, set course for Bir Hacheim. The route of Sell's column ran through a German strongpoint about which he fortunately received warning from an Italian prisoner. He decided to rush it and ordered his men to open fire while still on the move and to keep firing until they got through. As soon as they heard the approaching vehicles the Germans sent up flares, turning night into day, and in their ghostly light, for all the world like clusters of giant chandeliers, the column raced ahead with every ounce of speed the drivers could squeeze out of the trucks. The enemy opened up a murderous fire and in some of the vehicles took a heavy toll of casualties. But the armoured cars and carriers managed to silence most of the strongpoint's defenders, and once past it the firing ceased as quickly as it had begun. Not least of the obstructions and hazards which all columns had to face were the minefields and slit trenches which could not be seen in the dark and which sometimes brought the speed of the vehicles down to that of walking pace. Andrew Clarke's column ran into one minefield when some of the trucks had to be abandoned. A party of thirty-seven men under R.Q.M.S. Thomas Lightfoot set out to march to safety. But after a few miles they caught up with the column again which had been slowed down because of the number of slit trenches. They were lucky. On foot their chances of reaching safety were indeed forlorn. Meanwhile the rest of the Battalion under the C.O. did not have to fire a shot.

After waiting in positions astride the bridgehead until 2 a.m., they received the order to disengage and moved off south into the desert. By the night of the 16th of June the whole Battalion had arrived at Fort Maddalena.

The 9th Battalion, together with the 6th Battalion's rear party under Ferens, had not followed the rest of the Brigade. This was because some days previously it had been moved out of the Brigade area to a position east of 69 Brigade. When the withdrawal took place the Battalion was therefore given the option of either breaking out through the 8th Battalion's bridgehead or of taking the coast road to Tobruk. By the time the Battalion was due to move the amount of firing and the number of burning vehicles made it clear that the enemy was fully alive to what was taking place; so Colonel Percy decided to exercise his option and withdraw along the coastal route.

The Battalion moved in two columns, one under the C.O., the other under Major Campbell Slight, the second in command. They moved on parallel routes, towards the El Agheila and Gazala passes respectively which they reached about daybreak. The C.O.s column was at first shelled by the South Africans until it gave the recognition signal; then as it moved down the escarpment on to the coastal plain it was attacked by Stuka divebombers. Slight's column arrived at the Gazala pass just as the Sappers were preparing to mine it, but as it moved on into the coastal plain it came under heavy artillery fire from the top of the escarpment. Both column commanders then realised that the Germans were across their route and both columns diverged as they turned from the road and made for the rough dune country near the coast. There seemed little chance of getting through unopposed but the dune country would suit the infantry better if it came to a fight.

A fight there was to be. As the head of the combined column reached El Mrassus, some sixteen miles west of Tobruk, it was heavily engaged by German infantry astride the track with support from tanks near the coast road and artillery on the escarpment. Colonel Percy, realising that quick action was the only chance of success, immediately ordered an attack by such forces as he could collect from the nearest troop-carrying lorries. At the same time he sited a number of anti-tank guns to protect the stationary column. The attack which was led by Campbell

Slight was at once successful. The infantry, helped forward by bold use of Ferens' carriers and close support from a South African 25 pounder firing over open sights, made a determined attack which routed the enemy and resulted in a bag of thirty prisoners. Then, when the German tanks attacked the rear of the column, a 2 pounder anti-tank gun and several 25 pounders opened fire and knocked out seven of them. The enemy's resistance crumbled away except for the artillery on the escarpment which had ranged on the track and hindered any further progress. But again Slight came to the rescue. He got in touch with a South African artillery battery some 3,000 yards east of the scene of action and arranged for sufficient support to enable the column to push ahead. Once over this obstacle, the Battalion split again into two columns and set out to join the rest of the Brigade beyond the frontier. They reached it, after passing through Tobruk, on the 16th, and the following day moved into a Brigade camp at Bir Thalata.

For the average member of the Brigade it was far from clear exactly how the battle was going. Apart from the knowledge that the Division was to concentrate on the Egyptian frontier little else was known. There was no news of Tobruk but it was assumed that the famous little Libyan town would hold out as it had held before. When, early on the morning of the 21st of June, the bitter news of its fall became known, it was like a slap in the face to every man of the Eighth Army. Here was a disaster of the first magnitude and it meant that the retreat, far from being over, had only just begun. It meant that the frontier position was untenable because it was too easily outflanked to be held by infantry without a strong mobile reserve; and it meant, too, that Mersa Matruh—some twenty-five miles further back—would have to be abandoned for very similar reasons, not least because, with practically no armour, the Matruh escarpment might well prove to be a trap. So before long the whole Brigade was on the move eastwards once again; and by the 25th was in position with the rest of the Division on the escarpment south-east of Matruh. The town itself was held by the 10th Indian Division.

Meanwhile Rommel's forces had not been slow to follow up their advantage. The best part of three German and seven Italian divisions were available for the drive into Egypt; and there were the equivalent of barely five British divisions opposing them. By the 27th of June the Germans had bumped the Matruh defences and been brought to a temporary halt; but their main armoured force swept on past the town, by-passed the 10th Indian Division and the 50th Division, and pressed ahead against the bulk of the Eighth Army which was withdrawing to El Alamein. The two Divisions round Matruh were thus isolated and the German Commander, banking on another Tobruk, proceeded to act accordingly.

The bulk of this fighting fell upon the D.L.I. Brigade in general and the 9th Battalion in particular. At 2 a.m. on the morning of the 27th the Battalion received news that the German armour was approaching its positions. Soon after, one platoon position was attacked by a patrol. Then at 5.15 in the morning the Germans launched an all-out attack with overwhelming numbers of infantry supported by tanks and artillery. They seemed determined to destroy the Battalion and oblivious of the casualties they suffered in doing so. Fierce hand-to-hand fighting lasted for some hours; but the Germans kept renewing their attacks and as time went on the Battalion's resistance began to lessen. Quite early in the action a German tracked vehicle towed a light gun to within close range of one of the Battalion's 2 pounder anti-tank guns, sited on a forward slope in front of the infantry positions. The Battalion gun crew opened fire and put it out of action with a round through the engine. The Germans replied with another mobile gun and either killed or wounded the men manning the 2 pounder. They then moved forward towards the damaged tractor and tried to get the light gun into action against the infantry. But one wounded member of the Battalion's gun crew, realising the danger to his comrades, could not see their actions pass unchallenged. His name was Private Adam Wakenshaw; and his courage and devotion to duty on this day won him the Victoria Cross. He had already been severely wounded. But despite these wounds and the intense mortar and artillery fire which swept the gun site, he managed to drag himself to the gun, load it with one arm and fire five rounds. The German tractor was set on fire and the light gun damaged. Then a near miss killed the gun aimer, who had been helping him, and blew Wakenshaw himself away from the gun with further grievous wounds. Even then he was not deterred. Again he dragged himself back to the gun and again he placed a round in the breech; but just as he was ready to fire a direct hit on the ammunition killed him and finally silenced the gun. The battle raged on and surged around the Battalion positions. By 7.30 a.m. the three forward companies were completely isolated; and as time passed one by one they were overrun. At 9 a.m. the rest of the Battalion—mainly Headquarters and Headquarter Company—was ordered to withdraw and ultimately reached Division where they formed part of the defence of that Headquarters.

In the evening, when the fighting was over, the body of Adam Wakenshaw was found stretched out beside the ammunition box of his gun. His was bravery indeed, and his shining example of gallantry and devotion marks a glorious page in the annals of the Regiment and of the British Army.[1]

The loss of the 9th Battalion was a grievous blow to the Brigade; but so fierce had been their resistance that the Germans did not exploit their advantage by switching the attack against the 8th Battalion whose flank was by now dangerously exposed. During the lull in the battle the Brigade received orders to take part in a large scale raid by the 5th Indian and 50th Divisions that night. There was to be an attack southwards across the German and Italian lines of communication and the force was then to return to Matruh. The attack took place as planned and both the 6th and 8th Battalions took part. Without doubt it caused confusion among the enemy ranks, but many felt almost as much among their own. At one stage of the advance a German armoured car unwittingly glided into the middle of an 8th Battalion stationary column and parked alongside one of the anti-tank guns. The gunner could hardly believe his luck and put it out of action at point blank range. On another occasion Captain Francis Pitt of the 8th Battalion found a German lorry driving alongside his own; fortunately he spotted it just before the German spotted him. Such incidents were frequent during the night. Not a few trucks and men were missing when the Brigade returned to its positions at daybreak.

By the 28th the position of the Division was precarious. The Germans were closing in and once again it was all but surrounded. Orders were given for a withdrawal that night to

[1] The gun itself now stands in the courtyard of Brancepeth Castle.

be executed in much the same fashion as at Gazala but under far less favourable circumstances. The day passed comparatively quietly; though a detachment of the 6th Battalion had a brush with an enemy force of armoured cars and infantry which was very successfully repulsed. It was not without its anxious moments; but its successful outcome owed a great deal to Regimental Sergeant-Major Arthur Page who commanded a a mixed platoon of clerks, cooks and others in a most aggressive defensive action. He himself was wounded in the leg, but as well as conducting his own sniper's war against the turrets of enemy armoured cars, he got an abandoned anti-tank gun into action, knocked out the enemy commander's car and killed its occupants. His " bag " included a large number of enemy maps and papers.

This small force which was commanded by Major Dick Ovenden was able to withdraw without let or hindrance in time to rejoin the rest of the Battalion ready for the break-out that night. Their destination was to be Fuka. The Brigade—and indeed the whole Division—was divided up into a large number of small columns for the night's operations. But conditions were very different from those at Gazala. The enemy was in close contact and was German, not Italian; they consisted not of infantry but armour; instead of a dark night there was bright moonlight; and the route to be covered involved debouching from a few steep 'wadis' into a plain held by the enemy.

Soon after dark the Brigade set out. For the 6th Battalion the journey was successfully accomplished with only minor interference. But the 8th Battalion was less fortunate. Shortly after starting out it ran into a German ambush as the columns moved through a wadi on their climb up the escarpment. Up went enemy flares and soon all hell seemed let loose. Some troop carriers burst into flames as men jumped out and returned the fire; the rest pushed ahead over the top of the escarpment where they had to run the gauntlet of German machine gun fire. One troop carrier stuck and blocked the way. But somehow it was pushed over the top. The C.O. and Adjutant stood on the top of the escarpment and acted as traffic policemen. Down in the wadi Regimental Sergeant-Major Jennings soon had the situation under control. First of all he got Bren guns positioned to answer the enemy fire. Then he himself mounted a 2 inch mortar and sent bomb after bomb to fall with amazing accuracy on the top of the escarpment where the German gun crews were out in the open and unable to dig in owing to the rocky ground.

Thanks to the R.S.M., and to Private George Fearon, who kept a Bren gun in action for over an hour with remarkably accurate shooting, most of the battalion column got clear of the wadi. But of those who received the full force of the initial German fire few survived, and most of 'D' Company were either killed or captured.

Once clear of the death trap in the wadi the Battalion, now divided into some dozen or more small columns, set course for Fuka. One of them ran parallel to a German supply convoy for several miles. A lone three-tonner at one moment drove alongside a German Mercedes staff car into which a Corporal, sitting atop the driving cab, calmly tossed a grenade as the two parted company. But Fuka was already in German hands and several columns, not being warned, were there captured. The rest were diverted to El Alamein, the cluster of buildings soon to become the symbol of a new spirit in the desert which was to turn defeat into overwhelming victory. But for the moment the 50th Division was really in no fit state to take part in any further fighting. It had suffered over 8,000 casualties since the Gazala battle opened; its transport was on its last legs; and a rest and refit was what its officers and men badly needed. The Division was therefore withdrawn behind the Alamein line and took no part in repulsing Rommel's attack of the 1st of July. The D.L.I. Brigade found itself in a rest area not far from Alexandria and there it remained until early in September, save for a few days towards the end of the month when a composite battalion under Colonel Battiscombe took part in an abortive operation under 69 Brigade.

This latter was an unfortunate one for the Regiment. The composite battalion had an impossible task, was completely ill-equipped for it and was in fact thrown together to plug a hole at a time when the Eighth Army had still not recovered from the disasters of recent weeks. Each battalion in the D.L.I. Brigade found one company but, of course, the battalion as a whole had never worked together and equipment was so short that only two wireless sets were available.

The battalion's task was to carry out a night attack in

conjunction with the East Yorkshire Regiment and some Australians. No daylight reconnaissance was allowed in order not to lose surprise. The route for the attack was supposed to be lighted by a neighbouring South African Brigade, but the lighting was not a success. The attack was supposed to be silent but at the last minute the orders were changed and a barrage laid on. Gaps in the enemy minefield were supposed to have been cleared but in the event were not. All told, much went wrong. The East Yorkshires lost direction and one company of the D.L.I. Battalion lost touch with both the others. The remaining two companies found difficulty in keeping contact. In the moonlight, however, the battalion advanced, as it was meant to do, for 5,000 yards, but the Germans let them pass and then cut off their line of retreat and communication. When daylight came promised tank support failed to materialise and the battalion found itself isolated, hemmed in on all sides, and after a vigorous resistance the survivors, including the C.O., were captured. Most of the East Yorkshires and the Australians suffered a similar fate. It was a sad end to months of hard fighting.

3

ALAMEIN TO MARETH

The retreat to El Alamein was the nadir of the Eighth Army's fortunes. But in August the new firm of Alexander and Montgomery ushered in a fresh period of hope and optimism. General Montgomery's forceful and colourful personality wrought a rapid transformation of the Eighth Army. The period of dogged defence and retreat was soon to give way to one of spectacular advance and triumphant victory.

The new Army Commander made it clear from the start exactly what it was that he required. Rommel's final bid for Cairo was expected at any time—the Army Commander hoped not within the first fortnight—and it would be firmly repulsed. He explained exactly how he anticipated it would be made and the counter action to be taken. Once it was defeated, a great British offensive would be launched for which plans were to be prepared at once and for which a corps d'élite of one infantry and two armoured divisions was to be trained behind the line.

Rommel launched his attack on the night of the 30th of August. He did exactly as Montgomery predicted. So did the Eighth Army, with the result that by the 3rd of September Rommel had turned about and the final bid for Cairo had failed. This short, decisive action marked the final turning point of British fortunes in Africa. Thereafter it was to be one long tale of victory.

The D.L.I. Brigade took no active part in this battle. On the 4th of September it moved into the Alamein line and took over positions vacated by the New Zealanders. Bill Watson, a Territorial officer of long service with the 6th Battalion whose father and great-grandfather had served in the Regiment, had succeeded Sammy Battiscombe, while Jos Percy now commanded the Brigade and his place as C.O. of the 9th had been taken by Andrew Clarke from the 8th. But the rest of the 50th Division remained in the Delta training their newly arrived reinforcements and did not move up till early in October. On the 19th and 20th of October General Montgomery addressed all officers down to lieutenant-colonel and explained his plan. Most of the previous desert offensives had started with an outflanking movement round the enemy's southern flank. This one was to be different. The initial attack was to be a frontal one. Both opposing Armies were firmly entrenched in the style of the first world war: their northern flanks rested on the sea, their southern on the Quattara Depression. The Eighth Army's initial assault was to be in the south, in order to draw the German armoured reserve away from the north, while at the same time a slow, methodical advance in the north was to drive a hole in the German positions to allow the specially trained armoured force, consisting of the 1st and 10th Armoured Divisions, to penetrate through it. The Army Commander made it quite clear that for the first seven to ten days a " dog fight," or " killing match," would take place before the enemy defences finally gave way. This was a critical period when the enemy must not be allowed to regain the initiative. He then gave details of the formidable strength of the Army in guns, tanks and ammunition—all of which had been pouring into Egypt during the past few months, together with reinforcements; and he concluded by declaring that he was absolutely confident of the result of the battle.

Two days later every man in the Eighth Army was let into

the secret. Enthusiasm ran high. Each man felt certain they would succeed, but few realised to what extent. So it was that, on the night of the 23rd of October, the battle of El Alamein began with the mightiest concentration of artillery fire yet put down in the war against Hitler.

The D.L.I. Brigade was in reserve for the first part of the assault. It formed part of the force in the southern part of the line and its part in the attack was not planned to take place until another division, the 44th, had gained a foothold in the enemy positions. Apart, therefore, from a small raid by a company of the 9th Battalion, the Brigade spent a comparatively quiet night and for the next few days was busily engaged in preparing its attack. Then news came through that the plans were changed. Things had gone well in the north, whereas the 44th Division had struck a sticky patch in the south. The German and Italian positions had taken a very severe battering and it was felt that they would cave in when subjected to a final heavy assault. It had therefore been decided to exploit the success in the north, to pull the Brigade out of its present positions—and, temporarily, out of the 50th Division—and for it and a brigade of the Highland Division to attack together to a depth of some 5,000 yards in order to reach the line of the Rahman track.

On the 30th Brigadier Percy held a conference and outlined the plan. Thirteen field regiments and three medium regiments —some three hundred and fifty guns—were to support the operation. The frontage of the attack was about 4,000 yards and such a concentration of artillery on so narrow a front was unprecedented. The guns were to put down a creeping barrage and the troops were warned to keep close up to it. The attack was a vital one, as the whole of the 10th Corps, with its armoured divisions, was waiting to stream through the gap once it was made.

Operation " Supercharge "—for that was what it was called —was originally planned for the night of the 31st of October and then postponed for twenty-four hours. The Brigade moved to an assembly area at Tel el Eisa Station during the 1st of November and, just as the sun was setting, moved off to its forming up positions some seven miles further on. The sandy track had been churned up by so many tanks and lorries that in some places the powdered sand was over a foot deep; and by the time battalions had covered three or four miles every man wore a mantle of it.

The attack was due to begin just before one in the morning. The 8th and 9th Battalions—on the right and left respectively—were to lead the way; and the 6th was to follow them and mop up any isolated enemy posts left in the wake of the advance. After reaching the first objective, there was to be half an hour's halt for reorganisation, during which the 6th Battalion was to execute a complete right wheel so as to take up positions facing north, while the rest of the Brigade faced west. The boundaries between the D.L.I. and Highland Brigades were to be marked by red tracer shells fired by Bofors guns every two minutes along the line of advance; and red tracer fired from rifles and Brens was to be used as a general recognition signal.

The Brigade had nearly two hours to wait after reaching its forming up position. This gave plenty of time for the usual checking up, but it meant that after the hot march there was time to feel the effects of the cold night air, not to speak of the usual suspense of waiting. The night was quiet and, save for the distant sound of R.A.F. bombers pounding enemy gun lines and transport, there was little to break the stillness. At 12.45 a.m. round came the rum ration. There was plenty of it and it was more than welcome. Ten minutes later the troops got to their feet, forward companies spread out along their white tapes and, as the minutes ticked by, shuffled about as they anxiously waited for the guns to open fire.

It was deathly quiet when at five minutes past one the silence of the night was shattered by the British barrage. " In the first few seconds only a dozen or so guns opened fire and then the full weight of the barrage joined in. The infantry looked behind them to see an amazing sight. The whole night to the east was broken by hundreds of gun flashes stabbing into the darkness. The shells whistled overhead to burst with a deafening crash in the target area, and from then, until the barrage closed about three hours later, the frightful shattering noise went on continually."[1] As Colonel Watson, of the 6th Battalion, wrote afterwards, " It was as if the giants of some other world were

[1] " The 8th Battalion The Durham Light Infantry 1939-45 " by P. J. Lewis and I. R. English, p. 148.

cracking their huge whips and hurling lumps of metal through the air. In every twelve yards there was a shell-hole." The partial moon was completely blotted out and visibility reduced to fifty yards.

The Brigade advanced into the smoke and dust of this inferno. From somewhere on the left came the skirl of the pipes from the Scottish Brigade. In the 9th Battalion one company commander, Major Teddy Worrall, kept the company under control by the sound of his hunting horn. Over the wire and into no-man's land they went. Spandaus fired tracer on fixed lines through the smoke and dust, German flares went up and in reply artillery and machine-guns which had escaped the barrage gave answer. All along the line men stumbled and fell, but still the line moved forward close up behind the barrage. Hardly a minute passed without a call for stretcher bearers. The noise of battle was deafening.

The leading companies at last reached the German positions. The barrage had done its work well. German and Italian dead littered the area and many of those who had survived were morally shattered and almost hysterical. But the companies did not stop to consolidate; on they went in the wake of the barrage. Casualties were not light. The two leading companies of the 8th Battalion had by 2.30 a.m.—when they arrived at their first objective—lost five officers and over a hundred men. Indeed, in the smoke and dust the battle had largely become a series of isolated actions between sections or individual men who came upon successive German posts and platoon positions. Private James Brown of the 8th Battalion, though wounded himself, disposed of the occupants of one German post single-handed with his Tommy gun; Sergeant Albert Dunn of the 6th Battalion did the same with another, only the weapon he used was his bayonet.

Whereas the brunt of the 8th Battalion's fighting had fallen on the leading companies, in the 6th Battalion it was the right hand company only which ran into any real resistance. It was a little time before this resistance was overcome at the cost of considerable casualties, one platoon losing its commander killed, all its N.C.Os killed or wounded and all but five of its men. While dealing with these casualties the medical officer was wounded and later, while tending the wounds of Regimental

Sergeant-Major Page, who had accounted for at least one enemy position with his rifle and bayonet, both he and the medical sergeant were killed and, unhappily, the Sergeant-Major too. Strange to relate, the 9th Battalion also lost their medical officer and sergeant in somewhat similar circumstances. The former was an American volunteer and much liked in the Battalion.

As each succeeding small post was rushed, the pace of the attack increased. In the almost uncanny light, not unlike a thick pea-souper fog, figures could be seen moving about whom it was impossible to identify as friend or foe. But by 2.45 a.m. the first objective had everywhere been reached and a quarter of an hour later the barrage and the troops moved forward again on the last leg of the advance. The 6th Battalion wheeled right, soon reached its objective and dug in as best it could facing north.

At 4 a.m. the barrage stopped and everyone dug madly in order to be well below ground level by dawn when a German counter-attack was anticipated. New Zealand Sappers did a fine job clearing gaps through the minefields for tanks, carriers and anti-tank guns to come forward; as the mines were only anti-tank mines the infantry was able to walk through them. So thoroughly was the job done that Maurice Kirby of the 6th Battalion, for instance, had all the battalion fighting vehicles up by 5 a.m. By a quarter to six, when the first flush of dawn could be seen in the eastern sky, the British armour could be heard moving up towards the gaps in the minefields. The desert tracks, so recently crowded with marching infantry, were now jammed with long lines of tanks nose to tail. In the opposite direction went the ambulances, one after another, crammed with wounded; and not far off long processions of bedraggled and dejected Axis prisoners shuffled away into captivity. The 9th Battalion alone had taken over four hundred.

As it got light, things became lively again. At 6.30 a.m. 9 Armoured Brigade moved through the infantry positions and out towards the enemy beyond. The tanks opened fire on the enemy anti-tank guns, but the latter replied with great vigour and it soon became apparent that there was still a strong screen of German 88 millimetre guns as yet untouched. Some twenty Grant and Sherman tanks were knocked out before the British 25 pounders came into action against the gun crews. During the morning there was intermittent small arms fire and shelling of vehicles following up the armour on its way through the minefield. About mid-day eighteen light bombers of the Desert Air Force began a series of bombing attacks on the German positions, which they kept up at forty minute intervals for three or four hours. The effect on the enemy was devastating, and after some hours a hundred and fifty Germans got out of their trenches and walked into the 6th Battalion's lines to surrender. However, the 88 millimetre gun screen was still an obstacle to the tanks in the area and, though it was clear that elsewhere some armour had got through and a desperate tank battle was raging on the Rahman Track, the situation in the Brigade area was little changed by the afternoon. During the late afternoon a further attempt was made by the tanks to pass through the 6th Battalion, but again without success; though the effect of their fire on the German positions immediately at hand was not without its effect and another ninety Germans surrendered to the Battalion, including an immaculately dressed Commander of the Panzer Grenadiers.

The Brigade had now completed its task and during the early evening received orders that it was to be relieved that night by the New Zealanders. 'C' Company of the 8th Battalion which, under Captain Ian English, had borne the brunt of the latter part of the Battalion's attack, was withdrawn to new positions during the afternoon. It had reached a rather exposed position during the darkness somewhat ahead of the rest of the Battalion and during daylight could only be reached in the normal manner by armoured vehicles. The number of wounded in English's care was considerable and it was essential to evacuate them as soon as possible. Food and ammunition were also running short. The Company and all the wounded were in due course brought back into the sector held by the rest of the Brigade; though a raid by Stuka dive-bombers, which occurred simultaneously, made the operation a trifle uncomfortable!

There was some very heavy shelling on the Brigade area just before it got dark, heavier in fact than anyone had yet experienced. As Colonel Watson said: "It fell all round Battalion Headquarters and was horrible while it lasted, but seemed rather like the enemy's final effort." For the Brigade that indeed was what it was. Their relief was completed just before 2 a.m. on the 3rd of November, and the three Battalions, sadly depleted, marched back to their concentration area of the night before—in the words of the 9th Battalion War Diary—" tired, hungry, happy and triumphant." For them the battle of El Alamein was over.

*   *   *   *   *   *

The battle now sped away to the west. An attack by the Highland Division on the night of the 3rd of November prised open the last German defences and enabled the armoured divisions to pour through. The pursuit was on and during the next fortnight the Eighth Army covered seven hundred miles. Rommel pulled out fast, but only a torrential rainstorm, which bogged down all vehicles from tanks to supply lorries, prevented Montgomery from trapping the fleeing Afrika Corps by cutting the road at Fuka and Matruh. One by one the well-known places—Buq Buq, Sidi Barani, El Adem, Tobruk—were left behind. On the 8th of November came the joyful news of the Anglo-American landings in Algeria; on the 20th Benghazi was occupied; and on the 23rd the enemy had been forced out of his positions at Agedabia and had fallen back to Agheila, of evil memory. Even here, however, where so many previous advances had been brought to a halt, Rommel did not stay to fight, but pulled out and established his forces at Buerat, a little more than half way between Agheila and Tripoli.

The D.L.I. Brigade took no part in the pursuit proper. It moved forward some twenty-five miles to secure El Daba and seize the Axis store depots there: but it went no further. It was, however, in El Daba that the 9th Battalion made a remarkable find. While in the Gazala line Captain Tim Chamberlain, of the 6th Battalion, had lost a silver cigarette case engraved with his initials, the Regimental badge and an inscription from his mother. He, alas, was killed on patrol in the Alamein line; but the 9th Battalion on entering a German dug-out at El Daba found the cigarette case lying on the table. Some seven months had elapsed between the loss and the find and the places were three hundred miles apart. After reaching El Daba the Brigade, like the rest of the 50th Division, remained behind to clear the battlefield. At one moment, indeed, the fate of the Division hung in the balance because the manpower position had become so acute after Alamein that one division had to be disbanded to reinforce the others. Fortunately, this fate befell another. The Brigade moved forward early in December and spent Christmas not far from Tobruk. New Year's day saw it on the move again for Agheila, but a violent storm on the 3rd of January halted the columns and ultimately caused the Brigade to be diverted to Benina, a few miles inland from Benghazi. The storm had caused such havoc in Benghazi harbour that it was impossible to maintain the four Divisions planned to be used in the attack on Buerat and the 50th Division, which was to have been one of them, spent the next seven weeks helping to ferry forward supplies with its divisional transport and training for the operations it was shortly to be called upon to carry out.

On the 15th of January Montgomery attacked at Buerat; by the 17th the German resistance had been broken; and on the 23rd, in the early hours of the morning, the Eighth Army entered Tripoli, having advanced over 1,400 miles and inflicted some 75,000 casualties upon the enemy. It was three months since Alamein.

Rommel now withdrew across the Tunisian frontier. There he prepared to hold the defences of the Mareth line and assembled the German 15th and 21st Panzer Divisions, partly equipped with the formidable Tiger tanks, in readiness for an all-out attack on the advancing Eighth Army. On the 17th of February British forces occupied Medenine, an important road centre across the Tunisian frontier; and six days later Rommel attacked them, only to be firmly repulsed after failing completely to penetrate the British positions. This was a decisive battle; after it Rommel left for Germany, to take no further part in the African campaign, and the Eighth Army set about preparing for the next move—an attack on the enemy positions in front of Mareth.

The Mareth defences were unique in the African theatre. The so-called Mareth line had originally been constructed by the French to protect Tunisia from attack by the Italians from Libya. It had been laid out so as to exploit the defile formed by the close approach of the Matmata Hills to the Mediterranean. The hills, 2,300 feet at their highest, run from north to south and then bend away to the north-west to form the El Hamma gap.

"Except for a few tracks running through narrow passes, these rugged, broken hills formed a natural barrier to wheeled transport and at the same time dominated the whole western end of the defence system. In the coastal sector the line had been based on the Wadi Zigzaou, a horrible obstacle, widened and deepened to form a tank trap and covered by enfilade fire along its whole length by a complicated system of concrete and steel pillboxes, gun emplacements and blockhouses. The strongpoints, formidable affairs of concrete two or three feet thick, were supported by a well revetted trench system, linked with deep dug-outs and funk holes."[1]

The main road crosses the Wadi Zigzaou, of which the last five miles has running water throughout the year, seven miles from the sea. It runs through Arram village, which was one of the strongest redoubts in the Mareth positions. In the sector chosen for the 50th Division's attack there was no similar road and crossing, though there were crossing places which had been used in fine weather. The whole divisional area had the disadvantage of being overlooked by the enemy whereas observation of the enemy was impossible; and knowledge of his positions depended on good air photographs and what French officers could remember of them.

151 Brigade left Benina on the 2nd of March and arrived in rear of the main Eighth Army positions on the 13th. The Brigade was now commanded by Brigadier Beak, who had taken over from Brigadier Percy shortly after Alamein. The latter left to the regret and with the good wishes of all: he had served with the Brigade as Brigade Major, Battalion Commander and Brigadier since 1938. Command of the three Battalions had remained unchanged since Alamein, but reinforcements of officers and men had reached each of them, some only arriving at Benina. Battalions were thus fresh and rested and the period at Benina had been well spent preparing for the Mareth battle. As one company commander put it, this proved to be "the most valuable training which we had ever had and did more towards raising that high morale and confidence so necessary in battle than anything I have ever experienced either before or since."

The stage was now set for the assault on the Mareth line.

[1] "The 8th Battalion The Durham Light Infantry 1939-1945" by P. J. Lewis and I. R. English. p. 168.

The French had always maintained that it could not be outflanked; but, like so many pre-war beliefs, this was soon proved without foundation. In fact, early in January, the Long Range Desert Group had already found a way round and, while the 50th Division delivered the frontal assault, the 2nd New Zealand Division was to carry out a wide left hook to outflank the line and push through to El Hamma in rear of it. Whichever thrust went best could then be reinforced.

The main attack was to be made by 151 Brigade, supported by the 50th Royal Tank Regiment. A preliminary operation was, however, necessary to drive in the outposts covering the main approaches to the Wadi Zigzaou, and this was carried out during the night of the 16th of March by 69 Brigade, part of the 51st Division and 201 Guards Brigade. Generally, the attack was successful and at any rate left the southern side of the Wadi in the hands of 151 Brigade.

The Wadi Zigzaou runs to the sea through a mass of quicksands; it is sluggish and muddy, with high banks, and fordable in places. Beyond it was an anti-tank ditch, then a mass of trenches, then a number of French blockhouses; these last looked more formidable than in fact they were, but the other obstacles were serious. 151 Brigade was to make its attack on the area between and including the strongpoints of Ksiba Ouest on the right and Ouerzi on the left—the two strongpoints being about a mile apart. The 9th Battalion was to capture Ksiba Ouest and the 8th Ouerzi; once they had captured these objectives, Valentine tanks were to cross the Wadi by causeways, followed by the 6th Battalion whose task was to deepen the bridgehead. Some careful patrolling was carried out by the Brigade on the night of the 18th of March: the patrols examined the bed of the Wadi, crossed it and had a look at the anti-tank ditch beyond. They found the slopes leading down were mined, as was the Wadi itself: there was water in it, but at places it had a firm bottom. Under the very noses of the enemy they reconnoitred the most suitable crossing places and obtained a fair idea of the general lay-out of the defences.

There was a full moon on the night of the 20th of March. At 10.30 p.m. a subsidiary attack was launched by 69 Brigade, on 151 Brigade's left, to secure an area known as the Bastion which overlooked the rest of the divisional positions. Half an hour later the 8th and 9th Battalions moved off to begin the main attack. Enemy shelling on the forming up places caused some casualties, as did some mines lying undiscovered on the tracks leading up to it. The 9th Battalion on the right met a hail of fire from artillery, mortars and machine guns as it moved forward towards the Wadi: but, fortunately, a great deal of it was very inaccurate. Tanks fitted with flails—known as Scorpions—rumbled forward and with the gapping parties led the way through the minefields. These were successfully cleared. Then ' C ' Company, under Captain Charlie Goulden, crossed the anti-tank ditch by means of ladders, waded across the Wadi and reached the far side without serious loss. Here they encountered Italians, who were entrenched in strong dug-in positions, and it required some vigorous hand-to-hand fighting before the position finally caved in. ' B ' Company—Worrall's—was meanwhile advancing through the minefield on the British side of the Wadi nearly fifteen minutes behind schedule. On the way Worrall, who was using his hunting horn with great effect, as at Alamein, was hit in the chest, but decided to go on and patch the wound up at the objective. Knowing that he was committed to a timed artillery programme, he decided to make up the lost time by taking a chance on the minefield, and he led his company through the last part of it without waiting for it to be cleared. This bold gamble came off and there were comparatively few casualties.

The Company reached the far side of the Wadi at a point where the bank was very steep. As they began to struggle up it a burst of very heavy fire came from Ksiba Ouest and within a matter of minutes rifle and machine-gun fire poured in enfilade down the Wadi as the troops struggled desperately to gain a foothold. For a moment it was touch and go; then some men formed a human ladder and the rest scrambled up the bank and over the top. Once out of the Wadi they made for Ksiba Ouest itself, which they had been ordered to attack from the rear. " Here," in the words of Worrall himself, " the fire was quite bloody. I told Corporal Bell to crawl forward and cut the wire. Scotty White, Sergeant Randall, Corporal Daly and myself lay beside two palm trees and tried to cover him. We couldn't have taken those pillboxes unless somebody had cut that wire, and the bullets were missing by inches here. My horn had got bunged up with sand, so I couldn't blow the Company on. A lot of them had temporarily stuck and slowed down crossing the Wadi and getting up the anti-tank ditch.

"At last Bell said, 'I've cut the wire, Sir.' We made a dash for it and by sheer luck got into their trenches fifty yards beyond the wire. We went up these. When we got near the pillboxes, I put Randall and Daly with two Brens to fire at the slits, while White and I led a party up the trench towards them, throwing 36 grenades at each corner. To my joy, suddenly about fifty Italians appeared with their hands up. I then saw that the Bren guns had set the pillboxes on fire, at least the two left hand ones. More Italians surrendered, among them a Major and a Captain." This was about 2 in the morning.

Worrall then went back to the rest of the Company in the area of a pillbox over on the right. Here the same tactics were tried. "The Italians came rushing out in our faces," says Worrall. "I tried to make one put his hands up, but found I was unarmed; I had lost my revolver and, worse still, my hunting horn. However, no Italian fired! This time I determined there would be no need to go back and we swarmed over all three strong points quickly. We took about eighty prisoners and pushed them out of the fort along the trench to the road." So before daylight the Company was in possession of Ksiba Ouest and the rest of the Battalion had established its bridgehead.

Like the 9th, the 8th Battalion was heavily shelled in its forming up area, but by some miracle not a man was killed and after fifteen minutes the firing stopped. Then, thirty-five minutes after the opening of the barrage in support of 69 Brigade, the Battalion moved forward in the wake of the Scorpions. Colonel Jackson was, however, far from satisfied with the rate of advance and told Ian English of 'C' Company to "get a move on and ignore the blasted Scorpions: there aren't any mines on this side of the Wadi." He had scarcely uttered these words when a deafening explosion eloquently signified that this was merely wishful thinking; but the funny side was not lost on those who heard him!

The leading companies reached the Wadi which they found wider and deeper than had been expected. It meant wading, in some places chest high, and the enemy shelling was increasing; though, fortunately, the middle of the Wadi had not as yet been subjected to very heavy fire. Once across, 'A' Company (Captain Chris Beattie) made for Ouerzi. It had to cross a minefield first and here Beattie and a number of others were wounded. Then came the anti-tank ditch. Down came the scaling ladders and over went the Company; and, finally, through increasingly heavy artillery and machine-gun fire, the platoons doubled across the open, firing Brens and Tommy guns from the hip, to close with the defenders. It was not an easy task to clear the Ouerzi post. The trenches leading to and from it were very deep and it was difficult to follow their lay-out. The area was partly cleared of its Italian garrison but, despite all efforts to dislodge them, a band of intrepid young Fascists held on behind the concrete and steel of the innermost part of the fort. So 'A' Company had no option but to share its newly won positions with them.

'C' Company, under Ian English, on the other hand were making remarkably good progress. Once over the Wadi, it was found impossible to make effective use of the Sappers' mine detectors, as the noise of battle was so great that the buzz in the earphones could not be heard when a mine was detected. Besides, there were so many shell fragments lying about that the detectors could not distinguish between the mines and them. So English led the way through the minefield and, like Worrall of the 9th, found that boldness pays. Casualties were surprisingly few.

It did not take long to cross the anti-tank ditch. Only two ladders were used and the Company nipped across them immediately the supporting barrage lifted from the enemy pillboxes. They met very little opposition and were soon on their objective and digging in. Indeed, their most uncomfortable moment was when they found themselves in the middle of a British artillery barrage. Fortunately, terrifying as it was, there was only one casualty.

Meanwhile, the Battalion had suffered a grievous loss. The Colonel had been killed in the Wadi. He had gone there with the Intelligence Officer, Lieutenant Richardson, while the two leading companies were crossing. Very early on both of them were wounded by shelling and it was reported that they were lying helpless on the bank of the Zigzaou. There were a dozen or more wounded men not far from them. The enemy guns were shelling the Wadi very heavily and a search party, sent out from Battalion Headquarters, was unable to locate any of them. Whether the C.O. died from his original wounds or was hit while lying exposed to shell fire in the Wadi, will never be known but his loss meant the loss of a very gallant officer, quite fearless and deeply respected by officers and men alike. His death came as a great shock to the whole Battalion.

When the news of the Colonel's death reached the reserve company—still on the home side of the Wadi—Captain Peter Lewis, the commander, decided to carry out the original plan, which was for his company to cross the Wadi and reinforce 'A' Company. As the Company had no mine detecting team, it, too, had to take a chance on the minefield. Lewis led his men across the Wadi without trouble, as the enemy fire slackened; but once across their tale is a chapter of accidents. First the leading platoon commander stepped on a mine and was killed instantly; fragments from it wounded Lewis; and then, to make matters worse, the explosion brought down a fierce concentration of enemy defensive fire on the Wadi, followed by a deluge of machine-gun fire. Men began to fall thick and fast, some killed, some wounded, and within a matter of minutes only one officer—Lieutenant Randall—was still on his feet. Lewis ordered him to take what was left of the Company across the anti-tank ditch to join 'A' Company in Ouerzi. With the help of Company Sergeant-Major Matthew Brannigan, this was what Randall did, but the wounded had to be left where they lay on the banks of the Wadi. There, for the next ten minutes, these unfortunate men were subjected to a vicious hail of fire from machine-guns, mortars and guns. One 105 millimetre German gun did terrible destruction and only a few, one of whom was Lewis, lived to tell the tale.

By daylight on the 21st the overall situation on 151 Brigade front was not altogether unpromising. The 9th Battalion had reached its planned objectives and so had the 8th: both battalions had paid a not unreasonable price for their success. However, the 8th as well as losing their C.O. had their second in command wounded almost immediately after he took over command of the Battalion; and it was not till the afternoon of the 21st that Major Bob Lidwill of the King's Regiment and a senior company commander, who had remained back in charge of the

The grave of Private Adam Wakenshaw after the battle, with the gun he manned

Private Adam Wakenshaw, V.C.

Imperial War Museum
Men of 151 Brigade re-enact the crossing of the anti-tank ditch in the Mareth Line

Imperial War Museum
Men of the 6th Battalion on board the " Winchester Castle " on the way to Sicily

151 BRIGADE IN THE MIDDLE EAST AND SICILY

Battalion's reinforcements, came forward to take over the Battalion which—as it turned out—he was to command for over a year. But although both battalions had carried out their allotted tasks, there was another side to the picture. The timing of the operation was badly out. As a result, the 6th Battalion was compelled to wait in a narrow gap through the minefields throughout the night, as it could not move into the forming up place which was full of vehicles. There it lay, fully exposed to the shell fire of the enemy, unable to dig in owing to the rocky ground. Thirteen men were either killed or wounded without a shot being fired; and one signaller was killed at the C.O.'s side. The 6th Battalion's move was, therefore, called off until the following night: but although both the 8th and 9th Battalions were across the Wadi Zigzaou, both now had to be supplied and reinforced and crossings over the Wadi had to be constructed for tanks and transport. This proved a difficult and hazardous task, for the Wadi was still under heavy indirect fire from enemy machine guns and from artillery. The Sappers laboured valiantly building a causeway, but they lost a lot of men doing it; and then, when it was complete, only three Valentine tanks managed to get across as the fourth smashed the fascines, sank and blocked the way. Worse still, it meant that the troops on the far side of the Wadi had no anti-tank guns.

The enemy had obviously been shaken by what had happened and during the day did not launch his expected counter-attack. But he did begin filtering back through tunnels into some of the positions round Ouerzi. The 8th Battalion therefore spent the day conducting a vigorous guerilla warfare against these marauders, in which three men—Sergeant William Crawford and Privates William Higginson and " Mick " Michael—played a very prominent part. Each was able to claim a satisfactory ' bag ' at the end of the day. The 9th Battalion, on the other hand, spent a comparatively uneventful day until about 7 p.m. when some two hundred and fifty Bersaglieri decided they could not face another Eighth Army artillery barrage and walked in to surrender.

That night the attack was resumed. The 9th Battalion was relieved in Ksiba Ouest by the East Yorkshire Regiment from 69 Brigade, so that it should be free to attack Ouerzi Est and another post to the east of it. The 6th Battalion's objectives were the two forts of Ouerzi Ouest and Zarat Sudest. The 8th Battalion had no active part to play, but was fully occupied keeping a number of enemy probing attacks at bay.

Two companies of the 9th Battalion attacked at 1.30 a.m. The first had little difficulty in capturing the unnamed post, but the second found the Italian garrison of Ouerzi Est full of fight and it took over three hours of stiff hand-to-hand fighting before the success signal could be given. The Company took over a hundred and twenty prisoners, but their own casualties were heavy and a bare thirty-five men, with little ammunition, were all that were left fit to fight. The 6th Battalion, however, secured both their objectives comparatively easily, but suffered heavy casualties from enemy artillery fire on the anti-tank ditch which was used as a start-line. 'C' Company under Captain Tony Eardley-Wilmot, who was himself killed, lost all its officers save one and he was wounded next day. Ouerzi Ouest was found to be a position of considerable importance, with a commanding view of the countryside; but Zarat Sudest was larger than anticipated, with an intricate system of deep intercommunicating trenches, resulting in platoons and sections easily becoming detached and out of control. During the night the causeway over the Wadi was repaired and over forty tanks crossed into the newly won bridgehead.

As the sun came up on the morning of the 22nd the turning point of the battle was reached. The real key to the bridgehead position was still the Wadi Zigzaou. Unless supplies could be got across it, the position could never be maintained against a determined counter-attack, especially if it was supported by armour. Unfortunately, the tanks, in getting over the Wadi, had so damaged the crossing that the anti-tank guns had not been able to follow them—a serious disadvantage. The enemy had also been able to leave behind several snipers—some on the east bank—who succeeded in stopping all work in the Wadi once it became properly light.

Soon after first light, the R.A.F. reported enemy troop movements near the woods around Zarat. At 11 a.m. the 9th Battalion could clearly see German tanks forming up opposite Ksiba Ouest. But throughout the morning any enemy attempts to move forward were stopped by artillery fire. Then a disaster occurred. A short, but very heavy, shower of rain caused the water to rise in the Wadi and prevented the Air Force from using its airfields. At 1.30 p.m. the enemy attack began.

The attack was launched by the German 15th Panzer Division and elements of the 90th Light Division. They advanced in three columns, one on Ouerzi Est, the second between Ouerzi Est and Ouerzi Ouest and the third along a shallow valley between Ouerzi Ouest and Ouerzi. Each column consisted of tanks and large numbers of infantry. The main effort at first was directed against the Valentine tanks, and a fierce battle continued throughout the afternoon between the opposing armour; but the old Valentines were no match for the German 88 millimetre guns and by late afternoon thirty of them had been put out of action. Meanwhile, the infantry attacked Ouerzi and got round behind it, but the 8th Battalion fought back with great vigour and were still in possession at dusk. The 9th Battalion, however, was not so fortunate. By 3 p.m. the German infantry and tanks were all round Ouerzi Est and, after firing all their ammunition, the remaining defenders withdrew to the anti-tank ditch under a smokescreen. Those in the unnamed post were not directly attacked and held on till nightfall. The company of the 6th Battalion in Ouerzi Ouest received the full brunt of the attack. The company was without officers and commanded by Sergeant-Major Watts who was never heard of again; and it fought till all its ammunition was used up when the survivors struggled back to the anti-tank ditch. A second company—each Battalion had only three—between Ouerzi Ouest and Zarat Sudest found itself in the wake of a German force attacking from Zarat, and though it hung on as long as possible was similarly forced back in the late afternoon. The third company, under Captain George Wood, held fast in Zarat Sudest till 6 p.m. when, also with ammunition exhausted, it followed the others back after the enemy had worked round behind it.

By evening the position in the bridgehead was extremely serious. Communication with the troops there was almost non-existent: wirelesses had been knocked out and telephone lines cut. There was little ammunition, the few remaining tanks had had to withdraw to the Wadi and the troops only had their rifles and grenades against enemy tanks. The different companies—or what remained of them—of the 6th, 8th and 9th

Battalions were each isolated, though in some cases mixed up. A German armoured 88 millimetre gun had been brought up to within two hundred and fifty yards of the anti-tank ditch in the 6th Battalion area but small arms fire—which was all that was available—could make no impression on it. Ammunition, too, was running out. Dick Ovenden of the 6th Battalion visited Colonel Watson at Battalion Headquarters—a joint one with that of the 9th Battalion—just before midnight to ask for more and was given the last box. He was killed on the way back to his company. Shortly afterwards two Vickers machine-guns under Colonel Watson's personal command fired their last belt. Then another enemy attack came in on the left flank accompanied by intense mortar and artillery fire mixed with smoke. After that it was just a question of how long the enemy could be kept at arm's length; Bren guns were jammed with dust and everybody knew that when dawn came the ditch would be rushed and it would be the end. Though very heavy casualties had been inflicted on the Germans by both infantry and guns, they were not enough to stop them. All told, the general picture was pretty obscure to those on the other side of the Wadi and, about 4.30 a.m., the Divisional Commander ordered 151 Brigade to withdraw to the Wadi, leaving the East Yorkshires still in Ksiba Ouest as a pivot for an attack which it was hoped to resume the following day. The withdrawal was successfully carried out in the early hours of the 23rd and by first light all three Battalions were east of the Wadi; though one mixed company of 6th and 8th Battalion men had had to attack with fixed bayonets through a minefield in order to cut their way out.

It was a bitter blow to have to go back after three days of gallant fighting. Despite the ferocity of the battle, the order to withdraw came as such a surprise to many that a number of officers and N.C.O.s could only be convinced of it by the word of their C.O. But although at first it was intended that the Brigade should reorganise preparatory to launching a further attack, those who made their way back in the early hours of the 23rd had, in fact, completed their part in the battle of Mareth; and, indeed, the battle itself was now over. The counter-attack by the German Panzer and Light Divisions was the enemy's undoing. It cost him dearly and he had to leave his armour to hold the line. So he had none to face the New Zealanders when, after gradually working their way through the Matmata Hills, they suddenly appeared at El Hamma. Although their initial attack was held, General Montgomery moved up the 1st Armoured Division to reinforce them and sent the 4th Indian Division after them. By the 27th of March the enemy along the Wadi Zigzaou had pulled out and the Highland Division, who had relieved the 50th Division on the 23rd, occupied Mareth. Two days later the Eighth Army captured El Hamma and Gabes and the enemy sped away to the west to man the Wadi Akarit, some fifty miles beyond the Mareth line.

The battle of Mareth will long be remembered as one of the toughest operations assigned to any formation during the late war. The gallant stand north of the Wadi Zigzaou against overwhelming odds, after an attack against positions in which most of the advantage lay with the enemy, drew the German armour out of position and directly facilitated the success of the New Zealanders' flanking attack. The fighting of those three days in March tore grievous holes in the ranks of the Durham Brigade. Three rifle companies of the 6th Battalion were reduced from three hundred all ranks to sixty-five, and the other two Battalions' losses were of a somewhat similar nature. Not all, of course, were killed, and many rejoined their comrades later. This was certainly one of the most savage actions which the Regiment had to fight and one in which it can claim to have played a notable and glorious part. A sergeant in the Green Howards writing home to relatives in West Hartlepool about this time used these words: "The Scots lads of the Highland Division are good lads with bags of 'go'; the Aussies have plenty of dash; the New Zealanders are easily the finest soldiers in the desert; but when things are at their worst, when everything looks lost and men are going down left, right and centre, give us the Durham Light Infantry." It is a fitting tribute to those members of the Regiment who fought and died at Mareth in March, 1943.

*   *   *   *   *   *

The days of the Axis forces in North Africa were now numbered. It was not long before the Eighth and First Armies were to join hands and deal the final blow. Although there was still some bitter fighting ahead, 151 Brigade was to play a comparatively minor part in it. The attack on the Wadi Akarit was launched on the 6th of April. The 6th Battalion was borrowed by 150 Brigade as an additional reserve battalion for that Brigade's attack, but 151 Brigade as a whole remained in reserve. At dusk on the 6th, through some unpleasant enemy shelling, the Battalion moved into a gap between the Highland Division on the Djebel Romana and 150 Brigade on Hachana ridge. Through the gap, next morning, poured the New Zealanders on the way to Tunis and the Battalion contented itself with rounding up hundreds of prisoners and a great deal of loot. It returned to 151 Brigade on the 8th while an exhausted and demoralised enemy withdrew northwards towards Enfidaville with the Eighth Army in hot pursuit. A few hours after breaking through at Akarit, it joined up with the Americans, and, four days later, with the First Army. As the British forces closed in on Enfidaville on the 17th of April, it looked as if the D.L.I. Brigade would be required to take part in the attack. But, in fact, the 50th Division was wanted elsewhere and before it was able to take part in the final stages of the North African campaign the whole Division was whisked away over the 1,300 miles from Enfidaville to Alexandria, there to prepare for the assault on the soft underbelly of Europe. The invasion of Sicily was at hand.

4

SICILY

It took three weeks to get from Enfidaville to Alexandria. Once there 151 Brigade indulged in some well-earned leave, each man taking his choice between Alexandria and Cairo. Both cities—the fear of war banished—had returned to normal and officers and men were able to wallow in the pleasures of civilisation. Thereafter the Brigade started work once more and moved down to the Bitter Lakes for training in combined operations. Command of the three Battalions remained unchanged; Watson and Clarke having commanded since a month or so before Alamein and Lidwill since Mareth. Command of the Brigade had, however, changed shortly after

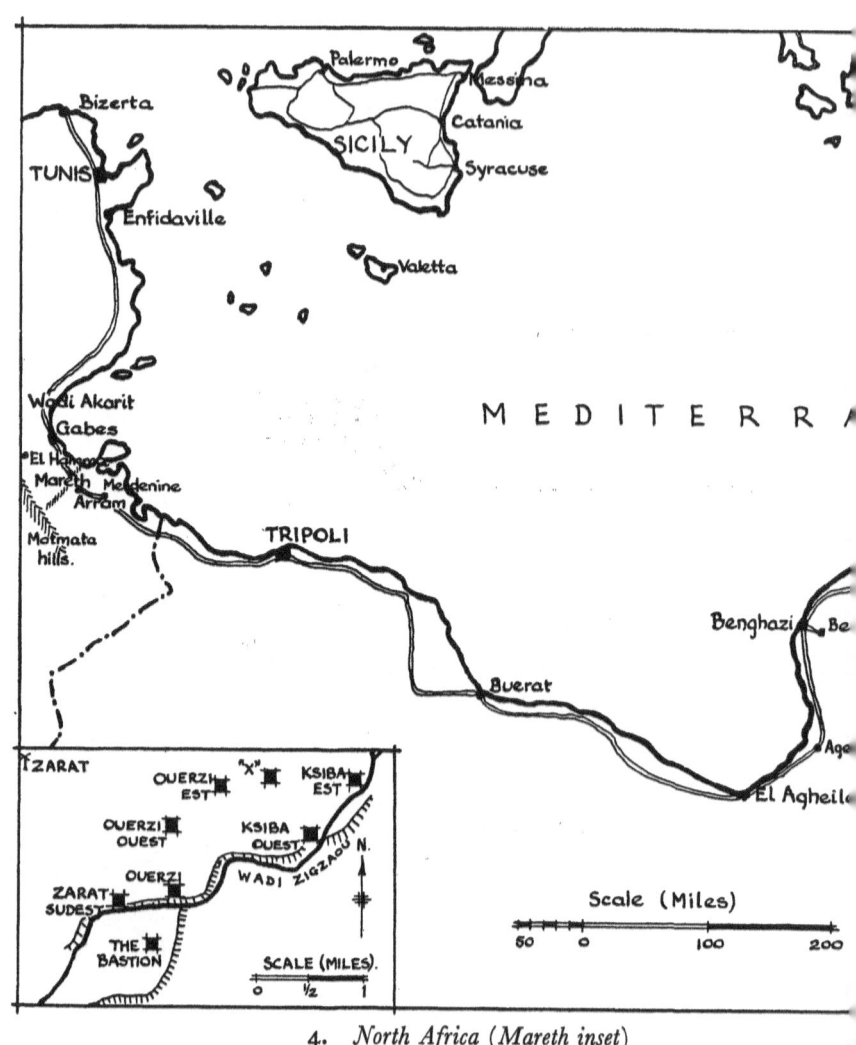

4. *North Africa (Mareth inset)*

the battle of Mareth when Brigadier Beake handed over to Brigadier Ronnie Senior who was to remain with the Brigade until after the invasion of Normandy more than a year ahead. Between the 22nd of May and the end of June the whole of the 50th Division was put through an intensive course of training for landing on hostile shores. On the 30th as part of a convoy carrying the assault troops for Sicily it sailed away from Port Said: and once out in the open sea the well kept secret of the convoy's destination—known hitherto to only a few—was divulged to everyone. Maps, models and aerial photographs were brought out and officers and N.C.Os set about studying the varied problems that faced them.

The D.L.I. Brigade had been chosen as assault Brigade. The two forward battalions—the 6th and 9th Battalions—were to land at 2.45 a.m. on the 10th of July on the beaches before the small town of Avola in the south-east corner of the island. The Brigade's task was to secure a beachhead for the landing of the rest of the 50th Division, and once the 6th and 9th Battalions had mopped up the beach defences the 8th was to land and the Brigade was to occupy a covering position north-west of Avola.

The convoy reached its assembly position off the beaches shortly before midnight on the 9th. The journey had been a memorable one. So far the weather had been perfect and, to everyone's surprise, enemy planes were virtually non-existent. True, there had been six air raid alerts, but only one hostile aircraft and that was a very high flying reconnaissance plane on the second day out. For the first five days the convoy from Suez was not a large one; but soon after midday on the 9th it was joined by others from Malta and North Africa and for a short while the broad expanse of sea was filled with ships of all shapes and sizes—so many, indeed, that it seemed that there was scarcely room for all of them to lie off the shores of Sicily. But this last day brought something more than the joining up of the convoys. The wind freshened and by midday a heavy sea was running. That night it blew half a gale, though for a time, at sunset, the wind dropped a little. As the sun went down the summit of Mount Etna could be clearly seen rising above a bank of low cloud; then there was darkness; and, not long after, in the glimmer of a half-moon, the outlines of planes and gliders were just visible as the airborne troops passed overhead.

From blacked out ships, in the early hours of the 10th, each Battalion climbed into landing craft suspended over the dark, storm-tossed waters of a sea whipped up by an offshore wind. There was considerable delay in getting craft away. There was a good deal of sea-sickness, too, especially among those in landing craft which had to circle the parent ship while waiting to form up before leaving for the shore: and the choppy sea resulted in many boatloads being drenched to the skin. In fact, due to weather, a great deal went wrong with the landing as a technical operation and parts of it were not unlike a rather chaotic exercise. At 2.45 a.m. the leading troops had not reached the shore and as time passed the naval officers in charge of the landing craft realised that many of the boats had got scattered, flotillas were no longer together and some craft were quite out of touch with their neighbours. Added to which most naval officers were uncertain as to their exact whereabouts. All this was largely due to the fact—learnt subsequently—that the convoy had stopped much further offshore than intended or realised; some put the distance at twelve miles offshore instead of seven. The extra distance and the heavy sea between them had put the timing badly out and resulted in the forward battalions being put ashore higgledy-piggledy and in the wrong places.

The 6th Battalion began landing at 4.15 a.m. exactly one and a half hours late. Companies did not all land together, some platoons were landed with companies other than their own and only Colonel Watson, and part of his Battalion Headquarters, arrived at anywhere approaching the right place and, when they did so, found the beach was under fire and so dropped a smoke canister overboard and ran in further north where half the 9th Battalion had landed previously. The rest of the Battalion was landed in scattered groups at distances varying from 3,000 to 6,000 yards south of the correct beach. Fortunately there was little opposition. The Italians seemed to have been taken by surprise, though as one of 'A' Company's boatloads approached the shore it had the pleasure of extinguishing an enemy searchlight with a burst of Bren gun fire.

The 9th Battalion was a little more fortunate, but not much. It, too, was an hour and a half late, but at least two companies were landed together within five hundred yards of the right beach

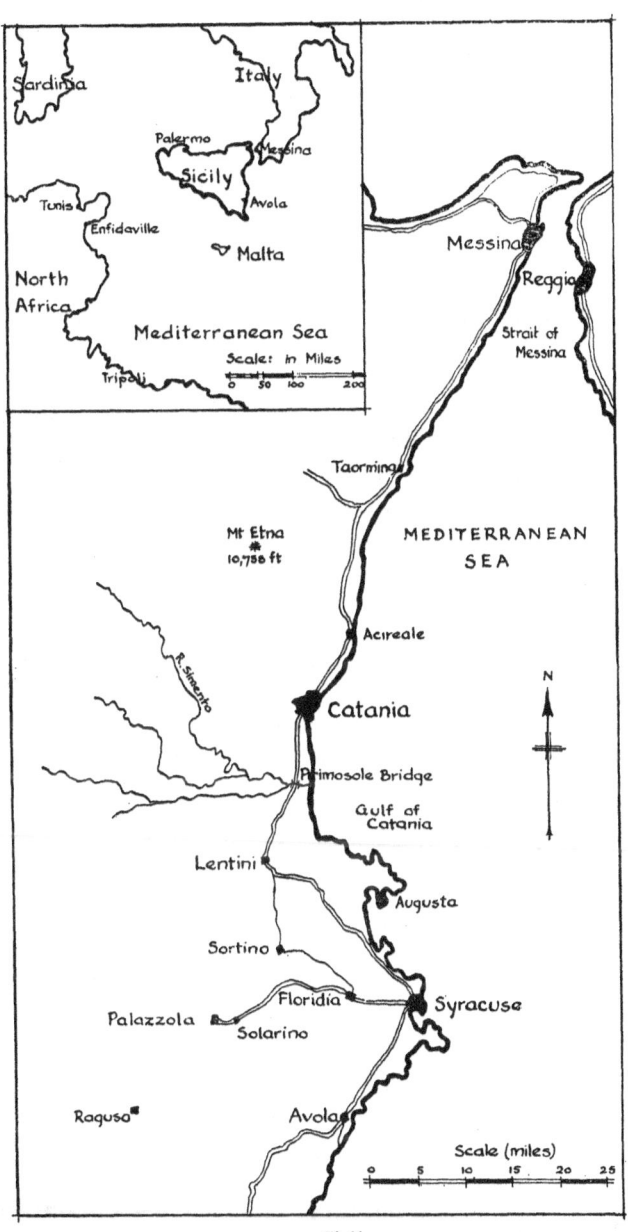

5. *Sicily*

and the C.O. did not get separated from the rest of the Battalion. However, the remainder of the Battalion was landed in scattered parties at from 3,000 to 4,000 yards too far south, but in spite of this the main beach was cleared fairly easily of enemy, although hostile shelling prevented it from being fully used for some little while.

Despite this rather disconcerting start both battalions quickly reorganised themselves on shore. As soon as it got light it was possible to discern a number of landmarks which indicated the true position, and the various scattered companies began sorting themselves out and mopping up such enemy resistance as they had encountered. The garrison troops of the beach defences were Italian and many were only too willing to give themselves up; and the local population was extremely friendly once it was realised the invaders were not German! The 6th Battalion was pleasantly surprised to meet with a company of American parachutists who had been dropped in the wrong place and were only too glad to join up and co-operate with them. They were a splendid body of men and one of them attached himself to Colonel Watson as his personal bodyguard, while the rest formed themselves into an additional company and placed themselves wholeheartedly under the Battalion for the next twenty-four hours.

At dawn the 8th Battalion landed in one piece to the north of what was originally intended as the 9th Battalion's beach. It found itself in another divisional area but at once turned south and made towards Avola. Both the 6th and 9th Battalions had secured Union Jacks from the Royal Navy before landing. By 8 a.m. the 6th Battalion's flag was fluttering from the top of Avola Railway Station and by 10 a.m. the town was in the hands of the 9th Battalion whose flag flew triumphantly from the Town Hall. So by midday the Brigade was in occupation of the high ground overlooking the beaches, each battalion having reached its pre-arranged positions. Despite an unfortunate start all had gone well and casualties had not been heavy.

During the night of the 10th the Brigade received the good news that elsewhere the landings had been successful. Syracuse was in Eighth Army hands by nightfall and though the Americans had met some tough resistance from German troops around Gela, the Allied operation had been carried out substantially according to plan. The next task for the 50th Division was to thrust inland beyond Syracuse along the road running through the hills from Floridia through Sortino to Lentini; thence along the road which crosses the Simeto river by the Primosole Bridge and into the plain of Catania. To speed the advance an airborne attack had been planned for the night of the 13th of July to capture and hold the vitally important Primosole Bridge —fifteen miles distance from Catania itself—where the airborne troops were to hold fast until the arrival of the advancing infantry.

The advance was led by 69 Brigade. The going was hot and thirsty. The road was narrow, winding and dusty and only really fit for one-way traffic. For much of the way it runs along valleys dominated on both sides by precipitous hills; in the hills it is bordered by stone walls and in the valleys by olive groves. The D.L.I. Brigade occupied positions in and around Floridia and Solarino on the 12th of July while 69 Brigade moved on to capture Sortino. The 6th Battalion, however, was counterattacked by the Italian Napoli Division, first with tanks and then with infantry. Neither attack was successful. The tanks—some five in all—careered down the road from Palazzola as the Battalion was moving forward: four were knocked out but one reached Floridia, shooting up Colonel Watson's jeep and wounding the medical officer on the way. It ended its career by running into a lamp post! The infantry attack was launched after the Battalion had moved into its new positions and it was stopped by artillery fire. It was returned in good measure on the following day, the 13th, at first light. Then the Battalion, supported by the 98th Field Regiment and the 44th Royal Tank Regiment, set upon the Italians who were so demoralized that their positions were overrun by 5.30 a.m. The Battalion's casualties were light but included two company commanders, Captain Dominic Parker, wounded in the lungs, and Captain Jimmy Chapman who was unfortunately killed—a very serious loss so early in the campaign. At 8 a.m. two sections of carriers and a troop of tanks, under Captain Bobbie Pringle, went forward through the completely disorganised resistance along the road to Palazzola while the reserve company started a sweep to round up snipers and any enemy who attempted to get away to the hills. These operations met with complete success. They resulted in the destruction of the Napoli Division, the capture of several hundred prisoners, including the Divisional Commander, and a mass of equipment. By nightfall Sortino had been occupied by 69 Brigade, who had pushed on towards Lentini, and 151 Brigade was moving up behind them.

During the night of the 13th part of the 1st Parachute Brigade was dropped in the area of the Primosole Bridge. It removed the demolition charges placed there, but as, unfortunately, many of the troops had been dropped wide of the target only a small force was available to hold the bridge against repeated German attempts to recapture it. It was, therefore, essential for troops of the 50th Division to reach the Bridge sometime during the 14th or at latest by nightfall. As 69 Brigade had so far borne the brunt of such fighting as there had been during the advance, 151 Brigade now took over from them. The three Battalions set out on a forced march of some twenty-five miles, the 9th Battalion leading followed by the 8th and then the 6th. By afternoon the 9th Battalion was well over half way and by dusk, together with 4 Armoured Brigade, it was within a mile of the bridge.

The paratroopers had bad news to relate. All day they had fought back repeated counter-attacks with success; but at about 7.30 p.m., just two hours before the arrival of the 9th Battalion, lack of ammunition had forced their sadly depleted force to withdraw in the face of another counter-attack. With demolition charges removed, of course, the bridge could not be blown and the paratroopers were near enough to prevent the enemy planting any more. But the battalions of 151 Brigade were too tired after their forced march to fight a battle that night and the Brigadier decided to postpone any such attack until the following morning. It was not Italians with whom they would have to deal but Germans of the 3rd Parachute Regiment, most of whom were veterans of the Crete and Russian campaigns and all of whom had been flown from the Italian mainland only a short while before.

The country round about the Primosole Bridge is flat and open. The road running north from Lentini runs along a ridge and from about 1,000 yards south of the bridge a good view is obtainable not only of the bridge itself but also of the country beyond it. The bridge was four hundred feet long with a superstructure of iron girders about eight feet above a sluggish, reed-bordered river. North of the bridge were two small farms, one on each side of the road, each consisting of two or three buildings and a barn. The road beyond the bridge could be seen running absolutely straight, between two lines of poplars, towards Catania. North of the river are thick vineyards, dotted with olive groves, to a depth of some four hundred yards; beyond them lies open country. Nothing, however, could be seen of the enemy positions nor of a sunken road some few hundred yards north of the river; indeed such cover as there was lay all on the enemy side of the bridge, for the British side was completely flat and open.

Both the 8th and 9th Battalions tried to snatch a few hours rest during the night. The 6th Battalion was still some way behind, after clearing up at Solarino, and did not arrive till later on the 15th. But at 4 a.m. the 9th Battalion was attacked by some Italian armoured cars which penetrated as far as battalion Headquarters before being halted. The Battalion anti-tank gunners quickly came into action and soon put an end to this desperate Italian bid from which there were few enemy survivors.

Sharp at 7.30 a.m. the Battalion attacked as planned, supported by the fire of two Field Regiments. But the companies advancing over the open ground were heavily machine-gunned before they reached the river bank and lost a number of men. Only a few platoons were able to cross the river and where they did so ran into heavy resistance from Germans concealed in the vineyards and lining the sunken road which hitherto no one knew existed. Many were drowned in the river as they crossed. After fierce hand-to-hand fighting the Battalion's precarious hold north of the river was finally broken and those men who had got across were driven back, leaving their dead and wounded behind them.

After this first encounter it was clear to the Brigadier that the bridge was a tougher nut to crack than had been hoped. Although a further attack by the 8th Battalion was planned for later in the day news had been received from Corps Headquarters that there was no immediate urgency for the capture of the bridge provided that a proper footing was secured on the far side by the 16th of July. Another daylight attack would be suicidal; so the 8th Battalion's attack was postponed and timed to take place by the light of the moon at two o'clock the next morning.

The Battalion was fortunate in having the help of Lieutenant-Colonel Alastair Pearson—C.O. of the Parachute Battalion—in this operation. The information he provided was invaluable, and he offered to lead the attacking companies over the river at a crossing place he knew of, some hundred yards upstream from the bridge. Two companies were to cross here, then move back

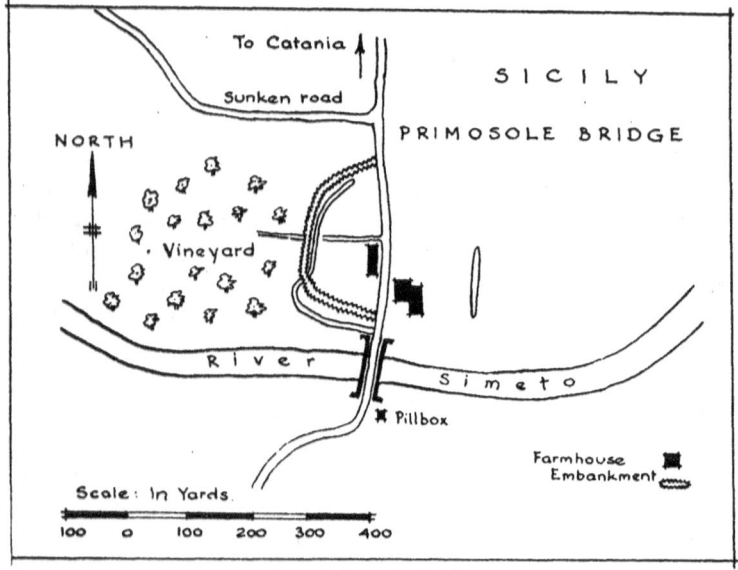

6. *Primosole Bridge*

towards the bridge and when once they had captured it the rest of the Battalion was to cross over it.

For an hour and twenty minutes before Colonel Pearson guided 'A' and 'D' Companies across the river the guns put down concentrations upstream of the bridge and a squadron of tanks and a platoon of machine-guns joined in the overture. For the last ten minutes every gun was concentrated on the area of the bridge. Then at 2.10 a.m. the two companies waded the river at two points fifty yards apart. Once across, the thickly planted vineyards made movement difficult—it would have been difficult enough by daylight—and platoons had to shout their numbers to maintain contact. However, the unexpected form of the attack took the Germans by surprise and when the Companies reached the bridge only a few of them were encountered. So far so good. Both Companies established themselves across the Catania road, though ' A ' Company had to run the gauntlet of Spandau machine-gun fire to get there; and once in position visibility was limited to only a few yards due to the thickness of the vines, shrubs and tall grass. Constant vigilance was needed to keep the Germans at bay.

Now it was the turn of the rest of the Battalion to cross the bridge. Colonel Lidwill, who was with the leading companies, had arranged a number of alternative signals for bringing up the Battalion; but when he got back to the bridge every one of them broke down. The mortar flares had got separated from the mortars; the wireless sets had got " drowned " during the crossing; and an R.E. carrier with wireless which came up to the bridge received a direct hit. Just at the critical moment, however, a War Office observer turned up at the bridge riding a bicycle. It was rather like a fairy tale but the C.O. despatched him back to the Battalion to tell it to come forward at once.

All this had caused delay and dawn was not far off when the rest of the Battalion crossed the bridge. Once over it ' B ' Company moved along the ditch on the left and ' C ' Company along that on the right of the road. They had gone scarcely a few hundred yards when all hell was suddenly let loose and the Battalion found itself engaged in the most savage hand-to-hand fighting it had ever experienced. Concealed Spandaus opened up at point blank range on the leading troops of ' B ' and ' C ' Companies; and but for the ditch hardly a man in either company would have survived. As it was the whole of ' B ' Company's leading platoon was written off.

Both Companies rallied quickly. ' C ' took to the fields on the right and began outflanking the enemy; ' B ' got its Brens into action; and a handful of men under Lieutenant A. F. Jackman charged the leading German posts. Jackman was badly wounded and most of his men killed or wounded; but the Germans withdrew. Then both sides set to with bayonets, grenades and automatics. Company Sergeant-Major Brannigan killed several Germans within the same number of minutes. British and Germans fired at trees by mistake thinking they were men. Some of 'B' Company advancing through the vines were shot down at point blank range while others crept up behind unsuspecting Germans and shot them where they stood or lay. It was a grim game of hide and seek and within twenty minutes both sides had fought themselves to a standstill. The front of 'B' Company and the Germans facing them suffered casualties of almost one hundred per cent; and only the dead and the wounded remained in the area of the fighting. The Company had gained some ground but there were only about forty men left unhurt and the Germans still held the sunken road of which the attackers still had no knowledge. Once they discovered it, after it got light, the survivors of 'B' Company withdrew to an embankment surrounding the farm on the left of the main road; and 'C' Company, whose casualties were equally heavy and included every officer, moved back behind them. Nevertheless, the Battalion had established itself in a position three or four hundred yards deep to the north of the bridge, and there it waited for the German counter-attack which the old hands knew would not be long delayed.

The attack came as soon as it was light. It was made against 'A' Company among the grapevines out on the right flank. The Company was heavily outnumbered and because of the closeness of the country the Germans were able to get very near before they attacked. The result was that two platoons were overrun and after more fierce hand-to-hand fighting these platoons were forced back to the river—which some men swam —and the rest of the Company had to withdraw towards the farmhouse on the right of the road. By six o'clock in the morning the Battalion as a whole held a precarious perimeter some hundred yards deep which they knew it was vital to maintain until reinforcements arrived.

They had to fight hard throughout the day to hold it. The Germans launched a number of counter-attacks, but they were all repulsed. The Battalion mortar platoon fired over six hundred bombs and accounted for dozens of snipers. To tackle a German pillbox, Corporal David Scriven at one stage led a tank by crouching outside on the top of it and from there directing the commander inside. At the end of the day the Battalion was still where it had been that morning.

Night fell and the Brigade prepared to deliver the coup de

The Commander of the Italian Napoli Division after capture by the 6th Battalion

Primosole Bridge

The 9th Battalion enter Catania

Imperial War Museum

Men of the 16th Battalion ferrying transport across the Volturno

Imperial War Museum

grace. This was the task of the 6th and 9th Battalions who, shortly after 1.30 a.m., forded the river upstream from the bridge in the area where the 8th had crossed the night before. They had little difficulty in crossing; but once on the far bank they encountered savage resistance from the German paratroopers who stood and fought it out until they either shot down their assailants or were shot down themselves. Movement was not easy through the vineyards and companies got split up in the thick undergrowth. As they fought their way forward in the moonlight they cleared up opposition in their path but inevitably left pockets of resistance on the flanks. 'B' Company of the 6th Battalion, under Captain Reggie Atkinson, had just such an experience. Once in the vineyards it met intense automatic fire from the Germans in the sunken road and one platoon was virtually wiped out. Nevertheless, the rest of the Company pushed on and actually got into the sunken road and cleared the Germans from it. Then they struggled on, using bayonets and grenades, to a position beyond it on the left of the Catania road. There, approximately one platoon strong and entrenched in a shallow ditch and a large shell crater, Reggie Atkinson and the remnants of his company were able to engage any Germans trying to advance up the road to reinforce the bridgehead and—what is more—to prevent any in the bridgehead from withdrawing from it. At dawn the Germans managed to infiltrate back into the sunken road and for a time they made things difficult for the Company; but for three and a half hours the enemy were kept at bay and finally driven back. This gallant action very materially influenced the course of the battle.

'A' Company of the 9th Battalion was less fortunate. It started out only two platoons strong and almost at once came under heavy fire. The advance was not made any easier by loose telephone and barbed wire lying among the vines; but the Company pushed on towards the main road and captured a machine-gun post and three prisoners. Then, crossing the road to more open ground, they were fired on from a white farmhouse, so attacked and took nine more prisoners; by which time the company commander, Captain Hudson, found he had only fifteen men left.

Heavy fire was then opened on this small party from their right rear. So they began to withdraw towards the main road.

As it began to get lighter, fire was opened on them from the road itself but Hudson, recognising the commander of another company advancing on the far side of the road, managed to attract his attention and signal to him to attack the post on the road. This they both did but were halted by very heavy fire. Hudson then found himself both short of ammunition and with only seven unwounded men left, so he ordered them to make their way back to the Battalion as best they could. He himself was wounded and was soon afterwards taken prisoner.

At about 6 a.m. the Germans counter-attacked with tanks, but the attack was broken up by shell-fire; and shortly afterwards both the 6th and 9th Battalions reported they were well beyond the bridge. At 7 a.m. some Sherman tanks crossed into the bridgehead and broke through the grapevines shooting at everything in sight. The effect of this added support was felt at once. The sunken road was quieter than for twenty-four hours and gradually white handkerchiefs began to appear in increasing numbers along the length of it. The Germans had had enough. By midday all resistance had ceased; over one hundred and fifty Germans had surrendered; and their dead on the ground numbered over three hundred. The area around the bridge was a regular hell's kitchen; it was littered with smashed rifles and automatics, torn pieces of equipment, bloodstained clothing, overturned ammunition boxes and the bodies of British and German dead. It was a scene of terrible destruction and telling evidence of a bitter struggle in which neither side had asked or given any quarter. There can have been few better German troops in Sicily than those who held the bridge. They were Nazi zealots to a man, but they fought superbly well and as their Battalion Commander was led away into captivity Colonel Clarke of the 9th Battalion quietly shook him by the hand. Apart from the British paratroopers the brunt of the fighting had fallen on the 8th Battalion who owed much to the conspicuous leadership of their C.O., Lidwill, and to the countless deeds of individual heroism which space forbids recording here. But when at the end of the fighting the three Battalions counted their casualties they had lost between them five hundred killed, wounded and missing.

The D.L.I. Brigade was now withdrawn south of the river Simeto for a short rest while other troops of the 50th Division moved up in their place. But it was soon realised that the Germans were in strength before the city of Catania and the Army Commander decided to shift the emphasis of the attack further west where other troops of the Eighth Army were advancing towards the southern slopes of Mount Etna. For two weeks, therefore, the 50th Division remained on the defensive in the positions it had reached. It was a comparatively quiet period save that the 9th Battalion suffered a grievous blow when both the C.O., Colonel Clarke, and the second in command, Major Bill Robinson, were killed by an unexpected German mortar barrage. Both were a grave loss to the Battalion.

Meanwhile to the west the advance was going well; and on the 4th of August the 50th Division moved forward again. By midday the 8th Battalion had captured some hundred and sixty Italian prisoners and during the night the Germans evacuated Catania which was occupied by the 6th and 9th Battalions during the early hours of the 5th. The 9th Battalion moved in from the seaward side, along the sea front and through the business part of the town. The city's surrender by the Mayor was actually accepted by Captain Brian Gardner at 8 a.m. The 6th Battalion entered from the Mount Etna side through the railway station northwards. At first everything was quiet and deserted but very soon the whole place was awake and crowds of excited Italians swarmed everywhere, welcoming the troops and showering upon them wine, fruit and flowers while at the same time many paid off old scores by looting the shops and houses of well known Fascists.

Once past Catania a new type of fighting developed which was to last for the rest of the campaign. Instead of open country, high terraced hillsides covered with grape-vines and stone walls transformed the fighting into a series of advanced guard actions against ambushes laid by German rearguards. It was a nerve-racking experience and casualties were not light. The inhabitants of the villages through which the battle passed were, however, glad to see the advancing soldiers. The leading platoon of the 6th Battalion, on approaching the small village of Aci S. Filippo, was met by the Mayor bearing a document with the following inscription:

ENGLISHMEN

We dwell at Aci S. Filippo and we have come here for telling you that the German soldiers have gone away from our country, where still are mines at the road, for this reason we caution you to be attentive and to remove the mentioned above mines. All people are happy in receiving you and they pray you to respect them.
Hurra! Englishmen!
England for Ever!

The days of the Axis forces in Sicily were clearly numbered and towards the middle of August the campaign became a race between the Eighth Army and the Americans for Messina in the north-east tip of the island. The Americans won by a short head, capturing the town on the 16th. Sicily was won. The D.L.I. Brigade moved to the south of Taormina, there to relax among the lemon groves and obtain a pleasant respite from the strain of recent weeks. The troops rested, bathed, wrote letters home, each preparing in his own way for the invasion of Italy which to all seemed the inevitable next step for the 50th Division. In fact, however, this was not to be; they had seen the last of fighting in the Mediterranean; for eight weeks later, to everyone's surprise and delight, they set sail for England.

CHAPTER FIVE

The 16th Battalion in North Africa, Italy and Greece 1942-1945

I

TUNISIA

THE 16TH was a so-called " Dunkirk " battalion. It was formed during the months following the collapse of France and was composed for the most part of recruits straight from civilian life who were called up in three batches in July 1940. Apart, therefore, from a small cadre of officers and N.C.O.s, some of whom were from other Regiments, this was a battalion which started from scratch and which trained together from the elementary stages until it reached a standard of efficiency which earned it distinction on the field of battle from Tunisia to Tirol. It owed much to two commanding officers in the early stages; to Colonel Morrough-Bernard who formed it and by his persistence obtained a substantial share of good reinforcements from the Depot; and to Colonel Murray, of the Grenadier Guards, who took command in March 1941 and welded this material into a really fine battalion.

Originally the Battalion was brigaded with the 14th and 17th Battalions—units raised at the same time and in the same manner—but at the end of August 1940 it was ordered to leave them and join the 46th Division, with which formation it remained till the end of the war. Together with the 2nd/4th King's Own Yorkshire Light Infantry and the 5th Sherwood Foresters it comprised 139 Brigade. After a period of intensive training, first in East Anglia and then on the south coast, the 46th Division joined the First Army and the Battalion, commanded by this time by Lieutenant-Colonel Richard Ware of the Regiment, found itself at the end of November 1942 preparing to go overseas and take part in the fighting in North Africa. The original Battalion of raw recruits had become in the preceding two years a highly efficient fighting unit and many officers, N.C.O.s and men had been posted to it from the Regimental Centre at Brancepeth to bring it up to full strength.

The Anglo-American expedition to north-west Africa, under General Eisenhower, landed on the 8th of November in three general sectors of which the easternmost was Algiers. The First Army's objective was the city of Tunis itself. The 46th Division did not take part in the initial landings and, indeed, did not enter the fray for several months. The Battalion thus landed at Algiers on the 3rd of January, 1943. The Allied advance in Tunis had by that time reached to within almost fifty miles of that city. But the original landings by the British and Americans in the previous November had not resulted in the quick capture of Tunis that was hoped for. The First Army had had a tough nut to crack; and its task was made the more difficult by the temporising of the French, many of whose senior commanders seemed unable to decide exactly where their duty lay. Had the French garrisons nearest Tunis itself resisted the German reinforcements which began to pour in as soon as the invasion became known, Tunis would have fallen three weeks before Christmas. As it was the German air transports landed unopposed, the build-up was rapid and the Allied drive was held and stabilised in the last week of 1942. The positions held by both sides were to remain virtually unchanged until the final phases of the campaign.

The Battalion reached the fighting area on the 17th of January after a journey by road and rail of some four hundred miles. It had rested for a week on the way at a transit camp where steps had been taken to improve physical fitness after the sea journey. Positions were taken over on the evening of the 17th from the 6th Battalion The Queen's Own Royal West Kent Regiment. They were sited on the foothills which led up to three prominent features occupied by the Germans. These three features—known as Green Hill, Baldy and Sugarloaf—dominated the road from Sedjenane through Jefna to Mateur and marked the furthermost point reached by British troops in the initial dash to Bizerta. To start with things were pretty quiet and the Battalion was able to settle down and accustom itself to the noises of war in easy stages. For the first six weeks there was little activity beyond patrolling and, as the Germans did little, the Battalion and the other two Battalions comprising 139 Brigade became master of the "no man's land" between the opposing armies. Gradually the Battalion began to acquire the experience which can only come from contact with the enemy, but its task was no easy one as the effect of being constantly overlooked and sitting at the bottom of a hill looking up was mentally wearisome; the slightest movement was the target for shelling or mortaring; and the physical effect on muscles and feet of restricted movement in the evil living conditions of mud and slush, caused by the winter rains, was considerable. Each night Captain Bert Newman, the Quartermaster, and Regimental Quartermaster Sergeant Larry Gaines carried out a major operation in supplying the Battalion; for this entailed a fourteen mile journey through an area where the nearest supporting troops—who were French—were six miles distant. The Battalion was introduced to shell fire, too, in easy stages; for there were a large number of 'duds', reputedly of Italian manufacture. At the same time there was in close support a number of small calibre mountain guns which helped to maintain morale by engaging one or two irritating, if perhaps less serious, targets— the occasional Arab who showed his partisanship by scanning the battalion positions with binoculars, the odd German infesting Jefna Station, and what, for a short while, appeared to be a German latrine. But there was plenty to impress upon everybody the nature of the struggle—some disabled carriers just ahead of them, relics of the first dash for Bizerta; the columns of German troops which could now and then be seen marching along a road beyond Sugarloaf; and the complete mastery of the air by the Germans which made movement along the road in daytime unpleasant and the lot of the dispatch rider far from enviable.

The lull was broken towards the end of February. Reports had been coming in, mainly from Arab sources, that more Germans were arriving in the area between Jefna and the sea; but they were conflicting both as to numbers and as to apparent intentions. However, on the 26th, French soldiers from those troops responsible for the eleven miles of country between Sedjenane and the sea began to trickle back into Sedjenane and report that they had been attacked by the Germans in

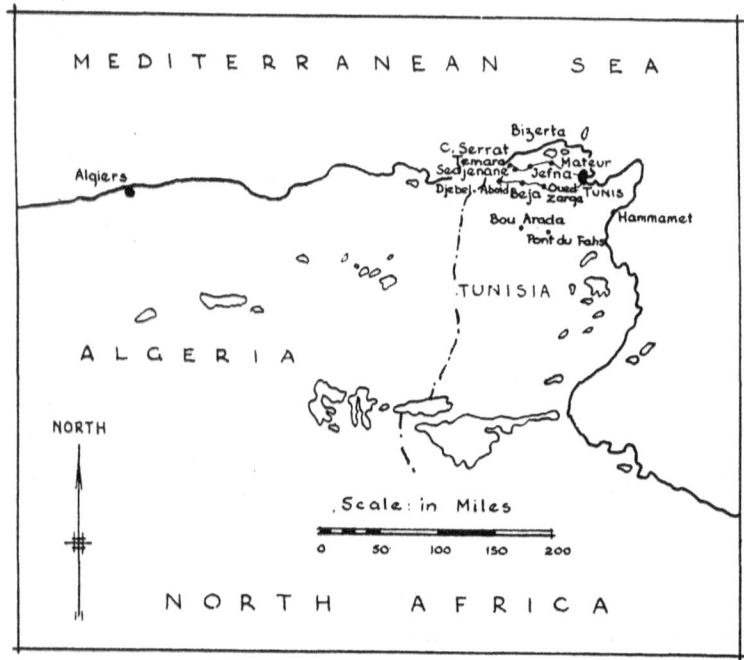

7. *Tunisia*

Monopoles, a small village on the Cape Serrat road six miles north of Sedjenane. It was as a result of this that the Battalion received its first orders for full scale action. It was to advance along the Sedjenane-Cap Serrat road and retake Monopoles which, it was thought, might only have been occupied by a strong fighting patrol.

These orders came at an awkward moment. It so happened that the Commanding Officer and all company commanders had been required to make a reconnaissance of another area into which it had been expected the Battalion would have to move. This meant that the Battalion would have to go into its first full scale action without them; and so it was that in the early hours of the 27th of February, with Major David Bannerman in command, the first brush occurred with the enemy on the hills separating the valley of Sedjenane from the valley in which Monopoles lay. At about 7 a.m., when the leading company had reached a point where the road ran into a kind of saucer formed by the hills, the enemy opened fire. There seemed to be about a company of them. The leading company, 'A' Company, was brought to a standstill and suffered a large number of casualties—which included all officers and Sergeant Major John Plemper—both in the inital encounter and in the German counter-attack which followed. Meanwhile, 'C' and 'D' Companies began to work round the flanks and skirmishing between the two forces continued for the rest of the day. By nightfall the only tangible gain was by 'C' Company on the left, who had managed to establish themselves on the hills with only a few losses. But 'D' Company on the right had been less fortunate, and though they had tried to press on with great determination against a stubborn enemy, it was decided in the evening to bring them back on to the plain again. So far from occupying Monopoles with a fighting patrol, as was at first thought, the enemy was in some strength occupying the hills round it from which he could look down on Sedjenane village lying in the plain a mile and a half away to the south. The German troops were Parachute Engineers, first class, highly trained individual soldiers, and they held a dominating position.

By the 28th the C.O. and company commanders were back with the Battalion. 'A' Company, who had sustained the heaviest casualties, was amalgamated with 'D' Company to produce a composite company of about ninety men. Apart from 'C' Company, who were holding on to what they had captured, the Battalion lay up in the woods just west of Sedjenane. It was from here that the next move was planned—an attack designed to exploit the initial gain by 'C' Company and to occupy the high ground to the north of Sedjenane from which the place could best be defended.

At six in the morning on the 2nd of March this attack was launched. The composite 'A' and 'B' Companies, together a force of about a hundred and sixty men, attacked up the hill under a heavy concentration of artillery. 'C' Company began to advance from the positions they already held, and a company of the 6th Battalion The Lincolnshire Regiment, lent for the occasion, formed the reserve.

This attack was pressed home with great determination but in vain; it was a bitter contest but only few survived it. From the two forward companies only one officer and about eighty men returned. Both Sergeant-Majors—Miles Etherington and George Broadhead—were killed and the surviving officer was wounded and evacuated at once. Apparently these two companies had reached the top of the first slope without difficulty and it was here that the few prisoners who came back to Battalion Headquarters were taken. But they then found themselves faced with a series of machine-gun posts sited in depth and stretching back into the undulating ground which formed the top of the hill. The companies themselves were unable to bring artillery fire down on those positions which had not been covered by the preliminary barrage because the wirelesses of both forward gunner officers had failed. So as they advanced into this defensive system they found themselves subjected first to severe mortaring and then, as they crawled up to deal with the machine guns, to repeated counter-attacks from the flanks, and even the rear, by German riflemen who were held back in the hollows of the undulating ground. 'C' Company, on the right, met with similar difficulties and in their case, too, very few survived. The attack failed, though not for want of trying, but a fine battalion had been decimated.

On the afternoon of the 2nd of March what remained of the rifle companies—barely a hundred men—gathered together in the 'B' Echelon area while Battalion Headquarters and Headquarter Company prepared the defence of Sedjenane in company with the battalion of Lincolns. Though the brunt of the subsequent battle for the village was borne by the Lincolns, a vigorous action was fought by Major George Ballance and Lieutenant Brian Lax of the Battalion, together with twenty men of the carrier platoon, in a small Arab village about half a mile north of Sedjenane. Here they were attacked for three hours and only withdrew at nightfall when the village was ablaze and their ammunition exhausted. They had killed over fifty of the enemy before they went and had frustrated a dusk attack planned to take place on Sedjenane from the north.

Sedjenane was evacuated two days later. It was subsequently learnt that in the area where the bitter fighting of the last four days had taken place the Germans had used two battalions, only one of which still existed when the fighting was over.

So serious was the manpower problem at this time that no period of rest or reorganisation was forthcoming for the Battalion. On the 10th of March Lieutenant-Colonel John Preston of the K.O.Y.L.I. succeeded Richard Ware as Commanding Officer, and the Battalion was organised into two composite companies until it received reinforcements. For the next two months it was moved all over the front, coming under different brigades and divisions with bewildering rapidity and generally acting as maid of all work. On the 5th all available riflemen were formed into a composite company under Major Denis Worrall and sent to help the 1st Parachute Brigade. On the 17th all reinforcements were temporarily formed into a company under Captain Arthur Vizard and placed under command of the 5th Sherwood Foresters when the Germans attacked that battalion's positions near Temara. In a period of extremely confused fighting they suffered only a few casualties. Meanwhile the two composite companies seized some high ground south-east of Djebel Aboid which was later to be used as the pivot for the 46th Division's counter-attack and recapture of Sedjenane at the end of the month. For a while, shortly afterwards, one company even had a force of four hundred Frenchmen under its command; at least they were nominally Frenchmen, even though they included a complete platoon of Russians!

The Germans' March offensive, which had begun with the battle of Sedjenane, had won them some useful ground. Their greatest gains had been in the north and they had only been stopped short of the very important road junction of Djebel Aboid after they had pushed the British troops back some twenty miles from Green Hill. On the Beja front, to the south, a similar offensive had also been held at a place called Hunt's Gap. There was no doubt that from the German point of view Bizerta was now more secure, some important heights had been taken as also many prisoners and some valuable equipment. But the Allied Forces in Tunisia were daily growing stronger as new troops arrived; the 6th Armoured Division had been converted to Sherman tanks; and the forcing of the Mareth defences by the Eighth Army enabled troops to be switched from the latter to the First Army for the final death blow against the Germans in North Africa.

Early in April the Battalion moved to Oued Zarga under command of 38 Irish Brigade of the 78th Division. There they held a firm base for the attack which cleared the enemy off heights overlooking the Oued Zarga-Medjez el Bab road. On the 9th they were placed under command of 12 Brigade of the 4th Division and on the 13th were rushed to Sidi Nsir where 10 Brigade was attacking. It was during this period of general post that on one night the 2nd Royal Irish Fusiliers of 38 Brigade of the 78th Division were relieved by the 6th Black Watch of 12 Brigade of the 4th Division covered by the 16th D.L.I. of 139 Brigade of the 46th Division! As the Colonel caustically remarked, " sort that one out at the Staff College!" So it was something of a relief when, on the 16th of April, the Battalion returned once more to its own brigade at Gafor near El Aroussa to prepare for its part in the 46th Division's counter-offensive. The area it occupied was not in the front line and it looked as if the much needed rest was at last about to materialise. Not so, however; for on arrival orders were received that the Battalion was to take over the next night from the 1st Battalion, The King's Shropshire Light Infantry who were in the line already, and so the only respite it got was just two days and one night. The new position was just north of Bou Araba and east of the road which runs up to Goubellat. The Germans in this area comprised the Hermann Goering Division, a fine fighting force composed mainly of young and ardent Nazis who appeared to have been picked for their size. They had been holding their positions for two months and had had plenty of time to prepare the defences. The 46th Division's plan was to punch a hole in these defences through which the 1st and 6th Armoured Divisions would be pushed with Tunis as their objective. Although at first it appeared that the Battalion would not be required to play an active part this was changed at the last minute, and they were once more taken out of their own Brigade and placed for the purposes of the attack under the command of 128 Brigade.

The Battalion's objective was Sidi Barka, a feature on the extreme left of the enemy's position. The Barka was something of a hog's back. To look at from the British lines it was a narrow sort of hill sloping gradually up to a conspicuous circle of stones which marked the summit. The slope was in fact several hundred yards long, but was deceptive when looked at from the west. Starting at the foot and running up the centre of the hill was an outcrop of rock and between the end of this spine and the highest point there was a small saddle. To the left of the Barka were the rest of the Brigade's objectives, hills like it, not high but with long rolling slopes. To the right lay the broad plain through which ran the road eastwards from Bou Araba to Pont du Fahs.

The information collected by the K.S.L.I. about the enemy was excellent. The round circle of stones on the very summit was an observation post which relied for its safety more on its natural strength than on concealment. It had often been shelled unsuccessfully. Two hundred yards behind it on the gradual reverse slope was a large patch of cactus and one or two unused buildings. These concealed the main enemy positions and protected the post from attack in the rear.

At half past three on the morning of the 22nd of April the Battalion began its attack, supported by a heavy artillery barrage. The attack was made on a two company front with the spine of the Barka as the dividing line between them. Soon after dawn the two leading companies had got very close to their objective but not right on to it. Colonel Preston had been told that some Churchill tanks would be available when it got light and that, if he was in trouble, he could rely upon the support of at least one troop. But this additional aid did not materialise as the complete squadron ran on to a minefield early in the action and all but one of them had either been hit or had its tracks blown off.

As it got lighter the observation post which had resisted the shelling began directing enemy artillery and mortars on to the forward companies with increasing accuracy. Major Arthur Martin, commanding the right hand company, was killed with Private Frank Chambers as they both attempted to crawl to within grenade range; so was Sergeant-Major Wilson Wales; but Lieutenant Tom Reynolds quickly took command and with the help of Sergeant Donald Threadgold held the company in an awkward position and successfully contained the enemy.

By 8 a.m. the Battalion had only gained a foothold on the western end of the Barka and had made no further gains by nightfall. It had suffered about a hundred and twenty casualties, many of whom were indebted to Lance-Corporal Calderbrook who did some magnificent work evacuating wounded under constant mortar fire. But the Germans had had enough. In the early hours of the next morning they pulled out and 'A' Company, who had been working their way round the flank during the night, were in possession of the observation post by mid-day without suffering any losses. The positions there were formidable. The post itself was blasted out of rock and sunk well down into the ground. The cactus concealed slit and communication trenches, and some good dug-outs beneath the ruins of the buildings. It also sheltered two heavy mortar positions.

This action was virtually the end of the Battalion's fighting on the shores of North Africa. The German defences were rapidly crumbling. After a few days' rest the Battalion moved to the Goubellat sector under the command of the 1st Armoured Division. Here the weather began to get hotter; and battle-dress was called in and exchanged for shorts and shirts. Apart, however, from patrol clashes the Battalion saw no more action. After as fierce a baptism of fire as any unit experienced in its first campaign, it emerged tough and battle-hardened but, ironically enough, ended the campaign as it had begun it, in a quiet sector of the front.

2

ITALY

From May to September the Battalion got a well-earned rest from fighting. The Axis forces laid down their arms in North Africa on the 13th of May. On the 20th the Battalion took part in the great victory parade in Tunis. The victory was duly celebrated by an extra issue of rum and a number of wild rumours about leave and a good time for all. A pleasant fortnight was spent by the sea, during which the Battalion welcomed the Prime Minister and Mr. Anthony Eden; and then in June it moved back to Blida, near Algiers, where it was reinforced and began training in earnest. This went on till August when a move was made to Bizerta. It was quite clear that another operation was in the offing and no one was surprised when, at the end of August, orders were received for the invasion of Italy.

The decision to invade Italy was the result of the rapid success of the Sicilian campaign which has been recorded elsewhere in these pages. General Eisenhower had resolved to land at Salerno, near Naples; and the 46th Division was chosen to form part of the British 10th Corps in General Mark Clark's Anglo-American Fifth Army. The Division was scheduled to land on the beaches of Salerno on the morning of the 9th of September when 128 Brigade was to undertake the initial assault and the Battalion, as part of 139 Brigade, was to pass through them.

The Battalion embarked from Bizerta on the 8th of September and received the news that the Italians had capitulated. Whether this would mean a better reception on the Salerno beaches was therefore a matter of considerable speculation on the part of everyone. But it did not. The opposition which met 128 Brigade on landing was stiff, even though it was not very well co-ordinated; and the two leading companies of the Battalion, who landed early the same day, spent most of it skirmishing with the enemy and helping the assault troops as best they could.

The remaining companies landed next day and by then the whole Battalion had no difficulty in reaching its first objectives. The enemy seemed to be collecting his wits and the first twenty-four hours ashore were quiet. It was not until the evening of the 11th, when the Battalion had moved through Salerno and had occupied some high ground bordering one of the roads leading out of the town, that the trouble really started. 'B' Company, who were trying to move forward to a new position, ran into small parties of enemy moving here, there and everywhere and were unable to make further progress during the night. They successfully withheld a small counter-attack the following morning; but 'A' Company who tried to work round to their left was forced to give some ground later in the day after suffering about twenty-five casualties. The next day or so till the 15th was a ding-dong struggle on both sides. Attack and counter-attack succeeded each other. In one of them some Panzer Grenadiers managed to establish a foothold in 'D' Company's area and it took two counter-attacks—the second led by Major Frank Duffy, the company commander—before the situation was restored at the cost of only one man wounded. These attacks on the 15th were the peak of the German efforts to disrupt the Salerno bridgehead. They were made all along the 46th Division's front and the Battalion played a very full part in stemming the tide and pushing the enemy back.

On the 23rd of September the battle for Naples began. The Battalion was given the task of clearing the northern exits of the Vietri defile, a few miles north-west of Salerno, so that the 7th Armoured Division might pass through to Naples. The Battalion's objective was a hill some six hundred metres high which lay to the left of the valley. The hills to the right were assigned to the 2nd/4th K.O.Y.L.I. and the 6th Lincolns. 'B' Company was to capture Hill 600 while 'D' Company was to secure a spur which ran at right angles to it down to the road. The rest of the Battalion was to move up behind them and the attack was to be a silent one though with concentrations of artillery at call. The 6th York and Lancaster Regiment were to co-operate by securing Dragone—a village just forward of the British lines—Monte di Amica, a low hill forward of that, and Corpo di Cava, a village at the foot of Hill 600.

The Battalion concentrated just behind the York and Lancasters during the evening of the 23rd. At 1 a.m. on the 24th they began to move forward. Dragone was reached without incident and then, at 3 a.m., 'B' and 'D' Companies began their advance to the final objectives. This advance was carried out with great skill over very difficult country. The route to Corpo di Cava lay along a tortuous track through a deep ravine; and while a platoon of York and Lancasters engaged the enemy the Lincolns and K.O.Y.L.I. ran into fierce resistance on the right. However, the two D.L.I. companies managed to make their way through to Hill 600 which they occupied—much to the Higher Command's surprise—by 6.30 a.m. Nevertheless, this skilful piece of infiltration through the enemy's positions put both companies in this difficulty: they could only be reached during the hours of daylight by a patrol which was prepared to fight its way through. This kept a platoon under Lieutenant Ronnie Sherlaw busy throughout the afternoon, and there was some vigorous fighting before, with the help of a platoon of York and Lancasters, the village of Corpo di Cava was cleared. Among the prizes was the Prefect of Salerno who had been sheltering in the crypt of the church and had the nerve to present himself in due course and demand a jeep to return him to his beloved people!

At about 5 o'clock in the afternoon the enemy brought up three tanks along the road past 'D' Company's position; they were supported by infantry. But rifle and machine-gun fire dispersed the infantry and medium artillery fire the tanks —though the men of 'D' Company swore that they and not the tanks were the main targets for these concentrations! When darkness fell once more the Battalion was firmly in its newly acquired positions, though the supplying of the forward companies with rations by a specially organised jeep column under Major Denis Worrall was a difficult and hazardous operation.

By the night of the 25th of September the Vietri defile was cleared sufficiently for 128 Brigade to push up the valley. 'A' Company managed to get into positions beyond 'D' Company and on the right the York and Lancasters were making quicker progress. From the Battalion's point of view the bouquets were due to 'B' and 'D' Companies who had outsmarted the Germans at their own game of infiltration; and morale was very high when on the 6th of October, in the wake of the 7th Armoured Division, the Battalion drove into Naples to be greeted by showers of apples from crowds of excited and enthusiastic Neapolitans!

After the fall of the city the Germans fell back some twenty miles to the north and prepared to defend the line of the river Volturno. The Battalion soon left Naples behind them and spent the next week patrolling the river bank with a view to finding a suitable crossing place for a divisional attack due to begin on the 12th of October. Their task was to secure an objective some four hundred yards from the river bank, then to strike across country and cut the main coast road running north from Naples. After their successful experience at Vietri, Colonel Preston asked to be allowed to make a silent crossing. The Sherwood Foresters were to make a noisy attack further up the river as a diversion but in the Battalion's area all the artillery, though it had previously registered all known enemy positions, was not to fire until the Germans had realised what had happened.

The attack began on the evening of the 12th. It began well. 'A' Company was quickly across the river, having found R.S.M. Thomasson waiting for them with the assault boats on a three ton lorry within two hundred yards of the crossing place: and the first the surprised Germans knew about it was when the first objective was reached. In fact one German joined on behind one file of men moving forward, presumably under the impression that it was one of his own working parties returning to its lines. The Company had only a few casualties, though the commander, Captain John Morant, was one of them. The rest of the Battalion followed them, though not without difficulty. The river which was about a hundred yards across, though only four feet six inches deep, was fast flowing and some of the boats performed a number of alarming and perverse evolutions in mid-stream. Unfortunately, too, one man panicked and lost his head upsetting the boat he was in and nearly drowning its occupants. His shouts aroused the enemy who opened up with machine guns and *nebelwerfers*, but fortunately he was firing blind and had selected the wrong place for this defensive fire. However, when 'B' and 'D' Companies came to cross the river they decided not to wait for the boats but to wade instead—not a pleasant experience as the night was cold and the enemy had begun to mortar the crossing place. At this point the gunners opened up and within an hour of dawn breaking the Battalion was firmly in position on the far bank and on its second objective. It had been stopped going on to the third.

The country over which the attack was being made was very open and flat and intersected by a number of canals. As further progress in the dark was unlikely, everybody was ordered to dig in so as to be protected from enemy fire once it got light. Things had not gone so well on the flanks and indeed, though it was not known at the time, the situation generally was rather precarious. Apart from the Americans at Capua, no other unit had succeeded in crossing the Volturno and holding its positions. Of their neighbours the Foresters had been heavily counter-attacked and so had the Leicesters. The German machine guns were still giving a lot of trouble and a fighting patrol was sent out under Lieutenant Russell Collins to do something about them. Its mission was highly successful and produced sixteen prisoners including three officers, two warrant officers and eleven other ranks with wireless and telephone equipment. This deprived the Germans in this sector of a vital link in their communications and was virtually the turning point in the battle.

Throughout the day the Battalion was shelled spasmodically and the few local counter-attacks were beaten off without difficulty. It owed much to Lieutenant Mike Fruer, of the 70th Field Regiment in support; thanks to his skilful shooting from a most dangerous and exposed position the enemy was the more easily kept at bay. Indeed, the Germans seemed at a loss as to what to do and though all preparations were made to meet a counter-attack once it got dark, none came. The following afternoon a squadron of Sherman tanks was landed from the sea and together with the Leicesters on the left flank mopped up what remained of the enemy and the Brigade bridgehead was then complete. On the 21st, a tired but triumphant Battalion was relieved by the Divisional Reconnaissance Regiment and went out of the line for a few days' rest.

Their first month in Italy had been a successful one for the Battalion; but it had not been without casualties. Companies were beginning to feel the effects of gaps in their ranks. Nor was the period out of the line a long one, for the enemy was gradually giving ground under the Allies' relentless pressure and there was little respite for troops constantly on the attack. The 25th found them taking over positions from the Rifle Brigade ten miles north-west of Capua; on the 28th they began the crossing of the River Teano—a tributary of the Volturno; and on the 1st of November they had entered Casale, a village on the southern slopes of Monte Croce, where the jubilant and thankful inhabitants garlanded the Colonel with prickly roses. Then on the 2nd they moved back to Carinola for a well-earned rest which lasted for some little while. The Teano crossing had sapped the numerical strength of companies and during the latter stages it had become necessary to amalgamate the four rifle companies into two composite companies. This rest period gave everyone a chance to reorganise and, indeed, some well-earned leave in Naples. It was a much refreshed Battalion—reinforced by Sergeant-Majors Leslie Thornton and

Joseph Hunter and a large number of men from the 70th Battalion—which returned to the line once again ready to play its part in the attacks on the German " Winter Line " in December.

December was an important month for the Allied Armies in Italy. The Germans had been ordered to hold their so-called " Winter Line " at all costs; and it was during December that the Allies breached it. In order to open the way to Rome it was necessary to cross the Garigliano River and capture the important Camino feature to the north. Monte Camino is but one of a number of craggy heights which block the approach to Cassino from the south-east. At the foot of these peaks, on the southern side, lies the village of Calabritto and around it the so-called Calabritto basin. From the north-east a spur—somewhat crudely named ' Barearse Spur '—ran down into the basin and its western lip was formed by another ridge of hills, known as the Cocurruzo Spur after the village of Cocurruzo which lay beyond it. The whole feature was known as the Camino Massif; the topmost height was named Monastery Hill; and the Germans had been ordered to hold all of it until at least February of 1944.

Two British Divisions—the 46th and 56th—were available for the attack, together with an American brigade. The 56th, which had already got on to Monastery Hill but had had to retire again due to supply difficulties, was to capture Camino itself and its surrounding peaks. The Americans were to operate to the north of them while the 46th Division was to advance into the Calabritto basin, occupy the Cocurruzo Spur and Capture Croce and Mortola.

The attack began on the 1st of December. For most of it ' B ' Company were detached from the rest of the Battalion and put under command of the Sherwood Foresters. They occupied positions on the lower slopes of Barearse Spur while the rest of the Battalion remained in reserve at La Murata, a village on the road to the south. Only slight progress was made to begin with. The leading battalions ran up against wire and machine guns firing in enfilade and mines in profusion. But on their right the attack by the 56th Division met with greater success. The enemy appeared to be caught on the wrong foot, and by dawn on the 3rd had yielded two important heights at the top of Barearse while the Americans had taken their objectives without much difficulty. This enabled the Leicesters and Foresters to make some further gains, but by evening the Leicesters had run into more wire and machine-guns, 'B' Company of the D.L.I. had been heavily shelled and mortared, George Ballance its commander had been killed, and all were forced to draw back slightly. The 4th saw an unpleasant change in the weather. Torrential rain turned slit trenches into duckponds, wireless sets ceased to function and the sunken track through the positions became a river. Then, to make things really unpleasant, the Germans heavily shelled both the Leicesters' and Foresters' positions and killed a number of men. But this did not stop the advance of the 56th Division. By the 5th it had occupied the heights to the east of the Cocurruzo spur and an opportunity now occurred for acceding to the representation, made by Colonel Preston the previous day, that the Battalion should move through the 56th Division's area and attack the Cocurruzo spur from the enemy's left flank.

At 11 o'clock in the morning of the 5th the Battalion set off together with a company of the York and Lancasters under command. Their objective was the two heights Point 620 and Point 683 which lay between the Barearse and Cocurruzo spurs. These two heights were held by troops of the 56th Division and it was from their area that the attack was to be launched. The move into these positions was to be made when it was dark, and at last light the C.O. showed his company commanders their tasks from positions behind Point 683. The Cocurruzo ridge itself consists of a row of three small peaks; the first and nearest to Point 683 was Point 430, the second immediately beyond it was nicknamed Dick, and the last and lowest was Point 420. 'C' Company was to attack Point 430 at first light; 'A' Company would move through them to capture Dick; and finally 'C' and 'D' Companies would take Point 420. Observation posts were to be established on Point 620 so that artillery and mortar fire could support the attack, and the troops of the 56th Division were ready to assist with medium and light machine-guns from Point 683.

The Battalion was in position under the lee of Point 620 soon after 8 p.m. As it turned out Higher Command decided to alter the timing of the operation so that the attack could be made while it was still dark. As a result 'C' Company could report at first light that it was on Point 430, such opposition as they had encountered having come from their right flank, from the south-western slopes of Point 620 and the saddle between that feature and their objective. Soon after first light 'A' Company were ordered to move up on 'C' Company's right and on to the second pimple, Dick. Their advance, however, was held up by opposition on their right, and about 10.30 in the morning they reported they could make no further progress till they had dealt with it. Colonel Preston then ordered 'D' Company to move to the left and with the help of pressure from 'A' Company to tackle the final objective—Point 420. A fire plan was quickly arranged with the gunners and the company started to move forward. However, they soon ran into trouble from enemy fire from positions further south which had been outflanked by the Battalion's march the previous day, and although these were shelled by the gunners they were able to hold up 'D' Company's advance till nightfall. Meanwhile hand-to-hand fighting had broken out on Point 430 and Dick where the enemy had about a platoon on each feature. But some Germans withdrew in the direction of 'A' Company who took about eighteen prisoners. As soon as it got dark the C.O. was able to push the company of York and Lancasters through on to Point 420 which they occupied by midnight without opposition.

The attack had taken the Germans in the flank and, apart from cutting the ground from under their feet, had saved the loss of many British lives. On the morning of the 7th the enemy had abandoned Cocuruzzo village and 'C' Company was able to move in. Although it took another forty-eight hours before the whole feature was cleared, from the Battalion's point of view the battle was at an end. All their objectives had been taken and from civilian reports later it was learned that the enemy had swum the Garigliano in disordered retreat.

This was the Battalion's last major engagement before the New Year although it remained in the line till the beginning of 1944. Then followed a period of chopping and changing and an uninterrupted spell of six weeks' fighting lasting till the early part of February. But rumour meanwhile was coming into its own and it was no surprise when, on the 13th of February, a

THE 16TH BATTALION IN N. AFRICA, ITALY & GREECE 151

move back from the fighting line was ordered and everybody was told they were in for a longish period of rest. That was a welcome relief. The 46th Division was destined for the Middle East, and it was a tired but happy Battalion which heard the news that it was to sail for Egypt and embarked from Naples on the 21st en route for Port Said.

*   *   *   *   *   *

The Battalion remained in the Middle East from the end of February until the end of June. From Egypt it went to Palestine and from Palestine back to Egypt. It was a period of rest and training with leave to Cairo thrown in, together with some aid to the civil authorities when rioting broke out in Tel-Aviv. There was only one event of any note and that was a sad one for everyone. At the end of June Colonel John Preston was appointed to be G.S.O.I. of the 78th Division and bade farewell to the Battalion. Although this was promotion it was little consolation to his many friends, nor, if the truth be told, to the Colonel himself. An extremely popular C.O. among officers and men alike he had commanded the Battalion with distinction from Djebel Aboid to Camino. Now he was taken away just as they were about to return to the battlefield once more. Everyone knew he would be greatly missed.

The 46th Division returned to Italy at the beginning of July. Denis Worrall, lately second in command, became the new Commanding Officer. For the first few weeks after their arrival training continued in rear areas and it was not till the middle of August that on a visit from the Army Commander—General Sir Oliver Leese—they learnt what their next task was to be. Much had happened in Italy during the past six months. Rome had fallen to the Allies in June and Florence in early August. The Germans now held a strongly fortified line which stretched through difficult mountainous country right across the Italian peninsula from the east to the west coast. This was the so-called Gothic Line and it was the Eighth Army's task to breach it and break the enemy's resistance in northern Italy. The invasion of Normandy had, of course, taken place early in June, and now the Armies in Italy were being milked for the landings in southern France. Success was therefore more likely to be achieved on the flatter and more open country near the Adriatic Coast than in the mountain fastnesses of the Apennine ridge. The Battalion, therefore, found itself in action again at Petriano, a village just short of the River Apsa and some twelve miles as the crow flies from the coastal town of Pesaro.

The Apsa is a tributary of the River Foglia which flows into the sea at Pesaro. The Apsa was crossed without difficulty on the 28th of August and the Foglia shortly afterwards. But the Battalion was soon involved in some heavy fighting round Mondaino, two or three miles further north, though by the 31st it had, with the aid of the Sherwood Foresters, managed to penetrate a further three miles to the village of Il Poggio and the Serra ridge just beyond it. These gains were not obtained without casualties and between the 27th of August and the 5th of September losses amounted to nine officers and a hundred and twenty-eight men. But there had been an advance of over twenty miles in the preceding week, almost as many prisoners had been taken as there were casualties and the prepared defences of the Gothic Line had been nicely dented.

The Battalion was relieved on the 5th of September, as indeed was the whole of the 46th Division, by troops of the 1st Armoured Division. But two days' heavy rain and increasing German resistance prevented any further break-through; and, by the 10th, after a short-lived rest, the Battalion found itself committed once again round the village of Gemmano. Gemmano stands on a prominent ridge just south of the River Conca, some three miles from the road along which the Battalion had been advancing up till the 5th of September, and about the same distance north-west of the Serra ridge. The main ridge itself is comprised of numerous smaller hills and dips which were the scene of some very bitter fighting. Along the road which runs across the open slopes of the ridge are four villages—from east to west Villa, Gemmano, Borgo and Zollaro. Zollaro is further away from the other three and more isolated. West of Borgo, between it and Zollaro, are two hills separated by a dip containing a cemetery. That nearest Borgo has a farmhouse on the top of it and was known as Hill 414. That nearest to Zollaro is bare on top save for a large Cross and was known as Hill 449. These features were the scene of some savage fighting during the three days following the 10th of September.

The Battalion occupied Gemmano village that night to allow the K.O.Y.L.I. to push on to Hill 449. This they succeeded in doing but the enemy infiltrated back as the night wore on causing considerable confusion, particularly when they managed to get troops back into part of Borgo village. For a few days there was a stalemate and everybody lived in holes in the ground amid constant shelling and the stench of rotting corpses. Fortunately, an attack by the 56th Division north of the River Conca had met with some success and so the weight of the attack was shifted to the Conca Valley so that Gemmano was encircled round its left flank and the Germans began to pull out.

The Battalion's route took them through the small Republic of San Marino, and as the advance quickened an increasing number of prisoners gave themselves up. Their morale was low and as a result the Divisional Commander did everything in his power to maintain the pressure. The Battalion crossed the Rubicon, known now as the River Uso, on the 24th of September; on the 26th it occupied a hill with two farms on it where it had to resist repeated counter-attacks in one of which Germans and D.L.I. occupied different rooms of the same farm; and on the 27th it was relieved and went back to reorganise. Casualties had been heavy and there were only sufficient men for three companies. Indeed so heavy had the Division's losses been that the Infantry Brigade of the 1st Armoured Division was disbanded to provide reinforcements.

The first flush of enthusiasm engendered by the news from France and the early successes against the Gothic Line was by now beginning to wane. The prospect of another winter campaign loomed large and, as the battle progressed, the number of rivers to be crossed and hills to be captured seemed to increase just as did the fierceness of the fighting. Efforts to encourage everyone included the oft-repeated tale that the next ridge was the last before the Lombardy plains. But it was told so often that rumour had it that the enemy kept a large team of bull-dozers specially devoted to creating fresh ridges as he fell back! At all events the first half of October saw the Battalion cross the Fiumicino river and seize another series of hill features. And by the 15th it was in position for an attack on Cesena, the first really large town which the 46th Division had been required to take. In the early stages the Battalion was held in reserve, though it experienced some very heavy shelling of its positions. But in the early hours of the 19th it was committed and began the assault on the Monastery at Madonna el Monte which stood on some high ground on the outskirts of Cesena.

The Battalion had a company on the Monastery feature by daybreak and prepared at once to capture the bridge over the River Savio which runs through Cesena's western suburbs. This was to be achieved with the aid of two squadrons of tanks but met with some difficulty. Determined, if unco-ordinated, resistance was met in the streets and infantry and tanks had to combine in the slow deliberate business of routing out snipers house by house. By 2 o'clock in the afternoon the two leading companies had penetrated well into the southern part of the town, but any further progress was held up by enemy in positions on high ground to the south-west from which it was possible in some degree to control the town and the approaches to the bridges.

It was not till 4 o'clock the next morning, after the Leicesters had attacked these positions and captured some seventy prisoners, that the Battalion could push its way through the town and capture the castle which overlooked the river. By this time the Germans had pulled out, having blown all the bridges over the Savio as they went. They also left a time bomb in the castle; hence the blunt comment by Colonel Worrall over the wireless to the company which had successfully occupied it—" Well done; now get out for obvious reasons."

The Battalion, like the other units of the Division, received a tremendous welcome from the inhabitants of Cesena. Women and children clapped and shouted and flung their arms round the necks of the troops. Italian partisans paraded the streets proudly displaying their armbands. The old folk were more subdued but showed their gratitude by placing bunches of flowers on the bodies of those who had given their lives in the relief of the town. All through the day the town was heavily shelled but it did not interfere with the general clearing up which the troops were carrying out and during which a patrol of 'B' Company captured seven German soldiers having a shave in a barber's shop.

On the evening of the 20th the 46th Division was relieved by

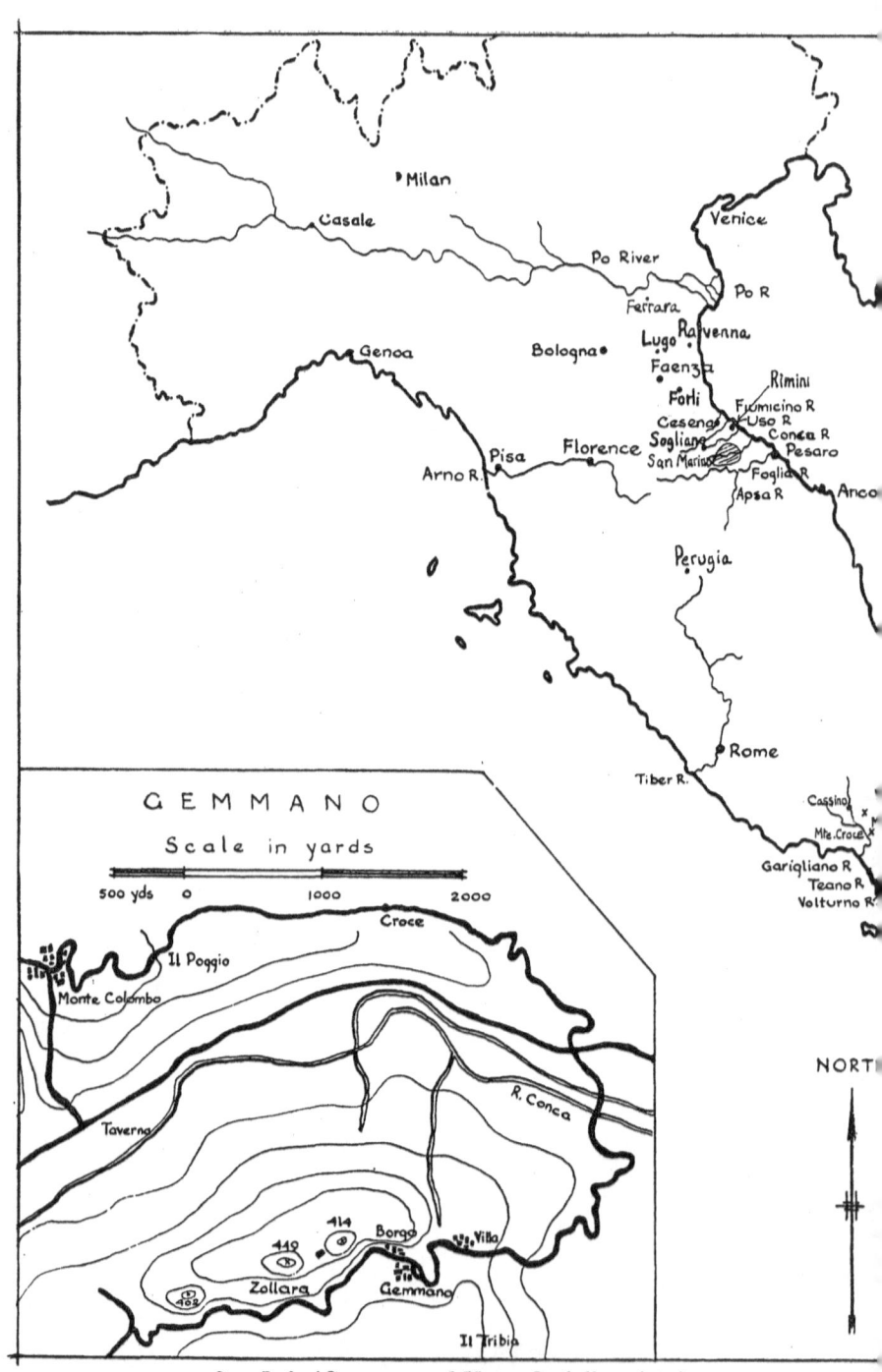

8. *Italy (Gemmano and Upper Garigliano inset)*

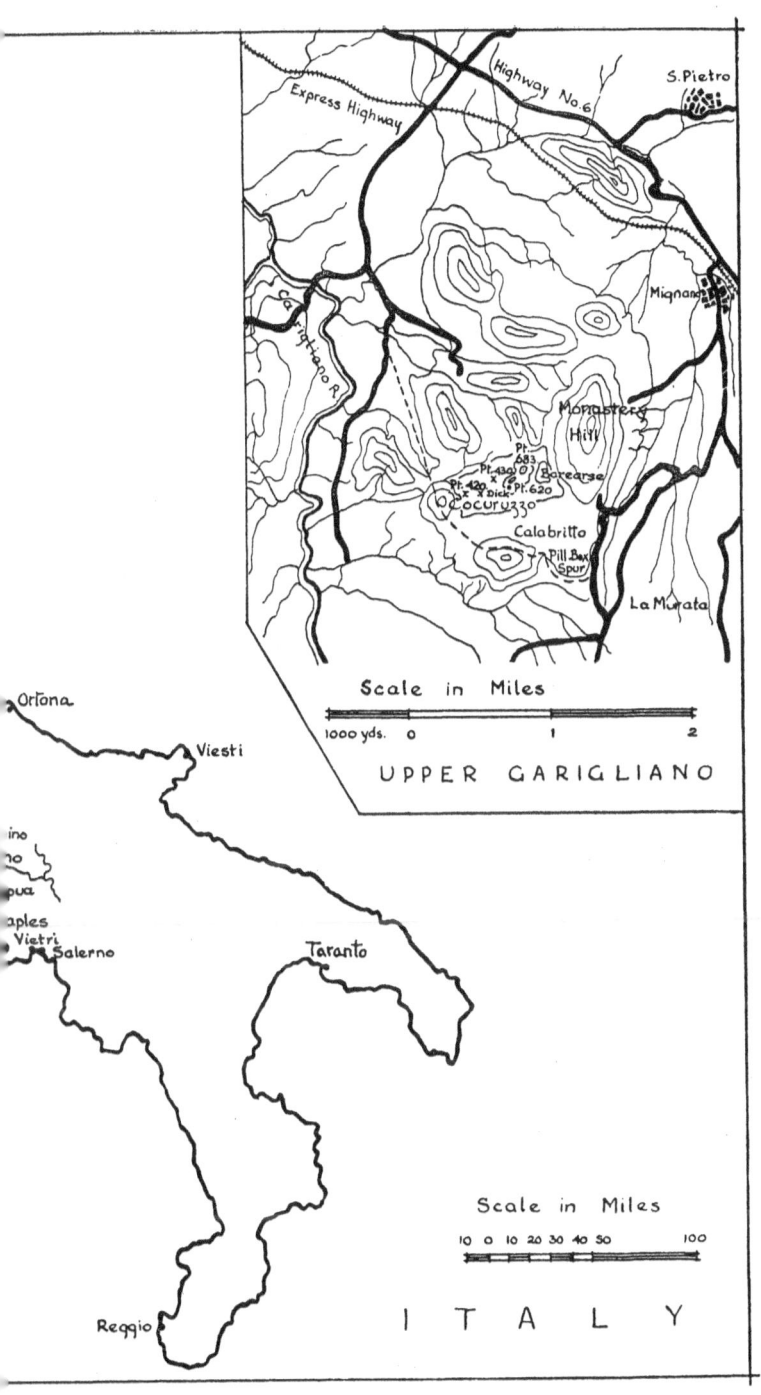

the 4th Division and the Battalion went out for a rest to Montefiore, a village not far from Gemmano. The Mayor and population did their best to entertain them, the battalion concert party and the mobile cinema worked overtime, the R.S.M., all C.S.M.'s and Colour Sergeants were, with the C.O.'s blessing, packed off on leave to Rome, and parties of officers and men were able to pay a visit to the 1st Battalion some forty miles away with the 10th Indian Division.

Back into the line they went on the 1st of November: and this heralded an advance towards the Balzanino Canal through a morass of mud and slush caused by the winter rains. Heavy shelling had made the tracks impassable by ordinary transport and even mules and a team of oxen, borrowed from a local farmer, found the going hard. On the 14th the Battalion launched a diversionary attack on some enemy-held farmhouses to cover the building of a Bailey bridge over the Balzanino Canal. This attack was not successful because to reach their objectives the troops had to cross some eight hundred yards of flat, open plain and just before they started out an R.A.F. dive-bombing attack, meant for the Germans, was directed by mistake on the company positions. It was clear that the Germans were holding a line of some strength and it was not till the 22nd that, after a rest and reorganisation, the farmhouses succumbed to the Battalion's share of a Brigade attack. Then followed some confused and bitter fighting which resulted in the crossing of the Cosina river and a further advance towards Faenza. But once the crossing was complete and the bridgehead established the Battalion had little further part to play. On the 27th it moved back to Forli and though almost at once some wild rumours began to circulate as to the future, everyone was too tired to care. However, what eventually happened astounded everybody; for just as plans had been made to move to Ancona everything was changed, advance parties were called for and the Battalion found itself on the way to Rome. Once there frantic preparations were made for travel by air; and within thirty-six hours the whole Battalion was in planes bound for Greece.

3

GREECE

The Battalion landed at Kalamachi airfield, just outside Athens, on the 3rd of December, 1944. Its task, with the rest of 139 Brigade and other troops from the Italian front, was to maintain law and order in someone else's quarrel; for Greece was on the verge of civil war. At the time when the Battalion arrived open hostilities had not yet broken out between the two rival political factions, E.L.A.S.[1] the left and E.D.E.S.[2] the right wing movement. But the E.L.A.S. Army, which had been trained by British officers and armed with British weapons in order that it could fight the Germans, now threatened to effect an armed coup d'état, in support of Russian Communism, by occupying Athens and taking over the government of the country. They had selected this moment as the most opportune because, as the Germans had just been forced to withdraw from Greece, there was virtually no organisation in being in Athens capable of assuming immediate control of the situation. At the request of the Greek Government the British Army intervened, though when the Battalion landed at Kalamachi negotiations were still going on between the E.L.A.S. leaders and General Scobie, the British Commander on the spot. Nevertheless, local clashes occurred, and continued to occur, between E.L.A.S. forces and the Greek gendarmerie—whom E.L.A.S. accused of collaboration with the Germans—as well as between armed bands of E.L.A.S. and E.D.E.S. supporters: so full scale intervention became inevitable.

At first the Battalion was deployed in the neighbourhood of the Acropolis and actually had a platoon round the Parthenon. But as the situation deteriorated and fighting between E.L.A.S. and E.D.E.S. grew more general it was withdrawn from the city proper and sent to the sea-front at Phaleron. The rather

[1] The partisan forces controlled by the Socialist-Communist National Liberation Front were called the Greek People's Army of Liberation (Ellenikos Laikos Apelftherotikos Stratos).

[2] The Greek Democratic Front (Ellenikos Demokratikos Ethnikos Syndesmos), a body which, though Socialist in doctrine, was also strongly nationalist.

unorthodox methods of civil war puzzled the troops, used to the stark simplicity of fighting Germans, particularly as it was difficult to distinguish friend from foe when many E.L.A.S. troops wore a mixture of uniforms and some none at all. Added to which the battlefield was nearly always inhabited by women and children who could not be evacuated.

As full reports of the cruelties inflicted by the E.L.A.S. forces became known, any doubts anyone may have had as to the respective merits of both sides were quickly dispelled. Despite strenuous propaganda by E.L.A.S. supporters and reports of the dissension caused by left-wing British members of Parliament at home, the Communists were soon seen in their true light.

The Battalion's task was to keep open the road from Athens itself to the coast. To do it they had some tanks to help them, and quite invaluable they were despite the disturbing habit adopted by many E.L.A.S. women of lying in the road across their path. Amid scenes reminiscent of the struggles of the Suffragettes the troops soon became adept at removing them! While the Battalion kept the coast road open, the Leicesters held the area of Piraeus and awaited the arrival of an Indian Brigade to strengthen the perimeter.

By the 13th, companies were located along the sea-front between the hill of Loftos Kostello, overlooking Piraeus harbour, and Phaleron. Ships of the Royal Navy lay anchored in the bay, sweeping the coastal area with their searchlights at night and prepared to act as artillery when required by the troops ashore. During the night of the 13th the Battalion experienced its first full scale encounter with the E.L.A.S. forces. Every company was attacked as well as Battalion Headquarters where clerks laid aside their pens to take part in the defence of the Headquarters building. The attackers were in large numbers and used sticks of dynamite to demolish the walls of buildings. In one company area a platoon kept them at bay for several hours till their ammunition ran out, when some of the survivors were taken prisoner. This company owed much to Private J. Peckett who very gallantly contained the enemy throughout the night from his position at a road block, and in the early hours of the morning volunteered to go through a fire-swept street to get further supplies of ammunition for the besieged defenders. But the Battalion held its ground and by morning, when the attacks petered out, it had the consolation of knowing it had inflicted heavy casualties upon the enemy.

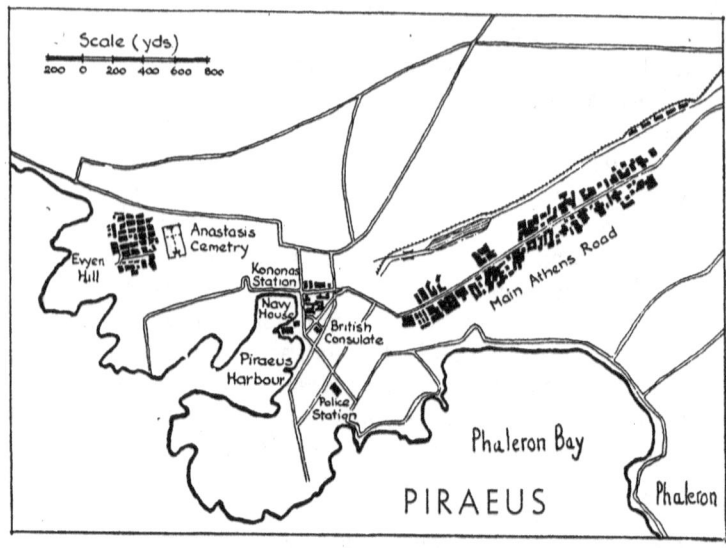

9. *Greece—The Piraeus*

By the 15th a battalion of the 4th Indian Division had been landed at Piraeus and had made its way across Loftos Kostello to link up with the Battalion. It was also possible to keep the coast road open for armoured vehicles during the day-time. As the E.L.A.S. troops were cleared from an area the attitude of the Greek population took on a marked change and became one of undisguised friendliness. Once any chance of retaliation by E.L.A.S. was gone the British troops were welcomed as liberators. One young girl of seventeen attached herself to one of the companies and worked devotedly at its washing and mending. Even when an attack was in progress it was difficult enough to persuade her to stay behind.

On the 22nd the British forces received further reinforcements in the shape of the 5th Indian Brigade who landed on the north of Piraeus harbour and two days later had linked up with the Leicesters to complete the perimeter. Meanwhile the Battalion, with tanks and armoured cars, advanced up the line of the railway which runs from Piraeus to Athens. Every building had to be cleared systematically and each night the whole battalion front was wired off to prevent enemy infiltration into the areas cleared. As the Battalion pushed ahead food and medical supplies were brought forward for the civilians in the cleared areas; and the Quartermaster was kept busy organising soup kitchens. As far as the civil population was concerned the soup kitchen was probably a better weapon than the rifle.

Christmas Eve and Christmas Day were comparatively quiet and on Boxing Day Field-Marshal Alexander, the Supreme Commander, paid the Battalion a visit. The arrival of reinforcements was beginning to make itself felt, and in the first few days of the New Year the advance quickened and increasing numbers of prisoners and supply dumps were captured. By the 6th of January all E.L.A.S. resistance in Athens had ceased and the city was given over to great rejoicing. But there was little respite for the Battalion. The E.L.A.S. forces had taken to the hills and mountains and in other parts of the country were still active. So on the 7th, within a few hours of receiving an order to move, the Battalion found itself on shipboard bound for Patras in the gulf of Corinth where it arrived after a stormy passage round the southern Peloponnese on the 9th.

E.L.A.S. forces were still in Patras but they were given an ultimatum to leave it by six o'clock the next morning; and much to the surprise of everyone this was complied with. So when the Battalion landed on the 10th there was no opposition and the city was peacefully occupied. The Battalion's task was to occupy Araxos aerodrome in the north-west corner of the peninsula, which it did on the 13th without trouble. On the 14th a general truce was declared throughout Greece and all fighting ceased.

The Battalion had in fact fired its last shot in anger. Although it had yet many miles to travel its war was to all ntents finished. In February it moved back to Athens where for two months it remained on occupation duties of every description. Then, on the 13th of April, it boarded the M.V. " Ville d'Oran " and sailed once more for Italy.

* * * * * * *

When the Battalion landed again in Italy the Allied forces had broken through to the Po Valley, but by the time it had reached the fighting area the Po had been crossed and the Allies were advancing rapidly against negligible opposition. Indeed the German Army was so disorganised that it was unable to form another line to stem the onward surge of the Fifth and Eighth Armies; and so it was that when the capitulation of the German armies in Italy was announced the Battalion had not again been committed. On the 8th of May the war in Europe came to an end and thereafter the Battalion's duties consisted of the hundred and one tasks which beset an army of occupation. After its fair share of moves it arrived in Vienna, the first unit of the 46th Division to do so, and it was there that during January and February of 1946 it was disbanded. It had travelled far since the day when, as a collection of raw recruits, it had been raised during the stern days of 1940. But though the life of the Battalion ended when the war ended, it had gained well-earned distinction in some of the most arduous fighting in Africa and Italy, and had added further lustre to the name and fighting traditions of the Regiment.

CHAPTER SIX

The 2nd Battalion in India and Burma 1942-1945

I

INDIA

WHEN the 2nd Battalion returned from the Dunkirk beaches it needed a complete reorganisation. Only three officers of the Regiment remained—Captain Oswald Pearson, the Quartermaster, and Second-Lieutenants Hugh Lyster-Todd and J. W. Rudd. With them were the medical officer and the Padre, Dick Rice, who was to stay with the Battalion for another four years. They and a hundred and eighty odd men comprised the Battalion in its concentration area at Huddersfield and to it came Lieutenant-Colonel Ivar Wiehe, of the Regiment, as Commanding Officer. Few battalions owe a greater debt of gratitude to a C.O. than did the Battalion to Ivar Wiehe. It was his great personality which re-formed and re-made it and prepared it once more for battle. Reinforcements soon began to flow in and over five hundred officers and men—most of them of the Regiment—were shortly gathered together to bring the Battalion up to strength. Many of those who had been sick or wounded returned from hospital or convalescence and two senior officers of the Regiment, Major George Stobart and Major Michael Hanmer, were posted to it between June and the end of the year, the former becoming second in command in September. Bill Hutton, out of hospital and fit again, became adjutant.

The Battalion spent the next two years on home defence duties, still as part of the 2nd Division. For most of that time it was stationed on the Yorkshire Coast in and around Bridlington, save for one month when it was taken from the 2nd Division to be reorganised as a motor battalion in the 42nd Armoured Division near Bury St. Edmunds. This involved an immense amount of work so it was something of a surprise, to say the least of it, when barely a month later the orders were rescinded and the Battalion returned to the 2nd Division with orders to mobilise for overseas. It was at this moment, just when he was about to have the opportunity of commanding the Battalion on active service, that Colonel Wiehe was ordered by the doctors to take a prolonged rest and had to relinquish his command on account of ill-health. He had worked like a slave since he took command in 1940; but he had worked too hard. A strict disciplinarian and a fine soldier, with the Battalion as his one great interest, he said farewell to it to the great regret of officers and men alike. Few more respected C.O.s can have commanded a battalion. He was succeeded by George Stobart, who was himself succeeded as second in command by Major Jack Theobalds of the Oxfordshire and Buckinghamshire Light Infantry. Shortly afterwards the Battalion moved south to Cheltenham, and in April 1942 sailed from Glasgow they knew not whither. Bags and baggage were mysteriously marked " Destination X "; and khaki drill and topees were duly issued; but despite much speculation during the early part of the voyage, varying from the Western Desert to Palestine, the final port of call turned out to be Bombay in India where the Battalion disembarked on the 2nd of June.

From Bombay the Battalion was sent to Ahmednagar in the Deccan. There it was to spend several months getting used to the climate and training hard for whatever job it might be called upon to carry out. In some respects it was a period of anticlimax for, with the war situation as it was and with Japan knocking at the gates of India, everyone had imagined that within a short period they would be in action. Instead, they found themselves apparently committed to an indefinite period of routine training and this, together with the frustrations of a soldier's life in war-time India, was to many irksome. Many rumours were current as to exactly what the 2nd Division would be called upon to do, the most popular being that it was destined for Persia, but nobody really seemed to know and nothing unusual in fact took place.

Not long after its arrival the Battalion was instructed to train itself in jungle warfare. This was difficult, for the country round Ahmednagar is flat and open, there are few trees and the ground consists largely of cotton soil which turns quickly to thick mud in the monsoon rains. At the same time 6 Brigade, of which the Battalion formed a part, was told that it had been selected to train as an assault brigade for a seaborne landing operation; and from September onwards each of its battalions was sent on a short course in watermanship and amphibious landings at Lake Kharakvasla, some eighty odd miles away in the Western Ghats, where the Combined Training Centre, India, was located. Then, in October, training was taken a stage further. The Battalion found itself moved from Ahmednagar to an area north of Bombay where further work in boats could be combined with training in proper jungle more resembling that which would be met in a country such as Burma. In the middle of the month the Battalion underwent a period of training in landing craft from a camp in the coconut groves bordering the seashore twenty miles north of Bombay; and when that was finished it returned inland to its camp in the jungle. Not long afterwards the Brigade, which was composed of the same three battalions as it had been in France, was joined by a fourth—the 1st Battalion The Royal Scots from 4 Brigade—to form an independent Brigade Group complete with supporting arms; by which time it was clear that something more than mere training was in the offing. Early in December the whole Brigade concentrated on the coast and towards the middle of the month began moving, unit by unit, to a destination which, to all but a few senior officers, was said to be Colombo by way of Madras.

The Battalion, commanded now by Colonel Jack Theobalds, who had succeeded George Stobart in August, boarded a train in Bombay on the 17th of December. Its true destination was not Madras but Chittagong in Eastern Bengal, where it was due to arrive at 10.30 a.m. on the 23rd. In keeping with the vagaries of the Indian transport system it in fact arrived at 5 p.m. on Christmas Day, having spent a whole day in a siding without an engine and feasted on a Christmas dinner of bully beef and biscuits. Within a few days of its arrival officers and men were let into the secret of the task that lay before it. It was to prepare for a seaborne landing on the island of Akyab which lay some hundred or so miles to the south.

Chittagong in pre-war days was known as the jewel of

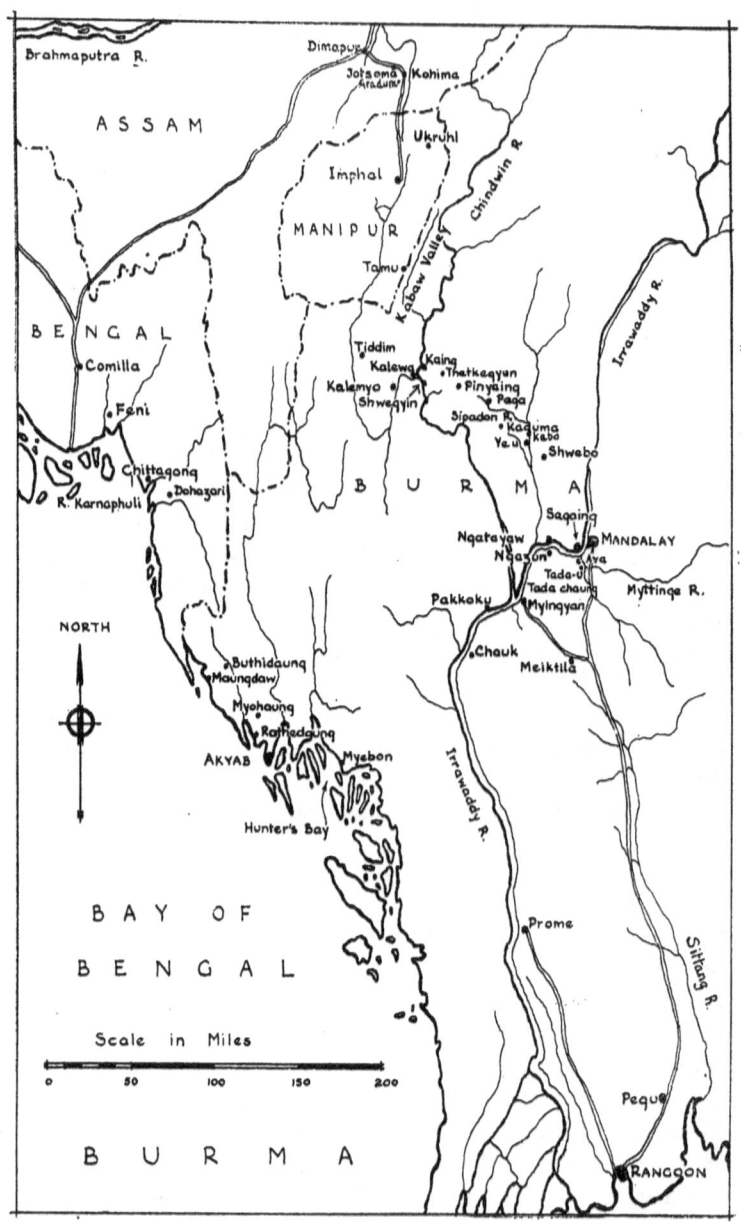

10. *Burma*

Bengal. It was far from being a jewel in December 1942. As a result of the Japanese invasion of Burma the previous summer the British forces had withdrawn north of Chittagong to the area of Feni, a small town with an aerodrome some hundred miles away. Only a small garrison had been left in Chittagong which it was intended to abandon if the Japanese advanced so far. Chittagong lies a few miles up the Karnaphuli river. Before the war its main occupation was the export of rice. As a result of the British withdrawal all the dockside installations had been destroyed and a large part of the population had removed themselves to places of greater safety. So both port and town presented rather a bleak and desolate appearance when the Battalion saw it for the first time at Christmas 1942.

The Arakan theatre of operations—that is to say the area south of Chittagong and north of Akyab—is a mixture of coastal plain, rivers and jungle covered hills. It is highly malarious. The Japanese had not in fact advanced beyond the Burma border which was some seventy miles south of Chittagong. Instead, they maintained two small garrisons in the villages of Maungdaw and Buthidaung—just south of the border—and concentrated the bulk of their defences in the Arakan upon the immediate approaches to Akyab itself. Most of the fighting, therefore, which was about to take place was confined to the country lying between the Burma border and Akyab island.

The grain of the country runs from north to south, dividing the area into two combat zones. The first—in which the Battalion was to fight—was that of the Mayu peninsula, bounded by the Naf river valley and the coastal plain on the west and by the Mayu river valley on the east. The width of the coastal plain varies between several miles in the area of Maungdaw and a few hundred yards at Foul Point on the tip of the Mayu peninsula. The greater part of the plain consists of paddy fields intersected by innumerable streams known as chaungs. Here and there hillocks rise from the paddy fields and the whole landscape is dotted with villages set among trees and bamboo clumps. The main chaungs are tidal and some are several hundred feet wide. Not a few are fringed with mud banks and mangrove swamps. The coastline is part mangrove swamp, part sandy, surf-ridden beach. Down the centre of the peninsula runs the Mayu range consisting of numerous steep ridges covered by dense bamboo jungle. The average height of the peaks is 1,500 feet but owing to their steepness the hills are cut by innumerable watercourses which in the rains become raging torrents and in the dry season provide possible pathways across the range. The second zone was that of the Kaladan valley. It is similar to the Mayu valley but less accessible and its hills are higher and more difficult to cross. The Battalion never reached it, but the fighting which took place there had an important bearing on the course of operations in which the Battalion itself was to be involved.

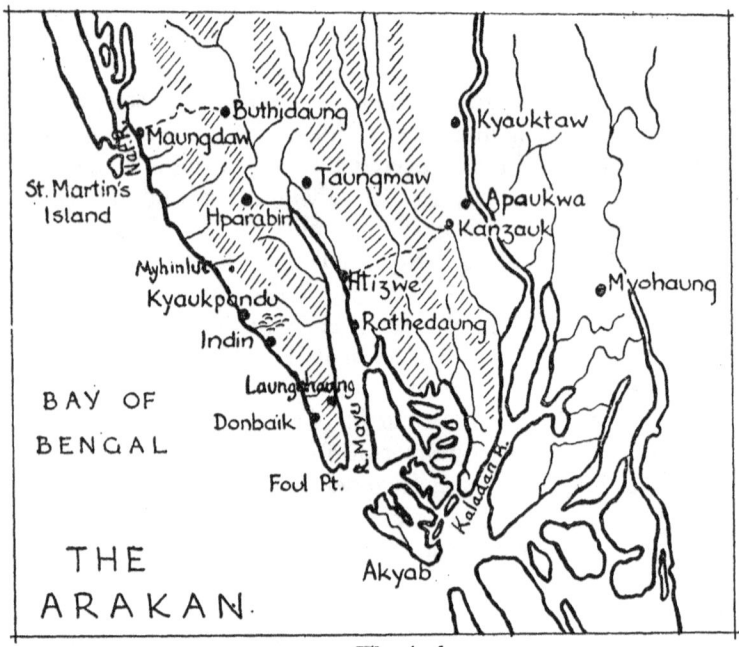

11. *The Arakan*

Early in December the 14th Indian Division had advanced across the Burma border with the object of seizing Maungdaw and Buthidaung, securing the Mayu peninsula and advancing down the Mayu valley to within striking distance of Akyab. As there was a grave shortage of naval landing craft for the seaborne attack on Akyab it was necessary to have a convenient land base from which heavy stores could be ferried over to the island. Foul Point was to be this base and its capture by the 14th Indian

Division was a pre-requisite for any seaborne attack being launched. This proved to be the stumbling block of the whole campaign. For one reason or another the 14th Division never succeeded in capturing Foul Point. The Division occupied Maungdaw and Buthidaung on the 14th of December 1942. As it went forward a rough road was built; but even administrative difficulties can scarcely explain why no contact was made with the Japanese till the 1st of January. On this day the two leading Brigades, one advancing down the east bank of the Mayu river, the other down the Mayu peninsula proper, met opposition at Rathedaung and Laungchaung, the latter village being only five miles north of Foul Point. On the 4th of January a patrol of Bren gun carriers advancing down the west side of the Mayu range actually reached Foul Point and saw no enemy; but on the 6th the troops who followed up the patrol encountered fairly stiff opposition at the village of Donbaik, about six miles north of Foul Point on the west side of the range. Whatever the Japanese strength—and it was not thought to be very great—it was enough to withstand a full-scale battalion attack at Donbaik on the 18th. By the end of the month the whole Division was at a complete standstill.

Meanwhile the Battalion—and the rest of the Brigade— remained in Chittagong busily carrying out landing exercises and preparing for battle. On the 27th of January the C.O. carried out a reconnaissance of the Akyab coast line from a naval motor launch; and on the 1st of February a party of thirty officers and men inspected a Japanese prisoner of war in Chittagong hospital! But as each target date arrived and the operation was postponed, doubts increased as to whether it would ever take place at all. Hardly a week passed—sometimes it was only a day or two—without some modification in the plans for the assault. By the end of January 1943 the chances of sailing seemed as remote as ever; and by the second week in February the assault on Akyab was called off. Instead it was decided that 6 Brigade should move south from Chittagong to Maungdaw where it was to prepare for a landing behind the Japanese defences at Donbaik so as to secure Foul Point from the sea where an attack from the land had so far failed. And so the Battalion left Chittagong on the 13th of February; and after a somewhat chaotic journey, throughout which it appeared that no preparations by the lines of communication staff had been made for its move, arrived at Maungdaw some two days later. Burma had been reached at last.

2

THE ARAKAN

It was not long before the Battalion, or at least part of it, was in action. Once it had settled in near Maungdaw and begun preparing for the landing south of Donbaik, it was ordered to select a platoon to carry out a special task. This platoon, commanded by Lieutenant Terry Bardell, was to embark in two naval motor launches on the 20th of February and carry out a raid on Myebon, a village used as a Japanese reinforcement camp some fifty miles south-east of Akyab. The camp and village lay at the head of a long, narrow waterway called Hunter's Bay. The boats sailed south from the Naf river, entered Hunter's Bay and drifted silently up to Myebon under cover of darkness. On the jetty near the camp stood a Japanese soldier. The leading motor launch slowly approached the jetty, still drifting, and a sailor, unable to stand the suspense any longer, shouted to the Jap, " sling out a rope." The Jap, taken by surprise and, it must be admitted, somewhat unexpectedly, complied with the request! Then he saw the troops on the deck and took to his heels. He did not get very far. The platoon jumped ashore without opposition and set about burning the village and camp and blowing up any important buildings such as the Post Office. Papers were seized and then the whole force withdrew in the resulting confusion as quickly as it had come without a single casualty.

The raid was highly successful and earned the participants the congratulations and commendation of the Divisional Commander. In fact, however, it was—despite months of specialised training—virtually the only amphibious operation any members of the Battalion were to take part in for the rest of the campaign and, as it turned out, for the rest of the war! On the 27th of February the seaborne attack on Foul Point was cancelled and the Battalion learnt that it was to be committed on land: 6 Brigade was to be placed under command of the 14th Indian Division for employment on the Mayu peninsula in an effort to succeed at Donbaik where everyone else had failed.

The move to the Donbaik positions was carried out by night and began at midnight on the 2nd of March. Earlier in the day the Battalion ' O ' group[1] had gone on ahead by truck. The Battalion marched the fifty miles to Donbaik in three stages, marching during the night and resting each day in a staging camp on the way. Marching was not easy. The so-called road had been constructed by cutting away the paddy " bands " and the dried paddy fields in fact formed its surface. Throughout its length it was inches thick in dust, and in some places ankle deep; and it was extremely rough and bumpy.

The Japanese forward positions were based upon a chaung approximately one mile north of Donbaik village. This chaung runs inland but only contains water until it reaches the jungle and the foothills. There, almost dry, it twists in the shape of a crook before disappearing into the hills. The area between the crook—" Shepherd's Crook " as it came to be known—and the sea is flat open paddy, approximately a thousand yards wide. The chaung itself was a natural obstacle: but the Japanese had made it an excellent defensive position by building an intricate system of intercommunicating weapon pits, strong points and dug-outs, all of which supported each other by fire. Each of these positions was known by the target number allotted to it by the gunners—Sugar 4, Sugar 5, Monkey 16, Monkey 24 and so on—and the two strongest, S4 and S5, were situated on a small subsidiary chaung leading north from the main chaung towards the jungle, where it petered out near a prominent mound of earth. This mound was S5 and somehow within it the Japanese had constructed a dug-out or " bunker " position which was quite immune to all the normal fire of field artillery. The S4 position was equally strong—if not stronger— and it was thought to be a series of bunkers hollowed out of the banks of the main chaung. This was the strongest part of the defended area but, in order to prevent a flanking movement through the foothills, additional positions were constructed at certain important points, such as the junctions of dry

[1] Company Commanders and others required in advance to receive the C.O.'s orders.

nalas,[1] which could successfully impede a force moving round in this way, particularly by interfering with its supply columns. These latter positions, being constructed in the jungle, were extremely well hidden and did not open fire unless absolutely necessary. Furthermore, the whole of the chaung area was overlooked by the two commanding features, Hills 500 and 823, both of which were steep and densely wooded, both of which were held by the Japanese and both of which concealed mortars, machine-guns and guns which were able to put down defensive fire anywhere in the area by day, by night, or through smoke.

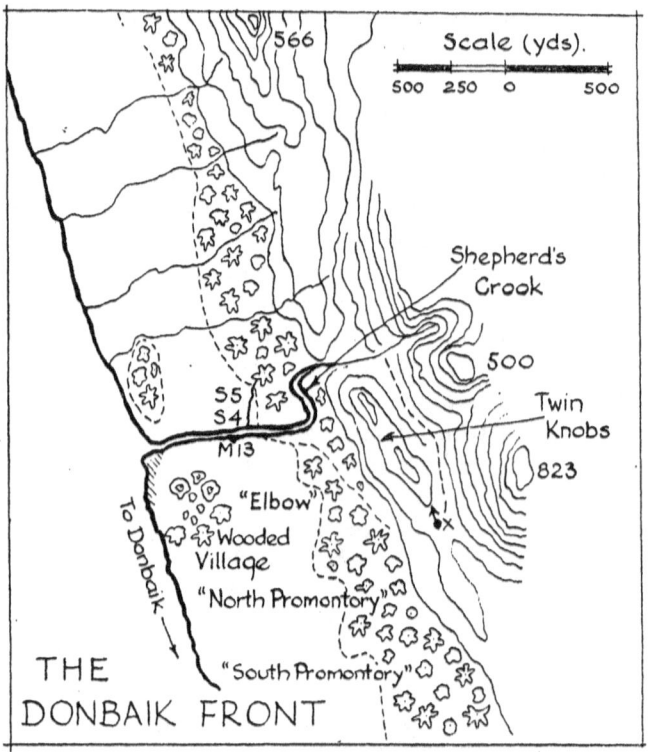

12. *The Donbaik Front*

Although the various positions in the chaung could be located from air photos by signs of digging, those in the hills remained completely concealed and only disclosed themselves when actually menaced.

[1] Stream beds.

Early on the morning of the 3rd of March the 'O' group, led by the C.O., did the rounds and went over the positions of the Punjab Battalion whom they were to relieve. First came a sweaty climb up Hill 566 for a grandstand view of the battlefield: from it could be seen the chaung, the enemy strong points and the innocuous cluster of huts which comprised Donbaik. Two previous attacks had already overrun the strong points and crossed the chaung; but the bunkers had closed their hatches and the heavy fire from Jap guns and mortars brought down upon them had made the position untenable and had forced a withdrawal to the original line. Casualties had been heavy and the bodies of the fallen still lay in no man's land for all to see. The Donbaik line had, in fact, already become something of a bogey.

After this first look round each company commander went to live with the company whose area he was to take over. This meant 'B' (Robert Allen) and 'D' (Phil Kelly) on the right, facing S4 and S5 and 'A' (Sean Kelly, deputising for Denis Hungate who was ill with malaria) and 'C' (Bill Hutton) on the left. The route to 'A' Company's position forked off from the main track to the chaung and in the angle of the tracks was a small narrow mound of earth surmounted by a blue cross bearing the words "Rasta nahin." "For some days," said Sean Kelly, "I passed this cross with feelings of silent respect for the unfortunate Indian soldier who lay beneath it until my slowly increasing knowledge of Urdu brought the realisation that the words meant 'No road this way!'" All the company positions were well organised and fairly simple to grasp once one had correlated all the twistings through the jungle necessary to get unseen from one position to the next. Some were already provided by nature in the form of dry chaung beds and many were deep enough for a man to stand upright unseen by the enemy in front. But in others it was a matter of dig or die and foxholes, dug-outs and occasionally sandbagged revetments were the order of the day. In the jungle visibility was often limited to a matter of feet. Routine was simple too; quiet by day, with sporadic shelling or mortaring, and active by night, but with the Jap doing all the night work! "There was a good deal of firing at night," wrote Sean Kelly—no relation to Phil —afterwards, " and it seemed to be all rifle and light machine-gun, plus 36 grenades; but try as I would I could see no sign of the Japs from the forward positions nor could I hear their fire. This 'Fifth of November' attitude was clarified and my suspicions confirmed when I talked to Phil Kelly in the chaung next day. His Indians fired off at least two thousand rounds each night, he said, presumably working on the theory that any dark patch might really be moving and that lead flying about in an unpredictable sort of way must surely discourage any snooping by the Japs. Moreover, said Phil's opposite number, they had some five thousand rounds in reserve and they would brass it all off their last night in the line. And I do believe they did."

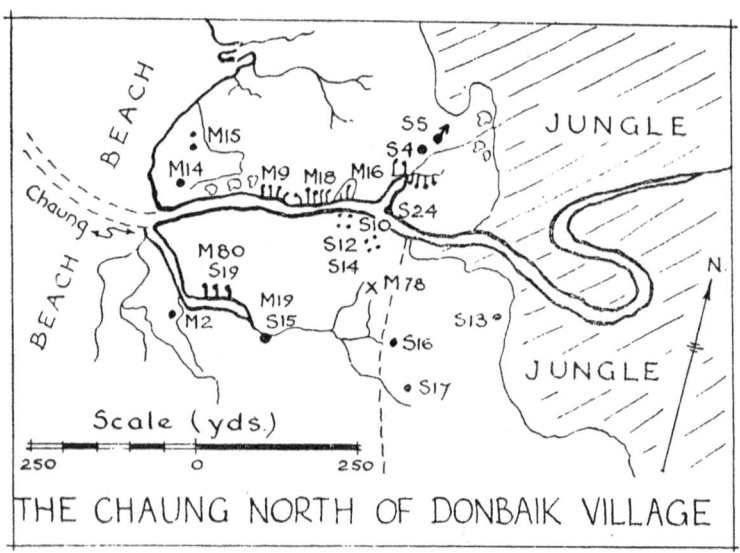

13. *The Chaung North of Donbaik*

By the morning of the 6th of March the remainder of the Battalion had arrived and in the course of the day moved into their positions. The Japs must have realised that there had been a change because at night there was not a sound and no random shooting betrayed the position of a foxhole. Within twenty-four hours the C.O. called a conference and disclosed the Brigade Commander's plan for the capture of Donbaik, the main assault on which was timed for the 18th. This was in essence that frontal attacks pure and simple were costly failures, as witnessed by the sight and smell of many bodies—British and Indian—lying in the open ground between jungle and sea, and that the Jap line must be by-passed by extending the Brigade flank on the left. The task of the Battalion was therefore to push forward company localities through the jungle below the feature known as "Twin Knobs." This was to be done as quickly and as quietly as possible without any outward show, so that a chain of company "boxes" might be established sufficiently far through the jungle for an assault to be launched on Donbaik with a minimum of activity against the strong points and bunkers.

The Battalion began patrolling from the moment it moved into position. Lieutenant Martin Wilson, commanding the Battle Patrol, had already been out beyond the main chaung with some of his men before the C.O.'s conference and was able to give a very clear picture of what he had learnt and seen. It was then decided that 'A' Company should be the first to move over the chaung to begin the outflanking build-up, and so the company commander, Sean Kelly, with Corporal John McLeary and three men set off on a patrol of their own to spy out the land. They made their way slowly from Shepherd's Crook into thinly wooded ground beyond, intersected by deep, dry, rocky nalas. There were many dead Indians there, the victims of a previous attack and a few empty Jap foxholes; but of Japs there was no sign. The patrol then moved up to "Twin Knobs"; still more dead Indians, but no Japs; but they found a good company area just forward of the upper end of the Crook where a tortuous nala and its shallow tributary offered a good all round position.

Next day a platoon of 'A' Company, under Lieutenant John Rolland, moved into this new area covered by a second. They soon dug themselves in, but during the night became the target of Jap jitter-parties who shot at and grenaded them. The following day the whole company moved in and by nightfall had dug, wired and camouflaged the complete position. They, too, were bothered at night by Jap parties with firecrackers and grenades; but they refused to be drawn and there were no casualties. By day all remained quiet save for fairly accurate mortaring; but the burst of the bombs was sharply upwards—one landed a few feet from Sean Kelly and Sergeant-Major Robert Suddes without damage—and only one man was hurt. Meanwhile the rest of the Battalion settled into its positions and by vigorous patrolling prepared itself for the attack to come. On the 13th, after a week in the line, it moved back, on relief by the Royal Berkshires, for a few days rest in the 'B' Echelon area. This, which contained the supply and water points, was a mile and a half in the rear; and the route between it and the front line was a mule path only. This path ran first through the jungle for three quarters of a mile and then debouched on to the paddy where it joined a motorable track which ran back, skirting the edge of the jungle, to the so-called main road. Part of this track was under observation from the Japanese positions and quite often came under shell fire from their guns. Motor traffic upon it was, therefore, strictly limited to essential vehicles. Supply of the forward positions was carried out by mules; and food and water were brought up each day. There was no water in the front line and what the mules brought was for drinking and cooking: for washing it was a case of saving a little from one's water bottle or waiting one's turn to go back to 'B' Echelon and a bathe in the chaung there.

While resting the Battalion received the final orders for the Brigade attack on the 18th. It and the Royal Welch Fusiliers were to lead it. The latter, who had moved into the jungle directly north and east of S4 and S5, and who at the nearest point were barely a hundred yards away from them, were to capture the eastern half of the chaung at 5.45 a.m. An hour later the Battalion was to capture the area of jungle known as "The Elbow". At 7.10 a.m. a battalion of an Indian Brigade, which had been placed under command, was to move forward through the jungle and secure as far forward as "North Promontory." Finally, at ten to eight, the Battalion was to exploit as far south as "South Promontory."

The attack began on the 18th at 5.30 a.m. with an artillery and mortar bombardment during which one hundred and twenty-four tons of shells were fired into the chaung area. Two days before, the Battalion had moved back into the line into positions ready for the attack. At 5.45 a.m. the Royal Welch Fusiliers went over the top, and most gallantly too. They overran the strong points but could not get inside them, with the result that they sustained heavy losses from Jap mortar and machine-gun fire. In fact, the pick of the battalion was knocked off in less than half an hour. Those who got into the chaung were isolated and later in the day had to be withdrawn; and in order to get them out their C.O. had to broadcast instructions through loudspeaker equipment in Welsh.

Meanwhile the D.L.I. attacked as planned. ' C ' Company was on the right and ' D ' on the left. The latter reached its objective with little difficulty; but ' C ' Company ran into strong opposition with all its platoons and lost some twenty-four men. Lieutenant Francis Greenwell led a dashing attack on one Japanese post blowing his hunting horn; but both he and Lieutenant James Freeman were wounded early on, as was Bill Hutton, the company commander, who received, for the second time, part of a mortar bomb in the same knee as on the Dyle in 1940. Only one platoon under Lieutenant " Ding " Bell reached the point of " The Elbow " and consolidated there; but the platoon remained isolated for some two hours. Sergeant Thomas Turnbull, the platoon sergeant, went forward to one section which had pushed well ahead of the rest and had been cut off by very heavy fire, and skilfully extricated them from a tricky situation, bringing a wounded man back with him. The rest of the Company under Sergeant-Major Martin McLane took up a position on the right of ' D ' Company. Then Robert Allen, with ' B ' Company, as yet uncommitted, moved forward on ' D ' Company's left and managed to push ahead without any opposition. Back near Battalion Headquarters the medical officer, Mattison—nicknamed " Joe the Joiner "—worked like a Trojan; and Dick Rice, the Padre, was an inspiration to everybody. By mid-day the Battalion had occupied most of the jungle comprising " The Elbow ", save near the edge where the two platoons of ' C ' Company had run into trouble.

The Brigadier visited Battalion Headquarters during the afternoon. The Brigade attack as a whole had not succeeded. The Royal Welch, despite their efforts, had failed to make any impression on S4 and S5 and the battalion of the Indian Brigade, though successful initially, had been cut off and was to be withdrawn that night. At the same time Colonel Theobalds was ordered to put in an attack on the remaining enemy position in " The Elbow ". This was to be carried out by a platoon of 'D' Company under Lieutenant Brian Cooke; but as ill-luck would have it Phil Kelly was shot through the head and killed by a sniper while reconnoitring the area of attack; and when the platoon reached its lying up position it was spotted by the enemy and engaged by them.

On the morning of the 19th, Brigade ordered the Battalion to consolidate its existing positions and make no further advance. A further attempt by the Royal Scots to take S4 and S5 during the night had failed and any hopes of continuing the attack as originally conceived were abandoned. The Battalion spent an uncomfortable day or so where it was, during which any obvious movement was sniped at; but this soon died down and things became comparatively quiet. " It's a most deceptive situation during a lull," wrote Colonel Theobalds at the time; "you practically never see a Jap and one can wander about quite exposed without anything happening except some occasional mortaring or shelling or the odd sniper. Their snipers were very active one day, but we certainly got four and they've been more cautious since then. Sergeant Turnbull spotted a couple only fifteen yards away from his position and bumped them both off. Sergeant Scott and Lance-Sergeant Stevenson were both killed trying to get at the Japs, but the trouble is that you can't find the way into their strong points, which really are immensely strong. After a number of direct hits by our guns, the old machine-gun pops up again, apparently quite unaffected. The chaps are all in very good heart and the principal criticism is that they so seldom get a chance of shooting at a Jap! At night the Japs wander around with crackers trying to draw our fire, but the men are very steady and refuse to be drawn."

The Battalion went out of the line on the 22nd for a rest. It received a welcome draft of reinforcements and made the most of the chance to clean up and reorganise. Captain Graham Holmes took over Phil Kelly's company and Captain Roger Stock the newly constituted 'C'. Then, on the 25th, the Battalion moved back into the line to relieve the Royal Berkshires on "Twin Knobs." As it did so it received some rather disturbing news which may have accounted for the comparative quiet of the Japanese in the area of Donbaik. On the other side of the Mayu range, and in the Mayu valley beyond, events were taking place which were shortly to have a profound effect on the course of the whole campaign.

Throughout the month of February the Japanese had been preparing an offensive, and even as 6 Brigade moved south to Donbaik the first blow was being struck. In the first week of March a Japanese force started up the lower Kaladan valley and gained control of it by the 8th. At the same time they began infiltrating round the flank of 55 Indian Brigade in Rathedaung and by the 11th a battalion had started marching from the Kaladan valley over the Kanzauk pass to fall upon that Brigade's rear at Htizwe. This right hook was only too successful. 55 Brigade was forced to withdraw across the Mayu river and by the 18th of March, when 6 Brigade attacked at Donbaik, the Japanese were in control of a considerable part of the eastern half of the Mayu valley. On the 24th they struck again. Eluding the Navy's river patrols, they crossed the Mayu, a regiment strong, and struck out over the hills with the object of severing the lines of communication of the forces on the Mayu peninsula and of establishing a road block near Indin on the west of the Mayu range.

This meant a withdrawal by 6 Brigade to meet the new threat. A scratch force composed of each battalion's carrier platoon was dispatched at once to Indin with a company, and shortly afterwards the whole, of the Royal Berkshires. The D.L.I. received its orders to withdraw on the 29th of March; forward positions were adjusted and thinned out; large numbers of booby traps were set; and the Battalion finally slipped away on the 4th of April, covered by Martin Wilson's Battle Patrol. As it did so news was received that the bridge over the chaung at Indin had been attacked by the Japanese and captured the previous night. At mid-day Colonel Theobalds went to Brigade and was told that the withdrawal was to be speeded up; all timings were put forward; and by 6 a.m. the following morning the greater part of the Battalion was in Indin and none too soon either. 'D' Company and the administrative parts of the Battalion were moving up behind and did not in fact join up with the rest of it till next day.

The bridge over the Indin chaung lay midway between Indin and Kyaukpandu at a point several hundred yards from where the chaung ran into the sea. Nearby were a number of small hill features, one of which overlooked and dominated not only the bridge but also the beach which, at low tide, provided vehicles with the only other means of crossing the chaung. At Indin there was a rest camp of bamboo huts; at Kyaukpandu lay the Headquarters of the forces in the Indin area commanded by the Brigade second in command.

The occupation of the Indin bridge was the first move in the Japanese attempt to prevent 6 Brigade's withdrawal from Donbaik. The bridge had been held by a carrier detachment which was easily overrun by approximately a Japanese company which established itself in the hills overlooking the bridge and successfully blocked the road. An early attack on the 4th by some troops from the rest camp was unsuccessful; but with the arrival of the rest of the Brigade it was planned to attack not only the area of the bridge but also the Jap positions on and around a feature known as Point 251 to the north of it.

The Battalion's objective was Point 251 and the attack was timed for the same afternoon. After hearing reports of the attack the previous day, stiff opposition was expected when the leading companies crossed the start line. However, there was only a little desultory firing from the enemy and the sole casualties were one man wounded and one 2 lb. fish which drifted down the Indin chaung as the troops waded across it! 'A' Company spotted a Jap rifleman up a tree as they waited to move off; but he was quickly despatched by Lance-Corporal Braveley with a burst of Bren gun fire. Otherwise the Battalion gained its objective without difficulty and 'B' and 'D' Companies reached Point 251 without encountering the enemy at all. No one could understand why the enemy had yielded so easily.

It was not until 4 o'clock the following morning that the reason became apparent. Then, quite suddenly, a strong Japanese attack was launched on the rear of 6 Brigade in the Indin rest camp and beyond it. The brunt of this attack fell upon the Royal Scots in the rest camp, into which the Japs streamed shouting in pidgin English "Royal Scots don't shoot!" A bitter battle raged in the moonlight in which friend and foe were inextricably mixed up. Brigade Headquarters was itself overrun and the Brigadier captured. It was not, however, till nearly 7 a.m. that this news reached Colonel

Theobalds who, as senior C.O., took command of the Brigade and handed over the Battalion to Major George Lyster Todd. Then the Battalion began to move back to help the defenders of the rest camp where it arrived to find the situation, if confused, certainly not out of control. The Royal Scots had suffered heavily, but so had the Japanese. By the time it was light the enemy was for the most part disposed among the clumps of bamboo which dotted the landscape and surrounded the clusters of huts forming Indin village and its environs and provided practically the only cover in the area. They were thus a sitting target for artillery and mortars.

At 10 a.m. George Lyster Todd issued orders for the withdrawal of the Battalion along the beach to Kyaukpandu that afternoon. The whole Brigade was to concentrate in the area of that village by 5 p.m. For the remaining few hours the Battalion joined in a wholesale slaughter of Japanese. The latter, for the first time in the campaign, had committed themselves in the open, and they were to pay for it dearly. The Battalion positioned itself where it could take a heavy toll of any enemy who might break out from the cover of the bamboo clumps. Then guns and mortars opened up on all the likely cover. It was Hobson's choice for the Japs; either stay under cover—for they had not had time to dig in properly—and be killed by the shells; or run for it and be slaughtered by rifles and automatics positioned round them like guns at a rat hunt. Many did run for it, screaming at the tops of their voices, and were shot down as they did so. Each company took a heavy toll, though Lieutenant Pat Rome's platoon actually brought in a live prisoner—a rarity at that stage of the war as the Japs preferred to die rather than be captured.

In due course came the order to pull out. Any stores which had to be left behind were destroyed and the columns of infantry marched off along the beach widely dispersed. The carriers leap-frogged along the line, taking up dismounted positions covering the flank toward Point 251. Tommy Bewick, the Quartermaster, was given a cheer as he rode by in a three tonner with his ' B ' Echelon which had been separated for some days. The truck's cabin was well protected by plates from a hydro-burner cooker! As the artillery limbers passed beyond the Jap dominated hills, the guns were unhooked and went into action firing smoke and high explosive to screen the thin files of infantry stretching as far as the eye could see. The Japs put up little resistance; what there was was confined to long range shelling, but the range was so extreme that the shells fell wearily on the wet sand and bounced slowly across the path of the marching columns. By 5.30 p.m. the Battalion was concentrated around Kyaukpandu and Colonel Theobalds had re-assumed command on handing over the Brigade to the Brigade second in command in the village.

The Japs had taken a beating at Indin. Of three battalions they committed there, two virtually ceased to exist and the third was reduced to eighty riflemen. At all events for one reason or another they made no major attack thereafter on the west of the Mayu range and for the rest of the campaign the Battalion's activities were confined to patrolling.

6 Brigade did not remain long at Kyaukpandu; in fact only long enough to cover the withdrawal of one of the 14th Division's battered Brigades which had been cut off in the hills to the east. On the 10th of April the Battalion was ordered to withdraw to Myhinlut where it was to join 4 Indian Brigade, the leading brigade of a fresh Indian Division which was moving in to replace the 14th. This was only to be temporary and, in fact, it lasted only a month; but it meant that for a while the Battalion was separated from 6 Brigade who moved back at once to within a mile or so of Maungdaw.

The Battalion took up positions at Myhinlut alongside the 1st/15th Punjab Regiment, digging in on the crests of steep bamboo clad hills which rose straight out of the Myhinlut chaung. They had barely completed the task when they were ordered to withdraw again with instructions to blow the bridge over the chaung when another Indian battalion had passed through them. Then occurred one of those maddening muddles when friend fires on friend; for the withdrawing Indians opened up on the men of the Battalion guarding the bridge, killing two and badly wounding Terry Bardell. The Battalion moved back to Lambaguna in not too good a temper.

The next three weeks were weeks of busy patrolling southwards and eastwards into the intricate scrub-covered foothills of the Mayu range. The Japs had been slow in following up and the patrols suffered few casualties. However, on one occasion a spirited encounter took place between a patrol of 'D' Company and a numerically stronger force of Japanese in which the latter were routed but in which the courageous Corporal William Houghton was killed. On another a patrol led by Corporal McLeary was ambushed, two men were killed, one—Private Terence McKeown—was thought to be missing but subsequently learnt to have been killed, and the Corporal himself was severely wounded. When he was hit he fell over a small rock-face into a jungle-covered nala with four wounds in his buttocks and stomach, another four in his right wrist and with his right palm completely shot away. When he came to, and despite these grievous injuries, he made his way back some three miles to Battalion Headquarters, complete with all his arms and equipment. He made his report to the Colonel in a very low voice as he lay on a stretcher and was then evacuated; but he died before he reached hospital.

Lambaguna had its lighter moments too, for it was here that rumour, assisted by Colour-Sergeant Richard Whittaker, really came into its own. Colour-Sergeant George Wood was constantly informed by the solemn faced Whittaker that the advance party of a relieving Chinese-American division was about to arrive—the identity of the force was changed periodically—and was constantly kept busy laying out his reserve rations and equipment ready for the take over! Needless to say, there was no such relief. Indeed on the east of the Mayu range the position was going from bad to worse. Between the 18th and 30th of April the Japanese pressed forward relentlessly towards Buthidaung; on the 3rd of May they occupied a vital feature dominating the lateral road between Maungdaw and Buthidaung which repeated attacks failed to regain; and on the 7th the troops of the 14th Division withdrew northwards and the enemy marched into Buthidaung. The Commander of the 26th Indian Division, who had now taken command along the whole front, realising that Maungdaw was liable to be outflanked from Buthidaung much as Indin had been when the Japs crossed the Mayu river, decided on a further withdrawal northwards to a line some fifteen or twenty miles away which was to be held for the approaching monsoon.

For the Battalion this was virtually the end of the campaign. On the night of the 11th of May, exactly a month after joining

4 Indian Brigade, they carried out one more melancholy retreat. They had the satisfaction, before going, of shooting up a Japanese patrol which, with typical arrogance, had the temerity to march up the road in threes. On the 12th they were once more united with 6 Brigade; within a fortnight back again in Chittagong; and within a month, with the rest of the Brigade, restored to the ranks of the 2nd Division in Ahmednagar. The short campaign, miserable failure though it was, had taught them many lessons; the Battalion had been blooded; and after the experience of Indin everybody felt that, man for man, they were the equal of any Japanese.

3

KOHIMA

When the Battalion arrived back in Ahmednagar it was to find itself once more committed to intensive training for amphibious warfare. While 6 Brigade had been occupied in the Arakan a force was being collected in and around Bombay which, under Lord Mountbatten's newly formed South-East Asia Command, was to strike against the Japanese in Burma from the sea. The 2nd Division formed part of this force, which consisted in all of four infantry divisions under command of the XXXIIIrd Indian Corps.

First, however, there was a period of rest and reorganisation. Everyone went on leave to such leave centres as India could offer. For some Bombay or Poona were popular; for the more adventurous a number of the many hill stations proved more attractive. After rest, reorganisation; and, not least, a course of medical treatment to try to mitigate the all too recurrent outbreaks of malaria which had attacked the whole of 6 Brigade in the Arakan and still persisted. The Battalion's sickness rate in this respect was the best in the Brigade, but, even so, over three hundred men succumbed to one attack and as many as fifty had four. Two unfortunate men had nine. The treatment given was, however, only moderately successful and in fact malaria continued to disrupt training plans for some months to come.

There were changes in the Battalion too. Early in July

Colonel Theobalds was promoted full Colonel and took up an appointment at Combined Operations Headquarters. Later, to everybody's great satisfaction, he became second in command of 6 Brigade. His loss was greatly felt, as his command and direction of the Battalion in the Arakan had made him extremely popular and won him the admiration and respect of all ranks. Regret was, however, tempered with the satisfaction that his successor, Lieutenant-Colonel Jack Brown, was himself a member of the Regiment.

From August until the end of 1943 the Battalion busied itself in amphibious and jungle training. In November it joined the rest of the 2nd Division in a large scale exercise from ships south of Bombay. Then, in the New Year, it left Ahmednagar temporarily and moved into camp in the jungle near Belgaum, only to receive, after barely a month, a sudden and unexpected call to return at once and prepare a second time for a move to Burma. These orders were in fact received at 9 a.m. on the 21st of March, 1944. The Battalion arrived back in Ahmednagar on the 25th; on the 3rd of April it was organised on a war footing and in the train bound for Calcutta; and on the 9th it was deployed round the airstrip at Dimapur in Assam some 1,200 miles from where it had started.

The suddenness of the move was amply justified by events. The war in Burma had flared up once more on a large scale and a Japanese offensive of considerable proportions was well under way by the time the Battalion—and the rest of the 2nd Division—arrived at Dimapur. The tale of this offensive had begun early in the previous month when a vigorous attack was made by the Japanese on the forces of the XVth Indian Corps in the Arakan. Somewhat similar tactics were employed as in the previous year and within a short while the British and Indian forces had been encircled and cut off. Then, according to the Japanese plan, they ought to have withdrawn in disorder leaving the way clear for a victorious " march on Delhi "; but the plan misfired as the troops stood fast where they were and to their rescue came squadrons of Dakota supply dropping aircraft. The British had learnt much from the disasters of the previous year and in a month of bitter fighting proved that to stand one's ground and be supplied by air was the most effective answer to the Japanese tactics of infiltration and encirclement. The attack was smashed. The encirclers were cut off from their own supply base and themselves encircled. Once the original plan went wrong, the Jap—brave, tenacious, stubborn but incredibly stupid—had no alternative course of action. Split up into penny packets, what remained of the attackers were systematically eliminated; the Jap dead ran into thousands and every day patrols would report coming upon groups of dead among the foothills or on top of the Mayu range. Within a short time the XVth Corps passed to the offensive and the decisive struggle was over. The Japs had suffered their first major defeat in Burma.

Despite the rough handling they had received in the Arakan, the Japs were undeterred from their design to invade India. In fact the operations in the Arakan were a subsidiary effort to distract and divide attention. The main plan, shaped as far back as 1943, was to be put into effect in the State of Manipur, immediately behind the central front. Known as Operation U, it had a threefold purpose—to cross the Indo-Burma border and seize the main Allied advance base at Imphal, destroying the British position on the central front; to cut the Bengal-Assam Railway, which was General Stilwell's supply line for the northern front, so breaking up the Northern Combat Area Command; and finally to overrun the Assam airfields and disrupt the airborne traffic over the Hump to China. The Japanese set great store on the outcome of their offensive. General Mataguchi's order of the day to the invasion forces summed it up in three sentences. "This operation," he said, "will engage the attention of the whole world, and is eagerly awaited by a hundred million of our countrymen. Its success will have a profound effect on the course of the war and may even lead to its conclusion. We must therefore expend every ounce of energy and talent to achieve our purpose."

Imphal lies in a plain 3,000 feet up in the heart of the Manipur mountains which wall off India from Burma. It is formed by an opening in the gorges of the Manipur river which tumbles through the Naga hills on its course to the Chindwin at Kalewa. The plain, which is about six hundred miles square, is shaped like a pear. To reach it from India a road from Dimapur winds through the mountains up to Kohima—fifty miles above Dimapur—and thence down into the plain.

To the south, roads continue through Tamu into the Kabaw valley and, further south still, through Tiddim to the Chindwin.

In the middle of March 100,000 crack Japanese troops were launched across the frontier. Their offensive was not unforeseen and the Indian Divisions of the IVth Corps, initially positioned along the frontier, were withdrawn into the plain to fight the decisive battle there. The Japs moved swiftly—more so than anticipated and in greater strength. By the end of March Imphal had been isolated and by the 4th of April so had Kohima. Indeed, in the latter case a whole Japanese division of some 15,000 men surged round a British and Indian garrison of just over 3,000 which, once eliminated, would leave the enemy free to sweep down to Dimapur and the Brahmaputra valley beyond.

Once again the air was to save the day. Already the 5th Indian Division was being flown from the Arakan to the aid of the Imphal garrison; and one Brigade of it—161—had been despatched to Kohima just before the Japs completed encirclement. A second division was flown after it, also from the Arakan. Meanwhile the British and Indian forces stood fast and prepared to fight it out; and the 2nd Division arrived at Dimapur to rush to their aid.

The village of Kohima stands 5,000 feet up in the Manipur mountains. The road from Dimapur winds tortuously up a valley to the saddle which comprises the Kohima ridge. The ridge lies, like a great dam, at right angles across the road, which turns and runs along the top of it. Beyond, it bends away again to resume its southward journey down the valley to Imphal. Along the crest of the ridge are a series of hillocks and rising above them commanding heights. The Kohima garrison held all of these at the start of the siege, but was gradually forced back as the battle progressed until only one, scarcely a mile in length, remained in its hands.

The task of the 2nd Division was twofold: to relieve the Kohima garrison and, having done so, to drive south to Imphal. Though only a quarter of its signal units had arrived, and with a still smaller fraction of wireless and telephone equipment, the Division advanced to the attack.

The Battalion began to move up the road to Kohima on the 15th of April, on which day their transport arrived after its long drive from the west of India. The vehicles had travelled some 1,200 miles, often over bad roads, and not a single one had fallen by the wayside. By the 17th the Battalion occupied reserve positions about two miles from the forward positions around Kohima; and the same night ' D ' Company had a clash with some Jap patrols and sustained the Battalion's first casualty of the campaign. Early on the following morning troops of 161 Brigade succeeded in gaining contact with the troops in the Kohima perimeter and the relief of the garrison began. There was, however, still much bitter fighting to come before it was completed. On the afternoon of the 19th ' B ' Company of the Battalion was ordered to attack a feature called " Terrace Hill " which commanded the road into Kohima and which it was vital to secure for the safe passage of the transport columns. The attack went like clockwork and the Company wrought havoc with the bayonet. Over fifty casualties were inflicted on the Jap and a quantity of equipment captured; but although the Company's casualties were not heavy, Robert Allen, its commander, was unfortunately among those killed. He had been well up during the attack, and when it was over went forward to organise the defence when a burst of machine-gun fire caught him in the chest. He lived only a few seconds and his only words, as the Padre reached him, were " well done ' B ' Company." He was a great loss so early in the battle. After this otherwise not unsuccessful start there was a lull for two days when first two companies and then the whole Battalion occupied the southern and western parts of the now aptly named feature of " Garrison Hill." Conditions were far from pleasant.

The Hill had to be seen to be believed. The immediate garrison of some two hundred had been completely surrounded for nearly three weeks and had been pushed back till they were crowded together on the last remaining feature. No wounded had been evacuated. Supplies had all been delivered by air and, though the hill had once been thickly covered with jungle, all that now remained were the limbless stumps of trees festooned with parachutes. The whole area was a mass of foxholes and it was littered with ammunition and water containers, unburied dead and all the sordid relics of battle. Some supplies were still hanging in the trees; but Jap snipers prevented them from being cut down. The Battalion's forward positions were overlooked by a feature known as "Kuki's Piquet," which was Jap held and which made daylight movement more than risky. Only the perimeter defences were tactically sited; the rest were deep dug dug-outs.

On the morning of the 22nd it was decided that 'D' Company—which was now commanded by Major "Tank" Waterhouse—should attack "Kuki's Piquet" at dawn the following

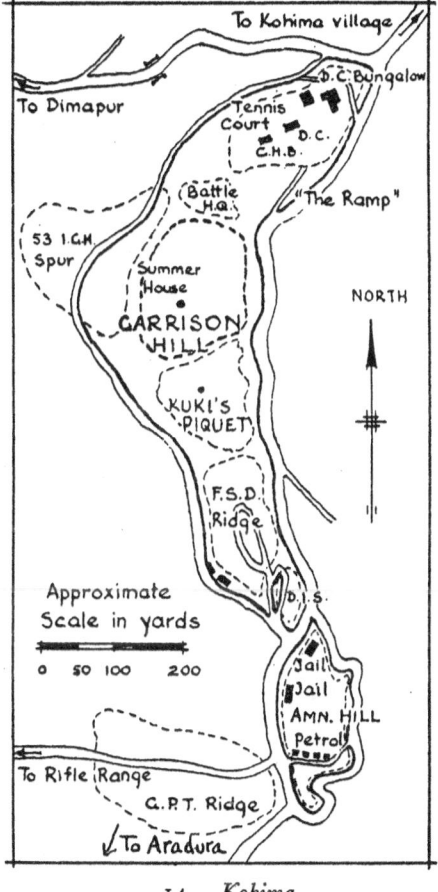

14. *Kohima*

day. Rumour had it that the Jap was pulling out, though why no one could understand. 'A' and 'C' Companies were then ordered up on to the hill, the latter to take over from 'D' who were to lie up for the night, the former to come into reserve to exploit whatever success was achieved. The relief was successfully completed under a heavy smoke screen and everyone settled down for a quiet night. 'C' Company faced the Japs on "Kuki's Piquet" with 'D' behind them in non-tactically sited bunkers, and 'A' and 'B' on a plateau about one hundred feet below.

Just before "stand-to" 'D' Company's attack was postponed owing to the failure of two small attacks which had been put in elsewhere by other troops of 6 Brigade. At about dusk the Japs put down about twenty rounds from a 75 millimetre gun and caused a few casualties; but otherwise all was quiet and remained so for the first part of the night.

At about 1.30 a.m. the Jap opened up on 'C' Company with mortars and grenades. "I turned over," wrote "Tank" Waterhouse afterwards, "and said to myself that it was nothing to do with me and tried to go to sleep again. It just didn't work and the noise increased. The 'C' Company platoon on the forward slopes was taking a good hammering. Jap automatics had all their L.M.G.s pinpointed and they were losing men fast. The situation was, in fact, getting serious. Quite a few trees were on fire, an ammunition dump was hit and the place looked like Blackpool on a summer night, plus a firework display." The Japs lengthened the range of their mortars, mixing smoke and high explosive, and then at the same time attacked the unfortunate platoon of 'C' Company in great strength. They came up the slope shoulder to shoulder with those in front wearing gas masks and throwing phosphorus grenades. They were shot down; but as soon as one man fell another took his place and by sheer weight of numbers the inevitable happened and they broke through in the centre. Lieutenant Jock Ainley, the platoon commander, was badly wounded and all in all the position was very confused. Then "Tank" Waterhouse brought 'D' Company into action. Rallying everyone he could, he managed to form a line somewhere around 'C' Company Headquarters and there the Jap was held. "Every now and then," he wrote afterwards, "we managed to push forward a little, but our casualties were heavy. We were now lying shoulder to shoulder and suffering very badly from spring grenades. Martin Wilson, second in command of ' C ' Company, was badly hit, but refused to be moved till the others had been evacuated. All line had gone and most of the wireless sets. Our gunner O.P. was killed and it took nearly two hours to get any defensive fire. About 4 a.m. we started to counter-attack the right flank. Bill Watson of ' D ' Company was killed leading one of these. He was last seen clubbing Japs with the butt end of a Bren gun. Willie Lockhart, my second in command, was also killed by a burst from an automatic. But the Japs were getting a good beating too; and we could hear them shouting and screaming just below us. They seemed to have had just about enough and some officer was trying to reorganise them to attack again. There was a short lull. Roger Stock, commanding ' C ' Company, and I had a cigarette together and talked of Teesdale and our next leave. Then the Japs attacked again. That was the last I saw of Roger; he went forward to his hard pressed Company and I back to collect the clerks and cooks. When I returned I was told that Roger had been killed and Pat Rome wounded."

Thanks very largely to " Tank " Waterhouse, the Japs got no further that night: they just held on to what they had. But about 5 a.m. Colonel Brown got part of ' A ' Company up from their positions on the plateau to try to regain the lost ground. The attack was made by one platoon and was led by the company commander, Captain Sean Kelly. They fixed bayonets, crawled into position and then went in. The top of the hill was flat and bare with pines on all sides as it sloped away. Lying on top of each other all over the hilltop were the bodies of friend and foe, all intermingled, and half of them had been set alight by the spreading blaze of the burning ammunition dump which in the darkness lit up the whole grisly scene. The platoon commander, Lieutenant Baker, and his sergeant, Bob Dunlop, were wounded right at the start: but the platoon went forward amid a welter of fire and grenades and began to clear the Japs from what were originally ' C ' Company's trenches. One section under Corporal Arthur Breden set about them with Sten guns and grenades. Breden and Kelly together bowled grenades into one Jap dug-out with telling effect. At one stage Private McLellan, a wee Scot in charge of a Bren gun, fell bottom first into a foxhole where he stuck, head and feet to the sky, swearing horribly. "Gie's a hand out Maister Kelly," he shouted; which request was complied with and, none the worse, he got his gun into action again. While it was still dark it was difficult to gauge exactly the attack's success: but as it got lighter the Japs opened up from "Kuki's Piquet" and Kelly, who had been wounded in the shoulder quite early on, returned to fetch up a second platoon to clear the right flank. While he did so, Breden and his section cleared the last of the trenches and got the remnants of the platoon into them. Breden was badly wounded in the legs, but nothing daunted, continued to direct operations sitting down. He was soon hit again, this time in the shoulder and chest, but he refused to give in and, dragging himself once again into a sitting position, tried to start firing his Sten gun. Just then he was killed by a mortar burst and the Battalion lost a very gallant N.C.O.

In due course up came the second platoon—Lieutenant Peter Stockton's—but Kelly resolved that they should not be rushed and pointed out the ground and laid on fire support. In they went, only to meet a hail of fire which the Japs, now it was lighter, were able to pour in from "Kuki's Piquet". It was soon obvious that they could not hold the place in daylight and so what was left of the Company was pulled up to the top of the hill where it occupied a rough line of pits already in existence. Stockton was killed, so was Private George Mathews his batman, his sergeant and two section commanders. The right hand section had ceased to exist.

Everyone now set to with vigour to improve the position, which consisted mainly of dug-outs without fire slits. While they did so, they were covered by two volunteer Bren gun teams, who lay out in front and kept accurate enemy fire away. Two of these volunteers, Privates Wood and Ward, were towers of strength and were always to be found volunteering for the most unpleasant tasks. But it was difficult to stop the snipers. "Every now and then there would be a crack," wrote Sean Kelly, "and nearly always a groan or a cry for help and the stretcher bearers would rush and kneel there where the man had been hit, dress him and carry him off. Lance-Corporals Spencer and Stokell, my two best, worked without ceasing: they had been at it non-stop since 3 a.m. If ever there were heroes, they were. What cold blooded courage! It's nothing to charge in in hot blood, but to kneel and do your job where a man has just been hit, and where you must be hit, too, if another comes, is the bravest thing I know."

So the day passed. The Pioneer Platoon was sent up to join 'A' Company to make up numbers and its sergeant, Charles Andrews, cool and energetic, held the left position together by sheer cheerfulness and courage: with Sean Kelly he conducted a private war against the snipers by firing grenades from a discharger cup into the trees. He was killed two days later and was a great loss to the Battalion. The carrier platoon, too, was thrown into the battle dismounted: their sergeant was unlucky to get two shots through the buttocks and was carried off, face down, amid a string of expletives which left no doubt as to his opinions of Japan and the Japanese.

The Japs' losses had been heavy, but so had the Battalion's. Out of fifteen officers of the three forward companies, only four remained—and Sean Kelly ultimately had to be evacuated for several days till his shoulder mended—while of 'A' Company's one hundred and thirty-six men on the morning of the 23rd, only sixty remained at nightfall. The other companies were in a similar position. Fortunately, however, the Jap did not attack again at once and for the next few days both sides stood their ground, licked their wounds and glowered at each other.

The Japs returned to the attack during the 27th. At about midnight they mortared the whole Battalion area, but particularly the positions occupied by the left hand platoon of 'A' Company. Then, about two companies of infantry assaulted that platoon's positions in much the same way as they had attacked 'C' Company a few nights before. The platoon was heavily outnumbered; the leading Japs carried bags full of grenades, but no weapons; and by sheer weight of numbers they reached the plateau on the top of the hill. " There," in the words of one company commander, " they went round and round shouting " Tojo " and blessing the Mikado: it was the old boy's birthday." And, finally, they settled down to dig in on the plateau though, thanks to the Battalion's resistance, not in very great strength.

The C.O. then ordered a counter-attack. It was to take place at first light and to be carried out by Lieutenant Francis Greenwell and the Battle Patrol, together with a composite force under Captain Tony Shuttle. The attack went in from two sides. Greenwell went over the top, as in the Arakan the year before, blowing his hunting horn. Guns and mortars pounded the Jap positions—the Battalion mortars alone fired over 1,300 rounds and inflicted heavy casualties—and the Japs took one look and ran. As bad luck would have it, they were able to take cover in a supporting smoke screen put down to mask " Kuki's Piquet; " but the situation was restored and the Battalion was master of the battlefield. Three days later it was withdrawn for forty-eight hours' rest and handed over to the Royal Welch Fusiliers.

* * * * * * *

The period of resisting Japanese attacks was now over. The 2nd Division turned to plans for throwing the enemy out of Kohima and advancing down the road to Imphal. The remaining two Brigades of the Division began a series of wide-sweeping attacks round the flanks, while to 6 Brigade fell the task of ejecting the Japs from the main Kohima ridge. The Battalion was chosen to make the first attack on what was known as " F.S.D. Ridge," which runs at right angles to " Garrison Hill " and parallel to the main Imphal road. The attack was planned for the 4th of May. ' B ' Company was to escort tanks up to " F.S.D. Ridge," where it was to consolidate. ' C ' Company was to follow as Brigade reserve and the rest of the Battalion as Divisional reserve.

The tanks moved off by road as planned, ' B ' Company across country, and in due course infantry and tanks joined up, having met no opposition: but when the Company began its attack on " F.S.D. Ridge " they came under heavy fire from enemy held features across the valley and it was some time before they could move. ' C ' Company coming along behind was then ordered to clear that part of " F.S.D. Ridge " which had been named " D.I.S. Ridge "; but they too came under heavy fire and met considerable opposition.

Meanwhile, the rest of the Battalion were moving up in carriers along the road to join the two forward companies with a view to forming a Battalion ' box ' on " F.S.D. Ridge "; but as the column reached the ramp leading from the main road up

Men of the 16th Battalion after crossing the Cosina River

The Arakan foot-hills near Maungdaw, looking towards the Mayu Range

Kohima, April 1944

'Kuki's Piquet' from 'Garrison Hill'

to the District Commissioner's bungalow, they came under heavy automatic fire and a barrage of grenades from those parts of "F.S.D. Ridge" which 'B' Company, having suffered heavily, had as yet been unable to clear. The C.O. then ordered the Battalion out of the carriers, which returned whence they had come: but orders were then received from the Brigade Commander to withdraw to "Garrison Hill" through positions held by troops of 5 Brigade in the area of the District Commissioner's bungalow. It was clear from the intensity of enemy fire that further advance on foot was impossible. A Jap 75 millimetre gun was shelling the ramp with great accuracy and one shell killed Colonel Brown himself. This was a tragic loss at a critical stage of the battle and it was not till late that evening that his place was taken by Major L. a B. Robinson, second in command of the Royal Berkshires.

Meanwhile, all was far from well with 'B' and 'C' Companies. The former had made its way along "F.S.D. Ridge" towards "Kuki's Piquet," but had suffered heavily from machine-gun fire. The latter, due to some misunderstanding, had tried to join a company of Royal Welch Fusiliers on "Kuki's Piquet," only to find that that particular attack had failed and the feature was still in Jap hands. Enemy machine-guns wrought havoc in their ranks and what remained of them linked up with the remnants of 'B' Company and the company of Royal Welch Fusiliers and went to ground on "F.S.D. Ridge" where further enemy fire made movement impossible. All attempts to get supplies to them and to evacuate wounded were in vain, though when darkness fell some of the more serious cases were removed on tanks and a few were carried down a nala leading to the Battalion's original forming up position. This small force remained dug in on the ridge for a further day and night until early on the 6th of May they were relieved by the Royal Berkshires and withdrew to join the rest of the Battalion, who had been ordered back to Dimapur for a rest and refit. So ended a further spell of savage fighting.

It was a sadly depleted Battalion which gathered together at West Point Sidings in Dimapur. There were only sufficient men for three rifle companies, each of only two platoons. Some thirty men from the rear details left behind at Ahmednagar arrived within a few days and helped to swell the throng. But the respite was only a short one and within ten days the Battalion, rested, reorganised and re-equipped, was in transport on the way back to Kohima.

Back in the line life was a little less arduous than previously, as the Battalion was occupied in garrisoning a number of features on the flanks of the main Kohima ridge in and around the village of Jotsoma. It was here that they came into close contact with the Nagas, those loyal and gallant hillmen who worked devotedly to aid the British and Indian forces in his campaign. Indeed, they even held some defensive posts themselves, armed with ancient fowling pieces and Jap and British rifles picked up from the battlefield. They are a wonderfully well built race, and no wonder; they sow, tend, reap and thrash their paddy in the valley fields two or three thousand feet below their villages and carry everything up and down on their backs. They are a proud and clannish people and the Battalion liked them immensely. Acting as stretcher bearers for 5 Brigade, they carried wounded out, 1,500 feet down into the Zuba valley and 2,000 feet up again to the main road with only one rest—a task which would have taken British bearers eight times as long and exhausted them for days as well.

Jotsoma made a good defensive position, though the Battalion was not there long and the defences were never tested. Francis Greenwell had good cause to remember Jotsoma, for he had the misfortune to get one hundred and nine fleabites there; while Sergeant Walter Hogg earned lasting fame and regard among the marriageable maidens of the village by his exercise of the coiffeur's art! The Naga girls wear their hair cropped until they marry and the cropping is done by their parents with a dah—a large knife—which makes the process painful. Sergeant Hogg was in great demand soaping, cutting the hair with scissors and shaving the heads of all those whose crowning glory was beginning to grow again.

Soon, however, everyone was on the move once more, as the Battalion joined 6 Brigade in the long, hard grind up the Aradura Spur, the last real bastion of the Kohima defences. The spur was covered with thick jungle and the Battalion formed a series of company defensive "boxes." The main opposition was from sniping, and vigorous patrolling was employed to deal with it. A party under Lieutenant Jack Burkmar found a number of Japs just behind a located sniper post in the act of cooking a meal. They attacked them with grenades and automatics and put an end to their destructiveness at the cost of only one man slightly wounded. The advance continued by a series of leap frogging movements; opposition was slight, though there was a steady drain of casualties from snipers. The weather was appalling. It rained almost continuously and the jungle tracks consisted for the most part of a mixture of mud and water. "The rains had now started in no mean fashion," wrote one officer, " and what with the Jap, the thick jungle, the hill and the weather, life was pretty unpleasant. However, having got practically to the top, some other units of the Division got behind the Jap, who very obligingly pulled out and saved us what would have been a most bloody battle on the crest. In spite of the fact that we didn't see a great deal of fighting on the way up, I liked this part of it least of all, as the jungle was very dense and you never quite knew where anybody else was; and wherever we went the Jap was always uphill, which is a beastly sensation." All supplies had to be carried by mule or porter—here the gallant Nagas were invaluable—but the mud made it a case of climbing two steps upwards and sliding back one. The steepness of the hillside made going for the mules difficult, and on one day a number of them fell over the side and down the steep drop, including one carrying the signal exchange.

The withdrawal of the Jap made it unnecessary to reach the crest of the spur; and the Battalion withdrew whence it came preparatory to taking part in the advance to Imphal: the battle for Kohima was over. As it did so, it suffered a loss which cannot pass unmentioned. The Padre, Captain Dick Rice, who had been with the Battalion since 1939, was ordered to leave the 2nd Division and take up the appointment of Senior Chaplain with the late General Wingate's Chindit Division. His departure was felt deeply by everyone "even by the most heathen," as one officer put it. Throughout the bitter fighting, both in the Arakan and of recent weeks, he had been quite magnificient, and wherever the struggle raged hottest, there he would be found tending the wounded and ministering to the dying. A gallant Padre is often an unsung hero of the battle; let Padre Rice's praise be sung here. He left the Battalion loved and respected by all.

It is perhaps necessary for one moment to turn aside to the wider picture of the Fourteenth Army's operations against the enemy. The battle in the Imphal plain was going well: once the Jap moved into it he was set upon with such ferocity by the Air Force and the troops of IVth Corps that he quickly retired back into the hills where he dug in and resisted stubbornly. As the battle went against him, troops of the 5th Indian Division began moving north towards Kohima just as troops of the XXXIIIrd Corps were breaking out of Kohima. The latter formation had by this time been reinforced by the 7th Indian Division from the Arakan; and the Division was ordered to march eastwards from Kohima into the jungle in a wide-sweeping arc to cut the Japs off from the Chindwin. At the same time the 2nd Division received its orders to drive straight down the road to Imphal, which it did, led by an armoured column, under a fire screen of guns, mortars, dive-bombers and fighters.

Not all that was going on elsewhere was clear to the Battalion, pre-occupied as it was with its own limited operations. After the Jap withdrawal, it waited patiently for the order to move forward. An entry in the War Diary of the 9th of June reads: " C.O. went down to milestone 58 to try to get the picture: moderate success." The rain continued to fall and the Battalion went on waiting. " Ready to move forward with the armoured column tomorrow," says the War Diary of the 14th; and then adds, " sudden invasion of the 2 i.c. by leeches led to hasty evacuation of the command post which was moved into a 15 cwt. truck! "

Although the enemy was now on the defensive, opposition was by no means negligible. Beyond Kohima he held the advantage in ground: the road to Imphal was carved out of the cliffside and moving off it meant going vertically up or down. The mountains here are immense and a Brigade could be swallowed up on any one feature; so discovering which the enemy occupied was like looking for a needle in a haystack.

On the 15th the long awaited move forward began. Trouble was soon forthcoming. At Khuzama, some miles along the road, one Japanese, with a magnetic mine strapped round his waist, leapt from the thick jungle on the right of the road on to the leading tank, blowing up both himself and the tank. At the same time fire was opened on the leading infantry, which halted the advance and involved the Battalion in quite a complicated manoeuvre to clear the road. The terrain was ideal for the Japs' rearguard action, and at one moment the Battalion would be leading the Brigade, then they would have to capture some Jap held feature and hold it, and no sooner was that done than the whole war would roar past them and they would be left miles behind till it was their turn to lead again. As each day went by the speed of the advance increased, turning retreat into rout. " It really was great fun," wrote one officer, "just like walking up partridges. We got them absolutely on the hop and the whole Battalion and attached troops were plugging away for dear life at the Japs, who were making off sideways up over the hill towards the Chindwin." Nevertheless, since the time that they had returned to the line, casualties had been steadily reducing rifle companies' strength and one of them totalled a mere forty-seven men when, on the 20th of June, a welcome batch of reinforcements arrived from an R.A.S.C. Company which had been disbanded to swell the ranks of the infantry.

To the Battalion fell the honour of linking up with the IVth Corps on the 22nd of June. 'A' Company took the lead as the Battalion moved off early on that morning. They were supported by tanks and carriers. Within a couple of miles the shooting started, but the opposition was not serious and turned out to be composed of those inmates of a Japanese hospital who were not too ill to walk. They had been told to go and stop the British Army until they were killed; and they had. They were disposed of without loss. The advance then continued; and, apart from a rather gentlemanly exchange of shots with some Japs clearing off over the hills and a brief encounter with a few more at milestone 108, the journey was uninterrupted! " Then," in the words of Sean Kelly, the company commander, " the tanks spotted more movements away forward where elephant grass gave way to trees and began to brass it up properly. Soon they stopped. A plaintive message relayed through many sets had reached them: we were brassing up the advance elements of the 5th Indian Division of the beleaguered IVth Corps! Imphal was relieved. We sat alone in the sunshine and smoked and ate. Soon the staff cars came purring both ways. The road was open again. It was a lovely day."

It was now merely a question of mopping up and scouring the countryside with patrols. Not all were as unfruitful as one whose exploits were laconically recorded in the War Diary: " battle patrol sent out to search villages Thumionkhongjai and Thumionkhuton for Japs. Didn't find Japs, but didn't find villages either." More often there would be traces of enemy or abandoned equipment and in some cases a prisoner might be captured. One patrol from ' D ' Company found twelve Japs in a basha, all quite exhausted and starved. The War Diary records that they " brought back one Captain, one Lance-Corporal and two superior privates as prisoners. One barbary Lieutenant shot. Remainder left." Of them Francis Greenwell wrote, " the company got four prisoners the other day—a thing we never got in the early days—an officer and three men all in a pretty bad state of repair. The officer was rather browned off and pretty uncommunicative, but the troops were very cheerful indeed, rather like dogs who expected a good hiding and got a good meal instead. They looked very much the animal type, and to see them sitting round the cookhouse eating away looked like the Chimpanzee tea party at the Zoo." However, these were isolated incidents. For the Battalion, at any rate, all serious fighting was for the moment over; and on the 4th of July it moved into a camp at milestone 86 where it remained until December.

The battle of Kohima had been arduous in the extreme. For the savagery of the fighting it may well be compared from the Regiment's point of view with the battle of Mareth. Losses had been grievous and in killed and missing the Battalion's were the heaviest in the Division. Over one hundred and fifty names of the Regiment are inscribed on the Divisional War Memorial on Garrison Hill.[1] The memorial takes the form of a huge monolith of natural stone, surrounded by a wall on which bronze plaques display the names of the fallen. Below it, in terraces, lie the white-crossed graves of the Divisional Cemetery. It is an impressive sight and the great stone—dragged to its position by the Nagas for miles across the hills as their own tribute to the fallen—looks down over the mountains and valleys which now lie quiet and tranquil. Time has mended the scars of battle and

---

[1] A Battalion War Memorial was also erected on Garrison Hill by the Battalion's Pioneers.

the Kohima landscape has regained the beauty that it had before the fighting. Cut into the stone are four lines which, in their striking simplicity, pay eloquent and moving tribute to those who fought and died amid those far away hills:

" When you go home
Tell them of us and say
For your tomorrow
We gave our to-day."

4

FROM THE CHINDWIN TO RANGOON

From July to December was a period of comparative peace. The Battalion made itself as comfortable as it could in its tented camp at Milestone 86. A new C.O. arrived in Lieutenant-Colonel C. A. Southey—although not of the Regiment he had served with the 17th Battalion in England—and Colonel Robinson bade farewell on returning to the Royal Berkshires as their new Commanding Officer. The Battalion was very sorry to see him go, for he had won their admiration and respect as soon as he took over command on Colonel Brown's death.

Rest, reorganisation and leave were the main preoccupations of the next few months as well as keeping dry: for the monsoon had arrived with a vengeance. Nor was training neglected. " This year " said General Slim, " we have thrashed the Japanese soldier, man for man and decisively. Next year we shall smash the Japanese Army." All training was devoted to making his promise a reality. Not least of the innovations for the Battalion was the formation of a Battalion Mule Platoon, a new departure which caused amusement and not a little confusion until the forty mules and those who looked after them had settled down in each other's company.

Although, however, the remaining months of 1944 were months of rest for the Battalion—as indeed for the whole of the 2nd Division—the war against the Jap was being vigorously pressed forward by other troops of the Fourteenth Army. The enemy was pursued to the frontier and then beyond it to the Chindwin river. Tired, exhausted, wracked by disease he gradually abandoned one position after another. By the beginning of December the 11th East African Division, who were leading the advance, had reached the Chindwin and, on the night of the 3rd, crossed over to establish the first major bridgehead. Once this bridgehead was established the stage was set for the drive to reach the open Burma plain: and the 2nd Division, fresh from its rest area in the hills moved down to the northern bank of the river ready to set foot upon the road to Mandalay.

The Battalion crossed the Chindwin on the 13th of December and marched downstream to Shwegyin some seven miles away. The rains were now over and the road was thick with dust. At Shwegyin it left the river and shortly afterwards joined the main road to Mandalay. This was well maintained, a good earth and gravel surface, and much easier going. Its verges were littered with scores of abandoned Jap transport and, indeed, at some points with wrecked guns and tanks left by General Alexander's Army in 1942.

The break out from the bridgehead was timed for the 20th and the task of the Battalion, as part of 6 Brigade, was to thrust eastwards along the main road as far as they could, if possible to Pinyaing, thirty-five miles away and half way to the plains. 'A' Company led the advance with orders to secure first a village which was seven miles ahead and then Thetkegyin which was twelve. This the Company did. There were no signs of Japs save for a few very dead ones and the print marks of the distinctive Japanese rubber soled boots in the dust. Thetkegyin was reached without incident and was found to be burnt out and silent.

Contact with the enemy was ultimately established on Christmas Eve by the Royal Berkshires who had taken over the role of leading battalion. It was surprising that there had been no opposition for thirty-five miles in country which was in many ways ideal for the defence, with extremely thick jungle and too many large trees to allow tanks to operate off the road. However, Christmas Day passed without the Battalion being involved in any fighting and even when, on the 27th, it became leading battalion once again it only experienced a brush with an enemy rearguard and one company had three men wounded. By the evening of the 27th the Battalion had pushed on beyond Pinyaing and occupied an island in the dry bed of the Sipadon Chaung.

The next day the Battalion left the main road in order to execute a left hook northwards while the rest of the Brigade and an armoured column drove on down it. Their route took them through several villages one of which, Paga, was on the Sipadon Chaung and reputedly occupied by a battalion of the enemy's 33rd Division. The 33rd Division were held in great respect; they were very tough and throughout the retreat through the rains their discipline remained unimpaired and they fought fanatically.

The track through thinnish jungle lay never far from the chaung but it was very bad, and the mortar carriers and jeeps found the going difficult. A small Jap rearguard party withdrew after slight opposition to 'D' Company after about ten miles' march; but real opposition materialised as the forward platoon of 'D' Company was half way across the four hundred yards wide chaung near Paga. The Company reacted quickly, putting down high explosive and smoke from mortars and trying to get covering parties to the flank; but the Japs were active with machine-guns and no immediate headway was possible. There was a long pause. Then, with supporting artillery in action and with 'A' Company crossing the chaung further up, the Battalion moved forward, the Jap withdrew and Paga was theirs. By then the sun was down and the moon was doing its best to shine through the gathering mist. "It was very cold and damp," wrote Sean Kelly. "The signal officer ran phones out and we closed the set. Pat—Pat Rome—a jazz fiend, sat up with the earphones on for almost an hour after I lay down, listening to Benny Goodman or some such man. He then lay down beside me and was snoring in five minutes. I was too cold about the feet to sleep easily and lay awake, hating Pat like hell!"

The Jap defence of Paga was typical of the sort of resistance he offered almost all the way to Mandalay. "Mainly light resistance," the communiqués no doubt called it, but it was stubborn and inflicted casualties. The truth was that the Japs had abandoned their intention of holding the advance west of the Irrawaddy. Besides the 2nd Division marching along the road to Shwebo, the 19th Indian Division was closing in further north and the 20th Indian Division further south. There, too, resistance was often bitter but the advance went relentlessly on, ahead of schedule, and the Jap defences crumbled.

On the morning of the 31st the Battalion was ordered to occupy a place called Kaduma. The airfield there had been seized by the armoured column earlier and the Royal Welch Fusiliers had raced ahead in trucks beyond it to seize Kabo Weir. The weir controls the irrigation of the great rice bowl stretching in a broad wedge down the Irrawaddy and the orders were to secure it intact if possible. It was something of a historic day for the Battalion. After five hundred miles of jungle since Dimapur the country now changed. About midday the Battalion debouched into the Burma plain. On either side the land was flat and open. Here and there were clumps of palm trees; and a few white pagodas stood out brightly against the blue sky and golden paddy. The jungle had been left behind at last.

The day will be remembered for another reason too. The Jap air force made its first air raid on the road. The leading company of the Battalion escaped with only one man wounded, but further back, where the cover was not so good, there were some twenty hit, though none really badly. However, it never rains but it pours, and not least of the casualties was the three ton lorry which for days had been following the marching column with the Battalion's load of Christmas beer!

Two days' rest followed the days of marching but on the 2nd of January, 1945, the Battalion relieved the Royal Welch Fusiliers at Kabo Weir. The Japs were still at the far side of it and for several days more continued to hold on. The weir was finally captured intact with the aid of an airstrike on the 5th; and the Battalion was treated to a further few days of inactivity before marching south to catch up with the leading brigades of 2nd Division who had passed through to capture Yeu and Shwebo. During this lull Colonel Southey said goodbye to the Battalion on posting to an appointment back in Imphal and he was succeeded by " Tank " Waterhouse who was to remain in command till the end of the war. Colonel Waterhouse had joined the Regiment as an emergency commissioned officer early in 1940 and the Battalion at Huddersfield just after its return from Dunkirk. He had remained with it ever since and had now the distinction of being the only war-time commissioned officer to command a battalion of the Regiment.

On the 15th the Battalion set off south-eastwards in the wake of the rest of the division. It marched for three days through the open rice bowl, moving usually in single file along the banks of the many irrigation canals. It must have smelt pretty opulent at this time as practically everybody was smoking the excellent Burma cheroots which were produced in the area at about three shillings a hundred. Anyway the advance continued enveloped in a cloud of blue smoke!

The crossing of the Irrawaddy was now imminent and the Battalion moved south to a village called Ngatayaw, which was less than a mile north of the river. For two weeks it busied itself with preparations for the crossing. Every night reconnaissance and ambush patrols were sent out, the former to gain information regarding the northern bank, the latter to lie up in wait for Japanese patrols who were crossing from the south to the north bank fairly frequently. One of these latter ventured into Ngatayaw one moonlight night with the result that a fortunate Corporal of ' D ' Company killed the officer and three men of the patrol and became the proud possessor of a fine officer's sword and an excellent Luger pistol.

The actual crossing by the 2nd Division was timed for the night of the 25th of February and the initial assault was to be by 5 Brigade. It went anything but smoothly. The rubber boats containing the first flights were many of them sunk before they got far from the home bank, and by the morning of the 26th the bridgehead on the far side consisted of little more than a company of Cameron Highlanders. However, things improved as the day wore on and the Sappers did wonders in getting tanks over on rafts; so that by the time it was the Battalion's turn to cross the situation was relatively stable.

The night before the crossing began the Battalion, oddly enough, had a visit from the divisional concert party; they were accompanied by Miss Frances Day, whose appearance was a real morale booster, not least, it may be added, when she stood conspicuously on the northern river bank and was only just restrained from crossing in one of the assault craft. In due course the Battalion crossed the river in dukws at about 2.30 p.m. and without a single casualty; but a few Japs were firmly embedded in the steep banks on the right flank of the crossing and inflicted heavy casualties on any craft carried downstream from the main crossing area.

The bridgehead was still very shallow and the Battalion dug in on the flat ground about two hundred yards from the river and a mile west of the village of Ngazun. The soil was very light and digging was easy. The fields were full of ripe tomatoes, so many in fact that it was possible to pluck them from one's slit trench; and they were a welcome addition to the half rations on which, due to the rapid advance, the whole Fourteenth Army was living. However, there was little time to sit still and two attacks were necessary before the bridgehead could be considered finally secure. One, which involved two companies, was put in on a ridge of low hills about three miles inland and took the position at the small cost of two men killed and an officer and six men wounded. Thirty-five dead Japs were counted in fox-holes on the position which, it was later learnt, the Jap commander had ordered a party of thirty-five men to hold to the last man and last round. The other attack, which was launched the following morning, was against a village about a mile to the south and was supported by tanks of the 3rd Carabiniers. Again it was successful, though the communications with the tanks left much to be desired. Sean Kelly had an unpleasant few moments climbing atop a tank and beating hard on the turret to draw the commander's attention while Jap bullets flew around him in all directions. Although the Japs were taking a beating they fought as fanatically as ever. One of the tank commanders was driving with his turret open when a Jap officer leapt from a bank on to the tank, decapitated the commander with his sword, climbed inside and stabbed the gunner to death and then fought with the driver for possession of the gunner's pistol. The driver fortunately won. In the same action a company commander of the Royal Berkshires—who were attacking parallel with the Battalion—was attacked by a large unarmed Jap who embedded his teeth in the company commander's throat.

Fanaticism, however, was of little avail in the deteriorating position in which the Japanese Army was in fact placed; and it is as well to recall the course of events elsewhere during the past few weeks. The 2nd Division's crossing of the Irrawaddy was in fact the last of several such crossings, all designed to delude the enemy as to exactly where the main thrust for Mandalay was to be made. The 19th Indian Division had crossed as early as the 14th of January, some forty miles north of Mandalay, and exactly a month later the 7th Indian Division—the spearhead of the reorganised IVth Corps from Imphal—had thrust across well to the south near Pakkoku, and with the 17th Indian Division was streaming towards Meiktila, an important base in the Japanese rear. Meanwhile another Indian Division, the 20th, had made a crossing a few days before that of the 2nd Division and to the west of it. By the beginning of March both Divisions had linked up; whereupon the 20th struck south and east while the 2nd marched due east towards the main Mandalay-Meiktila road ready for an attack on Mandalay from the south.

The Japanese Army had in fact been dealt a blow from which it was never effectively to recover. It was hardly surprising, therefore, that the sort of opposition which the Battalion met during the weeks following its crossing of the Irrawaddy was, for the most part, of a minor character and not very well co-ordinated. Between the 8th and the 24th of March the Battalion pushed east towards the Mandalay-Meiktila road, secured it, crossed it and then moved on to positions along the Myttinge river. Opposition, such as it was, was scrappy and consisted of occasional brushes with scattered enemy parties or the odd encounter at night with small bodies of retreating Japs who blundered into the Battalion's positions by mistake.

On one of these occasions two Japs on bicycles managed to free-wheel silently down the road through a section of machine-gunners and on through the Battalion position! Fortunately, however, they fell into a trench dug alongside the road, the occupant of which was a large corporal—" Big " Bowman of ' B ' Company—who strangled one and killed the other with his bayonet. And honour was satisfied.

On another occasion ' A ' Company was sent to the rescue of a convent which housed a community of Anglo-Burmese Christians under the care of some thirty nuns of all nationalities. The Japs had apparently been arriving in the village where the convent stood and been laying their hands on whatever they could. The nuns were very frightened and the Mother Superior had appealed for protection.

The village round the convent was large and the Company

could only hold one end of it and patrol. There was a stone church but the convent itself was built of teak. So when the Japs appeared on the night the Company arrived and began throwing phosphorus bombs in the village, it was not long before the convent as well as many of the tinder dry huts was alight. Aided by the nuns, who were a model of calmness, the Company shepherded all the women and children into the church and then set a guard around it. The convent went up with a roar and the Japs fired off everything they had. Altogether it was a nerve-wracking night; and it was a relief next morning for the Company to conduct their charges to the transport which had been sent to remove them to safety. As a parting gift, the Mother Superior presented the Company with what was left of the convent's collection of livestock. So when it was all over the Company marched back to the Battalion with the prospect of roast chicken and duck and with Sergeant-Major Joseph Noble carefully guarding two enormous geese which were christened George and Margaret.

By the 24th of March the battle for Mandalay, begun by the 19th Division on the 7th, was all but complete. Nor was the Battalion involved in the actual fighting in Mandalay itself. That task fell to troops of 4 and 5 Brigades who had seized Ava and marched into the southern part of the city. In fact the Battalion remained where it was for the rest of the month. The War Diary of the 28th could comfortably record: "The Battalion remained in the same area, resting and swimming in the Myttinge river; and sightseeing tours were arranged to Mandalay City."

Apart from the retreating Jap columns and a few stubborn pockets holding out, the north of Burma was liberated.

*   *   *   *   *   *

With the fall of Mandalay the Fourteenth Army was regrouped for the next stage of the advance in which Rangoon was inevitably the main objective. The IVth Corps, which had so successfully disrupted the Jap supply lines and their base at Meiktila, was now ordered to drive southwards along the main road to the capital; while the XXXIIIrd Corps turned aside and pushed down the Irrawaddy valley through the oilfields towards

Prome. So, on the 31st of March, the Battalion found itself on the move again making for Myingyan, fifty miles to the south-west and about fifty miles north of the oil town of Chauk. There it dug in and spent a comparatively peaceful week doing nothing in particular.

The Battalion had been in its new location only a few days when it received orders, which at first it could hardly believe, that the whole of the 2nd Division was to be flown out of Burma to Calcutta in order to act as follow up Division in the seaborne assault on Rangoon. This project was very welcome to everyone: at last there was a prospect of using some of the experience gained in two years' hard training in combined operations!

The flight began in the early afternoon of the 7th of April. That night the planes touched down at Dohazari, just south of Chittagong, now a busy base compared with the cluster of huts which the Battalion had passed through two and a half years before. Several days later, after a further journey by rail and river, the Battalion found itself in camp in a mango grove at Bandel some twenty miles outside Calcutta. Here for three weeks it re-equipped itself, fed off hospital rations to bring everybody back to full weight again, brushed up its knowledge of amphibious operations, and found a little time to drink and be merry and snatch a spot of leave in Calcutta. Then, on the 28th, the Battalion embarked from Calcutta docks in the transport " Dilwara " and steamed south towards Rangoon.

The assault on Rangoon in fact took the form of a sledge hammer cracking a nut. The convoy had only reached Ranree Island, just south of Akyab, when the news was received that the city had fallen, without opposition, to the leading troops of the 26th Indian Division—the Division chosen to carry out the initial seaborne assault. The Battalion therefore sailed quietly up the Rangoon river, disembarked at the jetties on the morning of the 13th of May and marched off to Jacob Barracks at Mingaladon through streets ankle deep in Japanese printed currency of all denominations.

As it turned out, the war had just three months more to run, though no one knew it then. But for the Battalion it was virtually over. For the next two months or so their main task was the occupation of various villages down river from Pegu, the rounding up of stragglers from the Japanese Army cut off to the west of the Pegu-Mandalay road and the chasing of bandits. On the 15th of June the Battalion had the honour of representing the 2nd Division in the victory parade before Lord Louis Mountbatten in the battered streets of Rangoon, and was the largest single contingent in a parade which included troops of many Allied nations. On the 20th news of a Japanese force crossing the Sittang river and the possibility of an enemy thrust towards Rangoon or Pegu resulted in more patrolling to the banks of that river. But, apart from an occasional exchange of fire with stragglers, there was little action of an organised kind. By the end of the month there was talk of repatriation and preparations were being made to replace those who were due to go home; a month later some were actually preparing to go. Then on the 15th of August Japan surrendered and all organised resistance in Burma ceased.

The Battalion remained for only a short time longer in Burma. Many of its members were due for repatriation, which the end of the war was now to accelerate. The Battalion as such moved back to India in September to reform with new officers and men for occupation duties in Japan itself. But it left those due for repatriation behind, and they in their turn sailed home from Rangoon in October. The Battalion which had fought from the Arakan to Kohima, and from Kohima to Rangoon, was in fact no more: and a new one was now to reform upon the bare framework of the old.

'A' Company of the 2nd Battalion link up with troops of the 5th Indian Division on the Kohima-Imphal road

Men of 'A' Company of the 2nd Battalion on Pagoda Hill, Yzagyo

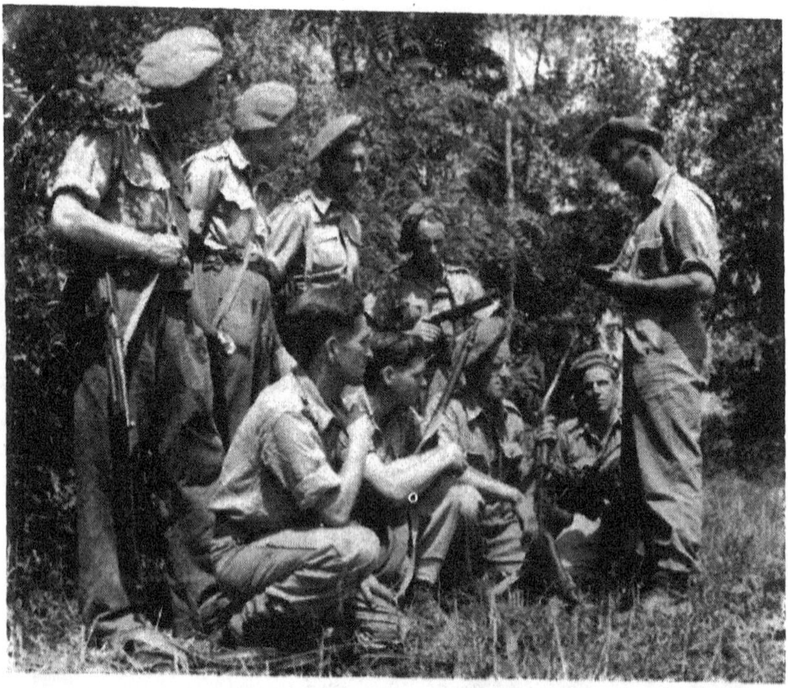

Imperial War Museum

A patrol of the 1st Battalion near Citta di Castello, Italy

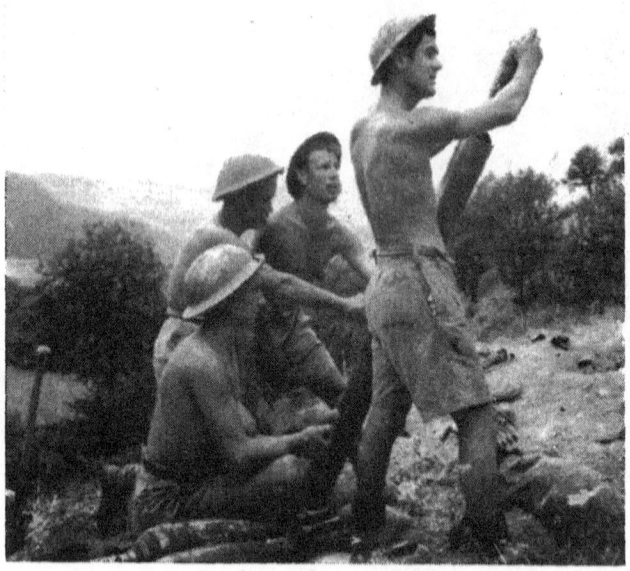

The 1st Battalion Mortars in action, July 1944

CHAPTER SEVEN

The 1st Battalion in the Mediterranean 1943-1945

I

COS

THE end of June 1943 found the Battalion once more back in Egypt. The tide of war had turned. The Eighth Army had smashed its way across the desert into Tunisia and, with the First, had swept the Germans and Italians from the North African shore. Already plans for the invasion of Sicily were in train and the assault forces—among them 151 Brigade— were rehearsing in the Gulf of Aqaba for the landing. But none of this was for the 1st Durham Light Infantry. While the battle of Sicily was being fought and won, the Battalion was absorbed into the usual cycle of Middle East training—in boats in the Bitter Lakes, on foot in Palestine and up mountain sides in Syria. In due course it joined the 10th Indian Division and by the end of August was encamped on the Syrian coast at Insayria. Here, in September, it received the glad news that Italy had capitulated: and shortly afterwards, under sealed orders, it was ordered to move to Ramat David airfield. There, in the early hours of the 16th, 'C' Company and Colonel Kirby climbed aboard transport aircraft and learnt that their destination was the Italian island of Cos in the Dodecanese.

The island was occupied by some 3,000 Italians and contained the only airstrip in the Dodecanese except for those at Rhodes. The Battalion's task was to seize the Cos airfield with a view to an air build-up for subsequent operations against Rhodes. What sort of a reception it would get was a matter of conjecture. A few German technicians were known to be on the island though in view of the capitulation of their country, the Italians were thought to have downed tools.

For the most part the island is a mixture of rugged and rolling hills. It is some twenty-eight miles long and six miles wide. An abrupt ridge of hard limestone extends from Cape Phoca at its eastern end almost to Antimachia in the middle. At its highest the ridge tops 2,800 feet. On its south face it is very steep and rugged save for the deep sheltered valleys which converge on Kardomena on the coast. Northward the steep crest is soon covered by soft marls and sandstones which slope gently down to a coastal plain intersected by torrent beds. At the bottom of the limestone ridge are numerous deep-seated springs and, though an aqueduct supplies Cos town, the principal village sites are decided by them. The southern slopes of the ridge are pastured, the upper are terraced for olives and vines and are fertile because they are watered. Over the rolling country below grow vines and corn.

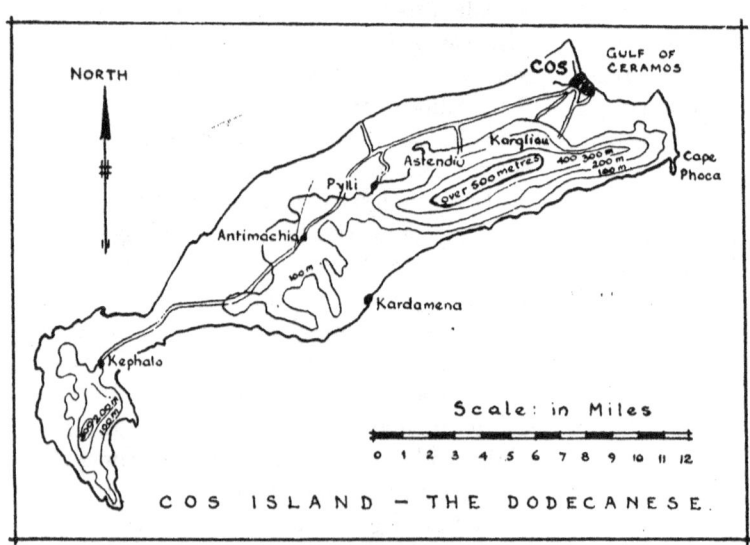

15. *Cos*

Just east of Antimachia—where the airstrip was sited—the limestone ridge disappears and the country forms continuous rolling upland from sea to sea. The northern coastline consists of open beach intersected by torrent beds; but the southern is mostly cliff and, below the main ridge, the hills overhang the sea and the coastline is dotted with dangerous rocks and reefs.

It was a lovely day as the first planes touched down on the airfield to find, to their pleasure, that a South African Spitfire squadron had arrived shortly before them, together with a company of Parachutists. But it was another two days before the bulk of the Battalion had arrived, and by that time the German air force was beginning to make itself more than a nuisance. Fighters began to sweep the island and bombers to drop their loads on the airstrip. So crater filling became a top priority in order to keep the strip in action; and 'C' Company was ordered to move into Cos town to help unload the ships which were beginning to bring in much needed supplies.

'A' Company was the last of the rifle companies to arrive and found the airstrip badly damaged and littered with burning aircraft. It was, however, still just usable. But the Company unfortunately lost one of its platoons on the way when the Dakota carrying it came down in the sea. The occupants were picked up by a Turkish cutter but, despite a dash by a Royal Naval motor launch, the Turks refused to hand over. It was suspected that they got head money! At all events the platoon had to spend a short while in internment in Turkey and 'A' Company had to get on without it!

The end of the first forty-eight hours found all the rifle companies except 'C' in position around the airfield; but neither Support Company nor the transport had yet arrived as they were due to come in by sea. The Italians did not prove to be actively hostile though they would not co-operate in any way. But German aircraft were increasingly attentive, and, indeed, made air support for the troops on the ground extremely difficult. An attempt was made to bring in Hurricanes and Spitfires and an alternative strip was begun on the outskirts of Cos and on the salt pans three miles away. Over a period two squadrons were landed but they were shot up as soon as they touched down; and though Beaufighter patrols were started they could only be maintained over the island for a short while owing to the distance from their base; and in any case they were no match for the more manoeuvrable Messerschmitts.

It was not till the end of September that the whole of the Battalion was concentrated in the island. By then enemy bombing had increased still further. Many of the planes were Junkers 88s, painted white and obviously diverted from Russia. The airstrip at Antimachia was straddled daily and casualties in men and stores began to mount. It became increasingly obvious that the air strip was useless and it was pointless to do anything about it without planes; and these did not seem to be forthcoming. So it was not surprising that orders were shortly issued to 'A' and 'B' Companies to move eastwards towards Cos town, leaving 'D' behind under Captain John Thorpe to hold the airstrip as best it could. 'A' and 'B' Companies' new area was in some olive groves about five miles west of the port and their new task was to help make another landing ground on the salt pans.

On the night of the 3rd of October there was more than usual German air activity. It was suspected that saboteurs had been dropped by parachute. As dawn broke the air was heavy with the throb of aircraft engines, small arms fire was heard along the coast to the north-west, and a battery of Italian 75 millimetres opened fire. Line communication between the Battalion and 'D' Company on the airfield was cut and—though it was not known until later—German parachutists landed at Antimachia. Colonel Kirby was in hospital while all this was going on and Hugh Vaux, deputising for him, ordered the Battalion to take up positions astride the main Cos-Antimachia road. The enemy could actually be seen landing on the salt pans and 'C' Company, which was in position on the edge of the town, was ordered to send a platoon to investigate a reported landing on the south side of the island. The carrier platoon, without their carriers though with jeeps instead, went forward at once from the Battalion positions; but they clashed head on with some Germans moving down the Cos-Antimachia road and Lieutenant George Sievwright, the commander, and his driver were killed by a burst of fire from point blank range.

The battle for the island had now really begun. Colonel Kirby, as soon as he heard the news, jumped on a motor cycle and was soon back with the Battalion. In the short time available before the Germans could arrive in strength, every effort was made to improve existing positions, though this was not easy as the ground was hard and rocky and only a few tools were available. Soon Stuka dive-bombers appeared and began bombing each company area; and as anti-aircraft weapons were few and far between, and as there were even fewer British aircraft, they were able to circle around at their leisure until a suitable target presented itself. Then German infantry were seen forming up in about battalion strength and the fighting began in earnest.

A pitched battle between the Battalion and the enemy raged throughout the day. Mortars supporting 'B' Company to the north of the road, opened fire with good effect. The Germans attacked frontally and tried to work round both flanks; and after stubborn resistance the leading platoons of 'B' Company were over-run and the Company lost touch with 'A' on its left, south of the road. Each company owed much to Regimental Sergeant-Major Flanagan whose untiring efforts kept them supplied with ammunition and to John Bush, the Quartermaster, who got food up to the forward areas despite intense fire and the shelling and mortaring of his stores area. But the fact was that the Battalion was heavily out-numbered and it was only a matter of time before it would be forced to withdraw if it was to maintain itself as a fighting entity.

Meanwhile, at Antimachia, 'D' Company fought hard against German parachutists before they too were over-run. The Germans landed in a number of places near the airstrip and were able to establish themselves before the Company could reach them. The Company fought until its members were almost all either killed, wounded or taken prisoner, though a few got away into the hills. John Thorpe and Sergeant-Major Wally Carr both managed to evade capture, but Thorpe had a severe wound in the back and was forced to surrender after several days in the hills. Carr was luckier and managed to escape from the island and rejoin the Battalion later.

By 5 p.m. the Companies guarding Cos—except 'A' Company, south of the road, who were still out of touch with the rest of the Battalion—were ordered to withdraw into the outskirts of the town itself. In the fluctuating fortune of battle heavy casualties had been inflicted on the Germans, but the Battalion had suffered too, and its strength now consisted of a little less than two hundred. 'A' Company, under Captain Jim Gray, had now only forty men left and it withdrew westwards to the area of an Italian 75 millimetre gun battery which was still in action though under heavy air attack. The Italians were hard pressed not only from the air but also from an infantry attack from both east and west made by Germans who had landed on the south-eastern part of the island. Gray offered his men's help in any capacity and remained alongside the Italians till it got dark. Then the Germans closed in on the positions, lit flares, began their evening meal and even sang songs! Gray collected his men and prepared to attack with the bayonet when a lone anti-aircraft gunner appeared with the news that the rest of the Battalion was in Cos. Gray, therefore, concluded that discretion was the better part of valour and set off at once with his men for Battalion Headquarters.

At the approaches to the town the remains of 'B' and Headquarter Companies had joined 'C' in forming a defensive perimeter. Fighting continued till it was dark. Captain " Beagle " Birchenough, with the anti-tank platoon, succeeded in preventing the enemy from working round the right flank though in the later stages of the afternoon his men had suffered many casualties. For a time they had been guarding an emergency landing ground which came under heavy fire from the enemy. Indeed, during the withdrawal Birchenough twice went back under fire and brought in two men who had been badly wounded; and when it was completed he went out alone to a wood where an abandoned Spitfire was concealed and set it on fire to prevent it falling into enemy hands.

It was a case of all hands to the pumps in the new perimeter. John Bush, after valiant efforts all day to keep the Battalion supplied, moved into the line with his staff—still wearing his green fore and aft cap!—and himself manned a forward post near the main road. Soon afterwards the C.O. summoned an 'O' Group under cover of some buildings on the outskirts of the town; but it had no sooner assembled than several enemy mortar bombs landed on the very spot and the C.O., Mark Leather— commanding Headquarter Company—and Jack Stafford were all wounded and John Bush so badly that he died shortly afterwards. This was a heavy blow: and when Topper Browne evacuated the wounded to a small convent hospital in the town, Hugh Vaux, who assumed command, ordered him to go to Force Headquarters for orders. As a result the Battalion was ordered to stand fast for the present but the new C.O. was to report to Force Headquarters at 8 p.m. for further instructions.

When Hugh Vaux returned from Force Headquarters that night he brought with him the last desperate instructions for a force which was outnumbered, badly in need of reinforcements which it would never receive, and completely lacking in air support. Indeed the orders which he brought signified the end of organised resistance on the island: for the Battalion was to split into small parties of about a dozen, make for the hills and rendezvous at the small village of Kargiou which lay between Cos and Antimachia, some three miles west of the main road. From there they were to carry on the struggle in the rôle of guerrillas.

Parties set off independently, carrying what they could in addition to weapons. One platoon with some mortars was left to cover the evacuation till two o'clock the following morning. In most cases each man had two bandoliers of ammunition and a tin of food and two blankets were carried by each party. Very naturally all movement had to be by night which did not make things easy: the country was rough and rocky, progress was slow, falls frequent and the language unprintable! Each party lay up during the day and kept a wary eye open for German patrols who were beginning to be fairly active in the hills; and, indeed, a serious game of hide and seek ensued. Several clashes occurred and some parties were taken prisoner. Many men were soon in no fit state to continue, having run out of food and had no sleep for days; others fell victim to malaria. Nevertheless, parties gradually began to arrive near Kargiou where they concealed themselves and posted sentries.

What remained of the Battalion by this time comprised a fairly mixed bag. There were only about sixty of them all told, but numbers were augmented by a few sappers and gunners and men of the Royal Air Force Regiment. What did not help matters, however, was the fact that the rendezvous—reputedly an Italian food dump—was occupied by the Germans and any hope of either a firm base or a supply of food was gone. The food situation was thus critical and water could only be obtained from springs which were few and far between. A curious dish of mixed margarine and jam was eaten with some relish for want of anything better and was supplemented, when opportunity offered, by mountain goat. What these survivors of the battle would have done without the help of Greek shepherds, who generously gave whatever they had, it is difficult to imagine.

When, after nearly ten days in the hills, it was clear that all was lost and that the survivors were unfit to carry out any further offensive operations, plans were made for escape from the island. The nearest part of the Turkish coastline was some ten miles away to the south and from it a lighthouse could be seen flashing each night with maddening persistence. At all events it was decided to build a raft and with it to ferry a small party across to Turkey, there to obtain boats with which to return and evacuate the remainder. A Greek carpenter was persuaded to help in this venture and he built a raft which was hidden in a cave near the beach.

A small party was in due course selected to make the precipitous descent from the cliffs above the beach down to the cave where the raft was hidden. It consisted of a sapper colonel, Topper Browne, two men from the Battalion, five sappers and two gunners. But when they reached the cave they found, to their surprise and delight, a Captain Milner Barry, of the Special Boat Service, who had recently been landed on the island to try to round up survivors. They were indeed glad to see him; and as it happened he had already picked up Captain Frank Armitage and Sergeant Fishwick, both of whom had been with the rearguard left at Cos to cover the Battalion's withdrawal. They had both had a few adventures too; for their party had been overrun by the Germans as they made for the foothills; both had been captured; and both had managed to escape.

Milner Barry's timely arrival somewhat naturally caused a change of plan: for he brought the glad news that a naval caïque was due to put in to the island the following night to take him off with any survivors he had collected. It was doubtful whether it could accommodate everybody but at any rate they were all speedily assembled in the cave and the final decision as to how many could go aboard was left to the skipper of the caïque when it should arrive.

The boat was timed to appear at 2 a.m. and with naval precision it arrived on time. The skipper decided to embark everyone and so, by means of a rubber dinghy, some eight officers and sixty men clambered aboard and set off out to sea. It was the 13th of October, ten days since the Germans landed on the island and the end of a hard and gruelling struggle against the enemy and against Nature herself.

It was not, however, quite the end of this adventure. The

caïque made straight for Turkey and shortly before dawn everybody was told to dispose of their arms; for a secret base was their destination and the Turks would only permit a landing on the pretext that those brought ashore were ship-wrecked hospital cases. The base—used by the Special Boat Service—was in direct wireless touch with London and was closely supervised by Turkish soldiers who refused to fraternise. From here the men of the Battalion were taken, again by caïque, to Castelrosso, passing on their way under the very noses of the Germans at Rhodes and within sight, incidentally, of enemy aircraft landing and taking off on the airfield there: it was not a particularly comfortable journey, not least because of a severe storm which blew up and, as one officer put it, made the voyage not unlike one of St. Paul's journeys in these waters. It was a relieved, if scruffy, party which landed at Castelrosso three days later.

But the Battalion's travels were still not at an end. A short stay on the island in billets, shared with a company of Italians who had deserted from Rhodes, allowed everybody to make up for lost sleep; but not perhaps for as much as many would have liked because their arrival appeared to coincide with a succession of enemy air raids. These had their lighter moments —if one may put it that way—particularly when Captain Armitage mistook a deep trench latrine for an Italian slit trench with most unfortunate results for himself and his neighbours. But that is by the way. While everybody enjoyed some rest and relaxation the C.O., Hugh Vaux, was flown by sea plane to Middle East Headquarters to report on the operations; the men of the Battalion continued their journey without him; and they were not reunited until they finally arrived in Egypt.

From Castelrosso the next stop was Cyprus. Embarkation took place in an air raid and the caïque in which the journey was to be made had to be shared with the Italian deserters and some fifty women and children. The skipper of the boat was a Greek who had been shot up by enemy aircraft on a previous trip and had a nasty wound in his chest. The weather was again extremely rough and the scene in the hold had to be seen to be believed. Sanitary arrangements were primitive, to put it mildly, and at least one member of the Battalion preferred a precarious hold below the bowsprit to the provisions made on deck! However, after two days' sailing the weather improved even though the boat's engine broke down into the bargain. It was possible to sunbathe on deck and some even went overboard for a swim. Regimental Sergeant-Major Flanagan reached the peak of popularity because in some unexplained manner he was still the proud owner of some " V " cigarettes! But the offending engine was ultimately re-started and though, within sight of Cyprus, it broke down once more the caïque limped into the harbour of Famagusta two nights later and disgorged its human cargo with no further mishap. The men were ushered into the nearest transit camp and the officers into the St. George Hotel which at two o'clock in the morning rose to the occasion with turkey sandwiches, brandy, black coffee and feather beds! The age of wonders was not yet over!

2

ITALY

By the end of October the remnants of the Battalion were concentrated once more in Egypt at the Infantry Base Depot at Geneifa. They consisted of nine officers and one hundred and twenty rank and file. The burning question of the day was whether the Battalion would be sent home to re-form or whether the necessary reinforcements to bring it up to strength could be found on the spot. Any illusions about going home were, however, speedily dispelled by G.H.Q. who pointed out that there were nearly a thousand members of the Regiment extra-regimentally employed in the Middle East. True though this may have been, it was not easy to find the men in practice. Some were of low medical category; others were destined to rejoin 151 Brigade; and, to make things more difficult, a number of the existing Battalion were due for repatriation. By the 21st of November, when the Battalion moved from Geneifa to Mena near Cairo, its total strength was sixteen officers and just over a hundred other ranks. But from then on it began to fill out. At the end of November " Crackers " May rejoined as second in command from 4 Parachute Brigade in Italy; and in fact he took command while Colonel Vaux flew home to report on the Cos operations. At about the same time four officers and a hundred and fifty-nine other ranks arrived as reinforcements from the 17th Battalion in England, and it was possible to form two rifle companies and the basis for Support Company. Later, after the base camps had been combed for men of north country Regiments, two more rifle companies were able to be formed; Company Sergeant-Major George Scott rejoined from Malta as Regimental Sergeant-Major and 2nd Echelon, after a struggle, yielded up Quartermaster-Sergeant Jock Pirie as R.Q.M.S. By the end of December the Battalion was about four hundred strong and beginning to take shape.

In January Colonel Vaux returned from England and platoon and company training began. Yet the Battalion's future still remained in the balance. One scheme afoot was to send it as a garrison battalion to Khartoum: but this fortunately fell through and it continued to train with the object of joining a Division as soon as it was ready once more to fight.

By the end of March sufficient reinforcements had at last been received to bring the Battalion approximately up to strength. The men were from every conceivable Regiment—in fact twenty-nine different Regiments were represented by drafts of five or more—but slightly over a third were originally Durham Light Infantrymen. An increasing number of visits by Colonel Vaux to G.H.Q., talks with the Quartermaster and the re-appearance of anti-malarial tablets made it obvious that something was in the wind and, in fact, the C.O. had been told that the Battalion would move by the end of April. Everybody's guess was that their destination would be Italy; the only question was whether the Battalion would join a British division or the 10th Indian Division to which it was attached before the Cos adventure.

The Battalion began its final training early in April. At the same time it began drawing stores and equipment for battle. There was naturally a lot to be done; and just as everybody was fully occupied doing it, orders were received to move to Amriya near Alexandria. The Greek Brigade, stationed nearby, had mutinied and the Battalion was to form part of a scratch force to watch and then disarm them.

This was somewhat disconcerting at a time of packing up and drawing of kit, but it also afforded a first class opportunity for the Battalion to shake down before it left Egypt. This little episode did not, however, last long. It was over in about ten days; for just as the Battalion was about to lay on an attack it was relieved and went back to Mena to make final preparations for departure. On the 30th of April it set sail for Italy.

The Battalion disembarked at Taranto on the 4th of May and within a few days the C.O. took an advance party up to the 10th Indian Division which was in the line just north of Ortona on the Adriatic coast. The Battalion was to fill the remaining vacancy for a British Battalion in 10 Indian Brigade alongside the 4th/10th Baluch Regiment and the 2nd/4th Gurkha Rifles. Although it was hoped that there might be a few weeks for training under conditions similar to those in the line, this was not to be. Almost before it had collected itself, certainly before its transport was complete, the Battalion found itself taking over 10 Brigade's reserve positions from the 4th/10th Baluch. It was back in action again, re-formed and re-equipped in little more than six months.

The first few weeks in the line were comparatively peaceful. The sector was quiet. With the approach of spring it was beginning to wake out of its winter sleep; and anyhow, by the 7th of June, the 10th Indian Division had been relieved by the 4th Indian Division and the Battalion moved to Venafro for some mountain training. Whilst there " Topper " Browne—one of the originals—left to be repatriated, having been continuously with the Battalion since he joined it in 1922. By the end of the month the whole Division had moved forward to Perugia, which had just been captured, and the Battalion took over from the 2nd Rifle Brigade about one and a half miles north of the town. Battalion Headquarters was in the Villa Albini, owned by a certain Signor Sarti who was famous for his brandy and liqueurs, a large stock of which the Germans had fortunately left behind. Rome had fallen to the Allies on the 4th of June and the 10th Indian Division stood ready for an advance up the Tiber valley through the heart of the mountains.

" The average width of the Tiber valley above Perugia is somewhat under a mile. The lateral valleys which feed the great Roman river are of no particular length or depth: after entering the foothills they quickly deteriorate into bush filled gullies impassable to all but the goat footed. Two roads, one on each bank, follow the Tiber meanders. At intervals of from ten to twelve miles flourishing market towns have grown up around the sites of old castles and fortifications, usually on a bend or loop of the river. On the high ridges and saddle-backs small villages tightly cluster around the churches, whose towers or spires afford observation over miles of countryside ... At the end of June the cereal crops had been harvested and the luxuriant fruits for which the valley is famed were still unripe. On the high wooded crests the foresters were cutting and peeling pine, beech and larch logs, to be slid into the valleys on the first snows."[1]

Through this country the Battalion slogged its way for the next three months, beginning on the 2nd of July by occupying the Cardinal's Palace near San Giovanni—a rather surprising combination of Palace and Stud Farm which, with pictures slashed, curtains and carpets ripped and filth littering the floors and walls, provided a classic example of wanton destruction by the Germans—and finishing up towards the end of September facing the Gothic Line. By that time command of the Battalion had passed to "Crackers" May, for Colonel Vaux, after six years abroad, had returned to England on the 12th of September. At the same time Major John Taylor, of the Regiment, rejoined as second in command after an absence from the Battalion of over five years. By then, too, the Germans had been ejected from the upper Arno and Tiber valleys and had withdrawn into the shelter of their newly prepared defensive barrier on the wall of the High Apennines.

The Battalion had three months of hard if unspectacular fighting between July and September. Though unspectacular, casualties took their toll; and the Battalion was ultimately reduced to three rifle companies, each of which was under strength. Ordinary routine required a good many patrols. On one, in mid July, Lieutenant Wally Howard and one of his men were killed and Lance-Corporal Peter Thorogood was wounded trying to bring Howard in and in fact bringing in another wounded man. On another Captain Mitchell, a seconded South African officer, led a patrol a mile and a half into the enemy lines but on returning, after successfully locating certain enemy positions, trod on a mine which blew his leg off

[1] "The Tiger Triumphs: The story of three great Divisions in Italy." p. 88.

below the knee. As his wounds were being tended the patrol was attacked. He would have been a tremendous hindrance to the patrol on the way back, which involved crossing a river, and he gallantly ordered them to return without him but with the information they had won. He himself was, of course, captured; but he managed to smuggle a message to an Italian priest who delivered it to the Battalion when it later occupied the area. Yet again, in September, Lieutenant Ferguson and twenty men went out to discover the strength of the enemy in the village of Bulciano—and to occupy it if it was not held. The patrol was, however, seen and heavily engaged with small arms and artillery fire just short of the village. One man was killed and four wounded; and there would have been more but for magnificent shooting by ' P ' Battery of the Leicestershire Yeomanry directed by the Battery commander, Major Arthur Hazelrigg. The guns covered the withdrawal of the patrol and enabled Ferguson to get all his men, including the wounded, back to the foot of the hill by nightfall and without further loss. As it was impossible to bring the wounded up the slope in the dark, a party of stretcher bearers, led by Padre George Parr carrying a Red Cross flag, went down with mules at first light next day to bring them in. As a precautionary measure the divisional artillery and a medium regiment stood ready to fire on Bulciano but fortunately did not have to. The patrol owed much to Hazelrigg who, as a former cricket captain of both Cambridge University and Leicestershire, said that the nicest compliment paid to him during the war was Colonel May's thanks for this shoot: " Arthur, you shoot guns better than you play cricket."

At the beginning of September the Eighth Army had opened a massive offensive on the Adriatic front. During the last ten days of the month the 10th Indian Division was relieved from its positions inland and began to move at once, through torrential rain, towards the east coast to join in the battle there. By the 9th of October, after a fortnight's journeying which took it through the miniature Republic of San Marino, recently captured by the 4th Indian Division, the Battalion had moved into Sogliano across the Rubicon river to prepare for an attack that very night.

The countryside over which the Battalion now had to fight

lacked the substance of the Tiber landscape. " The hills were little more than bare, sharp ridges, slashed by precipitous ravines. The area was heavily populated; everywhere solidly built villages and farmsteads provided the enemy with ready made pillboxes and strongpoints. The village church with its observation tower and the high, thick walls of the village cemeteries, supplied the nodal points of such defences. As Allied artillery and aircraft were loath to attack consecrated ground, the Germans established their headquarters in sanctuary and enjoyed a measure of immunity during the early stages of any battle."[1]

The Battalion was to attack the feature known as Monte Spaccato. It was to do so by way of Monte Farneto—1600 feet high and protected by a maze of deep-cut watercourses— which had already been captured by other troops of the Division. Monte Spaccato was the next height after Monte Farneto in the direction of Cesena, the town on the river Savio whose capture— in which the 16th D.L.I. took part—has been related in a previous chapter.

It was not easy to get a good view of Monte Spaccato. Only one O.P., which was definitely unhealthy, gave good observation, and while Colonel May was making his " recce " it received a direct hit which wounded one signaller. It was clearly impossible to assemble the Battalion ' O ' Group at this spot so this had to be done further back near Sogliano.

The plan was to climb the steep south-east shoulder of Monte Farneto at night and move through a hamlet called Croce to Monte Spaccato, assembling there at first light. This the Battalion did in pouring rain, staggering up the slippery hillside and over two small torrents. At one stage Lieutenant Bernard Wallis, at the head of his company's mules, negotiated a hedge and, with a loud " follow me " to those behind, jumped what he thought was a ditch on the far side. He was more than surprised to land, complete with mule, in a sand pit about thirty feet deep: but fortunately neither was hurt! Many of the mule loads, however, had to be manhandled, as the mules could not make the slippery climb, but only one load was lost in a stream and by first light the Battalion was ready to attack.

Making use of an early morning ground mist ' A ' Company,

[1] " The Tiger Triumphs: The story of three great Divisions in Italy," p. 142.

under Jim Gray, reached its objective with few casualties, achieving complete surprise and even catching some of the enemy shaving! 'C' Company, on the Battalion's left, were less fortunate. As they were almost on to the objective a sniper killed Major Roy Menzies, the company commander, and Lieutenant Chris Harker, one of his platoon commanders. The only other officer, Lieutenant Lloyd Evans, was seriously wounded and had to be evacuated (six months later he talked his way back to the Battalion despite being blind in one eye and unsound in one leg!): and the Company was then heavily counter-attacked and forced to fall back to the positions held by 'B' Company in reserve. Meanwhile Battalion Headquarters and the Regimental Aid Post, in two houses near Croce, were having their share of troubles; for though not directly observed, they were accurately shelled throughout the day by medium guns which were obviously being ranged. After several close shaves and a number of casualties both were forced to move. It was later discovered that the fire was being directed from a church tower in the rear by a priest who was subsequently captured by the 2nd/4th Gurkhas.

Despite the slight setback on the left, 'A' Company was able to hang on to what it had captured though it was subjected to very heavy shelling. Lieutenant Ditchburn's platoon, established well forward of the main company position, was hotly engaged and resisted vigorously until lack of ammunition compelled it to fall back to the main company area. Sergeant Ernest Pluck and Privates Wilfred Hobkinson and Roy Gerry distinguished themselves in a fight which resulted in the platoon killing at least twenty Germans for the loss of only two killed and three wounded. However, the attack had done the trick and when, next morning, 'B' Company pushed forward to clear up on the left, it succeeded in reaching its objective without undue difficulty and occupied the castle at Monteleone. Here Lina Pagliughi—the well-known soprano—was among those in the refugio under the castle and, to everyone's amusement, marked the occasion by rushing up to Major Mike Hodgson, the company commander, throwing her arms around his neck and kissing him.

From the Battalion's newly won positions the road to Cesena drops into a steep valley covered on its far side by the village of Sorrivoli with a castle dominating it. After a few days the Battalion got a patrol into the castle and captured twenty-four of the garrison almost without firing a shot. Then, leaving the castle behind, it pushed ahead to a village from which could be seen the spires and turrets of Cesena itself. However, the Battalion never entered that city. It begged to be allowed to so that it might join with the 16th Battalion fighting there. But this was not permitted; and, apart from a few days' fighting when it was lent to Brigadier Arderne's Brigade for the crossing of the River Savio, the Battalion had a month's rest back in Sogliano before moving up to the Montone River on the 24th of November.

While they had been at rest the battle ahead of them had been going well as other troops of the Eighth Army drove on towards Forli. Early in November two British Divisions had stormed that town successfully and a fresh attack was now being planned, having as its main objective Faenza, the next important town on the highway from Rimini, on the coast, to Bologna. The 10th Indian Division had been ordered to establish a bridgehead over the Montone river through which the assault divisions could deploy for the attack on Faenza. The campaign in the mountains was now over. From assaults on precipitous ridges and infiltration along valleys and ravines the troops now turned to a different kind of warfare. " The Emilian plain beyond the Apennines was by no means a strategical and tactical paradise. This low land in centuries past had formed a great marsh. When the snows melted in the Apennines each spring immense torrents poured down through clefts in the foothills, seeking the Adriatic. This spate spread across the plain, engulfing large areas. As the countryside became populated it was possible to contain these seasonal floods by raising the river banks with ramparts of earth. The turbid water moved sluggishly to the sea, tending to silt rather than to erode. No deep channels were cut, and the levels of the river rose rather than fell. To confine the spring freshets the banks were built higher and higher, until to-day the line of the river is marked by great dykes standing above the plain."[1]

The ground near the River Montone is flat and open, heavily cultivated and intersected by a network of drainage

[1] " The Tiger Triumphs: The story of three great Divisions in Italy," p. 173.

ditches. The countryside abounds in vineyards, orchards and farms. All bridges had been blown, but the river was no grave obstacle as it was a sludgy stream about thirty feet wide. However, a soft mud bottom flanks the edges of the water and extends the gap to some two hundred feet. The Germans had breached the banks with the result that the land was flooded for about 1,000 yards east of the river. The only approaches were along built up roads, cratered or mined and covered by the fire of machine-guns and artillery.

The Battalion was ordered to cross the river in assault boats during the evening of the 24th. The area had been reported free of mines. This was, however, incorrect; for when, at 10 p.m., the leading company tried to launch the first boat it suddenly ran into a dense minefield as a result of which half the carrying party became casualties. To make matters worse the mines were found on inspection to be hidden in undergrowth which was too difficult to clear at night: so the Battalion had to wait till daylight when the Sappers came and lifted a hundred and fifty mines before clearing a couple of suitable gaps. The leading companies then crossed over without difficulty and by afternoon the whole Battalion was across, holding a perimeter about 1,000 yards deep which was later extended by the 2nd/4th Gurkhas. The perimeter was not, however, secured without a scrap. One platoon, under Sergeant McGary, had to fight hard to capture a certain farmhouse and, after suffering some heavy casualties, had to beat off two heavy counter-attacks during the second of which the Germans managed to gain a footing in the platoon area. McGary at once called for artillery fire on his own positions and though two of his own men were wounded it was so effective against the enemy that the platoon was able to regain control. Another platoon, however, was more fortunate. So unnerved were the enemy by the hideous screams of a pig which had been wounded by a stray bullet nearby that they surrendered without firing a shot!

By this time it had begun to rain hard and, worse still, the Battalion area was pretty heavily shelled. Evacuating wounded was no easy task for the first twenty-four hours and the dead were buried near the Regimental Aid Post by the river. Captain Marcus Howe, the medical officer, who was a tower of strength to the Battalion and saved many lives by his medical skill, was always prepared to move his R.A.P. as far forward as possible. On this occasion he was established across the river in the bridgehead where he looked after the casualties of the 2nd/4th Gurkhas as well as the Battalion's. The situation was not made any easier by the fact that ammunition for 25 pounders was restricted; but the Battalion was fortunate in having in support one 4.2-inch mortar platoon from the Fifth Fusiliers which fired over 1,000 bombs a day for three days until its supply was also cut to a daily rate of twenty-eight. Then, at last light on the 26th, a tank squadron of the North Irish Horse came down the road parallel to the river, having crossed with the 2nd New Zealand Division a little to the south-west. They approached firing vigorously from their tanks and it was some little while before the Battalion could convince them who they were and induce them to stop. Once there they were more than welcome and were of the greatest help in extending the bridgehead. In fact, two days later, when orders were received for two companies to cross the next canal line, their co-operation proved invaluable. How the Battalion was to get its tank support on the far side provided quite a headache for Colonel May because the bridge had been blown. But nothing was too much for the North Irish Horse. They borrowed an " Ark ",[1] dropped it into the canal and, though they had no experience with this machine of war, got two troops of tanks across soon after the leading rifle companies had crossed over. They were finally enshrined in the Battalion's heart when they took 2,000 cigarettes and a stock of chocolate to the forward companies most of whom had had to swim the canal!

Fortunately the Battalion spent only about a week in their newly won positions in the bleakness and damp of the Montone river bank. " On dark nights searchlights were deployed well up in the forward areas and struck their beams with a flat trajectory over the German lines to provide a substitute for the moon and to help patrols to move about at night. One evening just as a watery sun was setting and the mists were beginning to rise from the floods, a motor cyclist was found stranded on a very damp and deserted stretch of road in the forward area.

[1] A tank with a bridge in place of its superstructure.

" Do you want a hand?"

" Oh, I think I'll get it going soon," he replied.

" O.K. and who are you anyway? "

" Me Sir," came the answer, " I'm artificial moonlight, I am! "

There didn't seem much more to be said except to wish him a safe return to that searchlight of his." [1]

The final phase in the consolidation of the bridgehead took place on the 30th of November. ' C ' Company attacked a hamlet called La Capanna which was captured with few casualties; and the Baluch battalion was able to pass through with tanks to a depth of some two miles. ' C ' Company's operation had, however, provided one of the sad ironies of war; for during it a sniper from a haystack had killed Lieutenant Walker and three of his platoon. This was to have been Walker's final battle anyhow, for he was due for repatriation. But he had insisted on making this last attack though he had heard only that morning that his only brother had been killed, also in Italy, a few days before.

The past month's fighting had driven a large dent into the defences of the Gothic Line south of Faenza. Early in December four Army Corps struck at this wavering salient. The Canadians attacked to the north-east towards Ravenna; the Poles struck at the last high ground held by the Germans in the Apennine foothills along the ridges between the Lamone and Senio valleys; XIIIth Corps strove to pinch out the enemy east of the Senio; and Vth Corps, led by the 46th Division, drove on to Faenza. Beyond the Lamone the 46th Division came to a halt and was forced to engage in a slogging match which involved them in some of the hardest fighting of the war. On the 11th of December the 10th Indian Division was ordered to relieve them and take over the attack. On the 13th the Battalion found itself across the Lamone near Qartolo, south-west of Faenza, and on the following night attacked across a valley and a small tributary of the Senio river—known as the Canova—on to the Pergola ridge.

The attack began at 11 p.m. It was a Brigade attack with the 4th/10th Baluch on the left and the Battalion on the right:

[1] " There is an Honour Likewise: The Story of 154 Field Regiment (Leicestershire Yeomanry) " by C. E. Bouskell-Wade, p. 113.

and it was a silent one. The Battalion's objective was one farm on the right, known as Casa Barbiera, and two more—Casa Pozzo and Casa Pozzetti—on the left. 'A' Company was to attack Casa Barbiera and 'B' the other two.

The attack began well and both companies crossed the Canova before the enemy knew what was happening. As a result the latter's defensive fire came down behind them. This was a blessing to 'A' and 'B' Companies though not to 'C' who were moving up in reserve and ran into some of it. 'A' Company, meanwhile, almost reached Casa Barbiera together with the carrier platoon which was dismounted and attached to the Company to make up numbers. Some members of the carriers managed to reach a feature known as Point 168, but the Company as a whole was stopped by mines and Spandau fire after Private Holmes had cleaned up one dangerous Spandau post in a haystack with a lifebuoy flame-thrower. 'B' Company, on the other hand, ran into a thick minefield and stiff opposition, and though a few men reached Casa Pozzo they were killed and the attack beaten back. Just before first light 'C' Company was committed on the left but could make no progress; and it was therefore ordered to occupy the feature Point 147 which covered 'A''s right rear. Meanwhile 'A' Company got a foothold on Point 168.

None of the companies had been strong before the attack and the morning of the 15th found them no stronger. 'A' held Point 168 with the carrier platoon and 'C' in their rear. Both companies were commanded by Jim Gray because in occupying its positions 'C' Company had the misfortune to lose all its officers, Major Macaulay, the company commander, being mortally wounded, Lieutenant Thornley killed and Lieutenant Mason wounded. The remnants of 'B' Company were holding the ridge from which the attack had started and Battalion Headquarters with a defence section of seven men was with it. All day the whole area was heavily shelled and mortared, especially the 'A' Company positions where Gray's task was not made easier by his holding a dozen prisoners who could not be sent back in daylight. The company held on like grim death and beat back at least one counter-attack: and Gray, with a defective "tommy gun" and a handful of grenades, personally drove the Germans from some more weapon pits. Owing to the closeness of the enemy, air support was difficult; but on two occasions air strikes were delivered, and although some bombs were falling on his own positions Gray, for a time, refused to use his yellow smoke signals for the aircraft to stop because more of the bombs were falling on the Germans than on the Company.

The rest of the Brigade had met similar opposition to that facing the Battalion and the principal objectives had not in fact been reached. The gruelling fight, however, was not without its reward, for it had pinned down the Germans and allowed the New Zealanders, on the 10th Division's right, a clear run to the River Senio. The result was that when 'A' and 'C' Companies of the Battalion moved forward on the night of the 15th they were able to reach their objectives without trouble. The enemy had pulled out. The same night the Battalion welcomed back Private Barnett who had been captured the previous evening, and with him be brought eleven prisoners. He had been held in a farmhouse on the New Zealanders' front and, hearing the noise of tracks and seeing a New Zealand tank nearby, had persuaded his captors that the game was up and that they had better surrender!

The Battalion now went into reserve and remained there for a further week. It was very weak in numbers, with little over fifty men a rifle company even after receiving a few reinforcements. It remained in the Columbara-Pergola area while the 4th/10th Baluch pushed on to the River Senio near Tebano, and did not move up to take over from them until the 22nd. The wintry gales had slowed down operations to a standstill and the main activity consisted of shelling and patrolling. In order to prepare for a crossing of the Senio patrols were sent over the river nightly, which was a cold and unpleasant business involving swimming and wading. On one of these Sergeant Rasmussen of 'C' Company was the patrol leader. Reaching the spot on the river bank where he understood he was to cross he told his men, "jump in; it is only bottom high." This they did, only to find the water up to their necks—an uncomfortable start to a cold night's work. Indeed so cold was it that when, later during the night, the patrol tried to cross what appeared to be an unidentified track, the latter was found to be a water-filled drain frozen over by an inch of ice which, rather naturally, broke and gave everybody another wetting. Nevertheless, the patrol remained out for three hours—their clothes freezing to the ground whenever they lay up listening for the enemy—and ultimately launched a successful attack on an enemy headquarters. On returning it crossed the river at another spot only a short way from where it had crossed coming out. Once more everyone braced themselves for another ducking, but when they jumped found, to their surprise and satisfaction, that the water only came up to their knees!

As well as the weather the Battalion had to put up with a most unpleasant bout of shelling which was particularly heavy and resulted in a steady drain of casualties. At about 2 a.m. on Christmas morning the little farm housing Battalion Headquarters received a direct hit which completely demolished two rooms. Next day a rather superior officer arrived with some Indian Sappers to improve the road. " This is a nice quiet little place," he remarked, when a 120 millimetre mortar bomb landed on the roof of Battalion Headquarters and removed a few more tiles. Had it landed five yards away among the working party there would have been many casualties.

On the 28th of December an effort was made to move tanks up to Tebano; but the first two became bogged in full view of the enemy. Much against his better judgment Colonel May was ordered to send a protective patrol to guard them overnight, and within an hour the N.C.O. and four men—from the anti-tank platoon as they could not be spared from elsewhere—were all casualties. The Battalion's forward positions were on the lower exposed slopes above the river and were held by ' B ' Company. They, too, suffered their fair share of casualties. Mortaring from across the river was pretty heavy and Mike Hodgson, the commander, went forward to a farmhouse with four men to observe the enemy positions. As ill luck would have it, two mortar bombs dropped amongst them, killing one man and wounding Hodgson and the other three. At the same time the main company position received the enemy's full attention and the one remaining officer, Lieutenant " Solomon " Grundy, and several other men were wounded. Grundy insisted on remaining: but none of the wounded could be reached without considerable hazard. Their subsequent evacuation owed much to Padre Parr. Using a medical jeep and with volunteer stretcher bearers from the Pioneers, he drove forward as far as possible. Then he continued on foot with his stretcher bearers to the Company's position. He managed to get all the wounded back into the company area and then went round all the section posts. Finally, just before first light he was able to evacuate four serious casualties to the jeep and back to the R.A.P. despite the heavy mortaring which still persisted.

The Battalion remained in these positions for a few days longer—until New Year's day to be exact. New Year's Eve itself was a beautiful night with an almost full moon; and as if by common consent there was little or no harassing fire. The Germans could clearly be heard singing " Silent Night, Holy Night," across the river until midnight when they put up a wonderful firework display by firing every conceivable kind of tracer and flare into the clear night sky. This was, as it happened, a farewell display—at any rate for the present; and the Battalion marched out on the night of the 1st of January, 1945, to a rest area near Forli. There, on the 3rd, a somewhat overdue Christmas was celebrated with some first rate food and an extra week's supply of beer. On the 4th Colonel May flew home on a fortnight's leave to England as he, too, had been abroad for over seven years; and John Taylor took over command until May returned in the first week of February.

The Battalion's days on the river line were now about to end. It had little further to do until February and when not resting was only in reserve. In fact the 10th Indian Division was relieved by the Poles early in that month so that, in its turn, it could relieve another British Division in the upper Sillaro valley. The Germans still clung tenaciously to their strongholds in this area, including Monte Grande, which remained a key position covering the eastern approaches to Bologna. The Battalion was relieved on the 7th of February and a few days later moved off to Monte Spaduro, in front of Castel del Rio, where it took over from the 5th Northamptonshire Regiment. Although the distance was only twenty-five miles as the crow flies it involved a road journey in sleet and snow seven times that distance, mostly over roads deep in mud and with steep gradients.

The new area was a deer stalker's landscape, with high look-outs and deep scours. Everybody had an embarrassingly good view of everybody else. Monte Spaduro itself was covered with snow, and rations and ammunition either had to come by mule over three miles of track with coir matting on it, or round by road to a place called San Clemente ford and thence forward along a filthy track most of which could be directly harassed. From Battalion Headquarters at Casa Oppio to the forward companies only mule or man pack was possible. Though San Clemente ford could be crossed in daylight, because it was continuously smoked by the gunners, all movement forward except on foot was impossible.

A few days after arriving a bit of a thaw set in and bodies buried by the snow since October began appearing around the positions. The Battalion was also troubled by some excellent patrolling by the German Parachute troops who were opposing them. A smash and grab party seeking to identify the Battalion soon after it arrived gave one forward company a busy half hour: but the company gave as good as it got and the intruders finally fled, leaving a number of dead behind. On the 1st of March the Battalion moved once more into reserve finding a few night patrols only; but it was back in the line again a week later on the right of Monte Spaduro in the Casone area. It was bitterly cold and 'C' Company occupied a very high peak known as Little Spaduro. It took an hour and forty minutes to reach the company area from Battalion Headquarters; and one humorist erected a sign on the only safe and climbable route which read "Cyclists—one way only!" On windy nights, at this altitude, the frost was so severe that even the special cold weather oil used for weapons froze solid and automatics were often useless. Here there was even more trouble from the enemy's patrols, one of which captured a prisoner from a forward section almost unobserved, while another killed a sentry at a company headquarters. However, the Battalion had its revenge when an ambush patrol under Corporal Watson caught the experts and killed all three of them. They turned out to be a Lieutenant, a Warrant Officer and a Sergeant from the Parachute Corps Patrol School. On another occasion, however, the laugh was on the Battalion; for on one night a patrol thought they saw an enemy patrol on the snow covered slopes and stalked it with great care, only to find that their opponent was a harmless but hungry cow.

This game of cat and mouse continued throughout the month of March. It was soon discovered that the German Battalion opposite was in fact a penal battalion commanded by an officer named Fuchs who could frequently be heard "encouraging" his charges. Although several harassing shoots were organised to quieten him they never succeeded; but, by a series of shoots with Vickers machine-guns, the Battalion had the satisfaction of closing the track along which their opponents' rations were brought—a fact later confirmed by a prisoner who had a friend killed coming up with the mules. By the time the Battalion left on the 24th it reckoned it had the measure of the German parachutists. By that time, too, it had received a batch of reinforcements, mainly from disbanded anti-aircraft and coast defence units, which enabled the formation once again of a fourth rifle company. These reinforcements were absolutely first class. Not a few were volunteers of 1939 vintage and many were actually "Geordies," coming from a regiment originally raised in County Durham. Thus reinforced the Battalion looked confidently forward to the next important task – a great new offensive to destroy the German Army in Italy and make further major operations unnecessary.

The miserable Italian winter had departed with what almost amounted to dramatic suddenness. A procession of dry and glowing days, beginning early in February, enabled the final offensive against the Germans to be launched several weeks earlier than expected. This was planned in three phases—the first being an attack by the Eighth Army designed to draw as many German divisions as possible down to the Adriatic coast; the second involving the Fifth Army in an offensive from the mountains to capture Bologna and exploit into the Po Valley; and the third being a joint sweep into the Po Valley by both Armies.

The Eighth Army's offensive began early in April and it was well under way by the time that the 10th Indian Division, and with it the Battalion, joined the fight once more. Joined the hunt might perhaps be a more accurate phrase; for the Wehrmacht had dropped its guard and was staggering dizzily under an avalanche of blows. There was, indeed, little it could do to stem the tide.

The Battalion crossed the River Sillaro near Lugo on the

night of the 15th of April and pushed ahead the following day against light resistance. During the day some fighter-bombers attacked the German positions nearby and one, flying low, was winged by small arms fire. It landed in a field near the Battalion's R.A.P.: but it had scarcely done so before Marcus Howe had jumped into a jeep, driven up to the plane and rescued the pilot. " That's service for you " was the latter's apt comment! On the 17th one company reached the village of Portonovo to find that the Germans had just pulled out and that the Italian Partisans were busily shaving the heads of all the women who had " collaborated " with them. The company commander, Captain Norman Benson, was most distressed that he was unable to save the blonde tresses of one decorative creature who cast herself at his feet and asked for sanctuary! The same night the whole Battalion crossed the next river—the Qaderna—on the right of the New Zealanders who put in a highly spectacular attack with a regiment of crocodiles,[1] about fifty wasps[2] and some two hundred and fifty guns in support. Yet there was still " one more river to cross " before the Battalion could say it had fired its last shot in anger; and this obstacle was negotiated two days later. Once across the Battalion found itself held up just short of its objective by German rearguards; but as the Divisional Commander wanted the opposition dispersed before dark the leading companies were ordered back whilst two fresh Battalions were pushed in, supported by the whole of the divisional artillery. ' D ' Company, whose wireless set went ' dead ' because the aerial rod was shot off, was only pulled back in the nick of time, just before the barrage started!

This was the Battalion's last battle of the war. Ahead of them other troops of the 10th Division pushed on and were, indeed, involved in some of the campaign's bitterest fighting when crossing the Indice river. But despite being at notice to move, varying from twenty-four hours' to three, the Durham Light Infantry never again went into action. News of the Armistice in Italy reached them at about 7 p.m. on the 2nd of May whilst in comfortable billets in farms near Ferrara. They had come a long way since the day when a few scattered

[1] Flame throwing tanks.
[2] Flame throwing Bren carriers.

remnants had limped back to Egypt from Cos. A new Battalion had been created from the hard core of the old, and for a year in Italy had performed with distinction a difficult and unpleasant job in conditions of warfare which were far from easy. There was little spectacular about the Italian campaign: it was one long slog over mountain ridges and across rivers. Yet in this unpleasant job the Battalion was a happy one: and for that it owed much to its commanding officers. From September 1944 Colonel May commanded and the Battalion's history from that time was very much of his making. "There was a tremendous confidence throughout the unit in the ability of its Colonel," wrote one company commander afterwards. " Whatever order was given we knew that the battle was being fought so that the maximum possible use was being made of everything that was available. The greatest thing I would say in carrying out an order is the confidence that that order is the right one. We had that on all occasions." Now all the fighting was over; and in Headquarters Officers' Mess on the night of the 2nd some specially preserved port was brought out and passed round. The Royal Toast was drunk as marking an auspicious occasion: for by special custom no toasts are drunk in normal circumstances. Next morning a new Regimental flag, kept in cold storage for eighteen months in honour of this very day, was broken at the masthead. The war of ridges and rivers was over.

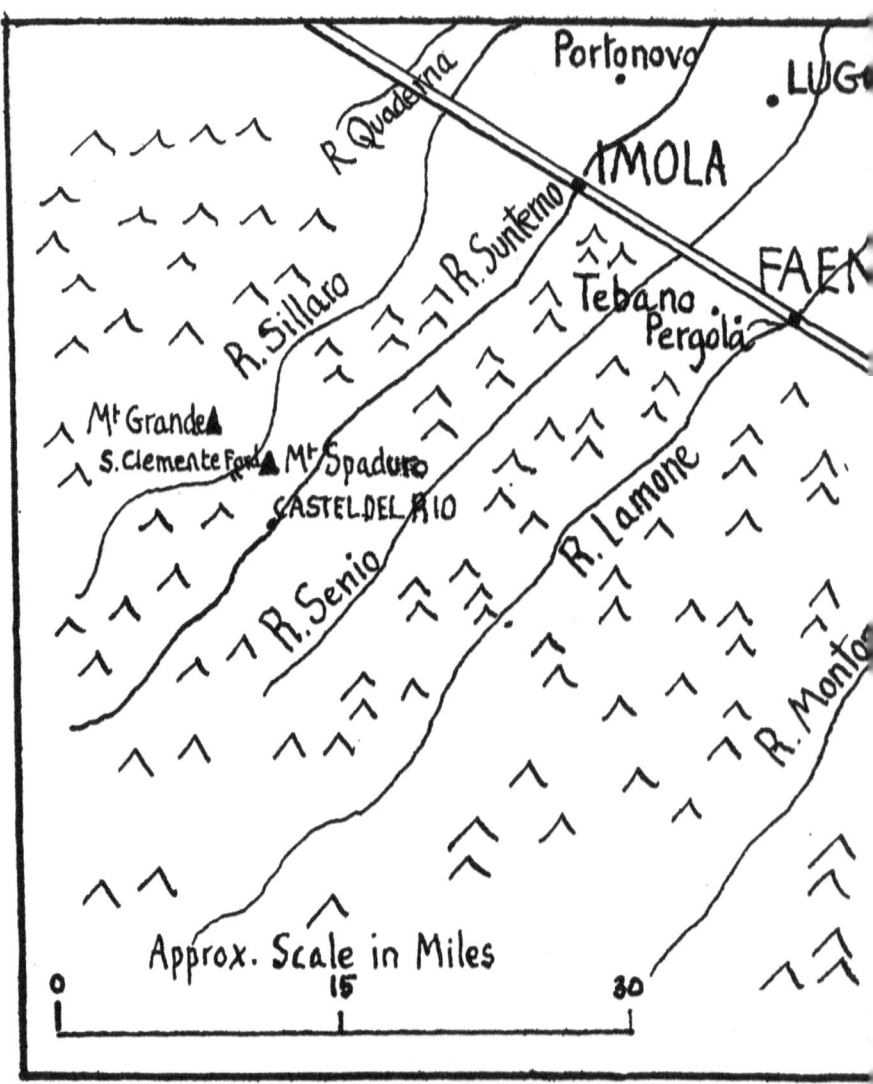

16. *North-east Italy*

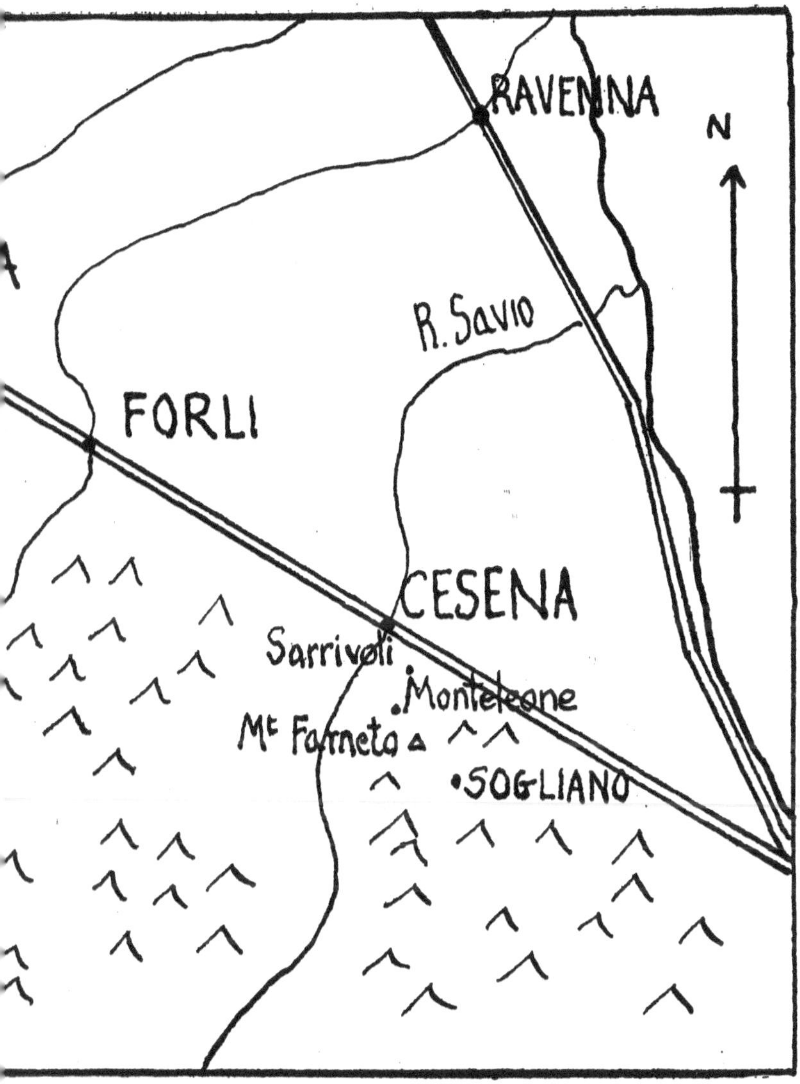

RAVENNA
N
R. Savio
FORLI
CESENA
Sarrivoli
Monteleone
Mt Farneto
SOGLIANO

CHAPTER EIGHT

The Durham Light Infantry in North-west Europe 1944-1945

I

151 BRIGADE IN FRANCE

WITH the invasion of Normandy began the last great campaign of the war; and there was much to be done to prepare those who were to take part in it. The Durham Brigade reached England early in November 1943, some thirty months after leaving it for the Middle East. Hopes of being stationed in the north were soon dashed and it was in Suffolk that they spent the next few months.

The Brigade had now to learn the new techniques of battle evolved with painstaking care over the past years by those responsible for planning the assault on the Continent. After a well-earned spell of leave, varying in length according to the individual's period of service overseas, each battalion settled down once again to a vigorous programme of training. In February General Montgomery visited and addressed the Brigade and from him they learnt that the 50th Division was once more to be in the van as one of the assault divisions in the invasion. This news was received with mixed feelings; for many felt, after so recent a reunion with their families, that one of the many divisions which had not yet been out of England might well have been chosen as the first to attack Hitler's Atlantic wall. Nevertheless, as the days passed and experience was gained of the new weapons and devices for the task, none failed to be impressed by the efforts that had been made for securing the success of the operation.

As spring approached, training was intensified. In April the Brigade moved to a concentration area near Romsey in Hampshire, and as the weeks sped by the tentacles of security tightened. Each battalion was given an Army Post Office number and names of locations were forbidden. A visitor's ban was imposed on the areas where the assaulting divisions lay and extended to a depth of ten miles from the coast. Finally, during the last week in May, all invasion troops were sealed in their invasion camps; and then, for the first time, the plans for the assault were disclosed to the officers and men who were to carry them out. Even then the maps and models contained code names and only C.O.s and seconds-in-command knew the exact area of the invasion.

The assault on the Normandy coast was to be made by five divisions—three British and two American—between St. Laurent, on the Cotentin peninsula, and the mouth of the River Orne. The British attack was to be preceded by the dropping of the 6th Airborne Division to seize vital crossings over the Caen Canal and the River Orne, and the American by two Airborne divisions in the area of St. Mère Eglise.

The British assault was to be carried out by the 50th Division, the 3rd Canadian and the 3rd British Divisions. To the 50th Division fell the task of penetrating the beach defences between Le Hamel and La Rivière and securing a covering position which would include Bayeux, on the west, and the area of St. Léger—a hill on the Caen-Bayeux road—on the east. The assault was, in fact, to begin on the night before D Day in the form of a pounding by Bomber Command of the most important enemy coastal batteries. This was to be taken up by light bombers and naval guns from the sea and was to be followed—just before the troops landed—by attacks on the coast artillery and beach defences by every available plane of the American Eighth and Ninth Air Forces. The assaulting craft would then run into the beaches covered by the fire of light naval forces and of 25 pounders and tanks in tank landing craft.

For the purposes of the landing the 50th Division had been reinforced by one additional infantry and one armoured brigade, giving it a strength of five brigades—56, 69, 151, 231 and 8 Armoured—and thus making it the largest division in the Second Army. The initial landing was to be by 231 Brigade on the right and 69 Brigade on the left on the beach, known as Gold Beach, between La Rivière and Arromanches. 151 Brigade's task was to follow up 69 Brigade and, once the initial objectives were captured, to join with them in securing the Division's final objective—the Caen-Bayeux road.

After a delay of twenty-four hours, due to bad weather, the Brigade set sail on the evening of the 5th of June. The 6th Battalion had suffered an unfortunate last minute casualty when its C.O.—Lieutenant-Colonel Arthur Green, who had succeeded Bill Watson before the Battalion returned to England—was packed off to hospital with a relapse of malaria on the very day of sailing. Major George Wood, his second in command, took over at once; but little reorganisation in the detailed plans was otherwise necessary. The 8th and 9th Battalions, however, were still commanded by the C.O.s who had brought them home to England—Bob Lidwill of the 8th and Humphrey Woods of the 9th who had succeeded Clarke in Sicily. The 6th and 9th Battalions were to land first, on the right and left respectively, and the 8th shortly afterwards as Brigade reserve. Although H hour was early in the morning, as follow-up brigade 151 Brigade did not expect to land much before midday: and so it turned out.

The landing craft sailed out from Southampton into a rough sea. Soon they were pitching and rolling in a most uncomfortable fashion. Every man will have his own impression and recollections of that memorable voyage, but there will be some common to all. None will forget the passage of the cold, wintry Channel and the seasickness which afflicted many; nor the curative effects of shell fire at the end of the journey. Only a few men were so incapacitated that they had to be carried ashore; but there were a few. None will forget, either, the vast concourse of shipping which was revealed as dawn broke; nor the first glimpse of the low, sandy, dune studded Normandy coast. As the ships moved in, the continuous drone of aircraft overhead could be heard and a sweet, comforting sound it was too. It seemed incredible that such an armada could lie off the coast of France almost with impunity. As it got lighter, ships and landing craft could be discerned as far as the eye could see and still more kept coming from the ports of southern England. As the landing craft carrying the 9th Battalion was negotiating a lane in the outer enemy minefield, there suddenly appeared off the port bow the ugly spiked shape of a mine. It did not seem to be secured; it was just drifting by. The helmsman swung

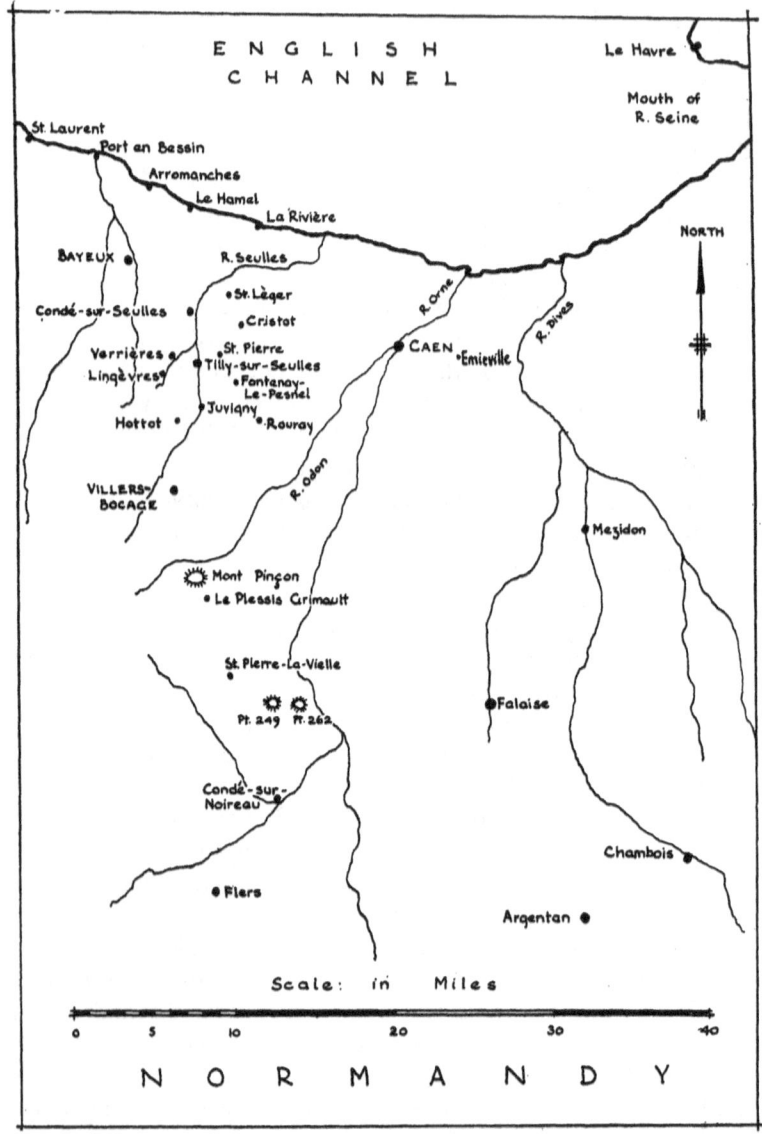

17. *Normandy*

his helm sharply to starboard and the craft heeled steeply over; and as it did so one man was heard to remark in a thick Geordie accent, " Look, 'Arry, a cow upside down."

By 9 a.m. it seemed that every inch of the Normandy coast was alive and breathing forth thick columns of smoke. " Away to the east," wrote one officer of the 9th Battalion, " about eight hundred yards from where our craft was due to beach, I could see a Sherman tank fitted with flails crashing its way through a minefield on a green slope just off the beach. What a Wellsian picture! It looked like a gigantic crab and as it crawled forward there was, every now and then, a burst of flame as it flailed a mine. Further to the right I could see orderly lines of men filing out of beached landing craft and then converging into thicker lines as they made for their pre-arranged beach exits. From that distance they resembled a nice, orderly football crowd until into their midst fell one or two mortar bombs and the resemblance ended. Yet the flow of men was in no way halted or dispersed. They looked, as indeed they were, inexorable and irresistible." It seemed that the assault, at any rate in the 50th Division's sector, had been successful.

It had. As in Sicily, the bad weather proved a blessing in disguise. The Germans had not believed a landing in such weather possible; and many of the coast defence troops were not on the alert. Unlike Sicily, however, each battalion was landed in exactly the right place, but all had to wade through anything up to five feet of water and some had to swim; so most of the 9th Battalion and at least half the 8th were drenched to the skin by the time they reached the shore. Once ashore, each battalion moved to an assembly area inland and from there sent off a mobile column of one company towards Bayeux. By nightfall all three Battalions were established to the south-east of Sommervieu. The 9th Battalion cleared the village; and the 6th Battalion's mobile column had successfully brushed aside some opposition on the way without difficulty. Both the latter Battalions had also taken a number of prisoners, mainly Russians with no desire to fight, and the 6th had collected its first spoils of war in the shape of a German Ford 10 h.p. car, which was proudly driven into the battalion area by Major Maurice Kirby. Two days later it had been repainted and adorned with the divisional sign and the Battalion's designation numbers.

By the evening of the 7th the Brigade had crossed the Caen-Bayeux road and the 6th Battalion was established just northwest of Condé and patrolling into it. During the afternoon the

Brigade Commander, Brigadier Ronnie Senior, had been ambushed in his jeep, wounded and forced to lie up to avoid capture. Although he managed to rejoin his Headquarters the following day, his wounds made it necessary for him to be evacuated and Colonel Lidwill, of the 8th Battalion, took temporary command of the Brigade. The same night orders were issued for a divisional mobile column to be formed to strike south from St. Léger to seize and hold Tessel-Bretteville, some six miles away, and thus threaten the important road centre of Villers-Bocage. To this column, comprised for the most part of 8 Armoured Brigade, the 8th Battalion was attached.

The Battalion moved off early on the morning of the 9th over the Caen-Bayeux railway and down the road towards the wooded and straggling village of St. Pierre. This was the bocage country; high thick hedges with small fields and deep ditches interspersed with orchards and narrow country lanes. It was difficult country and it was new to the men of the 50th Division. " Its dominant characteristic is the hedgerow—a bank three or four feet high with a ditch on either side and topped by a line of thorny bushes whose deep roots bind the earth into a wall which will rebuff even bulldozers. With these hedgerows bordering the fields and with stone walls enclosing the orchards, the country abounds in natural anti-tank obstacles and ready-made defensive positions for infantry, while its thick woods and copses provide secure cover for lurking tanks. Moreover, the villages, with their stout stone buildings and narrow streets provide formidable strongholds astride the roads and they cannot easily be by-passed."[1] Often there would be only a small field between friend and foe, yet each would be completely concealed from the other. Surprise was thus easy and one never quite knew where the enemy was; and that meant taut nerves and anxious hearts for prolonged periods. The bocage was ideal for the sniper and the man who lay in wait by the roadside with a *panzerfaust*.[2]

The Battalion advanced to within striking distance of St. Pierre, which was held by the enemy, and there prepared to attack. After a preliminary barrage from their supporting self-propelled guns, two companies—' C ' and ' D '—attacked

---
[1] " The Struggle for Europe " by Chester Wilmot, p. 301.
[2] German equivalent of the Bazooka.

the village and after a short but savage encounter cleared the enemy out of it. They lost quite a lot of men doing it; and in ' C ' Company four of its five officers were casualties. However, the village was theirs and they continued to hold it throughout the night. Then, early next morning and with great suddenness, the Germans launched a counter-attack accompanied by heavy shelling and mortaring. They had little difficulty in infiltrating for the village was overgrown and threaded with narrow, wooded lanes and tracks. The brunt of the attack fell upon ' C ' Company which was quickly overrun; and then enemy tanks and infantry attacked ' D ' Company and began to threaten ' B.' One section was annihilated but for Private Protano who remained firing a Bren gun until the attackers were driven off and the position reoccupied. At the same time the enemy made a determined effort to annihilate 'A' Company and Battalion Headquarters, which was only stopped by the concentrated fire of every officer and man in the area; and at one stage three enemy tanks, preceded by some cows, were only halted by the quick action of Lance-Sergeant Stanley Wallbanks —commanding a platoon of ' D ' Company—with a Piat gun whose gunner had been killed. The noise of battle rose to a climax as the morning wore on, the thunder of guns and mortars mingling with the short, sharp rattle of automatics; but the arrival of reinforcements from 8 Armoured Brigade helped to ease the situation and by midday the crisis was passed. The Battalion had been forced to surrender its forward positions but it still held most of the village, and by the time that Colonel Lidwill returned from Brigade to reassume command it was confident of staying there.

Stay there it did for another thirty-six hours, despite a further heavy counter-attack with tanks put in by the Germans the following day. The German tanks gave short shrift to the British tanks in support of the Battalion and they inflicted heavy casualties on ' B ' Company, mortally wounding Major Tommy Clapton, its commander, and seriously wounding Major Ted Dunn, the Battalion second in command. The Battalion was completely surrounded and Colonel Lidwill, who was at Brigade Headquarters for a conference, could only get back to it after a hazardous journey through the fields on foot. But every company stubbornly refused to give way and the enemy withdrew, leaving them masters of the battlefield for the second time.

By the morning of the 12th of June it was clear that the area of Tessel-Bretteville could not be captured without fresh troops. Moreover, the 7th Armoured Division, which had been coming ashore since the 7th, had advanced rapidly on the west of the river Seulles towards Villers-Bocage, but had been repulsed by the 2nd Panzer Division and forced to draw back. The 8th Battalion was thus in a dangerous salient and, in order to straighten out the line and re-group, both it and 8 Armoured Brigade were ordered to withdraw from St. Pierre the same day. The Battalion thus reverted to the command of 151 Brigade and moved back into Brigade reserve south of Bayeux, exhausted after days of hard fighting, but satisfied that it was the master of the Germans in Europe as it had been in Africa and Sicily. Casualties amounted to twelve officers and two hundred men.

So far the 8th Battalion had seen the heaviest fighting though the 6th and 9th Battalions had not been inactive. 'C' Company of the 9th Battalion had put in an attack on some positions at a place called Ellon, and with carriers and artillery support had reached their objective without difficulty. The 6th Battalion had established a platoon on the railway near Condé-sur-Seulles to stop the enemy infiltrating up the line of the river Seulles. The platoon fought a spirited action with some Germans whom it dispersed; then had to retire after the enemy had mounted a second and heavier attack; but was able to reoccupy the position a day later. On the 9th 'A' Company, on the Bayeux-Tilly road, captured a German staff car which drove unwittingly into their positions; followed this up by doing the same to a half track vehicle which made the same mistake; and finally rounded off the day by putting a Piat bomb into an enemy three ton lorry which did likewise. This resulted in an enemy attack with tanks the following day which was broken up by artillery fire and the Battalion's anti-tank gunners. The enemy withdrew, having inflicted few casualties on his opponents but having lost three tanks.

The Brigade now entered upon a period of fighting which many experienced officers regarded as one of the most unpleasant they had ever known. For nigh on two months it was to be at grips with not only the enemy but also the bocage;

and for half that time it was a case of static warfare in which little ground was given or taken. The 50th Division's attention was now concentrated on the Tilly-Hottot area and 151 Brigade's immediate objective was the road running south-west from Juvigny—a few miles south of Tilly—towards and through Hottot and beyond. The 7th Armoured Division had previously swept south-west of Tilly towards Villers-Bocage, and it was intended that the 50th Division should advance to relieve it.

The 8th Battalion had been withdrawn to rest and reorganise on the 12th. On the 13th the 6th Battalion advanced from Condé with the object of reaching the Hottot-Juvigny road. It soon ran into heavy opposition from which it was clear that the area between Tilly and the village of Lingèvres was a formidable defensive line held by determined troops. The burden of the day's fighting fell upon ' A ' and ' B ' Companies who lost between them fifty officers and fifty men either killed or wounded: and the Battalion was ordered to withdraw that evening to prepare for a Brigade attack planned for the following day.

The attack was to be simultaneous with another on the right flank by 231 Brigade. The 9th Battalion was to advance and capture Lingèvres and the 6th the neighbouring village of Verrières. If the 6th was successful, it was then to push south towards Hottot. The attack was to receive the full support of the divisional artillery and the R.A.F. were to strafe the orchards near Verrières and the road between Lingèvres and Tilly.

The 6th Battalion crossed the start-line at 10.15 a.m. on the 14th and worked across some open country between the bocage, well extended and supported by a squadron of tanks. The advance went well for about a mile when the leading Companies —' C ' and ' D '—were heavily engaged by machine guns in a cornfield just north of Verrières. The enemy was well dug in on the forward edges of a wood and held his fire until the leading troops were within a hundred and fifty yards. Then some twelve machine guns raked the advancing lines of infantry and for a while the attack was halted. Men began to fall thick and fast; artillery fire was called for and the gunners plastered the front of the wood; but some Germans still continued firing. Meanwhile both reserve companies were committed to the attack and slowly and surely the enemy began to give way. Nevertheless, it took five hours of hard fighting and fairly heavy casualties before the wood was cleared: and when it was, the enemy positions were found to have been dug into the sides of a ditch and so sited that they gave complete protection from anything but a direct hit.

The Battalion paused to reorganise on the line of the ditch. The Germans had departed leaving their machine guns, a large quantity of ammunition, some 75 millimetre guns and two half track vehicles; and from the general condition of the place it was clear that their departure was hurried. The guns were turned round to engage the enemy and ' B ' and ' D ' Companies moved on to clear Verrières village. The former went through Verrières without opposition, but both Companies were held up by strong resistance beyond it, though ' B ' got within two hundred yards of the main Tilly-Lingèvres road. That night the Battalion drew back to concentrate round Verrières itself and prepared for a further advance next day: casualties amounted to just over a hundred killed, wounded and missing.

Meanwhile the 9th Battalion had met with vigorous resistance in its operations against Lingèvres. On the 13th ' B ' Company had carried out a reconnaissance in force to test enemy reactions. These had been strong and the Company lost heavily, among its casualties being every officer. The main attack, however, began on the morning of the 14th simultaneously with that of the 6th Battalion. The Germans were disposed in a large wood which lay astride the Battalion's axis of advance to Lingèvres and only a few hundred yards from its forming up positions. 'A' Company (Major Charles D'Arcy Irvine) and ' C ' Company (Major John Hudson) were to attack the wood after a concentrated strafing from 25 pounders and Typhoon fighters equipped with bombs and rockets. The attackers had a field of stubble to cross and were to dash over it as the fighters finished their work.

The guns duly opened fire on the wood with great accuracy. " The wood literally danced in front of our eyes " wrote one officer, " and not three hundred yards away. The Typhoons each did one dive and released two bombs and ten rockets, straddling and plastering the wood . . . For what seemed a long time nothing happened, and then an enemy tank in the left hand corner of the wood fired and set on fire one of our Shermans. The fire was returned with good effect by the remaining two.

Another Hun tank opened up from the right hand of the wood, and then the wood came to life. Our leading troops were now in the middle of the stubble and were caught there by a withering fire from Spandaus and snipers; but still they kept going. A dash and we were in the wood; but the Hun had his plentiful Spandaus sited well back inside the edge of it."

Once in the wood bitter fighting ensued and progress was slow. 'A' Company on the left suffered heavy casualties, including all its officers. Colonel Woods, who was with it, ordered the two reserve companies to move up, one to pass through 'A' and the other to reinforce 'C.' But 'B' Company, who moved through 'A', also suffered heavily, losing all officers save one; and the C.O., after talking to the second in command over the radio, decided to reinforce the Battalion's right and was actually in the act of withdrawing the remnants of 'A' and 'B' Companies when a German mortar bomb landed nearby and killed him. By some freak of fortune the Intelligence officer, Lieutenant John Reed, who was with him escaped with little more than scratches. Yet, despite these losses and the bitter resistance, the two companies on the right, under the second in command, captured Lingèvres and by 12 p.m. what was left of the Battalion reorganised in defence of the village.

For three hours, apart from heavy shelling, there was a lull in the fighting during which the Battalion prepared itself to resist any counter-attack. Major John Mogg, of the Oxfordshire and Buckinghamshire Light Infantry, who had joined as second in command just before the invasion, at once took command after the C.O.'s death and, as it turned out, retained it for the rest of the war. The expected counter-attack materialised about 5 p.m.; it developed strongly on the left flank; and soon the forward troops were nearly surrounded. Things began to look serious until a call for air support was answered by Typhoons which strafed the enemy positions with bombs and rockets and the situation was eased. The Battalion stabilised its positions to include the road just west of Lingèvres and stretched out a hand to make contact with the 6th Battalion in Verrières. That night it was relieved by a battalion of 56 Brigade. Casualties amounted to some twenty officers and two hundred men.

The next stage of this slow slogging match concerned the 6th

Battalion once again. After its fight for Verrières, casualties had made it necessary for a reorganisation on a three company basis. On the 16th of June Colonel Green, out of hospital and recovered from his malaria, arrived to reassume command and George Wood, who had proved a first class deputy, once more became his second. On the afternoon of the 17th the Battalion was relieved by the 9th Battalion. This left it free to co-operate with troops of 231 Brigade who launched an attack on Tilly that same afternoon. The Battalion's task was to reach the Tilly-Lingèvres road and its route lay along the same path beyond Verrières where it had, in the last stages of the fighting on the 14th, met with so much opposition. It met similar opposition again and by nightfall was still held up, though 'C' Company, under Maurice Kirby, had reached the line of the road and were so close to the enemy that they were lobbing grenades from one side of it while the Germans were lobbing them from the other.

During the day's fighting the Commander of 151 Brigade—Brigadier Walton, Senior's successor—was wounded, and for a second time Colonel Lidwill of the 8th Battalion stepped in to fill the breach. A heavy fire plan was laid on to break the enemy hold round Tilly next day; and the following afternoon a fresh attack began.

The 6th Battalion had a splendid day. The attack began with a creeping barrage laid down by three Field Regiments. Each company was allotted a troop of tanks and, in addition, machine-guns mounted in carriers operated as light tanks. Once the attack began there was no stopping it. Tanks crashed through hedges, shooting into hedge junctions, and their support was magnificient. "The fire brought down on the enemy was simply terrific," wrote one observer, "and he was well and truly blasted out of his positions." Indeed, 'D' Company had the good fortune to see the Germans get up and run for it. The Battalion swept ahead and by 5 p.m.—after just on two and a half hours of fighting—was on its objective, the high ground south-west of Tilly, and had dug in. It had been the most successful attack of the campaign to date and the perfect co-operation of tanks, infantry and guns had given an immense boost to the morale and confidence of everybody; and, what is more, casualties had not been heavy.

Next day Tilly fell to the troops of 56 Brigade. It was a mere shell of a town, battered and ruined by shelling and bombing: for a while it had even been a target for the guns of H.M.S. Warspite. But although the enemy's grip on Tilly had been prised loose, he was still holding fast in Hottot to the south of it. It did not fall to 151 Brigade to crack this nut. Troops of 231 Brigade tried to do so without success, and on the 8th of July the men of 56 Brigade followed suit with no better luck. A further attempt by 231 Brigade on the 11th fared no better: and, indeed, the village was not occupied till the enemy made a general withdrawal on the 18th.

For 151 Brigade the period between the capture of Tilly and the middle of July was one of stalemate. That does not mean that it was one of inactivity. Far from it. But there was nothing spectacular: each Battalion was fully occupied harassing the enemy and probing his positions with patrols in the thick country of the bocage. A word has already been said about the countryside which, after the Desert and Sicily, was such an unfamiliar battleground to the men of the D.L.I. Brigade. For the following weeks the Battalions had their full share of it, and they learnt to appreciate it as first class infantry country to be made use of and not feared.

Everybody lived in slit trenches and kept clear of the houses which were apt to become artillery targets and were frequently booby-trapped. Carrier platoons were of little value as such and their men were dismounted and used as extra infantry. The gunners of anti-tank platoons had to be content with short fields of fire and, as there was no major German tank activity, with little shooting. The mortars, however, came into their own with a vengeance, learning to fire off the map instead of by direct observation and doing so with deadly effect. For the infantry proper there was plenty of patrolling for which air photos of the bocage proved invaluable. For all there were regular doses of shelling, mortaring and Spandau fire from the opposing Germans which caused a continuous trickle of casualties. Furthermore, life was not made any more pleasant by the large number of dead cows whose rotting carcases lay strewn all over the battlefield. They were some of the earliest victims of the clash between the opposing armies, but it was not always easy to dispose of them. In rear areas bulldozers came to the rescue, but nearer the enemy they proved a problem. Even if men could be spared to bury them there was the risk of the digging parties drawing enemy fire; and attempts to soak the carcases with petrol and burn them usually resulted in shelling by enemy guns and mortars. Thus all but the most offensive of the dead beasts had to be left alone, and the infantry nearest them had to put up with the smell.

On the 18th of July the Germans withdrew in front of 151 Brigade and the D.L.I. battalions at last moved forward again. This was as a result of a Second Army offensive in the Caen sector, on the 50th Division's left, and a successful attack launched by the American First Army on St. Lô in the middle of the month. By the 26th the 8th Battalion had reached the village of Ourville, which was captured after a sharp fight, and on the 27th 17 Platoon, established in the village, had to withstand a heavy German counter-attack which it repelled by accurate defensive fire. By the 30th the American offensive had got well into its stride and was to sweep south and then north in a great half circle towards Argentan. At the same time the British Second Army began attacking southwards to meet them, both Armies thus forming the great pocket around Falaise which was to be the graveyard of the German Army in France.

The task of the 50th Division was first to capture Villers-Bocage and then to strike southwards towards Condé-sur-Noireau. Villers-Bocage in fact fell to 69 Brigade on the 4th of August. The town had been smashed to pieces by a heavy force of Lancasters from Bomber Command and there was nothing left of it save rubble. But several miles to the south of it, lying sprawled across the road to Condé, was the dominating feature of Mount Pinçon, comprising one of the important bastions of the German defences in Normandy. When, on the 6th of August, the 43rd Division captured it after a very bitter struggle the road to Condé lay open.

Condé is a small town lying at the junction of two rivers and at a road bottleneck. The Americans sweeping round from the base of the Cherbourg peninsula, and the British and Canadians attacking south from Villers-Bocage and Caen, were gradually enveloping their German opponents who had been ordered by Hitler not to retreat. Condé was the town through which all

German troops now in the pocket would untimately have to pass if they were ever to be extricated. Its capture was thus one more step in the closing of the trap.

On the southern slopes of Mount Pinçon lies the village of Le Plessis Grimault. The road from the village slopes gradually downwards until it reaches St. Pierre la Vieille, nearly four miles away on the road to Condé. The 50th Division's plan for the advance was for the D.L.I. Brigade to advance half way to St. Pierre, for 69 Brigade to pass through them and capture the village and then for the D.L.I. Brigade to take the lead once more. That was the plan, but in fact it worked out somewhat differently.

The 9th Battalion's task was to hold Le Plessis Grimault as a firm base while the 6th and 8th Battalions advanced to the attack. Each battalion was supported by a squadron of tanks and the attack was to be preceded by a barrage provided by five field regiments. The enemy resisted stubbornly: and he shelled Le Plessis Grimault heavily as well as the road leading over Mount Pinçon along which each battalion had to move to reach its forming up position.

The barrage began promptly at midday with the usual whine and crash of shells. As the leading companies moved forward the Germans brought down artillery and mortar defensive fire which was not without effect. Colonel Lidwill of the 8th Battalion was badly wounded in the stomach and ' C ' Company of his battalion lost all its officers and a number of senior N.C.O.s so that Captain Gerald Maier of ' B ' Company had to take command of both. During the last 2,000 yards of the advance German resistance stiffened, and it was only broken by the determined use at close quarters of Stens, grenades and Bren guns fired from the hip. The 8th Battalion reckoned this as one of the most successful attacks in which it had ever taken part. It captured one hundred and twenty prisoners and on the whole its casualties were not unduly heavy. Ian English led his company relentlessly on through extremely heavy fire to be first on to the objective, while Sergeant-Major John Ineson of ' B ' Company personally forced at least fourteen Germans out of their fire positions. At all events, by 2 p.m. the 6th and 8th Battalions had reached their objectives and 69 Brigade was able to pass through them as planned. But it soon found itself held up by stiffening resistance, and for the next forty-eight hours

231 Brigade was brought in to continue the attacks on the high ground near St. Pierre.

Meanwhile, in the D.L.I. Brigade, it was the 9th Battalion's turn to attack. On the 11th of August it was ordered to capture two prominent features—Point 249 and Point 262—which lay to the south-east of St. Pierre and away from the St. Pierre-Condé road. The Battalion was to have the help of the 8th Battalion's carriers and Colonel Mogg planned to attack the two features with tanks leading the way, closely followed by the two carrier platoons, each taking on with their Brens and 2 inch mortars any anti-tank guns holding up the tanks. Once they had reached their objectives the rifle companies were to follow up as quickly as possible to occupy the position.

It cannot be said that everything went without a hitch. When the British artillery opened fire the Germans retaliated by shelling the start line. The Battalion's carrier platoon commander was one of the casualties. Then it was discovered that the forming up place was held by the enemy, although originally reported clear; and this meant a rapid change of plan and a new forming up place. Finally, while reconnoitring, the Colonel and Brian Gardner, commanding 'B' Company, ran into a German section post and only narrowly avoided capture. Once, however, the advance started in earnest at about 1.30 p.m. there was no stopping it; 'B' and 'C' Companies moved so fast that they overtook the tanks; and the Battalion was triumphantly on its objective by 5 p.m.

Next day the 9th Battalion was relieved by the Somerset Light Infantry and moved back to join the 6th and 8th Battalions in reserve. The long days of hard slogging through the bocage were virtually over. For five days the men of the Durham Brigade rested, relaxed and reorganised and then, on the 18th, moved forward on the first stages of a journey which, had they known it, was to lead them, almost unopposed, through northern France and over the Belgian border. Even as they rested, the Canadians away to their left and the Americans sweeping round from the south after their break-through from the Cherbourg peninsula, were steadily closing the trap on the Germans in the so-called Falaise pocket. On the 16th the Canadians entered Falaise itself; on the 17th they and the Poles, who formed part of the Canadian Army, reached Trun some ten miles south-east of it; and on the 19th the Poles met the Americans at Chambois, six miles east of the Falaise-Argentan road. The trap was closed. Within the pocket comprising an area bounded by the towns of Falaise, Condé, Flers and Argentan, were some 100,000 German troops who were subjected to a relentless pounding from all available artillery and aircraft as they desperately tried to battle their way to safety. Great was the slaughter of those sunlit August days. Long columns of German horse and motor transport, jammed on the overcrowded roads and lanes, gave the Air Forces targets which they had scarcely dreamt of. " The Germans moved along the roads until they were choked with dead horses and men and burning wreckage. Then they took to the fields across which they moved in columns of five or six abreast. At bottlenecks, such as gateways and stream crossing places, the traffic piled up and was then destroyed by shells and rocket firing planes. Swiftly destruction would spread across the entire field, until it was impossible for anything on wheels or tracks to move across it. In a day or two many fields became like the roads—simply impassable owing to the carnage and destruction. It was a battlefield that decided the fate of France."[1]

The advance to the Seine which began on the 18th was led by the 11th Armoured Division. To the 50th Division was given the task of protecting the latter's flank and mopping up any enemy left in the wake of the armour. The route of the Durham Brigade took them through the area of the pocket and each man was able to see for himself the havoc which the Allies had inflicted on the fleeing enemy. " Both sides and often the middle of the roads were jammed with wrecked lorries, guns, horses and tanks; dead men and horses lay about in grotesque attitudes, and here and there a truck or gun limber, which had been set on fire and was still smouldering. Abandoned staff cars and many other vehicles were packed with loot; field glasses, typewriters, pistols and small arms by the hundred, cases of wine and boxes of ladies' clothing. Many of the vehicles were untouched and could have been driven away, but no one had the time."[2] It was a sight few who saw it will ever forget.

[1] " The Path of the 50th " by E. W. Clay, p. 273.

[2] " The 8th Battalion The Durham Light Infantry 1939-45 " by P. J. Lewis and I. R. English, p. 271/2.

By the 22nd the 9th Battalion was in Chambois with the 8th sweeping the nearby Forêt de Gouffern, once used as the German Seventh Army Headquarters. Chambois itself appeared to be the meeting place of all the nations—Canadians, Poles, Americans, French, to say nothing of the Welsh from the 53rd (Welsh) Division! On the 23rd the men of the 8th Battalion joined the villagers of Bourth in a celebration of their liberation. The C.O.—Colonel Hugh Oldman, of the Green Howards, who had assumed command shortly after Lidwill was wounded—replied to an address of welcome in French; a band consisting of four cornets played the Marseillaise; and the officers of the Battalion sang 'God Save the King' unaccompanied, as the tune was not in the cornet players' repertoire. The advance continued, accompanied by a rapturous welcome from the enthusiastic French and an occasional exchange of shots with an odd party of itinerant Germans.

On the 29th of August the Brigade crossed the Seine where a bridgehead had already been secured by troops of the 43rd Division. Thence it moved northwards towards Amiens and Arras and the once familiar battle grounds of 1940. On the 31st 'C' Company of the 9th Battalion, in Beauvais, was attacked by some forty Germans who were successfully repulsed; and on the following day the 8th Battalion had a skirmish with some more in Picquigny, a town on the Somme north of Amiens and one which in 1940 had been a favourite spot with the Battalion for an evening's recreation. The town itself provided a scene of marked contrasts. Near the river men moved warily to keep under cover from German fire while just around the corner crowds of joyous townsfolk laughed and sang and danced in celebration of their newly won freedom. It was perhaps typical of the weeks of extraordinary progress that had marked the course of events since the break up of German resistance in the Falaise pocket. There had ceased to be any real front. Isolated pockets of the enemy kept surrendering, often in hundreds at a time. But every now and then a bridge would have to be fought for or a wood cleared; and this would cost lives. Thus the advance was not completely devoid of fighting or casualties. Yet the memory of the fighting, such as it was, must inevitably be overshadowed by that of the joyful scenes of liberation as the Brigade swept still further across

northern France and, on the 6th of September, crossed the
Belgian frontier on the road to Brussels and beyond.

2

THE 10TH AND 11TH BATTALIONS IN NORMANDY

For two years, after their return from Iceland, the 10th and
11th Battalions remained in England. For two long years,
mostly in Wales, they trained themselves for the invasion of
Europe. For a time they became mountain troops, and hopes
were raised that a special role might soon be allotted to them;
but as the months passed these hopes faded and they reverted
to the normal role of infantry. These were years of change, both
in organisation and in officers and men as well. Old faces
departed and new took their place. Each battalion had its share
of new C.O.s. In 1942 Brigadier Kirkup relinquished the
command of 70 Brigade of which both battalions still formed
part. Originally C.O. of the 8th Battalion, he had practically
raised the Brigade and had then taken it to France, reformed it
after Dunkirk, taken it to Iceland and back, and had longed to
take it into battle once again. His popularity was widespread
and he knew nearly every man in the Brigade; and his departure
at the end of his three years' tour of command was a sad occasion
for everyone.

As the years passed by the pace of training quickened; the
Battalions left Wales for eastern England; and by May of 1944
both were in camp in Norfolk ready for the fast approaching
assault across the Channel. Both were commanded by officers
of the Regiment, the 10th by Colonel "Jumbo" Sandars, the
11th by Colonel Michael Hanmer; both were highly trained
in the latest techniques of warfare; and both were eager to strike
at the enemy.

The 49th Division, of which it will be remembered 70
Brigade formed part, was allotted the role of a follow-up division.
Its task was to enlarge and exploit the foothold gained by the
assault troops. Moreover, 70 Brigade was to be reserve
Brigade, so detailed tactical planning before the troops landed
was unnecessary and, indeed, impracticable: but it was under-
stood that in any initial action the 11th Battalion would act as
Brigade reserve.

Final orders for the move to France did not reach the Battalions till the afternoon of D Day itself when, cheered by the news of a good start on the landing beaches, everyone hastened to put the finishing touches to his preparations. Apart from advance parties and vehicles, it was not, however, until the 11th of June that the Battalions actually set sail, after spending several days in a new concentration area near the port of Newhaven to which they moved on the 7th.

The sea voyage was without incident save for the sight of the " Mulberry " harbour being towed across the channel for a purpose which no one appreciated as they watched it. What was surprising, however, was the absence of any enemy activity. Indeed, when, on the 12th, both battalions waded ashore, armed like the complete tourist with Michelin guidebooks, francs and tins of boiled sweets, the war seemed far away. But this peaceful atmosphere soon changed. The march inland, for about six miles, was along narrow, dusty roads in blazing sunshine; and vehicles of all kinds, from dukws to Air Force lorries, streamed along them from the beaches; here Pioneers were filling in a crater; there signallers were repairing telegraph wires; everywhere were signs that though the battle had passed on, this was something more than an ordinary exercise!

The 10th Battalion was the first to draw blood. On the afternoon of the 16th it was ordered up to within a mile of St. Pierre where the 8th Battalion had had such a bitter struggle just a week before. Patrols moved into the village but found it empty, though they were sniped at from the hills and orchards beyond. Next day the Battalion occupied the village, but the enemy in the woods and orchards to the south proved troublesome and, after a night in close contact, a company attack under Lieutenant Delaney was put in on the morning of the 18th. This made some progress but not enough; and after an hour's hard tussle the company ran short of ammunition and had to pull back. On the following day another company had a crack, this time successfully, and it collected into the bargain the Battalion's first prisoners. But this only resulted in a period of stalemate during which both sides settled down to secure their positions and patrol with vigour. Night patrolling was continuous and there were frequent clashes. The Germans were expecting an Allied breakout and were very alert. They had

A patrol of ' B ' Company of the 1st Battalion moves off

Little Spaduro

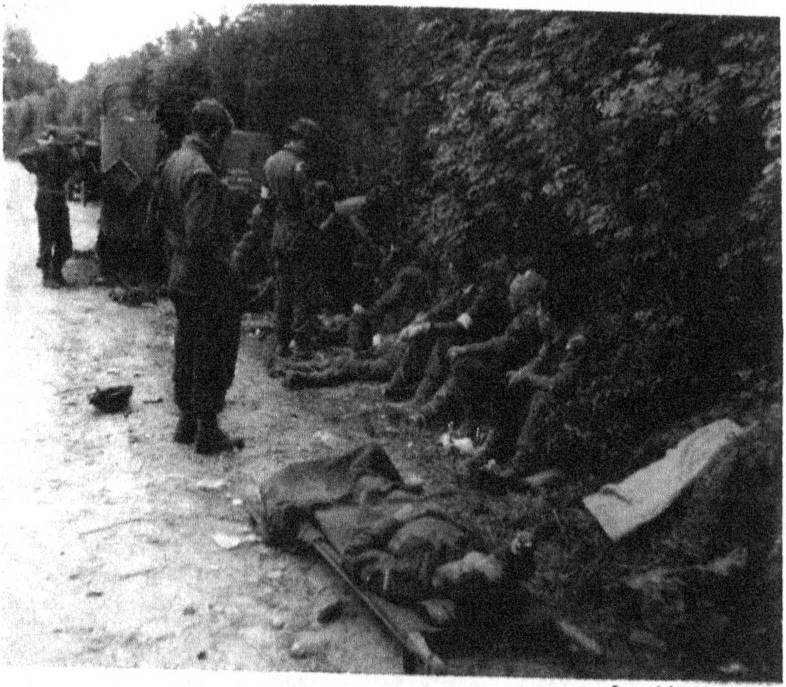

Imperial War Museum

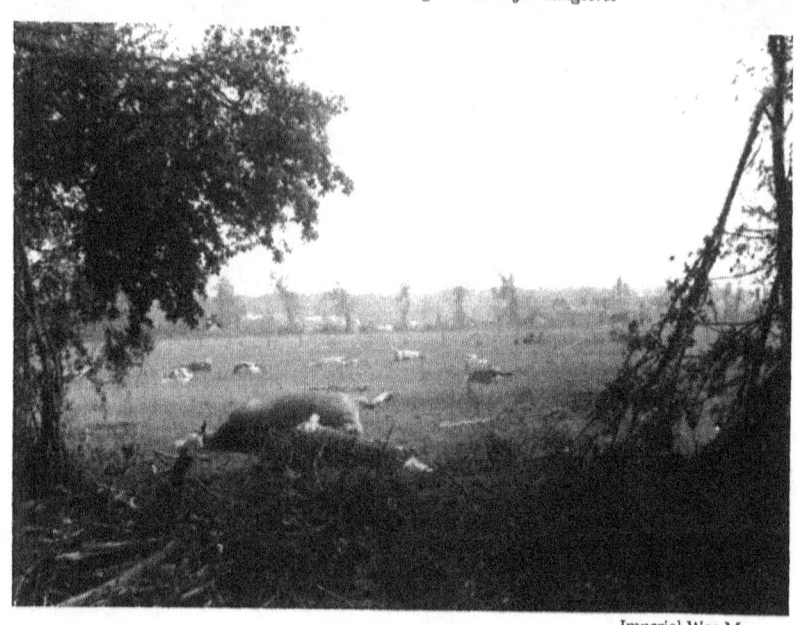

A Regimental Aid Post during the battle for Lingèvres

Imperial War Museum

Dead cattle near Fontenay-le-Pesnel

sentries posted about twenty-five yards apart which made it difficult to get exact information of their positions or to secure prisoners. But not impossible. On one night a newly arrived reinforcement officer and one private soldier together brought in a most talkative prisoner of Polish origin; and on another a platoon of ' A ' Company was involved in a lively little action in which the enemy brought up some tanks, one of which fell a victim to the Battalion anti-tank gunners.

Meanwhile, during these early days, the 11th Battalion had been enjoying a period of comparative calm. Whether by accident or design, it was lucky enough to be introduced and acclimatised to the atmosphere of battle by easy stages. From its first concentration area it moved up to the village of Duoy St. Marguerite; from there to the grimmer scenes of Cristot some two and a half miles north-east of Tilly; and then to join with the 10th Battalion in the battle of Rauray. This, however, is anticipating events a little. For, during the first week, with so much going on ahead of them, the Battalion waited eagerly to play its part, even though the days of quiet were not without incident. On the 21st of June, for instance, Battalion Headquarters was machine-gunned from the air and Corporal Morley, the M.T. corporal, wounded; and at odd intervals company positions were subjected to long range shellfire which was unpleasant not only because it came without warning but also because there was nothing with which to answer back! On the 23rd, however, the Battalion moved forward to Cristot to take over an area overlooking the Parc de Boislande. Here shellfire had denuded most of the trees of their foliage and the rich pasture was scored with the marks of tank tracks and pockmarked with mortar bombs. The enemy was close at hand and, in addition, over everything hung the overpowering stench of dead cattle whose bloated corpses, lying with their feet in the air, dotted the open fields round about. It was a sombre and depressing scene.

The main positions at Cristot were sited on a reverse slope. The Parc de Boislande extended down the forward slope and was a " no man's land " vigorously patrolled by friend and foe. Practically every subaltern did either a standing patrol during the day or night or led a fighting patrol to beat the bounds of the wood during darkness. It is difficult to convey any adequate impression of the eeriness of the Parc de Boislande. The undergrowth was unusually thick, making silent movement impossible, and the trees creaked in the wind in ghostly fashion. No wonder patrols sometimes returned to the Command Post wreathed in perspiration! One or two skirmishes occurred and in one Corporal Woodhead was taken prisoner, only to escape during some subsequent shelling and make his way back in stockinged feet to the Battalion's lines about a mile away. The grimness of Cristot will always be remembered by all who were there; but amongst much that was unpleasant there were more cheerful moments, and perhaps one of the best was when Captain Jack Pearson received a letter one morning in his slit trench asking him to play cricket for the Army against the R.A.F. As the match was "very important" he was offered a trial game in a British Empire XI!

On the 25th of June, in wet and misty weather, the 49th Division led one of a series of attacks by the Second Army between Tilly-sur-Seulles and Caen. The Division's task was to capture Rauray ridge, some six miles east of Caen, as part of a flank operation to assist the VIIIth Corps which was to thrust between Tilly and Caen in an enveloping threat to Caen itself. To begin with 70 Brigade was in reserve and the initial attack fell to others; but on the afternoon of the 26th it moved forward to Fontenay, a mile or so short of Rauray, which had been captured the previous day. The 11th Battalion was then ordered to go at once to the cross roads north of Rauray which was held by tanks of the Sherwood Rangers. They reached them just in time to form a rough defensive perimeter and dig in before darkness fell. But the fact that two enemy snipers refused to be dislodged even when tanks ran over their slit trench, was an indication of the fanaticism of the Germans opposing them and a foretaste of the trouble which lay ahead.

The Battalion had little information about the enemy. Indeed, it felt very much out in the blue. The nearest friendly troops were in its rear and there had been no time as yet to search any of the woods to west or east. Colonel Hanmer was thus faced with an awkward decision when at 10.30 p.m. orders were received from Brigade to find out if Rauray was occupied and, if not, then to move into it that night. A patrol was at once sent out to Rauray and the Battalion got ready, with some qualms, for an unreconnoitred night advance. Time was short and it was reckoned that a start would have to be made at 3 a.m. if the new positions were to be reached by daybreak.

At 2 a.m., however, news reached Battalion Headquarters that the officer in command of the patrol to Rauray had been wounded and captured, that there were an unknown number of Germans in the orchard round the village and that tanks had been heard in the woods nearby. Colonel Hanmer therefore decided against a hurriedly laid on night attack without proper reconnaissance and proposed instead to make his existing positions as secure as possible and then, by sending a strong fighting patrol forward at first light, to obtain a more accurate picture of the enemy positions and to occupy the village itself if possible.

Lieutenant Kenneth Hoggard's platoon was chosen for this task, supported by a troop of tanks from the Sherwood Rangers. Its move forward was preceded by a heavy barrage of medium and 25 pounder guns, but, unfortunately, to little effect. Very soon German 88 millimetres opened up and took a heavy toll of the tanks who were forced to beat a hasty retreat, leaving the platoon to battle on alone. This it did, and reached the centre of the village where Hoggard was himself badly wounded: but this did not prevent him sending back the valuable information that the enemy was holding Rauray with Spandau parties, snipers, at least two tanks, and some 88 millimetre guns on the flanks.

While the patrol was in progress the Germans began to mortar and snipe at the Battalion positions. As the morning wore on this intensified and movement of any kind became hazardous. The mortar fire was unpleasantly accurate but it was not till after the battle that the cause of it was discovered: for barely two hundred yards away was a cleverly concealed officer's sniping post, complete with sheets, mattress, chairs, flowers, wine and a telephone! Nevertheless, it was decided at about 11 a.m. to put in a battalion attack, even though this would have to be without tank support owing to the open ground in front of the village and the German guns concealed in the woods on the flanks. The guns had already knocked out seven tanks and two self-propelled guns earlier in the morning.

The attack began at midday. Platoons advanced in line abreast with fixed bayonets, 'B' Company on the right and

'D' on the left, with a platoon of 'C' Company ready for mopping up the village after the leading companies had reached its southern edge. The preliminary bombardment of the village and its environs again proved surprisingly ineffective and a murderous cross fire from Spandaus and mortars greeted the advancing columns. 'B' Company suffered heavily, particularly in officers and N.C.Os., but reached its objective with about fifty men left. It owed much to Corporal McArthur and Private Townsend, both of whom took command of their respective platoons when all the leaders had been killed and brought them through. 'D' Company, too, met stiffish opposition, but though Major Low, its commander, was killed, reached its objective without too many losses. It then remained to mop up and there was a good deal of it to be done. Snipers were as ubiquitous as ever, and even the Red Cross flags of stretcher bearers brought no immunity. The snipers, of whom about twenty were killed and one taken prisoner, were mostly teen-aged youths. All were heavily camouflaged and one, suspended by a rope from the boughs of a tree, was difficult to recognise even at close range. The prisoner was a typical Hitler Youth: he wept with rage at being captured alive and even spat when questioned by the Colonel. A search of his pockets produced a copy of "Mein Kampf."

A temporary lull now fell over the battlefield and the Battalion busied itself with badly needed reorganisation. Fortunately, there was no immediate counter-attack, and by nightfall much of the work was done. But thereafter the Germans tried hard to infiltrate; and for the next few days there was little rest or sleep for anybody. On one of them Major James Brewis, the sole surviving officer of 'D' Company, received severe wounds from Spandau fire, from which he later died. To encourage the men of a young company he personally took over a Bren gun and with a courage which reckoned naught of the consequences engaged at close range a German machine gun nest which was making movement in the company area hazardous. His place was promptly taken by Company Sergeant-Major Rochester, who, later on, was seriously wounded by mortar fire in equally gallant circumstances.

The 11th Battalion having thus secured Rauray, it fell to the 10th Battalion to attack through it on the 28th with the object of securing another feature in front of the town. Despite heavy artillery and mortar fire—and some German " Tiger " tanks—it achieved its object, thanks to some very gallant support by tanks of the Sherwood Rangers. One company commander was killed and another wounded, and one enemy counter-attack with infantry and armour was successfully beaten off; but the forward positions were very exposed and for the next twenty-four hours the Battalion spent an uncomfortable time being shelled and mortared by " moaning Minnies " and subjected on its right flank to continuous attempts by the Germans to infiltrate. After three days in close contact and with virtually no sleep, the Battalion was relieved by the Tyneside Scottish.

At dawn on the 1st of July the Germans launched their most determined and well planned counter-attack since the initial landing. They employed the resources of a whole division and seemed determined to punch a hole three to four miles wide in the British positions. The brunt of this fighting fell upon the 11th Battalion and the Tyneside Scottish. But the Battalion stood firm against all comers and the Tyneside Scottish knocked out over twenty tanks in its area. It was a day of bitter fighting. Among many outstanding incidents of a memorable day, one was an immediate counterattack, under Captain Robert Ellison, with a platoon of ' A ' Company, a troop of tanks and two sections of carriers under Captain J. B. Nicholson, which most effectively broke up a German attempt to infiltrate at the junction between the Battalion and a neighbouring Brigade. Another occurred early in the evening when, after some positions of the Tynside Scottish had been overrun, ' C ' Company was called up to counterattack. This went in exactly according to the book and could scarcely have been bettered at the battle school at Barnard Castle! It was personally led by the company commander, Captain Bill McMichael. While a platoon under Lieutenant Keith Pallister moved down a five sided field and engaged some Spandaus and a heavy machine gun, McMichael took the rest of the Company round the right flank. Down the alley between them tanks brought down covering fire. When Pallister got held up, McMichael dashed forward and threw a 77 grenade in front of the main enemy position. Unfortunately it was a blind; but Corporal Rowe of Pallister's platoon; quickly realising McMichael's plan, threw another with the desired effect and the Company was able to make short work of the Germans who made off in all directions. Not only was the attack successful but it enabled 70 Brigade to claim at the end of the day that it still held the same ground as when the German attack began.

On the 2nd of July the 10th Battalion moved forward once again to relieve the 11th and the Tyneside Scottish; but after twenty-four hours it, with the rest of the Brigade, was withdrawn for three days rest to reorganise and absorb reinforcements. The battle of Rauray was over.

A few days' relaxation was more than welcome. It was good to sleep the night through without interruption, and during daytime duties were kept to a minimum. Reinforcements—two hundred for the 11th Battalion and a hundred and fifty for the 10th—arrived and were quickly made welcome. Bayeux, almost undamaged, was conveniently near, and visits there to cinema and E.N.S.A. shows provided an attractive diversion. It was indeed a pleasant change to put on clean battle dress and shoes instead of boots and wander through the streets of that ancient town. After the grimness of Rauray, the sleepiness of Bayeux on a warm July day made the war seem a long way away.

The days passed all too quickly and on the 7th it was time to move forward again. The 10th Battalion moved up to take over positions in the Tilly area from the 8th and 9th Battalions of 151 Brigade, while the 11th followed them up in reserve; and as they did so five battalions of the Regiment—two of 70 Brigade and three of 151 Brigade—stood alongside each other in the line.

On the 11th of July the 50th Division launched an attack on the Juvigny-Hottot road; and the 10th Battalion was required to conform to the latter phase of this attack by seizing a wood surrounding a prominent house some three hundred yards to its front. The house appeared to be a key point in the German positions as possession of it would hinder movement in their rear areas, and the enemy thus fought hard to retain it. 'C' and 'B' Companies carried out the attack, but the former was only partially successful because its supporting flame throwing tanks lost direction and outpaced the infantry. The enemy, who beat a hasty retreat from the flames, was able to return before the men of 'C' Company arrived; and the Company suffered heavily moving across some open ground on the way, though some of them got near enough to the house to see German uniforms inside it and to intercept a German relief party. 'B' Company, however, was successful and encountered little opposition, and the Battalion as a whole remained in close contact with the enemy until the 13th of July when it was relieved by the 11th Battalion. The latter, incidentally, was only too glad to move forward into the line. For its own positions in reserve had become almost untenable from an overpowering smell which was thought at first to be something very dead but which, on further investigation, proved to be an abandoned Camembert cheese factory about a mile or so away!

Generally speaking, the position was still one of stalemate. The main effort to break the German positions was being made by the VIIIth Corps in the area of Caen; and for the next week or so the 49th Division had little spectacular to do. The enemy troops in the 70 Brigade area were a hotch-potch of all the nationalities of Europe. Interrogation of prisoners showed that German N.C.O.s were often commanding bodies of displaced Poles, Czechs, Dutch and Belgians, or, indeed, anyone who had chosen military service in return for such material comforts as the Wehrmacht could offer. Morale was not high and the prisoners had clearly little stomach for the fight; and in the darkness of one early morning a specially organised broadcast appeal was made to persuade those who were willing to desert. This resulted in thirteen miserable and rather tattered creatures staggering into the forward company positions of the 11th Battalion; and it was reckoned there would have been more had not the would-be deserters first to escape the attention of their German N.C.O.s, then cross a minefield and finally risk being shot on the way.

The lull in operations was broken by little other than routine shelling, which was always unpleasant, and the usual patrolling. At one moment detailed preparations—even down to type-written orders—were made for a set-piece attack: but nothing came of it. On one morning, too, Battalion Headquarters of the 11th Battalion found itself, by some strange mistake, the unwilling target of its own supporting artillery. Indeed, the Command Post received a direct hit, but was fortunately of such strong construction that its occupants escaped without a scratch; which, as one of them unkindly remarked, illustrates the ineffectiveness of artillery against prepared positions! Just to complete the excitement, German aircraft the same night dropped some bombs on the Headquarters; and the Adjutant, on returning to his slit trench after a spell as duty officer, found that in his absence it had suffered a direct hit.

As has been related already, the Germans withdrew in the Tilly-Hottot area on the 18th of July, for which the operations round Caen were partially responsible. As a result 70 Brigade was moved to the Caen area. Both Battalions by-passed the town, which was by this time a sad spectacle of rubble and devastation, and all the way had to move along a road which was uncomfortably under the eye of the German positions and, incidentally, under steady shellfire. The change from the countryside round Tilly was most marked. Gone were the close hedgerows of the bocage and in their place was a rolling, dusty plain, scored by a myriad of track marks. For a brief moment it might almost have been the desert, and notices appeared stressing the connection between speed and dust and shells, which might well have been salvaged from Tobruk!

The shelling was in fact particularly unpleasant, especially in the early stages of taking over these new positions: and it continued when, at the end of the month, both Battalions moved into Emieville about five miles due east of Caen. The 10th Battalion's Headquarters was in a luxurious old chateau complete with racing stables: but, being something of a landmark, the approaches to it were not altogether healthy. Unfortunately, even the rear areas were the target of the German artillery and the cooks of both Battalions found themselves boiling potatoes at one moment and diving for shelter the next. Though the supporting artillery did its utmost to give as good as it got, there was a steady drain of casualties, the 10th Battalion losing anything up to fifteen men a day. There were other irritations too; a mild form of dysentery affected many and with the hot August weather swarms of mosquitoes appeared, to make life in slit trenches almost unbearable. The medical services did their best to alleviate discomfort with ointment and lotion, but everybody tried to work out his own salvation, some with smoke, some by wrapping themselves in old curtains, some with attempts to construct flyproof trenches. Lance-Corporal Singleton, of the 11th Battalion, annointed his trench with petrol; but he soon became a casualty when, resting from his labours, he decided to light up and enjoy a quiet cigarette!

Patrolling, of course, continued unceasingly. Intelligence desperately wanted identifications. The 10th Battalion carried out one most successful sortie when, after shelling and mortaring the enemy positions and putting down a smoke screen at a specified time for two days running, the patrol went out on the third and caught the Germans napping. They brought back a complete enemy section. Later, on the 9th of August, after the German mortars had remained unusually silent, a platoon of the 11th Battalion sallied forth in daylight to see if the birds had flown. Again the enemy was taken by surprise and a prisoner quickly captured; but there had been no withdrawal—which was what the patrol wanted to find out. This sort of thing was especially valuable in view of the impending break out which was planned to take place in the middle of August and which, it was hoped, would end the long period of static warfare. It did. As has already been related, the Canadians in the east and the Americans sweeping forward from St. Lô to the west had opened the door for the break-through to the Seine: and, after six weeks at Emieville, 70 Brigade leapt forward eagerly on the morning of the 15th of August to join in the chase. Command of the 11th Battalion had by now passed to Lieutenant-Colonel Denis Hamilton—formerly second in command and a member of the Battalion since its formation in 1939; and Colonel Hanmer had gone to Divisional Headquarters prior to taking over the command of the 6th Battalion not long afterwards.

Little or no enemy resistance was at first encountered, the chief obstacles to the Brigade's advance being mines and bridges which had been respectively laid and blown with Teutonic efficiency. By the 18th the Brigade reached Mezidon on the River Dives. In that comparatively short time the devastation of the bridgehead was far behind. The birds, which had completely deserted the Caen area, were to be seen and heard again and as the columns made their way forward liberated Frenchmen, trundling handcarts piled high with mattresses and with bottles of cider swinging precariously from the axles, cheered them as they passed.

But at Mezidon the wheel of fortune turned. The town itself was clear of the enemy, but it was dominated by a hill feature, known as the Mont de la Vigne, some four miles beyond: and it soon became clear that it was upon this ground that the enemy had chosen to stand. The advance through Mezidon was led by the Tyneside Scottish and the 10th Battalion with the 11th in reserve: and it was not long before bitter resistance was encountered and a fierce encounter battle ensued.

Up till now the country had been pretty flat, but the advance had now reached the first of a range of thickly wooded hills. The road ran along the edge of the range, but between it and the Mont de la Vigne there were some six hundred yards of open fields intersected by two streams, each about twenty feet wide and, though fordable, with sheer banks up to twenty feet high. At the top of the hill was a chateau in a thick wood and below it an orchard sloping away towards the flat plain.

The leading company of the 10th Battalion ran into trouble as soon as it reached the orchard, where it was met with withering fire from close range. Major Keith Sanderson, the company commander, was hit in the face and rushed into the orchard. He was not seen again alive. The Company suffered heavily and lost most of its officers. Colonel Sandars decided to put in a two company attack as soon as artillery support could be arranged: and this was laid on ready to start at 8.30 in the evening.

The artillery fire came down very effectively and, apart from some rifle grenade fire at the second stream, which was very deep and fast flowing, there was little difficulty in reaching the orchard. "Then," as a member of 'D' Company put it, "hell was let loose from Spandaus firing from the hedgerows. I saw a lot of chaps fall wounded and the rest blazing away at the hedgerows. Cliff Thomas got to within thirty yards of one post, threw a grenade into it, got up to assault, but was killed outright by a Schmeisser[1] higher up."

Most of the Company had by this time closed in and were racing into the orchard firing from the hip and swearing profanely. Captain Riley, its commander, was knocked out by

[1] A German sub-machine gun.

a bullet through the shoulder, but the rest charged up the side of the orchard. Sergeant Brown, with the reserve platoon, cleared a cottage on the way and everybody reorganised just below the chateau for the final assault. As the last shells from the supporting barrage came down Private Jenn alone attacked three Germans in a post and took them prisoner. " We stormed the chateau," wrote one officer, " and Sergeant Brown and Private Ward did great work in clearing it. We captured fourteen prisoners in the chateau itself, including the German company commander and another officer. Corporal Fisher and Lance-Corporal Edwards both did extremely well in the attack, the latter knocking out several posts single-handed." But the price in men had been heavy. There were only about forty or so of ' D ' Company left to reorganise around the chateau and ammunition was short. Nor had ' C ' Company been much more fortunate. One officer had been killed and four wounded. Major Oliver Mason, the commander, was missing after personally attacking a position with a grenade. He was the last of the original company commanders and had commanded ' C ' Company since its formation as a young soldiers' company in England. It was learned later that he was wounded and captured and, later still, that the German hospital to which he went was overrun by Second Army: so he was happily rescued and evacuated to England. But now it was left to Sergeant Green and Sergeant Fullerton, with some eight men, to reach the Company's objective—which they successfully did—and for the rest of the Company to join them as best they could.

It was then dark; and the newly won positions were somewhat precarious and not easy to hold because of a ridge which extended to the left of the positions and which was higher than the chateau and thus overlooked it. Moreover, it was wooded and still occupied by the enemy.

There was no road up to the chateau. German patrols were encountered in the woods. The streams were difficult to cross in the dark and thus it took some time to bring up food and ammunition and to evacuate the numerous casualties. Everyone was tired and hungry. As the night wore on the German guns, which were only some two hundred yards ahead of the forward companies, were heard to limber up and withdraw. There was no doubt that the enemy had intended to hold the position at all costs and its loss had deprived him of a commanding view of the surrounding countryside. That, no doubt, was why, between 3 and 4 in the morning—just when, as it so happened, the food was at last arriving—a vigorous counter-attack was launched down the ridge and directed at the left of the two Companies.

The attack was well organised and extremely efficiently carried out by troops who obviously knew the ground well. It resulted in a confused melée of hand-to-hand fighting in the darkness. The Germans brought down a heavy mortar barrage and infiltrated a company under cover of it. Indeed, many of them attacked shouting in English and some were mistaken for troops of another Brigade who were expected to move up on the left flank but had in fact been delayed by the streams. From then on the situation rapidly deteriorated, for the Germans were liberally supplied with automatic weapons and the forward companies were still short of ammunition. Gradually each company in turn was forced back, fighting anyone they could identify. But when a second German company appeared, just as it was getting light, all who remained were ordered to fight their way out in small groups. This they successfully did and, as the sun came up, consolidated a firm front at the foot of the hill. The battle was over. The Germans did not follow up; and within twenty-four hours the Battalion had not only been relieved, but had received the sad and, indeed, bitter news that the battle of Mont de la Vigne had in fact been its last.

The news was sad indeed. On the 19th of August orders were received that 70 Brigade was to be disbanded. It was a decision which had in fact been taken some time before this last battle: for the initial planning of the invasion had envisaged the break-up of certain formations at this stage in the operations to conform with the general manpower situation. As General Montgomery himself told the Brigade, it was better to have a slightly smaller army of divisions up to strength than a large one with divisions short of men. So, as far as the 10th and 11th Battalions were concerned, the advance was therefore at an end; and it was now a question of withdrawing to a rest area until the arrangements for the final break-up were complete.

Anyone who has had experience of battalion life on active

service can appreciate exactly what this meant to those who had worked together so closely for so long. For four long years both Battalions had toiled hard to make themselves fit for war and now, after barely three months of active fighting, those who had been comrades in arms for all this time were to say good-bye. The blow was perhaps particularly unwelcome to the 11th Battalion who, unlike the 10th and the Tyneside Scottish, were still at full strength and maximum fighting efficiency. But orders were orders, and it was perhaps some consolation that, during the final disbandment in September, it was possible to dispatch each rifle company complete with its own officers. Not all went to battalions of the Regiment: and, indeed, most of the 11th Battalion were divided amongst the Green Howards, the Dorsets, the East Yorks and the Devons. Many of the 10th, however, found their way to 151 Brigade. Whatever their destination, all helped to play their part in the final battle for Germany and so, even indirectly, to represent the Regiment in the final downfall of the Nazi Reich.

3

151 BRIGADE IN THE LOW COUNTRIES

The Brigade crossed the Franco-Belgian frontier early on the morning of the 6th of September. The troop-carrying lorries made straight for Brussels and, as the Guards Armoured Division had already passed that way, the journey was peaceful. It was by no means uneventful, for the route was lined throughout with enthusiastic Belgians making the most of their liberation. Each battalion had to pass through Brussels itself to take up positions covering the city's eastern approaches. Their welcome from the inhabitants surpassed anything so far met with. It was a wonderful and heartening experience for all who took part in it though for battalion commanders an anxious one; for none could be quite sure how much of his battalion would emerge at the far end. From every window and flagstaff the Belgian national colours were once again freely displayed, after four years of Nazi occupation. Every conceivable able-bodied person thronged the streets to pay compliments and cheer the column as it passed. Those who could scramble on to the vehicles did so, and the rest lined the route so thickly that there was scarcely room to pass. Flowers and kisses were showered on all. In this latter respect some were luckier than others. Afterwards, Colonel Green of the 6th Battalion was heard to say to Reggie Atkinson, " It's amazing how out of all the innumerable women in the population of Brussels the only one to kiss me was an old woman of seventy ! " To which Reggie Atkinson drily retorted, " Well, Colonel, you are damned lucky. The only one to kiss me was an old man ! "

The Brigade stayed barely two days in Brussels but at any rate long enough to indulge in a little rest and recreation and to sample some generous Belgian hospitality. Very welcome it was too, but it was too good to last. Early on the morning of the 8th orders were received to move on again; for though there had been only scattered German opposition since the breakthrough at Falaise, the enemy had stiffened his resistance as the British and Americans moved forward into Belgium. Antwerp had fallen to the 11th Armoured Division on the 4th of September; but as the leading divisions pushed forward beyond Brussels opposition was met at the line of the Albert Canal. " Between this barrier and the next—the Meuse-Escaut Canal—the terrain lent itself to defence, for it is sandy heath broken by small streams and patches of swamp. Here the Germans concentrated on holding the main crossroads, establishing themselves in stoutly built villages which were difficult to by-pass and which could not be quickly taken by direct assault since the armoured divisions had not sufficient infantry or artillery. The defenders, mostly from parachute regiments, fought with fanatical bravery and were dislodged only when their village strongholds were demolished house by house."[1]

The Guards Armoured Division were the first to get over the Albert Canal, forcing a crossing at Beeringen on the Brussels-Louvain-Eindhoven road; but their bridgehead was heavily counter-attacked by German paratroops. At Antwerp all attempts to advance over the water obstacles north of the city were unsuccessful and so, after a regrouping of the forces in the Antwerp area, the 11th Armoured Division was switched to the Beeringen bridgehead and the 50th Division was ordered to make a new bridgehead over the Canal to the left of the Guards.

[1] " The Struggle for Europe " by Chester Wilmot, p. 486.

On the morning of the 8th of September 69 Brigade crossed the Canal between Steelen and Herenthals but was soon engaged in heavy fighting. It was then decided to commit 151 Brigade which was ordered to force a further crossing with the object of capturing the town of Gheel a mile or so north of the Canal.

To the 8th Battalion fell the task of the initial crossing. This was to be made by ' A ' Company in assault boats, silently and without supporting fire until opposition was met and the enemy positions located. No one knew what sort of resistance would be encountered but anticipations were that it would not be great. Once the 8th were across, the 6th Battalion was to pass through it and capture Gheel and, if opposition was light, exploit beyond. The 9th Battalion was to remain in reserve.

The 8th Battalion began crossing in the late afternoon of the 8th. After about a quarter of an hour two platoons of ' A ' Company had reached the far bank with comparatively few casualties. One or two boats were, however, holed. One, carrying Lance-Corporal James Hunter and his section, was sunk and two men were killed outright and three wounded. Hunter immediately dived into the water, wearing full battle kit, grabbed hold of a wounded man and swam with him to the Steelen bank. Then, regardless of enemy machine-gun fire which was sweeping the Canal, he dived in a second time and, with fire ripping the water all round him, rescued the second man. Finally he plunged in once again and brought the third man to safety. By the time that it was Company Headquarters' turn to cross the German fire had increased considerably, and as the members of it scrambled up the enemy bank Major Chris Beattie, the Company commander, received severe wounds from which he later died. His was a particularly sad loss as he had served with the Battalion since 1939 and was one of the original pre-war Territorial officers. As the Company advanced beyond the bank it ran into heavy opposition. From their positions in the hedgerows and road embankment the Germans opened deadly and accurate fire with Spandaus and light mortars. Casualties began to mount and within half an hour ' A ' Company had lost all its officers. But that did not stop it. Under the Company Sergeant-Major and Sergeant George Self the Company pushed on and occupied its objective; and despite heavy mortaring and machine-gun fire—Sergeant Self and two

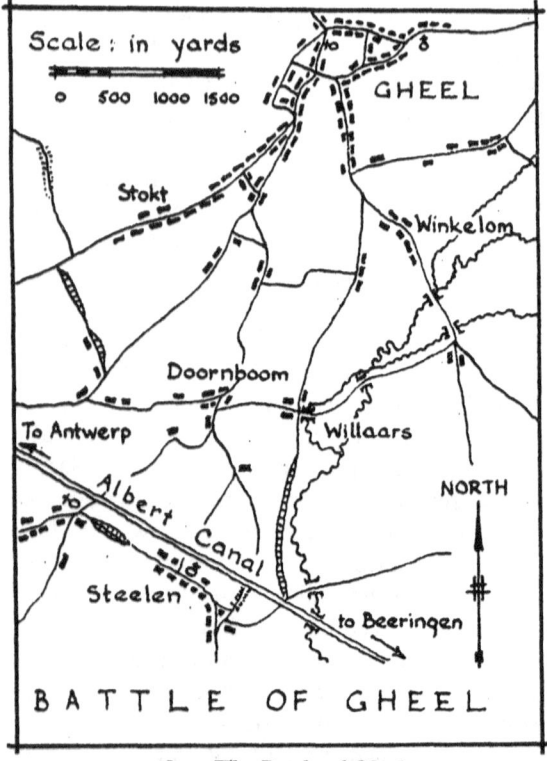

18. *The Battle of Gheel*

men together stalked and silenced two of them—the Company held steadfastly on to what it had gained.

At 5.30 p.m. 'D' Company crossed the river. They had an easier time of it than did 'A' and their casualties were light. So did the rest of the Battalion who crossed unopposed and were in position on the enemy bank by the time it was dark. Once there, the Sappers were able to begin the building of a Class 9 bridge, consisting of two ramps supported on canvas rafts with the ramps wide enough to carry a vehicle; and while the Battalion sent out patrols the Sappers set to work, though not without periodic interruptions from the fire of an enemy tank in position somewhere outside and to the flank of the bridgehead.

About 11 p.m. a sharp counter-attack developed against 'A' and 'C' Companies. The night was fine and there was a brilliant moon; and the scene was further lit up by burning

Imperial War Museum
Men of the 11th Battalion coming out of the line near Fontenay-le-Pesnel

The 9th Battalion before the attack on St. Joost

Lt. Col. John Mogg arranging for the safe passage of Gen. Wolz's surrender party near Hamburg

The Durham Light Infantry Memorial Garden, Durham City

buildings set alight by a German anti-aircraft gun which continually swept the area with incendiary shells. By the light of moon and flames the Germans advanced in open formation. They were met by withering fire from over a dozen Bren guns. But still they came on; and some got to within twenty yards of their opponents so as to throw their grenades. Then as suddenly as the attack had started it petered out. The Germans broke and ran, leaving their dead behind but carrying off their wounded. For the rest of the night the Battalion was left in comparative peace. It had won the first round.

Now it was the turn of the 6th Battalion. It crossed the Canal on the morning of the 9th, passed through the 8th Battalion and dug in in positions just south of Gheel. There was no violent enemy reaction at once; and indeed the Battalion had the day to secure itself. It was not till next morning, the 10th, that trouble started. Then the forward companies were subjected to heavy mortar and artillery fire and 'B' Company reported the Germans advancing with tanks in support. This resulted in an exchange of fire which lasted for an hour and a half at the end of which the Company reported the situation as easier. Meanwhile Colonel Green had received orders that the Battalion was to attack Gheel with support from artillery and tanks on a timed programme which was to begin at 2 o'clock that afternoon.

The plan was for 'D' and 'C' Companies to push through 'A' and 'B' behind the artillery barrage; but even before zero hour the Germans renewed their attacks on 'B' Company, infiltrating into and mortaring their positions. Indeed activity was so brisk that Reggie Atkinson, the commander, was unable to get to the Battalion 'O' Group. Then, just to make things more difficult, the enemy set upon 'A' Company on the right flank and succeeded in overrunning the forward platoons. It was an ugly situation and two sections of carriers were despatched to help restore it with all speed. 'C' Company, who were trying to move through 'A' to the front line, found the going difficult owing to withering Spandau and mortar fire: and the C.O. sent George Wood to this flank to reorganise the somewhat chaotic position there, which in due course he successfully accomplished.

On the left flank, however, 'D' Company had been able to launch the attack as planned and under Major Ken Wood had gallantly pressed on behind the barrage—in the face of determined resistance—and with the aid of tanks succeeded in reaching Gheel itself. Their progress did much to relieve the pressure on the right and, in fact, the Germans withdrew in front of 'A' and 'C' Companies, allowing them in their turn to move forward. So despite casualties the Battalion reached all its objectives; many enemy dead littered the battlefield; and 'D' Company was able to boast the capture of one hundred and sixty-five prisoners as well as a fair haul of enemy equipment.

The attack was a fine effort on the part of the Battalion, particularly after the early set-back on 'A' Company's front. Morale was high as everybody settled down to consolidating the newly won gains: but casualties had been fairly heavy and, as ill luck would have it, Colonel Green was himself wounded as he toured the company positions while the Battalion was consolidating and he had to be evacuated, leaving the Battalion once again in the capable hands of George Wood.

While the 6th Battalion had been battling for Gheel the 9th Battalion had arrived in Steelen and begun to cross the river. Once over, it was ordered to send a company to Winkelom, a village about a mile south-east of Gheel, with the rest of the Battalion following to secure a firm base for further advances east of the town. The Company had to fight its way to Winkelom against considerable opposition, but by late afternoon the Battalion was moving on to its objectives. Meanwhile 'A' and 'D' Companies of the 8th Battalion moved forward beyond Doornboom in the direction of Gheel so as to support the advance of the 9th Battalion. These two Companies ran into some German tanks and 'A' Company was caught in the open, its only officer, Captain Bill Ridealgh, being killed and its platoons somewhat disorganised. Thanks, however, to Sergeant Self who took command of the Company, the situation was restored; the Company drew back a little; and 'D' Company dug in where they were. With the latter firmly in position, the rest of the Battalion was able to advance as far as Stokt by nightfall.

As darkness fell the Germans launched a counter-attack on the 8th Battalion with unexpected suddenness. It was made by some two hundred men and about ten tanks and its ultimate objective was the Sappers' bridge at the Battalion's original crossing place. The enemy penetrated between 'D' and 'B'

Companies and even reached to within two hundred yards of Brigade Headquarters which was itself less than half a mile from the bridge. Going up the road to Gheel in a carrier Philip Hampson came on sixty men by the roadside who turned out to be Germans—somewhat to his surprise! One of them came running towards the carrier but was killed by Private Edwards firing his rifle from the hip. Later a mortar carrier, halted on the same road, was passed by a German tank but managed to turn round and race back past the tank unmolested.

The night was one of confusion; though it was soon realised that the attack was a full scale one on the Brigade positions. Each battalion stood to all night and there was a good deal of mortaring and shelling. The 6th Battalion captured a complete German patrol consisting of an officer and fifteen men. The 9th Battalion first heard that things were wrong from the 8th. All its companies were warned to expect trouble and 'D' Company was the first to get it. There was some sharp fighting in their area but with the aid of a troop of tanks the Company prevented the enemy from breaking through and finally forced them back towards Stokt. 'C' Company was pulled back to Willaars, nearer the river, and was able to neutralize a party of Germans and two tanks who had reached the Doornboom crossroads. But neither side was willing to move while it was still dark; so the position remained confused and uncertain throughout the Brigade area for the rest of the night.

Dawn came with a heavy mist lying close to the ground: but once it cleared the Germans were as active as ever. The men who comprised the enemy forces in this area were from the German Air Force. With the shattering of their armies in Normandy and the consequent need for their reorganisation, the German High Command had been compelled to improvise new forces to hold the Allies' advance. Among them was a Parachute Army which, in addition to parachute regiments, was composed of battalions raised from Luftwaffe air crews and ground staff. Not all were properly trained for ground fighting but they were all devoted Nazis, very young and very brave; and they fought, if not skilfully, at any rate fanatically.

About 10 a.m. the Germans who had infiltrated into the 8th Battalion area began to fall back. Some tried to get away on foot, some climbed on a tank, others on a self-propelled gun.

Sergeant Joe Middleton, seeing the latter covered with Germans, crawled some thirty yards with a Piat gun and with his first shot hit and knocked out the gun, killing ten of the enemy. Then he machine-gunned the rest of them—some thirty in all—who turned and ran for it, leaving their dead and their weapons behind. In all the Battalion captured fifty-four prisoners during the morning and counted twenty-seven dead bodies.

The enemy did not, however, draw back in front of the 6th and 9th Battalions. ' A ' Company of the latter was attacked by some fifty of them who, with the aid of tanks, were beaten off without much difficulty and with heavy losses, the Company capturing eight and counting thirty bodies. At the Doornboom crossroads there was something of a deadlock; neither side could leave without coming out into the open and the Germans were too close to ' C ' Company for an artillery shoot. But as the morning wore on they began to slip away as best they could, only to run into the 8th Battalion. The 6th Battalion had a very busy morning and daylight found a number of tanks of both sides milling around in its area. There were four quick " brew-ups " within less than a hundred yards of Battalion Headquarters, one Sherman disposing of two German Panthers and the new 17-pounder gun " opening up Boche tanks like cans of beans," as one officer put it. On the right ' B ' Company had to call for tank and air support to deal with an enemy tank and infantry attack; and this was at once forthcoming and helped to ease the situation for a while.

As the day wore on, however, enemy pressure around Gheel itself increased. The 6th Battalion was getting short of food and ammunition and generally was pretty thin on the ground. Carriers managed to get through to the forward companies with ammunition and Captain Winston Field was ordered by George Wood to collect as many men as possible from ' A ' Echelon and take them to Gheel to reinforce ' D ' Company who were in danger of being overrun. This Field succeeded in doing, though not without some anxious moments on the way. " If we were thankful to reach Gheel," he wrote afterwards, " Major Ken Wood of ' D ' Company was even more glad to see us. His men had been fighting against heavy odds in the fields in front of the town, across dykes into the town, and then from house to house inside the town, and now they were being heavily counter-attacked by the enemy who were numerous enough to cut off odd parties and sections in the street fighting. We loaded the wounded into three carriers and sent forty prisoners off with them right away—just in time as we soon discovered—and that left one platoon, Company Headquarters and my extra men."

Again and again the enemy shelled Gheel with heavy concentrations behind which moved his infantry; and again and again the attacks were beaten off by hard hand-to-hand fighting in the streets and houses, the fiercest fighting the Battalion had experienced since landing in France. At one stage some Germans were seen sheltering behind a disabled carrier which had belonged to the Sappers and contained a quantity of ammonal. A burst of fire from a Sherman tank blew up carrier and Germans together. Later, both the Company's anti-tank guns were put out of action, but by maintaining them in position the crews managed to bluff the enemy into thinking they might fire.

At last, however, continued infiltration by the enemy forced the depleted Battalion to fall back. Orders to do so managed to reach each company by carrier. ' D ' Company, though surrounded, fought their way out with bayonet and Sten gun. Their Headquarters had been in a café whose owner had told them the beer was theirs. "Just before leaving the square," wrote Field, " I happened to look in at our café: some of our supporting tankmen were keeping the pump handle busy! But perhaps the hardest thing for us to do was to leave behind in Gheel a pleasant looking girl, freckled and always cheerful, who, during the five years of war in Belgium, had befriended and helped with food and clothes and rest seven Allied airmen, all of whom had left letters of appreciation with her. Josephine, though only seventeen, had guided our men out of almost surrounded houses, had tended our wounded and had not flinched at the torn bodies of dying men. She told us she would look after those of our wounded, whom we could not take with us, in the town hospital until we came again, as she was sure we would. We pulled out leaving our two useless guns till last and met the relieving company of the 8th Battalion who had to fight to reach positions just short of the town."

The rest of the Battalion followed ' D ' 's example. ' B ' Company disengaged and retired with Reggie Atkinson somewhat annoyed at having to leave: his Headquarters, too, had been in a café! But 'C' and 'A' Companies—who on account of casualties had amalgamated—were apparently overwhelmed and thought to have all been killed or captured; and it was not till two days later that it was learnt that by sheer guts and determination Lieutenant Geoffrey Seggie had brought out the remnants of them, having fought from street corner to street corner through the town.

Though the 6th Battalion had been forced to fall back it still managed to keep a foothold in the south-eastern outskirts of Gheel and during the evening it was relieved by two companies of the 8th Battalion. The latter were heavily shelled and snipers who had infiltrated were active. One lucky man was Corporal Douglas of the Anti-Tank Platoon. He had a miraculous escape when he was hit by a mortar bomb which failed to explode and inflicted him with no more than a bruised shoulder. As it got dark the fighting was still pretty confused; but the worst was perhaps over and the 9th Battalion was able to report a comparatively quiet night.

One notable incident occurred during the evening. Captain Rory O'Conor of the 8th Battalion, who had been reported missing as a prisoner earlier in the day, turned up at Battalion Headquarters with a remarkable story of the events following his capture. He had been put in the charge of two young German airmen who escorted him aimlessly about the countryside, quite obviously hopelessly lost. They talked a lot about Gheel and asked O'Conor in bad French who was holding it. Knowing the 6th Battalion was there, O'Conor replied that the Germans held it and was promptly advised to lead the way there. After going some way the Germans got suspicious; but by pretending that south was north on his compass O'Conor managed to reassure the two ignorant young men, and they marched ahead until they met a British tank, when the Germans fled and O'Conor was rescued.

O'Conor was then ordered to report to Major Wood's Company of the 6th Battalion and with this Company, surrounded in Gheel, he held a corner of the town until, after five counter-attacks had been resisted, the Company was relieved and O'Conor rejoined his own Battalion.

The darkness brought a lull and welcome respite to the hard

pressed Battalions. It also brought news that on the following day the Brigade was to be relieved by a Brigade of the 15th Scottish Division. But even when daylight came the relief did not take place until the enemy had made one more attempt to disrupt the bridgehead and reach the river. This attack fell upon the 9th Battalion. One German force got between ' A ' and ' B ' Companies on the main road and another attacked ' A ' Company's forward platoon from three sides, while engaging ' B ' Company with machine-gun fire as a diversion. At one time both ' A ' Company's forward platoons were cut off; but they were extricated with the aid of some tanks and the whole Company re-formed to the south of its original position. The C.O. then ordered the ground which had been yielded to be recaptured before the relief by the 15th Division; and it was— within an hour. So the relief took place as planned and without undue disturbance.

On the 8th Battalion sector, too, there were signs of a further German counter-attack early on the morning of the 12th, and some enemy parties were observed forming up for it. It failed to materialise, however, thanks to heavy and accurate mortar and artillery fire; and though the Battalion's forward positions could not be relieved until after dark they were in due course handed over without incident.

The battle of Gheel was over. It had been of vital importance. The German intention had been to eliminate the bridgehead so as to open up the flank of the Beeringen bridgehead further east. Despite every effort they had failed to break the Durham Brigade's stubborn hold; and the troops that could have been deployed against the Guards at Beeringen were lost in three days of bitter attacks to reach the Steelen bridge. The support of the infantry by tanks and artillery had been quite superb even though, at the end, the gunners were down to their last few rounds and were running their own ferry service to Brussels for ammunition. But the real victory belonged to the infantry and the dogged resistance which in times of crisis had been the pride of the three Battalions from Africa to Europe. It speaks highly for their achievements in and before Gheel that when the Scottish Division attacked the town the next day they passed through it without firing a shot; the Germans had had enough and had made off northward. It was perhaps fitting, too, that when the 6th Battalion later re-entered Gheel to fetch the wounded and bury the dead the first person they met was Josephine. "We found a bottle of good Burgundy wine," said Captain Field, " and drank to Josephine and the 6th Durham Light Infantry."

A phase had ended with the battle of the bridgehead and a new one was now to begin, not only for the D.L.I. Brigade but for the whole of the Second Army. At home a large airborne Army had been assembled and General Montgomery had been awaiting an opportunity to use it. Now was the time; and the daring of his plan was only matched by the far reaching consequences which it would have were it successful. The object of the operations—which were outlined to the men of the D.L.I. Brigade on the 17th of September, the very day on which the operation itself started—was to " bounce " a crossing of the Rhine, isolate the Ruhr industrial area and then to penetrate deeply into the heart of the Reich.

Between the bridgehead at Beeringen and the eastern bank of the Rhine are five major water obstacles—two canals, the River Maas at Grave, the Waal at Nijmegen and the Lower Rhine at Arnhem. The plan involved laying a carpet of airborne troops across these waterways on the general axis of the road through Eindhoven, Veghel, Grave, Nijmegen and Arnhem. The troops dropped would form a corridor along which the XXXth Corps—composed of the Guards Armoured, the 43rd and the 50th Divisions—was to advance to Arnhem where a bridgehead was to be established by the 1st Airborne Division. The role of the infantry divisions was to take over the ground gained by the armour and to hold the flanks of the corridor secure against enemy attack. If the operation were successful the Siegfried Line, which petered out north of Aachen, would be outflanked and a powerful armoured force would be established on the edge of the North German plain. In fact, because of supply difficulties on the other fronts of the Allied Armies, the operation provided the last slender chance of ending the war in 1944.

The failure of this boldly conceived plan is now only too well known. The bridges between Eindhoven and Nijmegen were captured and the XXXth Corps advanced up the road towards Nijmegen without undue difficulty. But the Germans put up a vigorous resistance in Arnhem itself; and despite the gallantry of the 1st Airborne Division, the bridge there was never captured and the battered remnants of the Division had to be withdrawn across the Rhine.

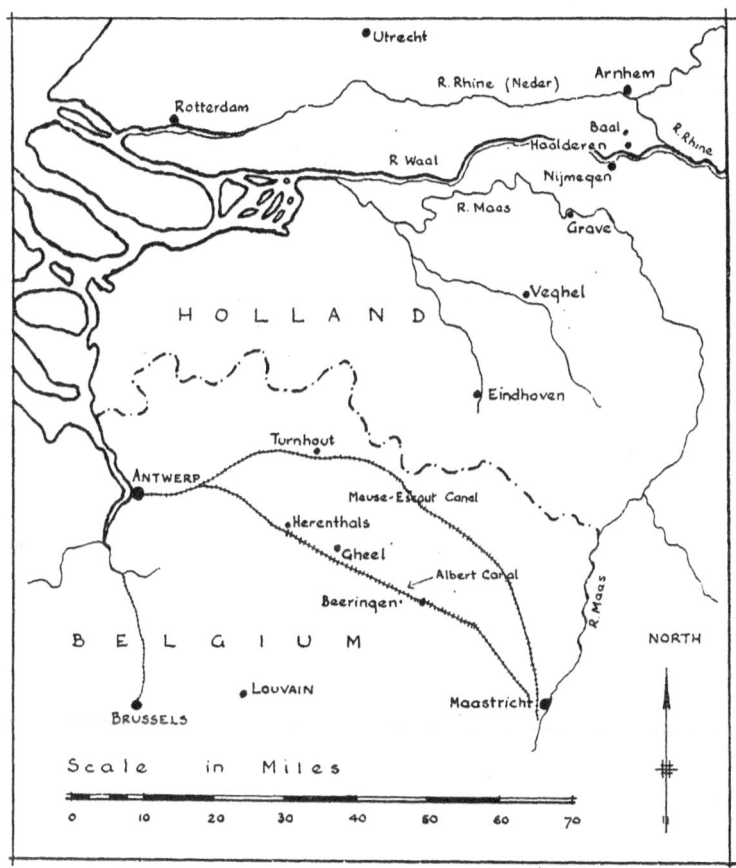

19. *The Low Countries*

The D.L.I. Brigade played a comparatively minor part in the XXXth Corps' northward advance. The 50th Division was reserve division and the Brigade its reserve brigade. Though on the move up the Germans had attempted—and on occasions succeeded in—the cutting of the road, the task of reopening it fell to others further forward on the line of march. So for the Durham Light Infantry the period between the 17th of September and the beginning of October was one of comparative peace and quiet.

The bridge at Nijmegen had been captured on the 20th of September by the American 82nd Airborne Division and the Guards Armoured had reached the town itself. But the failure at Arnhem and the withdrawal of the 1st Airborne Division transformed a vigorously resisting enemy around Nijmegen into an aggressive one. Tanks and infantry hitherto engaged at Arnhem were now freed for action against the Nijmegen bridgehead; and the recapture of the bridge there over the Waal was the enemy's immediate objective. To the 50th Division was allotted the task of guarding the bridge.

The D.L.I. Brigade reached Nijmegen on the 2nd of October and crossed the now famous bridge. " It was a magnificent structure, like a larger edition of the Tyne Bridge at Newcastle. No one stopped to examine it very carefully because . . . the Germans had a heavy gun in the Reichswald forest which shelled the bridge from time to time. It was about seventeen miles away and since the British had no gun capable of firing so far, and the R.A.F. Typhoons could not locate it in the forest, the gun had not been put out of action. When the Canadian Military Police arrived they summed up most people's feelings about the bridge by putting up notices which said: ' If you are going fast—go faster.' "[1] So each battalion moved quickly over to take up positions beyond the river in the country, known as " The Island," lying between the Waal and the Neder Rhine.

" The Island " was to be the Brigade's home for the next two months. It was also to be its last battleground of the war, though none yet knew it. It was an area of flat, rich pastures, mingled with orchards of apple and pear and criss-crossed by numerous canals and ditches—good land for farming, no doubt, but less well adapted for war. For it was overlooked by the high ground beyond Arnhem—though immediate observation of " The Island " was only possible from houses and church steeples—and the low lying ground meant that it was difficult to dig a trench deeper than two feet without striking water.

Early in the afternoon of the 4th a Brigade attack was launched to enlarge the bridgehead and to gain observation

---

[1] " The 8th Battalion The Durham Light Infantry, 1939-45 " by P. J. Lewis and I. R. English, p. 292.

over the flat, open ground beyond the village of Haalderen, four or five miles east of the Nijmegen-Arnhem road. The 8th Battalion attacked on the right towards Haalderen and the 9th on the left with the object of capturing Baal, another village almost due north of Haalderen. The attack was accompanied by some devastating close support from rocket-firing Typhoons and the now familiar barrage. It went well. The 8th Battalion had a certain amount of difficulty on its left flank to begin with, largely due to lack of experienced men in the company concerned; but this was only temporary and by 5.30 p.m. all objectives had been reached, sixty prisoners had been captured, and the old hands reckoned it had been one of the easiest attacks the Battalion had ever had to carry out. The progress of the 9th Battalion was somewhat similar. On the left flank ' C ' Company had to call for a repeat of the barrage to help them forward, but ' D ' Company on the right reached their intermediate objective within half an hour and the rest of the Battalion passed through towards Baal. As the advance made headway, German resistance stiffened and ' A ' Company encountered some heavy Spandau fire and lost all its officers save Captain Thomson, the second in command. But despite these set-backs all the Battalion's objectives had been taken by 4 p.m. and in addition to a hundred prisoners the booty included some nine anti-tank guns, mortars, bazookas and two half-track vehicles.

The 6th Battalion moved forward to the area of a factory in Bemmel, another village west of the other two, where for several days it carried out a series of active patrols, one of which was suddenly picked up at night by a searchlight and forced to make a somewhat hasty withdrawal. Their positions were not the most comfortable, chiefly because of the number of " overs " intended for the Nijmegen bridge which fell in the Battalion area: and even ' B ' Echelon had to admit it was now in the firing line.

On the 7th all three battalions moved back into Nijmegen for a few days' rest. Colonel Michael Hanmer, who had assumed command of the 6th Battalion a few days after the battle of Gheel in which Green was wounded, had as mixed a command as one could want for the defence of the bridge. It included anti-aircraft and anti-tank guns, searchlights, dukws for river patrols, a Field Security Section, Dutch Civil Police and four explosive experts! The bulk of each battalion's time, however, was spent in relaxation—hot baths, cinema and ENSA shows, and writing letters home; though the break did not last long and was all too soon over. On the 12th the Brigade moved back into "The Island" and began a longish period of static warfare involving each battalion in ten-day spells in the line, followed by three days out of it at rest. The object of this lull was to guard the Nijmegen bridge as a potential threat to the German defences in the north while preparations were made and the build-up prepared for an offensive the following spring. As the Germans, too, were ready for a respite to re-organise their shattered armies, both sides settled down to digging, wiring, laying mines and patrolling with the usual accompaniment of harassing fire from mortars and artillery.

The ground which the Brigade had to occupy was flat and marshy. The majority of the few large villages and scattered farmsteads had already been reduced to ruins by the fighting, which meant that the troops had to rough it in the open. Those who garrisoned that desolate salient during the winter of 1944 will long remember the weather and uncomfortable living conditions. The whole area was intersected by dykes, some of which were blocked by dead cattle; and when it rained, as it often did, the dykes became filled to overflowing. The first winds of winter soon stripped the orchards of their leaves and the men occupying them of their cover. Caught in the open it was often a case of deciding whether a shell would land a safe distance away or whether to jump into several feet of water in the nearest ditch or lie flat in a foot of squelching mud. Nor were conditions for patrolling ideal, as patrols often had to carry ladders or planks with which to span the ditches and this made movement—particularly silent movement—difficult, and an already nerve-wracking job more so.

So passed the weeks of October; and November brought heavy rain and little change from the established routine. Every now and then the stereotyped course of events would be broken by the sight of V-bombs speeding overhead to London, Antwerp or Brussels. Occasionally the enemy would be hoist with his own petard in this respect. The 6th Battalion War Diary records at this time, " flying bomb passed over Battalion

H.Q. in north-easterly direction. Engine cut out and a few seconds later loud explosion heard from enemy lines. Great satisfaction." On another occasion a diversion of a different kind was provided in the shape of the Regimental Band from Brancepeth which, under Bandmaster Frank Rose, arrived at Nijmegen in the middle of November and worked overtime at concerts, church parades and dances. Otherwise the standard routine continued uninterrupted.

Towards the end of November Rumour laid a very special egg. The 50th Division was to return to England, a piece of news which to those who had come safely through so much fighting with the most battle hardened division in the British Army seemed almost too good to be true. But true it was; and it was soon confirmed when battalions were ordered to prepare nominal rolls of men who were to go home with the battalion and those who were to remain behind as reinforcements for other units. For it was to the voracious demand for reinforcements that the 50th Division had now to be sacrificed. Not only that, but the time had perhaps been reached when the men who had been through the fire of almost every major battle from Gazala to the Rhine needed something more than a short period of rest behind an active and hotly contested front line. The Division was still to continue as an entity, though as a mere skeleton of its former self; for it was to return to England to act as a training division for reinforcements. The last battle in Europe was not to be theirs: though the demand for reinforcements meant that only those with the longest service would return home and the remainder would be scattered far and wide amongst the British Liberation Army. This was virtually the disbandment of the famous Northumbrian Division, as it certainly was of the Durham Brigade. The 6th and 8th Battalions, reduced to small cadres, set sail from Ostend on the 14th of December, arriving at Southampton the following day. But they sailed without the 9th Battalion who were chosen to replace a lorried infantry battalion in the 7th Armoured Division and were to have the privilege of representing not only the Brigade but the Regiment in the final collapse of Hitler's Germany.

The 6th and 8th Battalions spent the rest of the war in Yorkshire until, after the cease fire had sounded, both were disbanded. The 9th Battalion eventually reached Berlin, of which more later. But all three have risen again—though not as comrades in a newly constituted D.L.I. Brigade—and each to-day stands guardian of a fighting record of which they and the Regiment are justly proud.

4

THE 9TH BATTALION FROM THE WAAL TO THE ELBE

Leaving the 50th Division was a great wrench for the 9th Battalion which had been part and parcel of the D.L.I. Brigade through two world wars and the twenty odd years in between. It meant saying farewell to many old faces, though, in return, a few were welcomed into the Battalion under cross-postings from the 6th and 8th Battalions. But since the change had to be made, there were few divisions of which the Battalion would rather have formed a part than that of their comrades-in-arms of the Desert war, the " Desert Rats ", whose divisional sign had now to be substituted for the familiar " TT " flash. The Battalion left " The Island " during the evening of the 30th of November. By 2.30 p.m. the following day it had been completely reorganised for its new role of lorried infantry, had taken in and drafted out some two hundred men, had reshuffled its transport and was ready to move. At 4.30 p.m. it moved off to join 131 Brigade of the 7th Armoured Division at Dilsen in Belgium. Its comrades-in-arms in the Brigade were the 1st/5th Queen's and the 2nd Devons.

For the first month in its new role the Battalion was left in comparative peace. It was a period of static defence in the area north of Sittard—and so just inside the German border— where the flat, open ground provided a welcome contrast with conditions in " The Island " and where the lie of the land made any continuous defence line virtually impossible. Instead, villages were defended by company groups, with supporting arms, and the gaps in between them were covered by fire. The Battalion had the interesting experience of occupying ground in three different countries; for its rifle companies were in villages in Germany, its ' A ' Echelon at Sittard in Holland and its ' B ' Echelon at Dilsen in Belgium.

The Battalion undertook its fair share of patrolling; but plans for an attack, to coincide with an offensive by another division of the XXXth Corps, were called off when von Rundstedt launched his now famous "Ardennes offensive" against the Americans in the middle of December. Thereafter the Battalion was kept busy preparing defended areas to cover the Sittard-Maastricht road in case the Germans should accompany their attack on the Americans with another towards Maastricht. Any such fears, however, were not realised, and the Battalion spent Christmas in peace.

Christmas was not only spent in peace but in the next best thing to traditional style. The Christmas fare was first class, the local inhabitants provided decorations and a Christmas tree, companies held their own dances or socials, Headquarter Company laid on a children's party and the Regimental Band was present at the morning Church Parade. A reminder that the war was still on was, however, provided by a C.O.'s conference at 5 p.m. for a move forward on Boxing Day.

With the New Year of 1945 came the cold and the snow—and incidentally white snow suits which were invaluable for patrolling. But for the first fortnight of January there was no major activity apart from patrols; and on the 11th the Battalion moved out of the line to prepare for what came to be known as the battle of the Sittard triangle.

The object of this operation was to straighten out the German salient between Roermond, Sittard, Geilenkirchen and Heinsberg and to throw their line back across the River Roer to its junction with the Maas at Roermond. The resulting contraction of the line was calculated to free at least a division for work elsewhere and would also simplify the American Ninth Army's plan for crossing the Roer further south.

The Battalion's task was to capture the village of Dieteren and involved crossing two sizable streams on the way; which meant experiments and exercises beforehand for working out the best kind of portable bridging to be used. The attack was planned to take place at night on the 15th of January, but visibility was so bad due to fog that it was postponed till early on the following morning, despite an announcement to the contrary on the 9 p.m. BBC news!

Prior to the Battalion's attack a preliminary attack had been carried out on a village called Bakenhoven by a company of the 1st/5th Queen's. Though successful, the company called for reinforcements to meet a German counter-attack and 'D' Company of the Battalion, under Major Rumble, was sent to its aid. Therefore for the main assault the 9th D.L.I. was lent a company of the Queen's.

The attack began in thirty degrees of frost and under cover of smoke at 7.30 in the morning of the 16th. Snow lay thick upon the ground. Despite the Bakenhoven diversion it achieved almost complete surprise. Both leading companies—'A' and 'B'—advanced right into Dieteren without trouble, and 'A' Company captured intact a bridge over the second stream although it had been prepared for demolition. In fact, within three hours all objectives had been captured and what little resistance there was in Dieteren had been mopped up and twenty prisoners captured.

The Germans began to recover from their surprise during the afternoon; and though there was no counter-attack, shelling and mortaring were intensified. Dieteren in general and 'B' Company in particular received much attention, while the sites of the crossing places over the streams were shelled with unwelcome and—in view of the excellence of the smoke screen over the whole area—surprising accuracy. Nor was the German shelling the only difficulty, though it was the direct cause of another—the failure to bridge the first stream, known as the Vloed Beek, which meant that no vehicles could reach Dieteren itself. A scissors bridge was, in fact, erected by the Sappers, but the first vehicle to cross it—a flail tank—damaged it. A partial thaw had also set in and the approaches to the bridge were soon a sea of impassable mud. Carrying parties for ammunition and wireless batteries did their best until, eventually at midnight, the first vehicles got across and brought food and anti-tank guns to the forward troops.

Though Dieteren was firmly held, the same could not be said of the track back through the snow which provided the Battalion's tenuous link with the rest of the Brigade. With Germans in Susteren and Oud-Roosteren, Dieteren was too uncomfortably like an island fortress for the peace of mind of its defenders.

However, on the morning of the 17th the Queen's moved

forward to attack Susteren and, though they captured it without much difficulty, the Germans reacted with considerably greater vigour. After counter-attacking the Queen's and over-running one of their companies, they sent a party of infantry from the south up the line of the Vloed Beek towards the bridge site. A platoon of 'C' Company under Captain Tony Ashton and Lieutenant Bill Slee was sent out to deal with this threat and, even though the Germans got near enough to the bridge to knock out a bulldozer with a bazooka, fought them off and forced them back south after two hours' hard fighting in which the enemy had the advantage in numbers.

By now Dieteren itself was reasonably quiet; but the battle was going on all round it and other elements of the 7th Armoured Division were pushing forward against bitter German resistance. Nevertheless, 131 Brigade had succeeded in attaining its objectives and its next task was to complete the clearing of the main road as far as Schilberg. This was done by the 2nd Devons; but their column, advancing along the road, was held up and had to be reinforced by 'B' Company of the Battalion. 'B' Company commander took command of the combined force which linked up with the rest of the Devons at Schilberg next morning. 'B' Company returned to the fold shortly afterwards, having had no sleep and little food since the beginning of the attack on Dieteren, and was replaced by 'D' Company who moved out to guard the Devons' eastern flank where a German force was reported to be. The latter did not materialise; but once Schilberg was taken the battle began to extend and German resistance to become increasingly stubborn and effective. So effective, indeed, that a plan for the Battalion to push ahead towards Montfort was frustrated by the vigorous defence of Hingen and St. Joost, two villages which covered all the northern and north-eastern routes out of Schilberg. The task of cracking these two nuts at first fell to others, but although Hingen had fallen by the afternoon of the 20th the advance had come to a complete standstill and a prisoner said there were two hundred men left in St. Joost with orders to fight it out to the last man.

The Battalion was then ordered to make ready one company to continue the attack and seize the bridge between St. Joost and Steil. For this 'C' Company, under Major Willie Anderson, was chosen; and its orders were to move through Hingen, which had been secured as a firm base by the 1st Rifle Brigade, and make straight for the bridge without delay. This the Company did. It moved up to Hingen, made its way out and across the Krom Beek and then disappeared from view. Almost from the start its wireless set ceased to function. From that time onwards it was never seen or heard of again, and what happened thereafter can only be somewhat scrappily pieced together from the thirty survivors who eventually returned. It appears that the Company was split up by heavy shelling before it reached St. Joost and the different parties were then killed or captured piecemeal as they tried to fight their way back to Hingen. This was a most unfortunate set-back; but the C.O. at once ordered 'B' Company up to Hingen during the night with orders to attack up the main street to try to extricate what was left of the Company. The members of 'B' Company 'O' Group made a rapid reconnaissance by the aid of artificial moonlight but on their return had the misfortune to be leaning against the back of a tank when its turret was hit by a shell from a German SP gun. The tank was brewed up and the 'O' Group was lucky to escape with no more than temporary deafness. However, it never rains but it pours, and the next news 'B' Company received was that a German attack had driven the Rifle Brigade back some hundred and fifty yards or—in street fighting parlance—six hard won houses.

Despite these misfortunes the Company launched its attack at 5 a.m. with one tank as its support, but in the face of bitter resistance and a number of casualties it came to a full stop after capturing five houses. Despite heavy losses from shelling the Germans were dug in in all the gardens and were holding out in the cellars with very great determination.

When it got light 'B' Company was withdrawn and Colonel Mogg made a new plan. 'A' and 'D' Companies were to advance straight up the village, with 'A' in the lead and 'D' ready to pass through them, supported by two squadrons of the 8th Hussars and two troops of Crocodile flame-throwers. This worked well—at any rate at first; but by midday enemy resistance stiffened again; 'A' Company was held up and Major Sam Macartney, its commander, killed; 'D' Company tried to work round the left but the Crocodiles could not follow; and the whole advance came to a standstill once more. Throughout the morning the Germans continued shelling Schilberg and Hingen; 'A', 'B' and 'C' Companies were losing men; somewhat shaken, the thirty survivors of 'C' Company had got back; and generally the situation was pretty unpleasant. However, 'D' Company had one reasonably strong platoon in being, so it was decided to make one last attempt on St. Joost with the aid of the Crocodiles which so far had not fired at all.

Time was slipping by and it was last light when the attack finally went in. The Crocodiles set fire to each house as they came to it, and in less than half an hour 'D' Company was at the bridge and resistance in St. Joost was ended. A few of the German defenders were captured. Some managed to escape, but the majority were killed in the cellars in which they were holding out. The Company, expecting a counter-attack, concentrated on holding the bridge; but their patrols further up the village found no sign of the enemy and the Rifle Brigade pushed on to Steil without meeting any Germans at all. So ended one of the fiercest actions the Battalion had fought since it left Normandy and when next day it was relieved by the Devons the relief was as welcome as it was deserved.

So far as the Battalion was concerned, this was the end of serious fighting for some time to come. All it now had to do was to advance to Posterholt on the River Roer and there occupy defence positions opposite the enemy who was entrenched on the far bank. It remained in the area of Posterholt until the 21st of February, latterly under command of the XVIth United States Corps. These weeks were not without their discomforts—as when a thaw set in early in February and reduced every road to bottomless mud; or their excitements—as when the Battalion area was bombarded with rocket shells which left craters ten feet wide and five feet deep. But on the whole there was little to disturb a stereotyped defensive routine until, on the 21st of February, the Battalion was relieved by an American battalion and retired to Weert in Holland for its first real rest since landing in Normandy in June.

The Battalion remained in Weert for longer than had been expected and enjoyed several weeks of real relaxation. Although there was much training to do the local population was exceedingly generous and hospitable and everybody made many friends. As the weeks sped by, however, an increasing sense of urgency became apparent and an almost pre-D Day feeling, if one may use that phrase, pervaded the whole atmosphere of training and preparations. In the past weeks the Germans had suffered heavily at the hands of the Allies west of the Rhine and it was clearly only a matter of a very short time before Second Army crossed the river for a final drive into Germany to finish the war.

The planning and preparation for what everybody felt must be the final round began in great secrecy on the 23rd of March. The lavish supply of maps and air photos to an armoured formation was in marked contrast with the restricted infantry allowance of August and September 1944. The 7th Armoured Division was to come under command of the XIIth Corps for the operation. The Corps comprised the 15th Scottish, the 53rd Welsh and the 6th Airborne Divisions. The latter was to be dropped on the far bank of the Rhine while the 15th Scottish made the assault crossing at Wesel to link up with the airborne landings. Once the bridgehead had been established two columns were to break out of it—the 53rd Welsh Division directed on Bocholt and the 7th Armoured on Borken. The ultimate objective was the river Elbe where it was hoped to link up with the Russians.

Any secrecy about the date of the assault ceased on the morning of the 24th, when the whole of Weert turned out to watch the great airfleet, carrying the 6th Airborne Division, pass over on its way to Germany. By evening news reached the Battalion of the success of the first crossings. Opposition had been weak and the Airborne Division had dropped into the enemy's gun area and largely deprived him of artillery support. Next day the Battalion, this time as part of 22 Armoured Brigade, left Weert to the accompaniment of an enthusiastic send off by the local population, and moved once more into Germany in preparation for a crossing of the Rhine on the 26th.

In fact the Battalion as a whole did not cross the river till the 28th. To reach its destination it had to move through the biggest traffic block of the war. The whole of the British Army seemed to be trying to cross the river at Wesel and the delay caused to everybody was appalling. It was as well, too, that the Luftwaffe was merely a shadow of its former self! Captain Charles Peace was the first officer of the Battalion to reach the far bank and he was followed shortly afterwards by the C.O. and Intelligence Officer, Captain Bill Bailey—summoned to Brigade Headquarters—who were compelled to take to a motorcycle to get through the traffic. The C.O. steered and the I.O. was a somewhat unwilling pillion passenger in fear of his life. Once across, however, the traffic grew lighter, but the roads were crowded with long lines of prisoners being escorted back by men of the assaulting forces.

The Battalion soon learnt that the battle ahead of them was going so well that there had been a rapid change of plan: they were to move straight to an area just west of Brunen, there to be ready to push ahead as soon as Brunen was cleared. As in so many of the advances in this final campaign the Battalion moved forward in close conjunction with the 5th Dragoon Guards—its affiliated armoured regiment—with whom it had formed a close association. There were strong bonds of mutual respect and affection between both Regiments; officers and N.C.O.s were on the friendliest of terms; and teamwork was of the highest order. This move was carried out without much trouble. There was, it is true, a little opposition in one village on the way, but it was soon brushed aside and the most noteworthy incident of this early stage of the advance was the appearance of white flags and a civil population clearly astonished at the mass of equipment available to the Allied Armies. Then there were the prisoners, an uninspiring array with little fight left in them, and most of them apparently only too anxious to get away from the war. On one occasion an American stretcher bearer came down the road with twenty-five whom he had picked up on his way back from being a prisoner himself; while others turned up without any escort at all and were told to march down the road and report to the first British troops that they met. And they did, too.

Borken, the Division's original objective, was occupied by the Battalion the same day—the 28th—with little difficulty. The centre of the town had been reduced to rubble by the Royal Air Force and it took some time finding a way round. 'D' Company, working round the right flank, encountered little resistance; but the tanks round the left were held up and

'A' Company, under Major Stephen Terrell, moved up to help them and occupied the village of Gemen just north of the town. Here 'A' Company found the Germans seemingly unaware of their presence and were able to lay a highly successful ambush whose bag comprised a large number of vehicles, twenty prisoners and some miscellaneous casualties which included a German Field Cashier with 80,000 marks! At one stage during the night Stephen Terrell himself acted as traffic policeman in the centre of the village and directed enemy traffic into his own ambush.

From Borken the Battalion pushed ahead to Stadtlohn. Opposition was slight and, indeed, the greatest delay was caused by the rubble blocking the roads in those towns on the way which had been bombed by the R.A.F. One of them, Sudlohn, held the Battalion up a whole night while searches were made for a way round. Every road except one was blocked by rubble or craters and that one took some hours to find on foot in the dark. Once Stadtlohn was reached enemy resistance of a more formidable nature was encountered. The Germans had been ordered to hold the place for four days and two fresh battalions of Grenadiers put up a bitter resistance which gave the Battalion a day of really bloody street fighting. This battle was in fact the toughest the Battalion had to face during the whole of the campaign; but so effective were Colonel Mogg's tactics that German resistance was broken after only twenty-four hours' fighting. Instead of the usual drill of holding the enemy frontally and working round the flanks, the C.O. ordered one company to drive a wedge into the centre of the town—which it did—and then two more to branch off to the flanks in a sort of Y-shaped movement. This surprised the Germans and met with immediate success; added to which Lieutenant McNally of 'A' Company jumped on a tank and made a dash for a wooden bridge over the river which runs through the town and captured it intact. Most of the bridges over the river had been blown, nor was this one which the Sappers would normally have classified as fit for armour; but the tank commander was prepared to take the chance and within a short time the rest of his squadron had followed him. The capture of this bridge was vitally important to the attack as a whole because the crossing of the tanks dealt a heavy blow at the enemy's defences; but 'A' Company had to fight on the far side of it before they could link up with 'C' Company, on their left, who had forced their way over the remains of another bridge further west. During the day both Colonel Mogg and his second in command, Major Cramsie, joined personally in the battle, but whereas the Colonel bagged at least one German with a Bren gun, Cramsie was unlucky enough to be shot in the leg by a sniper. All told the Battalion killed several hundred Germans—'A' Company alone counted three hundred bodies—and the ambulances were busy all night evacuating enemy wounded. By the time it was dark and the town was finally cleared, Stadtlohn was a place which would always be remembered as the scene of a very bitter struggle. But the Battalion had the satisfaction of knowing they had bundled the enemy out of the town in a quarter of the time that the latter had intended, and that they had heavily defeated two of the best German battalions left on the Western front.

The Division was now regrouped in preparation for an advance to Rheine on the River Ems: and the Battalion became once more a part of 131 Brigade. On the 1st of April it set off in its vehicles in lovely weather and motored ahead at almost break-neck speed against negligible opposition. "It was terrific," one officer remarked afterwards, "white flags all the way." Indeed, the general character of the advance from the Rhine—at any rate on the XIIth Corps' front— left those who took part in it in no doubt that they were members of a victorious Army sweeping forward into country defended by a defeated and largely disorganised enemy. For the most part the opposition met was comparatively minor, but even where it was bitter, as at Stadtholn, it appeared to be uncoordinated with any overall plan of defence.

The Battalion reached Neunkirchen, an outlying suburb of Rheine, uneventfully. From there each company moved forward cautiously, uncertain as to what form the opposition, if any, would take. In fact nothing more serious was met than an occasional sniper, but when 'A' Company, who were leading, reached the Ems the bridge was blown up in their faces. As it turned out, however, this did not matter much as the 11th Armoured Division, which had been advancing on a parallel route to the east, had succeeded in securing one bridge over the Ems at Mesum and another over the Dortmund-

Ems Canal near Ibbenburen. So the Battalion found themselves with orders to withdraw from Rheine and to cross the Ems at Mesum where the whole of the 7th Armoured Division was to be diverted so that it might continue the advance through Ibbenburen.

Here again the Battalion was faced with some stiff opposition; for a German unit, formed from the N.C.O.s and Cadets of a Training School at Hanover, were entrenched north of the Canal on a steep and wooded ridge which overlooked the bridge over the Canal and commanded all the roads to Ibbenburen. The Germans had been fighting fanatically and had caused heavy casualties to a brigade of the 11th Armoured Division by a vigorous counter-attack against the bridgehead. A second counter-attack on the morning of the 2nd of April nearly reached the bridge, but the Devons were sent up to help relieve the pressure and successfully drove the Germans off that part of the ridge overlooking the bridge. It was after this that the Battalion was ordered to move south along the bottom of the ridge so as to clear another route and get round behind the Germans: and by nightfall of the 3rd 'C' Company had made considerable progress by getting within 2,000 yards of Ibbenburen itself.

The rest of the Battalion continued their advance early the following morning. There was a small river between them and Ibbenburen, and as they went forward they could hear the Germans fighting it out with others in the woods away to their left. 'A' Company was in the lead and was faced by a long row of farmhouses as it made its way forward. They had to fight for every one of them. In one encounter Lieutenant Taylor dashed forward to a wall sheltering a number of the enemy and polished off over a dozen of them with his Sten gun single-handed. The Germans, many of whom were instructors, were first class soldiers and even better shots. They worked in small and scattered parties and were thus difficult to pin down for treatment by artillery; and their excellent shooting cost the Company a number of N.C.O.s and the supporting tanks any tank commanders who put their heads up through their turrets. In fact it was usually necessary for the tanks to demolish a building and bury the defenders in the rubble before resistance ceased. One remark, made by one of these Germans, was perhaps enlightening. The man concerned was a warrant officer, badly wounded and buried up to his neck in debris. As he was being dug out someone asked him when he thought the war was going to end. " When we win," came the defiant reply; and it typified the fanaticism with which he and his comrades had been fighting and dying. But their fanaticism could not stop 'A' Company, nor 'B' Company, for that matter, who came up behind 'A' and passed through them; and, indeed, 'B' Company succeeded in pushing on to within six hundred yards of the river when orders arrived from Brigade to stop them. For there was another change of plan. Ibbenburen was to be left to troops of another division—the 52nd Lowland—and the Battalion was to be pulled out to rejoin the rest of the 7th Armoured Division whose leading elements had succeeded in by-passing Ibbenburen and were racing ahead to a town called Diepholz, some thirty miles away.

From now on the advance, gathering momentum all the time, went very much according to pattern. A sweep forward, brushing light resistance aside, would be followed by a day or more's hard fighting to overcome some particularly stubborn local opposition; and when that was done the victorious column would sweep forward again. From Diepholz the Battalion moved to Bassum. Here it had a fierce scrap in which Lieutenant Ingleton was killed—the first officer killed since crossing the Rhine—and forty-nine prisoners were taken. Then it swung north towards Wildeshausen, a town which lay right across the line of retreat of the Germans fighting the XXXth Corps, whose advance, to the west of the XIIth Corps, had not been so rapid and was being more bitterly contested. This was part of a general move by the 7th Armoured Division to disrupt the rear of the enemy on XXXth Corps' front. The Battalion successfully seized Wildeshausen and one of its prizes was, strangely enough, a vast store of gin; but having allowed the town to be occupied so easily the Germans seemed equally determined to try to get it back. Colonel Mogg narrowly missed running into a convoy of German tanks on his way to Brigade and had to remain there, cut off for one night, while the Battalion fought a vigorous action without him. All was well, however, and on the morning of the 12th of April it was possible to hand over the town to troops of the XXXth Corps before withdrawing to enjoy a complete day's rest and some much needed sleep.

The end was very near now. On the 17th the Battalion learnt that their final objective was Hamburg. On the 19th the first real signs of a complete German collapse began to be apparent. Prisoners taken were from very mixed units. Some were from the Hitler Youth and aged between thirteen and sixteen, some were old men too fed up to fight, some were just spiritless. Opposition, such as it was, was more sporadic and lacked cohesion. On the 20th the Battalion reached Hittfeldt, just short of Hamburg, where the advance came to a halt so as to clear up the vast salient which had been overrun during the preceding days and to prepare for a general assault on the city as soon as certain complementary moves by the XXXth Corps had been completed. The main body of the Battalion attacked Hittfeldt, while 'A' Company was sent off to seize the nearby village of Maschen. Neither place was secured without opposition. 'A' Company had to debouch from some woods and cross open ground, downhill, before reaching Maschen. At the bottom of the hill the Company held an 'O' Group. As Stephen Terrell began his orders a series of explosions occurred up the hill in the direction from which the Company had just come. "We're being shelled," said Ted Halliday, one of the platoon commanders. "Nonsense," said Terrell, "our own artillery is dropping short," and continued his orders. Then there were more explosions. "We *are* being shelled," said Halliday once more. "Be quiet," said Terrell. "I shan't believe we're being shelled until one falls right here." The words had scarcely been uttered when one did—or at any rate near enough to carry conviction; and the 'O' Group broke up with the brief command "Get into that—village!"

'A' Company captured Maschen and the Battalion Hittfeldt, but stubborn opposition was met in the area of Harburg and it was clear that the Division had now reached the German defence line covering the Elbe. However, it was clear also—a more comforting thought—that whatever the opposition the enemy was very short of good troops to man his new defences.

For ten days the Battalion stayed where it was. It sent out many patrols; indeed everybody in the Battalion took his turn, even the Transport Officer and the Regimental Quartermaster-Sergeant! Parties of enemy frequently gave themselves up, and on one occasion 'A' Company captured a complete platoon of Hamburg police who admitted they had only been waiting the chance to surrender. Then on the 1st of May, at about 7 o'clock in the evening, a large black car, flying an even larger white flag, was seen approaching a standing patrol in 'D' Company's area. A party was at once sent out to meet it and the occupants were discovered to be two officers from the staff of General Wolz, commander of Hamburg. They were duly escorted to Battalion Headquarters by Bill Bailey, the I.O., where, after consultation with the Colonel, it transpired that they wished to discuss with the Divisional Commander the shelling of a neighbouring factory which was near a military hospital. This was in fact not true, for when they reached Brigade they disclosed their real mission which was to arrange a meeting between General Wolz and anyone willing to accept the surrender of Hamburg. This was agreed to for the next day and a local cease fire was arranged until the matter was cleared up.

At 9 p.m. on the 2nd, therefore, Colonel Mogg met General Wolz at 'D' Company's standing patrol and took him first to Brigade and then to Divisional Headquarters. There it was discovered that in addition to the surrender of Hamburg the General had the authority of Admiral Doenitz to arrange negotiations for the surrender of all the Western Armies. As a result, at 8 a.m. on the 3rd, the Colonel and the I.O. met a still larger party consisting, among others, of Admiral Friedenburg, on behalf of Admiral Doenitz, and General Kinsel, Chief of Staff to C.-in-C. West, who were in due course escorted to Field-Marshal Montgomery. The war in the west was over. The Battalion led the way into Hamburg on that very afternoon and took over the Elbe bridges; on the 5th the Germans surrendered unconditionally; on the 7th the Colonel made the official announcement of the general surrender everywhere which was to take effect from the 9th; and on the 8th the Battalion let itself go in full and fitting celebration. It had been in at the death, as it had every right to be, and though later on—in July to be precise—it finally reached Berlin, the heart of the Nazi Reich, this was perhaps its most triumphant moment.

It shared the experience, symbolically if not in fact, with its absent comrades of the Durham Brigade with whom it had shared so much of the fighting of five long years. It shared it, too, in another sense, with those other battalions of the Regiment who had fought and beaten the Germans in various theatres and in various climes: for here, at Hamburg, the 9th Battalion represented the whole Regiment—and a Regiment, moreover, which with all humility can justly claim a record against the King's enemies which some may rival but none perhaps can excel.

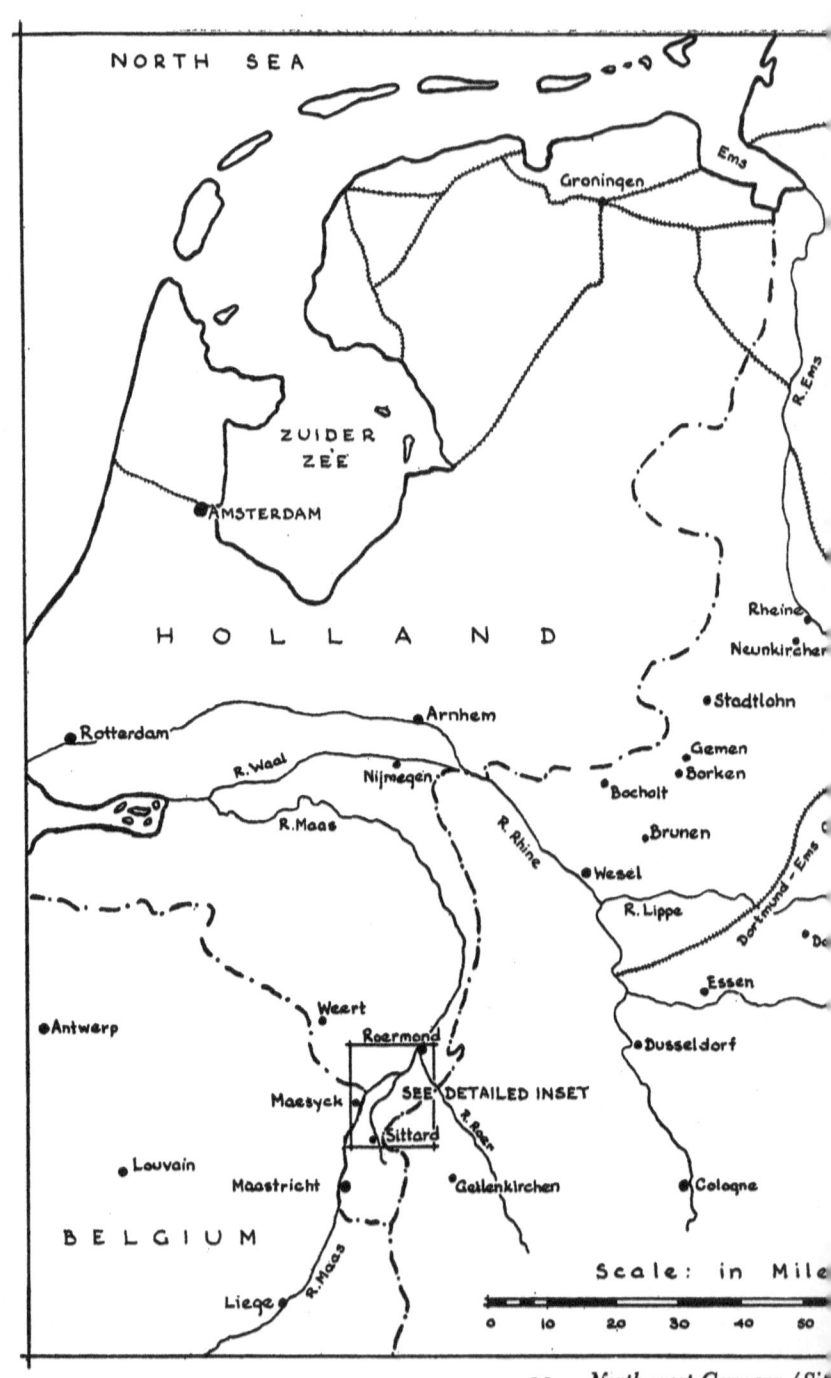

20. *North-west Germany (Sit*

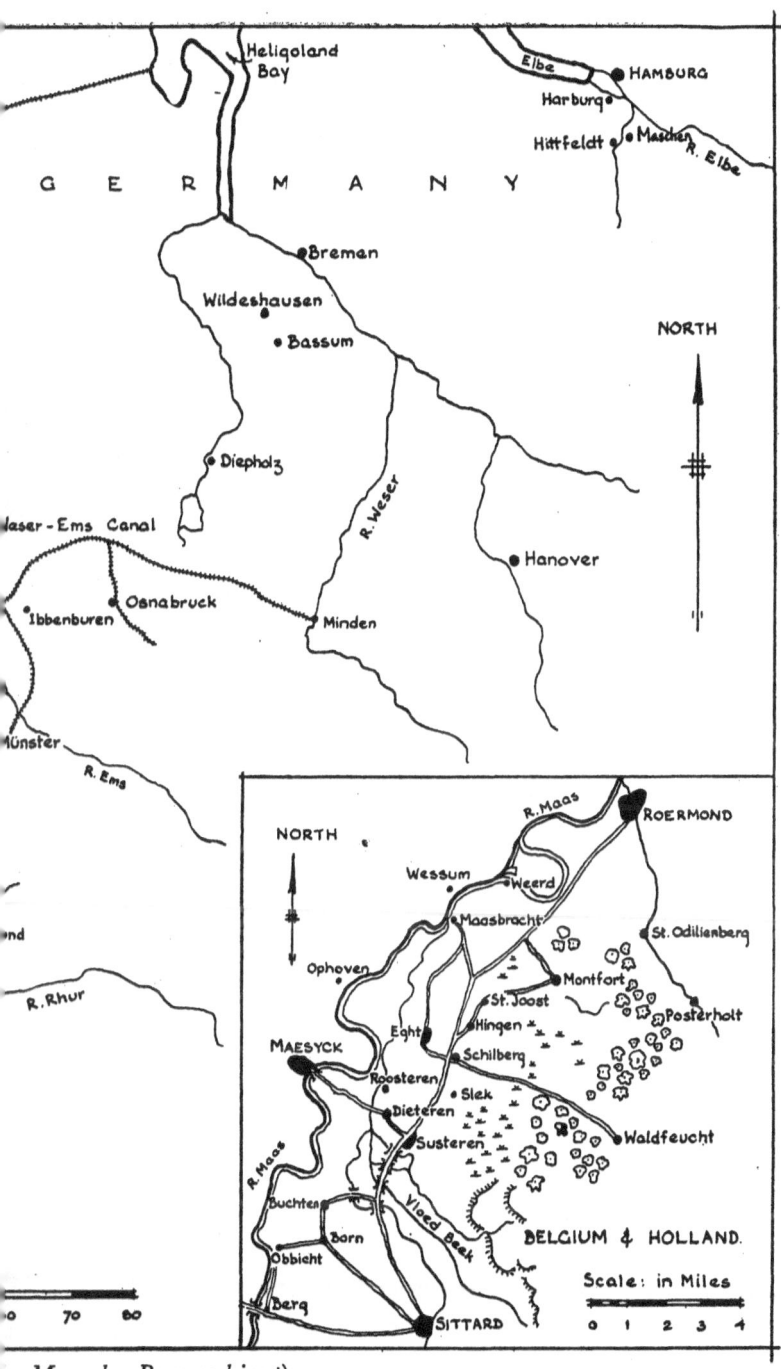

—Maesyck—Roermond inset)

CHAPTER NINE

The 5th and 7th Battalions

I

THE 112TH LIGHT ANTI-AIRCRAFT REGIMENT, ROYAL ARTILLERY

IN 1936 the 7th Battalion, which had hitherto served with the 50th Northumbrian Division, was invited by the War Office to convert into an anti-aircraft searchlight battalion. As a result, it became—to give the full title—the 47th (D.L.I.) A.A. Battalion R.E. (T.A.) and consisted of four companies. Thus the direct link with the Regiment was formally broken, though the many intangible ties remained and still remain. Soon after the outbreak of war the Battalion was transferred to the Royal Artillery as the 47th Searchlight Regiment, and so it remained, on anti-aircraft defence in the United Kingdom, until the 1st of January, 1942. It was then converted to Light Anti-Aircraft and assumed the title of the 112th Light Anti-Aircraft Regiment, R.A., and travelled south to Devon and Cornwall to take part in preparations for the landings in North Africa. However, the Regiment did not then go overseas and, indeed, returned to the north country for intensive battle training until, on joining the XIIth Corps as a field force unit, it began to prepare for the invasion of France.

Early in 1944 the Regiment received orders that only one battery would accompany the Corps to France but that the rest of the Regiment would follow on later. Thus it was that 366 Battery, under Major J. Storey, landed in Normandy on the 25th of June, to be followed by the rest of the Regiment on the 22nd of July. A week later the Corps Commander decided to use the Regiment as infantry, and thus for a few days at the beginning of the Second Army offensive towards Falaise the Regiment returned to its old and original role.

Early on the morning of the 30th they set off with rifles and

Bren guns without their guns and trucks. How they envied the drivers in the lorries which passed to and fro as they marched forward! They had their fair share of marching, digging and shelling. One battery picked up two bedraggled German prisoners. Though new to active service, some members were quick to exploit the opportunities of acquiring good French liquor, despite the somewhat ominous notice " Beware of Booby Traps " affixed to certain premises. They were, however, soon alive to this old soldier's dodge and were not long in placing similar notices to preserve their own hunting grounds.

On the 23rd of August the Regiment reverted to its accustomed role of artillery. Its infantry activities had been mainly confined to occupying and holding positions in support of the forward troops; but a fortunate coincidence had placed them during that time in a formation side by side with 151 Brigade to whom they had belonged in the days when the Regiment was an infantry battalion. During the days that followed, in the bitter fighting in the Falaise pocket, the Regiment was given a new role for light anti-aircraftmen—ground straffing.

After the slaughter of the Falaise gap, the Regiment took part in the pursuit, and, towards the end of August, one troop was sent to join 4 Armoured Brigade. It joined the advance on the 24th of August, after a hectic journey in which it got mixed up with the Polish Armoured Division and ultimately reached its destination across-country through farms and bogs. The countryside was littered with dead men and horses and, in the words of one member of the Regiment, " the smell could almost be seen."

The first day's advance was slow and the road seemed to be one long mass of vehicles nose to tail. There were only two speeds—flat out and stop. The second day's advance was swifter; vehicles moved at full speed for hours on end. By the 29th the troop was preparing to cross the Seine, which it did at 1 o'clock in the afternoon. The weather had changed and it was pouring with rain, and it remained so during the slow advance up the Seine valley and beyond. All that could be seen of the enemy were fires burning in the distance.

By the 31st of August the sun had come out again and everybody began grumbling about the dust! A great welcome was given to the advancing column by the French and it was wine, flowers and flags all the way. At St. Etienne the church bells were ringing, flags waving and the village green was packed with people. The troop crossed the Somme on the 1st of September, but when it woke up next morning discovered that something was very much amiss, as everyone else had gone and it was alone. It was then joined by one gun detachment which had got separated the previous day and had an amusing tale to tell. Apparently a small French boy had come to say there were Germans in a certain house, and was told to go away and not to talk nonsense. Quite undeterred, however, he promptly fired a round at the house, whereupon nine German officers and one private marched out and surrendered. One officer asked for a last cigarette before he was shot.

Next day the troop rejoined the XIIth Corps, and on the 4th of September reached the rest of the Regiment which was back near the Seine where it remained grounded for the best part of a month. It did not see action again until the end of September when, after a four hundred mile move, it was deployed before Nijmegen. Here there was plenty to do and some casualties. Jet aircraft were encountered for the first time. Just before Christmas, during von Runstedt's Ardennes offensive, there was a great deal of air activity by the Germans and in one attack Regimental Headquarters received a direct hit. Scares were frequent, and once over one hundred airborne objects were reported some six miles away; but they were mostly scares, and when, on New Year's Day, the Germans staged their biggest air effort the Regiment was unlucky and not a bird came its way.

The Regiment's next major activity was the crossing of the Rhine in March 1945. Although it had taken part in the initial attack on the Reich in January, it was withdrawn into Belgium in February for reorganisation. There two batteries went to a practice camp and on the 20th the third—364 Battery—heard, to its surprise and pleasure, that it was to be converted to Land Mattress Rockets. These formidable weapons were thirty-barrel projectors, all barrels firing simultaneously. A battery consisted of twelve projectors and its fire power was approximately equal to fifteen regiments of medium artillery; so the effect can well be imagined. The next month was one truly hectic rush—learning in a week from the Canadians what was supposed normally to be taught in four years; collecting the projectors; demonstrating in practice shoots to a stream of V.I.P.s fascinated by the new toy; and finally moving up into position on the Rhine. " What do you think of your new toys ? " said General Dempsey at one of the demonstration shoots. " Please never take them away from us " was the Battery Commander's enthusiastic reply: and that was the verdict of them all.

The Battery concentrated near Xanten, some 3,000 yards from the Rhine, during the early hours of the morning of the 23rd of March. All day it remained out of observation. Then at 6 p.m. an endless stream of vehicles began to pour towards the river. For hours this continued, tanks, motors, men, bridging equipment, crocodiles, buffaloes, weasels, dukws, jeeps, and boats moving forward through thick camouflage smoke screens which were burning for miles along the west bank of the river.

At 11 p.m. the pre-bombardment began and all hell was let loose as every sort of gun joined in. At 11.15 p.m. the Battery fired its first salvo. A salvo sounded like forty express trains passing through a tube station. When the attacking infantry heard it they went to ground until they learnt to whom this terrifying weapon belonged. Then they asked for more and when it came stood on their parapets and cheered. Thereafter a salvo was sent over every hour until 4.45 a.m. the following morning.

Meanwhile, the rest of the Regiment were taking part in the actual crossing itself. 366 Battery began crossing at dawn on rafts behind the 15th Scottish Division and were in action by 5.15 p.m. the following day without incident. They thus had the distinction of being the first artillery unit in the British Army to cross the Rhine. 365 Battery crossed forty-eight hours later, by which time 364 Battery had had an opportunity to see some of their target areas on the far bank of the river. Shooting had been excellent. There was a great deal of damage, fires had been started and the German population did not like the new weapon at all.

Thus ended the last major operation in which the Regiment took part. The advance continued and the cease-fire found it in the city of Hamburg.

2

THE 54TH SEARCHLIGHT REGIMENT, ROYAL ARTILLERY

The 7th Battalion was converted into an artillery regiment two years before its sister battalion, the 5th, followed along the same path. But, unlike the 7th, the 5th, which had also been part of 151 Brigade hitherto, was split into two—the 1st/5th and 2nd/5th—on its conversion, like the 7th, into a Searchlight Regiment. The Battalion as a whole attended camp in the summer of 1938 where it underwent preliminary training in searchlights with very inadequate equipment. Shortly afterwards it was split into two and to the 1st/5th, later to be designated the 54th Searchlight Regiment, came Lieutenant-Colonel David Marley as Commanding Officer. Intensive spare time training began; a company of A.T.S. was attached to the Regiment and rapidly made themselves an integral part of it; and in July 1939 batteries began to occupy searchlight sites in the Sedgefield and Guisborough areas. By the time that war was declared 413 Battery had deployed at Filey, followed by 411 at Malton and 412 with Regimental Headquarters at Easingwold.

Through no fault of its own the Regiment was fated to have a comparatively uninteresting war. It ultimately reached Continental Europe, but not until the end of 1944 and even then its adventures were uneventful. From 1939 onwards its activities were confined to the homeland, though they were not without their interest and excitements. After the bitterly cold winter of 1939, spent on isolated and exposed sites in the Yorkshire wolds, the Regiment said good-bye to David Marley on his going to command the 10th Battalion. He was succeeded by Lieutenant-Colonel J. K. Reay, an officer of long service with the old 5th Battalion, who had hitherto been senior battery commander and was to command until March 1945. With the arrival of spring and summer and the withdrawal of the B.E.F. from Dunkirk, the Regiment found itself undergoing special training in infantry tactics once more so as to fit into the general defence scheme for dealing with any type of German attack on the Yorkshire coastal area. This included making all sites mobile and even involved supplying some of them with taxis to make them so!

When the German air raids began in the summer and autumn of 1940 the Regiment found itself fully occupied. One of the enemy's favourite landfalls was Flamborough Head, and the troop site there was one of the first to be bombed. It so happened that the first man to reach the Lewis gun on this occasion was the cook, who scored several hits on the enemy bomber as a result of which the troop's morale, already high, rose higher than ever! Thereafter, the troop site at Reighton, several miles inland, received the attention of the enemy on frequent occasions, suffering a number of direct hits which wrecked equipment but fortunately inflicted no casualties. During the Battle of Britain the Regiment was credited with several German bombers destroyed by Lewis gun fire.

From 1940 until 1944 the pattern of life changed little. There were moves; and at one time the Regimental area extended from a few miles north of Scarborough to within a few miles of Hull and included the area bounded by York, Harrogate, Ilkley and Beverley. It speaks well for the spirit of all ranks that they continued to man their many sites happily, and without grousing, through the best part of four years, marked often by bad weather and, as the war progressed, by increasing spells of boring inactivity. Indeed, by the middle of 1944 the Regiment had reached such a high standard of efficiency that it was rewarded by being selected as the second Searchlight Regiment in Anti-Aircraft Command for overseas service. Orders to mobilise were received on the 16th of June and from the 21st it came under the command of General Montgomery's 21st Army Group. From June until October the Regiment underwent special training in the south and west of England in preparation for the move to France; first in Essex, then near Cardiff and, finally, at Perranporth in Cornwall. On the 27th of October warning was given that embarkation would take place at any time after the 5th of November; and, on the 11th, Regimental Headquarters and two batteries set sail from Tilbury for Arromanches in Normandy.

The ships moved inside the " Mulberry " harbour at Arromanches on the 16th and the troops disembarked. On the 18th the last Battery—413—arrived and the whole Regiment was ordered forward to Belgium to take part in the anti-aircraft defence of Brussels and Antwerp. By the 22nd Regimental

Headquarters was established in Brussels; 411 Battery was in Antwerp and 412 and 413 at Jodoigne and Louvain respectively. Their main task was the illumination of pilotless aircraft or, more familiarly, flying bombs.

The new Year saw a change in the Regiment's role which involved it in the defence of the approaches to the Scheldt and Antwerp. This meant occupying part of the Dutch coastline. New Year's day itself was marked by a very heavy low-level attack by the Luftwaffe on all airfields in the Regimental area, and every site was kept busy engaging enemy aircraft with its light machine guns. Later, 411 Battery, still in Antwerp, suffered a number of casualties from flying bombs of which some hundred and fifteen were estimated to have fallen in that area daily. Thereafter the task of the Regiment remained unchanged until, in May, the Germans surrendered and the war in Europe was over.

3

THE 113TH LIGHT ANTI-AIRCRAFT REGIMENT, ROYAL ARTILLERY

How the 5th Battalion came to be divided has already been told. The nucleus of the 2nd/5th Battalion was composed of the companies at West Hartlepool and Horden, together with a third raised at Easington; and the new unit was commanded by Lieutenant-Colonel O. J. Feetham who had been C.O. of the 5th hitherto.

In August 1940 the Battalion was redesignated the 55th Searchlight Regiment but it was not till December of the following year that it received its present title which it retained thereafter. By that time a new C.O.—Lieutenant-Colonel Bill Mather—had taken command, and it was under him that the Regiment was to serve throughout the rest of the war.

Like the 1st/5th and the 7th and, indeed, like so many units of the Home Army, the Regiment saw no service abroad until the invasion of Continental Europe. It is true that early in 1943 orders were received to mobilise for service overseas, but this proved to be a false alarm and the Regiment was redeployed in Kent against low altitude high speed fighter-bomber attacks. From the end of that year until the invasion itself it was occupied with intensive training under command of 100 Anti-Aircraft Brigade.

The Regiment embarked for the shores of Normandy with three Batteries—368, 369 and 370—and, after much shuttling up and down the coast, landed near Lion-sur-Mer. 368 Battery deployed at once at the mouth of the River Orne on the extreme left of the Allied flank, 369 at Langrune on the coast and 370 in harbour in readiness to support an expected thrust in the Cheux area. To that place it ultimately went, under command of XIIth Corps, and had an unpleasant baptism of fire, suffering a number of casualties and finding itself at a very early stage in an anti-tank role. Thereafter the whole Regiment moved up by stages to defend the crossings of the Caen Canal and the River Odon in preparation for the British break-out from the bridgehead. The months of June and July saw them receive their full share of attention from the enemy, but in return they were able to boast of more than twenty enemy planes destroyed and officially credited to the Regiment.

The Regiment, now in support of XIIth Corps, moved forward in the middle of August in preparation for the pursuit across France. In doing so they had their first experience of mines and booby traps on a large scale; but they were lucky in finding among their prisoners a number who were willing not only to point out where the mines were but also to lift them! Then the pursuit began. Transport scales were reduced and rapid moves became the order of the day. Through Falaise to the Seine; then with extra petrol for three hundred miles, double ammunition and "compo" rations to the Somme. It was a hectic move, accompanied by much order, counter-order and not a little disorder; but on the way the Regiment saw, for the first time, one of the new rocket-launching sites cleverly concealed in thick woods. From the Somme they moved to Lens and once there were ordered to send reconnaissance parties to Ghent. The C.O. and battery commanders duly set off, but they had scarcely departed when orders arrived that Ghent was still German and they were to go instead to Brussels. This meant a chase after the C.O. to arrange a new rendezvous and even when the Regiment duly arrived they were told to push on to Malines. Their reception along the route was typical of what all the liberating troops were receiving, but at Malines the crowd exceeded in joy and excitement anything as yet experienced.

The period of pursuit was now over. 368 Battery, who were deployed in support of the 50th Division, came in for an uncomfortable time first at Gheel and then on the Albert Canal, with the rest of the Regiment at Beeringen and Diest; but this did not last long, for the whole Regiment was concentrated in a harbour area to the rear of the Albert Canal and was placed under the command of the XXXth Corps to take part in the thrust designed to cross the three rivers at Arnhem and trap 250,000 Germans in western Holland. This was the operation in which the great airborne army was dropped to capture the Arnhem bridges; and its gallant failure now belongs to history. The Regiment had at least one anxious night, as they moved forward behind the Guards Armoured Division, when one evening they were ordered to deploy every man and gun in defence of the road as fourteen German Tiger tanks were reported to have broken through only a few miles away. All their fifty-four guns were deployed within half an hour; but the enemy did not appear, and though much traffic flowed back along the road, a quiet but eerie night was spent until, when it got light, more British armour moved up and the gap was closed. For the Regiment the advance came to an end at Nijmegen where they were allotted the anti-aircraft and river defence of the bridge. The remnants of the airborne division who had crossed the Neder Rhine were withdrawn, the road in their rear was repeatedly cut and the Luftwaffe was very active. There the Regiment remained for two months during which, after much aerial activity which had been designed as a distraction, the railway bridge was completely destroyed and a forty feet gap blown in the road bridge by German " frogmen " who swam down the Rhine and fitted torpedoes to it. Soon afterwards plans were made to counter the Germans' reported intention to breach the dykes and flood " The Island ", but before it was necessary for the Regiment to play its part it was relieved and went back for a rest to Exel in Belgium.

As for their comrades in the one time 7th Battalion, the major event of 1945 was the crossing of the Rhine. Earlier the Regiment paid a short visit to the Ardennes—indeed the move itself was begun on Christmas Day of 1944—where von

Rundstedt's counter-offensive was in progress and during which they were kept fully occupied by the Luftwaffe in temperatures involving anything up to twenty-eight degrees of frost. It was not very pleasant and no one was sorry to return once more to Holland, though with memories of a very happy co-operation with their American allies.

For the Regiment to take part in the Rhine Crossing meant that it had been honoured with every major forward anti-aircraft task since Normandy. It was hoped that this would be the last, and it was certainly expected to be the worst. The area approaching the crossing was wreathed in smoke to cover the vast dumping programme and the concentration of the assaulting forces. The guns moved up and at Marienbaum 369 Battery had the opportunity to operate as field artillery and fire their Bofors guns across the river! When the assault began early in the morning, the bridge over which the Regiment was to cross was damaged by a carrier falling over the side, so setting the operation back by several hours: but when it was repaired all three batteries were the first guns to cross over and were in action on the far side of the river by 6 p.m. Apart from the initial crossing there was little ground or aerial activity by the enemy; and what had been anticipated would be the hardest task of all turned out to be comparatively easy. In due course the Regiment left the Rhine and concentrated at Haldern with orders to be ready to move at forty-eight hours' notice.

The usual speculation accompanying any order to move at short notice was not really dispelled when instructions were received to move to a place called Belsen. No one had heard of it and the map reference was thought to have been given in error as it appeared to be some two hundred and fifty miles away inside enemy held territory. However, after travelling a hundred miles to Osnabruck the order was confirmed that the Regiment was to move to the concentration camp at Belsen near Celle.

Belsen was, in fact, in German held territory, but the British VIIIth Corps Commander had been approached by the German Commander of the First Parachute Army with the object of negotiating a truce so as to avoid a battle in the Belsen area. Typhus was, it seems, raging in the camp, and unless it was confined there was a danger that it might spread not only throughout Germany but into other parts of Europe as well,

Normal, but well armed, reconnaissance parties set out at once and were guaranteed safe conduct by the enemy. The Regiment itself arrived at Belsen on the 18th of April: and the scene which met their eyes had to be seen to be believed.

The internees—if one can give that name to the misshapen wretches who passed for human beings—were normally kept in separate " laagers " by sexes and nationalities; but they had all broken out of their usual confines and were mingled in an inextricable mass in the main camp. There were over 40,000 men and women still alive, all in an advanced stage of malnutrition and suffering from many diseases other than the typhus which was rampant; and there were some 13,000 unburied corpses. These latter were the victims of typhus, and their bodies were piled around the camp or left in their bunks alongside those living who were too weak to move. Those still alive were in most cases little more than human skeletons, their rags teemed with lice and they squatted and wandered unconcernedly among the dead. At least half of them were immediate hospital cases, most of them quite unable to feed themselves, and they continued, for the first ten days after the Regiment's arrival, to die at the rate of five hundred a day.

In addition to the inmates of the camp, there was a battalion of Wehrmacht about six hundred strong, some 1,000 Hungarian soldiers who were the camp guards, over 1,000 Russian prisoners and various other hangers-on and German families. There was also a hospital with over 2,000 German sick and, of course, a hospital staff.

The task which lay before the Regiment was two-fold; to bury the dead and to move all those who had the slightest chance of survival out of the camp and into a large Panzer training school and barracks which was not far away. Burial pits were dug by bulldozers and Bofors tractors and German lorries were used to move the bodies. As many as 1,700 were buried in one day and over 17,000 had to be placed in the mass graves before individual graves could be started. However, the compounds and huts were cleared of dead by the 25th of April. Those who were desperately ill but had a chance of recovery were stripped of their rags, wrapped in blankets and moved to the new barracks where they were washed, dusted and put to bed in a specially segregated typhus block. Many did not survive their treatment, but it was ultimately possible to move some four hundred a day in this manner. Those who could walk were given showers in the concentration camp and then moved by lorry to the new area where they were housed in barrack blocks by sexes and nationalities.

It can well be imagined what feats of administration were required by all ranks to achieve this formidable task. 'A' Troop, for example, was responsible for feeding and accommodating over 16,000 women; each cookhouse was run by a sergeant and provided some 2,500 people with three meals a day; while the Royal Electrical and Mechanical Engineers' detachment operated the electricity and water supplies and repaired the bakery in the Panzer barracks.

By the 19th of May the task was completed and the last inmate had gone. By the 21st the camp itself had been burnt to the ground. The war in the west was now over and, after ten days' rest on the shores of the Baltic, the Regiment turned its energies to the comparative peace and quiet of occupational duties in the area of Hanover.

CHAPTER TEN

The Durham Light Infantry in Home Forces

I

THE 14TH, 15TH AND 17TH BATTALIONS

THERE was one feature common to all these three battalions in their varied but uneventful existence. All became field force units at about the same time—though the 15th had been a Holding Battalion[1] before the other two were formed—and each one of them, during most of its life, was fortified by the hope and belief that one day it would go into action.

The 14th and 17th Battalions were brought into the world —together with the 16th whose tale has already been told— during the summer of 1940. They, too, were Dunkirk battalions. The 14th was formed at Brancepeth on the 4th of July. It was commanded by Lieutenant-Colonel " Ambrose " Appleby, of the Regiment, and comprised a cadre of some one hundred and forty-seven officers and men—mostly from the Depot—who left shortly afterwards for Scotland, where they moved into a tented camp near Edinburgh. The 17th came into being on the same day, but at the Depot of the King's Shropshire Light Infantry at Shrewsbury. Their C.O. was Lieutenant-Colonel H. B. Morkill, of the Green Howards, and their original cadre consisted of officers and men from no less than fifteen different Regiments. They too moved to Edinburgh alongside their comrades of the 14th and 16th Battalions. Each battalion then received a draft of approximately eight hundred civilians who had to be trained from scratch and welded together into an organised whole; and this each set out to do for the first three months of its existence.

[1] A Holding Battalion held men who had completed their Recruit Training before they were posted to active service battalions.

The task was not easy. Men were badly needed and the intake had not been as carefully vetted as in the case of more leisurely formed units: indeed the 14th Battalion had at least one man who arrived in an invalid chair and had been lame from birth! Equipment was short; broomsticks took the place of rifles; and a second suit of battle dress was unheard of. However, enthusiasm ran high amongst both trainers and trainees; the erstwhile civilians were soon sorted out and licked into shape; and by October both Battalions found themselves on coast defence near the English border.

In the New Year they moved south, still together, to join 206 Independent Infantry Brigade, and in February were stationed in and around Folkestone which was to be their home for nigh on two years. Here they were employed on coast defence and became past masters at the art of erecting wire, digging trenches, siting pillboxes and then of re-erecting, re-digging and re-siting according to the whim of whichever Divisional General was currently responsible for the coastal defences! In March, the 14th moved to Shorncliffe and for a time both Battalions were attached, as part of their Brigade, to the 46th Division which contained the 16th Battalion. Numerous exercises, marches, weapon training and co-operation with the Home Guard made up their daily round, as it did that of all who were destined to serve in the Home Army.

In July of 1942, after more than a year on coast defence, both Battalions left the sea and marched to the Gravesend area, partly for a large scale exercise in which the troops of XIIth Corps fought the Canadians and partly to carry out a special course of training for the Kent Home Guard. This was a pleasant and welcome change, but it lasted for only a month, after which both Battalions returned once more to Folkestone. Thereafter they went their several ways. In September the 14th moved west to Paignton in Devon and the 17th north to Otley in Yorkshire where it joined 164 Brigade of the 55th Division with whom it remained for the rest of the war.

In January of 1943 the 14th left the West Country for Hornsea near Hull. By this time its officers and men were constantly changing as its more long standing members were posted to active service battalions and in their place intakes were received from various sources; sometimes these would be recent recruits from Primary Training Wings, sometimes specialists of four months' service from the I.T.C. Then, in June, the Battalion moved to Durham City. In July Colonel Appleby, who had formed it and commanded it ever since, was forced to give up his command on the grounds of ill health, to be succeeded by Lieutenant-Colonel C. W. Oxley—also of the Regiment but hitherto commanding the old 12th Battalion, now the Tyneside Scottish. In fact, however, the days of the Battalion as such were now numbered; and by the autumn it had ceased to be a field force battalion on conversion into a Rehabilitation Centre. This was a result of the demands on manpower required for active infantry battalions which the increasing pace of the war made necessary. The Battalion, which now bore little resemblance to what it had been, was required to receive men of low morale and poor physique, including repatriates and ex-prisoners of war, and put them through a course which would fit them once again for service in field force units. This involved not only medical examinations but physical and military tests to decide the jobs for which their medical category and military capabilities suited them. To this task the Battalion now devoted itself and, interrupted only by changes in personnel and location, so it continued until the war was over.

After joining 164 Brigade at Otley in September 1942, the 17th never remained in one place for more than about three months during the rest of its existence. Like the 14th, it too was constantly required to provide drafts of officers and men for overseas. In the space of a twelve-month it moved with the Brigade to Leven, Hessle near Hull, Wadebridge in Cornwall, Penzance and finally Seaford. At Hessle the Battalion was inspected by the G.O.C. Northern Command, General Eastwood; and during the course of his tour he expressed some doubt as to whether the Battalion's mortars could fire accurately their sandfilled practice bombs on to a given target. One man was heard, in a stage whisper, to wager two shillings it could be done. The General heard him; accepted the challenge; and paid up when the task was successfully performed!

When the Battalion moved to Wadebridge in December its role of a mobile counter-attack force for the defence of airfields involved its dispersal over eighty square miles. As the New

Year approached there were hopes that it might in 1943 have a more active role to play. In February it moved to Penzance with a detachment at Land's End and, as it was allotted a mobile operational role, was no longer required to carry out coast watching. But the hopes of something more active came to nothing and soon faded. A move to Perranporth on the north coast in the spring was frustrated by a storm which blew the camp away. Instead, in May, the Battalion packed its kit and departed for Seaford in Sussex. There it came under command of a new Brigade Commander—Brigadier H. E. F. Smythe—who had commanded 6 Brigade in India with the 2nd Battalion in it and whose grandfather had commanded the 68th Light Infantry in the Crimea. The summer months were occupied with a spate of training; but as summer gave away to autumn the Battalion received the sad and unexpected news that it was to be disbanded. Colonel Morkill in due course addressed the Battalion and what he said aptly sums up the purpose and the achievement not only of his own Battalion but also, in many respects, that of the 14th with which it had so much in common. "The man," he said, "responsible for the formation of some sixty new battalions in June 1940 was very far sighted. They were formed at a time when it was essential to transform the civil population into fighting men at the earliest possible moment. The Infantry Training Centres could not cope with the task nor could they give the men Battalion, Brigade and Divisional training or the Regimental spirit that exists only in a battalion. Many of these battalions have served their purpose. This one alone has sent some one hundred and ten officers and 1,200 men to fight overseas. The present distribution of manpower among so many different and varied arms, together with the call made by war industry, has made it impossible to maintain all these battalions with the necessary reinforcements. Some must go and this Battalion is amongst those selected." Disbandment was completed in September, and a further six hundred officers and men went overseas to join other battalions of the Regiment whose deeds have been recounted elsewhere in these pages.

The 15th Battalion has been mentioned last not because its role was any less important but because its story is somewhat different and in one respect unique. It was not a Dunkirk battalion. Before being designated the 15th Battalion on the 9th of October, 1940, it had been the 50th Holding Battalion stationed at West Hartlepool—where it comprised, for the most part, men of the Regiment who had completed their training at Brancepeth—and before that the 3rd Holding Battalion. At the time of its conversion its Commanding Officer was Lieutenant-Colonel E. T. Heslop, of the Regiment. Conversion to a field force unit, therefore, was comparatively easier than the task facing the 14th and 17th. On the 14th of October, 1940, it took over its first operational role—the defence of Hartlepool beaches—and occupied a frontage of approximately ten miles from Blackhall in the north to the River Tees in the south.

From March 1941 until November the Battalion formed part of 217 Brigade of the Durham and North Riding County Division. This involved a period of intensive training during which, for a time, it performed the duties of Demonstration Battalion at the Northern Command Company Commander's school. Then, in November, the County Divisions were broken up; some battalions were converted into anti-tank regiments, some into anti-aircraft regiments and some into army tank battalions. It was for one of the latter that the 15th Battalion learnt, with some pleasure, it had been selected.

Official connection with the Regiment was now in a sense suspended, but only in a sense. The Battalion's new title was the 155th Regiment, Royal Armoured Corps (15th D.L.I.); and for a while it retained the Regimental cap badge and did not adopt the black beret. On the 19th of November it moved to Haydon Bridge in Northumberland under command of 35 Army Tank Brigade and thereafter plunged into a spate of reorganisation and training for its new role. This involved a great deal of hard work, most of it entirely new. Everybody had to undergo a War Office intelligence test to find out if they were suited to the new specialist role, and as an army tank battalion was smaller than an infantry battalion a number of officers and men were not required and had to be posted away. Some, too, were replaced by others from the Royal Armoured Corps; but taken all in all most of the old 15th comprised the new Tank Regiment.

For the first six months officers amd men were continuously dispersed on courses in gunnery, wireless, maintenance and the like, and when these were completed Regimental courses began.

It was not until July that any sort of normality was reached and by then training was sufficient to allow the formation of two troops per squadron and for troop training to begin. On the 1st of July the field service cap was finally exchanged for the black beret and the regimental badge discarded. But the D.L.I. flash was still retained on battle dress. Colonel Heslop, who had remained as Commanding Officer, congratulated all ranks on their achievements and warned them of future training commitments and of the need to be ready for action as soon as possible. The Regiment still looked upon itself as part of the Durham Light Infantry and it is significant that practically every man of the original 15th was a member of the Regimental Association and over two hundred and fifty names were submitted on the 1st of July of men wishing to join it.

On the 17th of July the Regiment moved to Gunnerton under canvas. Soon afterwards it was on the move again, this time to Penrith, to the accompaniment of pouring rain and oceans of mud. There it remained long enough to become accustomed to Lake District weather, to rain and mud, to tents instead of huts and to a N.A.A.F.I. without cigarettes. Someone discovered that Penrith enjoyed the third highest rainfall in the world and quoted as authority the Times Atlas. Whether or not this was true, the camp remained a sea of mud and welcome indeed were the huts that began going up in the New Year. However, a storm in January 1943 sent 'B' Squadron for shelter to Hutton Hall, Hutton-in-the-Forest—a pleasant billet save that the Hall itself was reputed to be haunted. One trooper swore he saw the ghost, though less credulous opinion thought it was an owl. At all events the visitation was not repeated. So time passed; and with it came spring and drier and more pleasant weather; and the Regiment blossomed forth from the kindergarten stage of training into a fully fledged and trained unit. In the process it had changed and re-changed its armament from Matildas to Churchills, from Churchills to Canadian Rams, from Rams to Shermans and back full circle to Churchills again. What is more, it had learnt not only the normally accepted role of a tank regiment but also a completely new and untried conception of the use of tanks in battle. The tanks were in fact altered and modified by mounting upon them strange and mysterious devices which for the most part were destined never to be used in action and are still in consequence presumably on the " Top Secret " list.

Throughout that long winter and the following spring the Regiment changed and re-changed its main equipment and devoted itself to a form of training, in the worst possible weather conditions, which put the emphasis on work by night. Night work became the rule save for a very occasional movement by day. It was a hard and trying time for all ranks; but everybody was sustained in their efforts by the belief that they were destined to play a vital and important part in the invasion of Europe. Many visits were paid to the Regiment at this time by the C.I.G.S. and other senior officers who watched demonstrations of the unit's proposed unusual and peculiar role. Indeed the Prime Minister himself was no stranger to the Regiment. At last, in May, it joined the 79th Armoured Division and became part of 21st Army Group. Hopes ran high for the future; but unfortunately they remained only hopes and by the end of the summer the Regiment was still where it was at the start.

In August Colonel Heslop was promoted full Colonel and left the Regiment to take up a new appointment. " The Regiment as it is to-day," said the current edition of the Regimental Newsletter, " is more than anything else a thing of his creation. When it does go into action there will be no means of measuring what it owes to his training. Many other things too will be remembered, above all, perhaps, the way in which he infused into the heterogeneous mass which from time to time served under him the spirit of the Durham Light Infantry. That spirit, despite the diverse origin of many of the men now serving with the unit, is still the cement that binds us together."

That bond was never to be submitted to the final testing. 1944 saw the last hopes of active service dashed. In April 35 Army Tank Brigade, and with it the Regiment, was taken out of the 79th Division—and thus out of the 21st Army Group— and placed under command of G.H.Q. Home Forces. It was a bitter blow for all who had trained so hard for two years in the hope of taking part in the liberation of Europe. A faint hope, however, still remained, and the Brigadier himself came to explain to the Regiment how the Brigade was still to remain in existence, to be re-equipped with Churchill tanks and to train once more as a field force unit. But even this hope was short-lived. The relentless demand for reinforcements for units already serving abroad was too great. On the 25th of May some four hundred officers and men were posted away to other regiments. All that was left was a small cadre which, in its turn, despatched others overseas for active service. This was virtually the end of the Regiment as such; but it survived both in name and as an entity, rather like the 14th Battalion, as a training cadre for recruits who had completed their primary training elsewhere and for the rehabilitation of those who had been wounded in north-west Europe. From the north it moved south to Newmarket and there remained till the cease fire sounded and it became one of the casualties of peace.

2

THE HOME DEFENCE BATTALIONS

The Regiment raised two so-called Home Defence Battalions, the second being carved out of the first and, after a short life, being re-absorbed by it. The parent unit was known as the 13th Battalion soon after its birth, and the 30th by the time of its disbandment; but in its three and a half years' existence its name was changed so frequently and its functions and its composition were subject to such variations as to make it, in this respect, unique among all the battalions of the Regiment. If more space is given to it than to its offspring, at first known as the 2nd/13th and latterly as the 18th, this is because of its longer life and parental responsibilities!

The 13th (Home Defence) Battalion, the Durham Light Infantry began life early in 1939 as the Durham Group of National Defence Companies. These companies were composed for the most part of veterans from the first world war with an average age of between forty-five and fifty and usually of low medical category. They were formed to provide guards for certain vulnerable points such as dockyards, airfields, railway viaducts and ammunition depots; and as their members lived locally they could sleep at home. Armament was limited to a rifle and a bayonet and a minimum of ammunition.

On the outbreak of war the Durham Group was renamed 41 Group, N.D.C. It was commanded by Lieutenant-Colonel

J. E. Stafford. Its total strength at that time was eighteen officers and five hundred and forty-nine men. Towards the end of August—the 22nd to be exact—the code word " Allenby " was received from the Territorial Forces Association which, being interpreted, meant " Call out key men for N.D.C." Out they came and the Group found itself organised with Headquarters at Messrs. Liddell and Stafford's offices in Newcastle— this consisted of the Colonel and Major R. Boys-Stones, the second in command, but with no staff—and companies at Sunderland, Gateshead, Durham, Bishop Auckland and Stockton-on-Tees. The majority of officers had no uniform; and no clothing, arms, equipment or stores had been issued or were available at the respective company headquarters.

The vulnerable points which were to be guarded had only been seen by the Commanding Officer. The order to occupy them was received on the 24th of August, eight were manned by the 25th and on the 29th the Group suffered its first casualty when Private G. R. Milburn was killed by a train while on sentry duty at Croxdale Viaduct. However, between the 22nd of August and the declaration of war the Group had enlisted— no one was enlisted before mobilisation—clothed, armed, equipped and organised into some kind of military formation over six hundred men who had taken up guard duties and were being fed and accommodated on some seventeen vulnerable points. This was no mean achievement.

These early days of mobilisation produced their lighter moments. One works manager, arriving late at night, was stopped by the sentry who said to him, " If you put your other foot out of the car I'll blow your——head off." He did not see the inside of his works that night. At one of the viaducts a permanent way inspector had to crawl up to a sentry on hands and knees to present his credentials. At another a sentry in the night challenged and halted the inspecting officer in the approved manner and then bade him to " advance and be reconciled." But these were the days when first war soldiering was with difficulty remembered and with even more difficulty applied once more in the new emergency. The fact was, nevertheless, that the veterans fulfilled an important function and, what is more, established as perhaps young soldiers could not have done, the most friendly relations with workpeople and managements at the works and other areas which they had to guard.

In September 1940 the Battalion which in December 1939 had been re-named the 13th Battalion had its name changed again when it became the 1st/13th and gave birth to its offspring the 2nd/13th. It reverted to the designation 13th when, three months later, the 2nd/13th became the 18th Battalion.

The original National Defence Companies covered the whole of County Durham and later extended to Northumberland. Gradually their area of operations was moved southward until, in 1941, the Battalion's responsibilities extended from Middlesbrough along the Yorkshire Coast to south of Scarborough; and at the same time its role changed from protection of vulnerable points against sabotage to that of anti-raid troops at, in the main, radio stations covering the Yorkshire airfields. During the same period—actually in 1940—the Battalion played an important part in helping to form the Young Soldier Battalions of both the D.L.I. and the Royal Northumberland Fusiliers; for it had hitherto been the custom to post such young soldiers as there were to a special company in the Home Defence Battalions, and the 13th thus provided a nucleus of both officers and men for the 70th D.L.I. and the 70th Royal Northumberland Fusiliers.

Changes among officers and men were as frequent as were changes in name and, indeed, in operational role. As 1941 progressed the Battalion was gradually converted from a low category unit to a full field force establishment. The older men were posted away and their place taken by younger men of " A1 " physical standard. In November the Battalion changed its name once again, becoming the 30th Battalion; and early in the New Year Colonel Stafford resigned his command and Major Boys-Stones was promoted to take his place. The Battalion owed much to their C.O. He was the first member of the Battalion and for three years before the war, practically unaided, prepared the ground for the formation of the Group which gave the Battalion life. Since 1939 Colonel Stafford had welded the independent companies into a unit with a very real esprit de corps which was able to meet every demand made upon it. Colonel Boys-Stones, who succeeded him, remained in command until final disbandment a year later.

The New Year saw the Battalion completely transformed

into a field force unit with a mobile counter-attack role in case of invasion. This involved posting all low category men to the 30th Royal Northumberland Fusiliers and taking from them all their fully fit men in exchange. From June, when the reorganisation was complete, until October the Battalion devoted itself to training and adapting itself for its new duties. Then as suddenly as so many of the other changes had occurred came orders that the Battalion was to be disbanded because the growing pace of the war overseas was making an increasing demand for the expansion of other arms of the service than infantry. Thus ended the life of the Battalion. It could boast that from a unit of elderly veterans there had sprung a Battalion with an average age of twenty-six and of "A1" physique. Now its men were posted almost without exception to every arm of the service except the infantry; indeed the majority went to the artillery. The news of official disbandment reached them in the first week of October, but actual dispersal was not due until the 20th of November. Such a period of waiting is always a test of morale and discipline; and it speaks well for the Battalion that till the bitter end they continued to maintain both and that their turn-out and bearing during the last days were a credit to themselves and to the Regiment.

There is little to tell of the 18th Battalion. Its life was short. It was formed from men of the 13th towards the end of 1940 and came into being as the 2nd/13th. Its Commanding Officer was Lieutenant-Colonel W. F. Simpson, who had taken the 9th Battalion to France early in 1940. The Battalion fulfilled the purpose for which the 1st/13th had originally been formed—the guarding of vulnerable points and airfields—and throughout its existence was composed for the most part of First War veterans and low category national servicemen. It began life in County Durham, them moved to Lincolnshire, and finally returned northwards to be re-absorbed by the 30th Battalion in November 1941. Its trials and adversities, its joys and sorrows were the common experience of all such units carrying out an unspectacular yet vital duty; but its various companies were so scattered that it was never really possible to live the normal life of a battalion. Save for one brief year, therefore, the story of the 18th is virtually the story of the 13th; and those who served with the one in most cases served also with the other.

3

THE 70TH (YOUNG SOLDIER) BATTALION

Young Soldier volunteer battalions were not new to the Army when their formation became part of the programme of expansion initiated during the months after Dunkirk. Such battalions had been employed towards the end of the First World War with considerable success and the Regiment had one as part of the Rhine Army of 1919.

When it became accepted policy to reform the Young Soldier battalions in 1940 the age for the ordinary call-up was still twenty. But there were many young men, with little outlet for their patriotic enthusiasm, who welcomed the opportunity to join the Colours before they became of conscription age. The possibilities of this potential were enormous; and they were superbly well exploited. All volunteers were required to be "A1" physically; and there flocked into the newly formed battalions a great mixture of ardent young men from all walks of life and all classes of society; some from Public and Grammar Schools, some from factory and field, a few from corrective schools and a sprinkling who had been advised to enlist by the Police! Such material required the leadership of first class young officers, with a backing of first rate N.C.O.s. It was not easy for the field force battalions to spare such men, and in consequence battalions at the start often had to be content with aged subalterns from the First World War—some over sixty years old—and low medical category N.C.O.s whom other units did not require. In the case of some battalions, this nearly ruined what was otherwise a first class venture.

The Regiment was, however, fortunate. Its Young Soldier Battalion—designated, as were they all, the 70th—was formed during December 1940 from a cadre of some forty officers and men from the Depot at Brancepeth. Lieutenant-Colonel Hubert McBain, hitherto second in command to Colonel Hasted at the Depot, was appointed Commanding Officer; and it was to his drive and enthusiasm from the outset that the Battalion's later name and reputation owed so much. This small cadre set off in deep snow for the Battalion's new Headquarters. These were to be five miles north of Darlington at School Aycliffe, an establishment originally planned as a mental home for children by the Durham County Council, built at enormous cost and barely completed. It made an ideal barracks. Everything was foolproof! A week later three hundred Durham youths, who had been held for the Regiment by its sister battalion of the Royal Northumberland Fusiliers at Newcastle, marched into the new camp. It was an unforgettable sight; for, although some of them were little more than mere children, their fore and aft caps worn straight on the head, their rifles at the trail and their quick regimental pace showed them to be Durham Light Infantrymen to the core!

By the spring of 1941 the Battalion was brought up to full strength and was, indeed, beginning to post away its twenty year olds to active service battalions of the Regiment. Its own role was the guarding of aerodromes and its first commitment was the large Bomber Station just south-east of Darlington at Middleton St. George. The defences of this airfield were taken over by the first company in April 1941; and then and there was established with the Royal Air Force a close and happy partnership which was maintained to the end. Before the end of the year two further companies took over the aerodromes at Scorton and Forrest Farm, Catterick, where every type of weapon from " Blacker bombard " to " Armadillo " was taught and used. The fall of Crete had emphasised the importance of aerodrome defence against parachute attack: and the work these Young Soldiers were called upon to do was considered of vital importance.

By the turn of the year the Battalion had reached a high state of efficiency. Over one hundred of its men had gone to Officer Training Units and had received their commissions. A type of young officer, as well as some active and competent N.C.O.s, had joined it who set a high standard and example to the young men who served under them. As a unit composed entirely of volunteers, morale was naturally high, and all ranks indulged in both work and play with great enthusiasm. A platoon of A.T.S. was formed at Headquarters to take over domestic duties and it proved to be a useful acquisition, particularly as the Battalion was the only such battalion to have this kind of assistance. On the aerodromes the good work went on, and winter gave way to spring, and spring to summer.

With the changes of the seasons came changes for the Battalion. Early in 1942 the conscription age was lowered to eighteen and, as a result, it was apparent that the role of the Young Soldier battalions would soon be ended. With the formation, at about the same time, of the Royal Air Force Regiment for the protection of airfields, the need for soldiers on aerodrome defence began to disappear. So it was that one after another the Young Soldier battalions were disbanded. However, such was the standing and reputation of the 70th D.L.I. that for them there was a better fate in store. Instead of disbandment, they were specially selected to be the first demonstration battalion for the newly formed G.H.Q. Battle School at Barnard Castle.

This honour—for such it was—was received by the Battalion shortly after Colonel McBain, who had done so much to establish its reputation, had bade it farewell on returning to Brancepeth to take command of the Depot. He was succeeded by Lieutenant-Colonel Peter Jeffreys, of the Regiment, to whom fell the responsibility for organising the Battalion for its new role, its move to a new camp at Barnard Castle and the handing over of its commitments on the several aerodromes.

Officers and men had been involved on a number of occasions in rescuing R.A.F. crews from aircraft which had crashed on or near the airfields. One of these occurred just before the Battalion left for Barnard Castle, when a bomber crashed on the aerodrome at which 'A' Company was stationed. Second-Lieutenant J. Tate dashed into the wreckage and succeeded in rescuing the rear gunner, though flames and exploding ammunition unfortunately prevented the extrication of the rest of the crew. At the same time, Private J. Parry, wearing, as it happened, P.T. kit of shorts and vest, flung himself on to the protective wire to make a way for the R.A.F. rescue party to reach the scene. The incident was a fitting close to a year's good service on the airfields, which earned the Battalion high commendation from the Air Officer commanding Bomber Command.

The Battalion quickly settled into its fine, newly built camp at Barnard Castle, and set about learning the numerous battle drills and other exercises required for the various courses run by the School. After three months the Battalion reckoned it had fired more ammunition relatively than any other battalion of the Regiment, active service or otherwise: and its demonstrations had been visited by a very large proportion of the Generals and senior officers of the Home Army, including the Commander-in-Chief. On the 4th of December the Prime Minister, the Secretary for Air and the Minister of Labour were among those who came to watch. But during this latter part of the year the personnel of the Battalion was beginning to change as increasing numbers of officers and men were sent to the Regiment's active service battalions at home and overseas. In November Colonel Jeffreys himself said goodbye on being posted to command the 10th Battalion; but the Battalion was fortunate in having as his successor a third C.O. from the Regiment in Lieutenant-Colonel George Fillingham.

The Battalion now entered on the last lap of its existence. Its role remained unchanged until its disbandment in August 1943 nearly three years after its birth. The Battle School Demonstrations were accompanied by a rigorous training programme to fit all ranks for active operations when they joined, in due time, the ranks of the field army. Spare time activities included an impressive performance of Shakespeare's " Henry V ", first given upon St. George's Day 1943, and later repeated at the Assembly Rooms in Durham as part of the " Wings for Victory " celebrations of that city. On the 6th of June the Battalion received a visit from General Paget, the Commander-in-Chief, and the letter which he wrote to Colonel Fillingham afterwards was a fitting tribute to the state of the unit at this time. " I wish to thank you," he said, " for my visit to your Battalion because it was a real morale-raiser to see such esprit de corps and keenness. Also I wish to thank you and your Battalion for the important part you have played in the work of the School of Infantry. Thereby you have made a very direct contribution to the winning of the war." This work was now virtually complete. In July the Battalion said farewell to Barnard Castle and moved to a new camp at Tow Law above Brancepeth. On the day the move was made it carried out its final demonstration at the School of Infantry, a demonstration which, while a spectacular success as such, was marred by a most unfortunate accident in which Lieutenant John Pestridge was killed by artillery fire. He was only twenty and this was his first Battalion on being commissioned. "He gave us his best from the moment he joined," read the notice of his death in Battalion Orders. The Battalion paid tribute with full military honours when he was buried at Startforth Church.

Tow Law saw the final disbandment of the 70th D.L.I. On the 10th of August the bulk of the Battalion, comprising fourteen officers and four hundred men, began the journey to Sicily to join 151 Brigade. The War Office sent a special cable to the Brigade telling them the men of the 70th were on the way. At 2 p.m. the Battalion paraded in camp for a final address by the C.O. and then all those on draft were given a few hours' leave without restrictions and ordered to be back on parade at 8 p.m. for the final march to the station. At 8 p.m. every man was there, and to the strains of the Crookhall Colliery Band—provided at very short notice by the Durham Miners' Association—the Battalion marched past a saluting base which contained, amongst others, Colonel McBain and Mr. Sam Watson of the Durham Miners' Association. The men marched to the station, entered the waiting train and bade their final farewells. As the train drew out, the band played the Regimental hymn "Abide with Me." It was a moving scene and an apt finale to what was in effect the end of a unique battalion. To those who were left fell the sad task of clearing and winding up. Then they in their turn departed for the 10th, 11th, 14th and 17th Battalions. By the 14th of September 1943 the 70th Battalion was no more.

Relatively few of those who went overseas in fact reached battalions of the Regiment. No doubt the reasons for this were the so-called exigencies of the service! But one batch reached the 16th Battalion; and Colonel Preston wrote of them: "I have had some excellent young officers and men from the 70th Battalion and I am sure Fillingham would be pleased to hear that they fitted right into the Battalion and have done excellent work." Meanwhile, a further batch of one hundred and fifty joined the 6th Battalion, the Lincolnshire Regiment whose C.O. wrote to Colonel Fillingham as follows: " . . . I feel you should know how well they are doing. My officers and I have been most impressed by their smartness, efficiency and, above all, their enthusiasm. They are a splendid lot and I only hope you will send me some more. They all volunteer for any patrol that is going, and two of the N.C.O.s—Corporal Ward and Corporal Dent—have particularly distinguished themselves. The former, with three of his men, brought in a prisoner on their first patrol, and yesterday the latter stalked an enemy platoon position with two others and, at ten yards' range, having failed to get a somewhat idle sentry to surrender, shot him and withdrew under heavy fire. If we got drafts like this one every time, the war would soon be over." No battalion could ask for a better tribute.

4

THE DEPOT

The Depot is the home of the Regiment, but for sixty years the Durham Light Infantry had shared one with the Royal Northumberland Fusiliers at Fenham Barracks, Newcastle. The resultant union had been a happy one, but it had nevertheless always been the Regiment's wish and very natural desire to have a Depot in Durham County itself. Many efforts had been made at one time and another, and in 1922 Lord Boyne had offered Brancepeth Castle to the War Office expressly for that purpose; but the offer was declined on grounds of economy. It took a second world war to bring the Regiment back into County Durham and it was in September 1939 that the Durham Light Infantry Training Centre—as it was now called—moved lock, stock and barrel to Brancepeth Castle which had lain derelict for close on a quarter of a century.

Lieutenant-Colonel J. O. C. Hasted must be acclaimed the founder of Brancepeth as it is today. Called back from the Reserve at the outbreak of war, he commanded the greatly enlarged Training Centre from September 1939 until his tragic death in January 1942. It was largely his guiding genius and infectious enthusiasm which turned this ramshackle old castle into the modern military depot it soon became.

For the first month or so the greater part of the unit was housed in tents in the Castle grounds and, while the various training companies were turning the great inrush of recruits into soldiers, military engineers began transforming the Castle itself. Few seeing Brancepeth today can visualise the problem which faced Colonel Hasted and the staff of those early days when virtually everything needed to be done. There was no water, no light, no proper means of heating and it took over two years at the cost of some £50,000 to modernise the building that is so appreciated today. To Brancepeth's first commanding officer and his staff the Regiment owes a great debt of gratitude.

Towards the end of 1939 the training companies left the Castle grounds and moved into billets in the neighbouring villages of Willington, Meadowfield, Spennymoor, Esh Winning, Ushaw Moor, and, in the case of one company, Durham City itself. The first bleak winter of the war was one of unending toil not only in the training of large numbers of recruits against time but also in expanding and keeping up to date the permanent staff of officers and N.C.O.s. But the steady routine of quiet peacetime training was soon to be broken with the defeat of the armies in France and the evacuation at Dunkirk. Late one night in May 1940 orders were received to make reception arrangements for one of the divisions from Dunkirk. This meant arranging billets, food and clothing for some thousands of men until the divisional staff could take over once more. Although this did not last long, from that time onwards the pace of training quickened and many of the more conventional methods were set aside. Intakes of recruits came and went. They found themselves firing their rifles within a few days of joining. Mobile Columns were organised to deal with parachutists and to defend an area round Durham City in case of invasion. Assistance was given to the newly raised Home Guard and numerous exercises were held to practise these various roles. In this Colonel Hasted excelled. It was his one ambition to command an active service unit once more and though this was denied him the role cast upon the Training Centre in case of invasion gave adequate scope to do the next best thing. Few who served at Brancepeth during this hectic and exhilarating period will forget the sudden surprise " mobilisations "—at all hours of the night and day—which the Colonel would spring upon his large but mixed command! Not all ranks looked upon them with the same enthusiasm as the Commanding Officer. In the middle of one exercise the private in charge of the Regimental pigs—part of the " Grow More Food " campaign in which many Army units joined—was heard to say to an officer, " It's all very well these schemes; but the pigs 'as got to 'ave their swill. And anyhow I've got flat feet." And though " these schemes " certainly upset the carefully prepared training programmes, they doubtless gave to all recruits a taste of what they would be called upon to do once they joined an active service battalion.

The Regiment expanded fast during the summer and autumn of 1940. The 1st Battalion was with General Wavell's Army of the Nile and the 2nd re-forming on the east coast. Drafts had to be provided for them and for the newly formed 14th, 15th, 16th and 17th Battalions. Reinforcements were constantly in demand for the Durham Brigade in the West Country and for the 10th and 11th Battalions in Iceland. In all these cases Brancepeth tried to satisfy the never-ending wants of battalion commanders. By the end of the year a new and modern hutted camp had been completed half a mile south of the Castle and the companies on detachment moved in. Thereafter the Training Centre worked together as one unit, with Headquarters, of course, still in the Castle. The new camp, with its thousands of trees, shrubs and flowers planted at the time, was, and is, one of the most attractive military sites in England; and at the same time great improvements were to be noted in the Castle. A fine collection of heads, asked for and sent from all parts of the country, decorated the main rooms; a well equipped stage was erected in the main hall; while in the great courtyard peacocks, muscovy ducks and other wildfowl added an attraction not often seen in military stations. Now and then the Provost Sergeant was kept busy tracking down the occasional miscreant that wandered too far beyond the Castle gates; and on one occasion a company was turned out at short notice to recapture a valuable Chinese pheasant which suddenly and without warning flew over the Castle wall.

In August 1941 a great change came over the Depot. In order to release accommodation for the many newly formed Corps of the Army, infantry depots were required to double up, and in some cases two Regiments had to share one depot. It was indeed fortunate for the Regiment that their newly acquired home at Brancepeth did not have to be handed over. Instead, the Duke of Wellington's Regiment was displaced at Halifax by the fast expanding A.T.S. and was merged with the D.L.I. in a unit which was given the somewhat prosaic title of 4 I.T.C. Together the two Regiments remained until the war was over in what ultimately became a happy and successful union. Colonel Hasted retained command of the combined units, but only for a few months; and his sudden and untimely death early in the New Year was as unexpected as it was tragic. A man of great personality, ability and charm, he had provided the inspiration for the great constructive work of the past two years; and now his death seemed not only a tragedy for Brancepeth but a disaster for the Regiment.

For a few months in the New Year Lieutenant-Colonel Duncan Paton of the Duke of Wellington's Regiment took command; he had originally been C.O. of their Depot at Halifax. But in May of 1942 command passed to a Durham Light Infantryman once again when Hubert McBain, who had been second in command in 1940, took over the command which he was to retain for the rest of the war. Under him the joint depot settled down into a fine working team, and though the strong esprit de corps of both Regiments still occasionally followed the wrong channels—not unlike the old Coldstream Guardsman who said he would rather bayonet a Grenadier than a Boche any day!—there grew up a strong friendship and mutual regard between the Regiment and the Duke's which was able to meet all the demands for high quality team work necessitated by the increasingly exacting role of the later war years.

In July 1942 a new system of Primary Training was introduced into the Army. This meant that every man who joined up carried out six weeks basic elementary training which was common to every arm of the service; and while it was going on he went through a highly scientific mental and physical test to discover in what arm of the service—infantry, tanks, gunners—he could be most useful. He was then posted to that arm at the end of the six weeks. The system was thus devised to ensure that there were, as far as possible, no square pegs in round holes.

The Training Centre was therefore saddled with a triple role. It had to train men for the D.L.I., men for the Duke's and at the same time undertake the six weeks' basic training for the newly joined recruits. This resulted in an increase in the size of the unit to over 2,500 officers and men with a permanent staff of six hundred, of whom a third were A.T.S. who took over every conceivable job from cook to driver.

The new system worked well—indeed so well that by the spring of 1943 Brancepeth had such a reputation that it was selected by the War Office for an experiment, known as the Brancepeth experiment, for the improvement of infantry recruit training. For three months, under the supervision of Professor Stevenson of Oxford University—an expert in time and motion studies—a highly successful examination was made of basic and infantry recruit training; and the result was a new infantry recruit training syllabus which was adopted by the whole of the Army forthwith.

Amid all the technical problems of training Brancepeth still remained very much the Depot and home of the Regiment and its many battalions at home and beyond the seas. A Regimental News Letter was produced to keep all battalions in touch with each other's affairs—a document incidentally to which this chronicle owes much—and the Regimental Comforts Fund was kept busy with a host of varied demands from an altar cloth for the Padre of the Durham Brigade to small games that could be played in a slit trench in Normandy, not to mention the many hundreds of parcels for prisoners of war.

Meanwhile some twenty battalions of Home Guard and of the Army Cadet Force, all of whom wore the Regimental Badge, rightly turned to Brancepeth as their Depot and mother unit. Each week-end found their officers and N.C.O.s at the Castle for short courses of instruction, and these meetings helped to make the already strong ties between the County and its Regiment all the stronger. These ties were still more firmly strengthened when, in March 1944, a great parade was held on Palace Green in Durham City at which were present representative contingents from all parts of the Regiment. Here the Colonel of the Regiment, Colonel Claude Matthews, received from the hands of the Mayor " in perpetuity the right, title, privilege, honour and distinction of marching through the streets of our city of Durham and Framwellgate on all ceremonial occasions with bayonets fixed, colours flying and bands playing." A similar ceremony took place shortly afterwards in Sunderland, the town where the Regimental Depot originally started, when the Durham County Council presented a citation recording its appreciation of the Regiment's achievement during the war. The war, of course, still had a year to run—and indeed some of its most bitter actions were still to be fought—but thenceforward the Depot's role remained unchanged and its task of turning out soldiers to feed the Regiment's many battalions continued unabated. It continued to the last to fulfil what to many may seem a dull and pedestrian task but which in the building of an army is, and always will be, a vital and indispensable role in the service of Queen and country.

Postscript

THE tale is told. The War is over and past these seven years. Many of those who served with the Regiment in those stern yet glorious days have long put aside their uniforms. For a time in the years that followed the capitulation of the King's Enemies there were some who sought to weaken the Regimental system of the British Army. The reorganisation that followed the war, moreover, resulted in the abolition of each Regiment's second battalion: and for four years, from 1948 until 1952, the 2nd Durham Light Infantry was no more, consigned to the shades of suspended animation! In the new Territorial Army the famous Durham Brigade has been broken up. The 6th and 8th Battalions comprise respectively a part of 150 and 151 Brigades of a newly constituted 50th Division. The 9th Battalion, as the 17th Parachute Battalion, jumps from aeroplanes as part of a Territorial Airborne Division. The 10th and 11th Battalions—the old second line Territorial battalions—have never been re-formed.

Yet in these days of uneasy peace, and especially in the recently intensified drive to make the nation secure, the Regiment is playing its part in full measure. On the 16th of April 1952, at Barnard Castle, the 2nd Durham Light Infantry sprang to life once more to take its place by the side of the 1st and to give the Regiment once again two Regular battalions. By the time these lines are in print it will no doubt have crossed the Channel to become part of the British Army of the Rhine. On the 30th of July 1952 the 1st Battalion, after a short stay at Brancepeth after its return from Berlin on the 1st of June, embarked from Southampton on the way to Korea, there to join the British Commonwealth Division. At home the Territorial Battalions, still basically volunteers but slowly attaining full strength with intakes of men who have completed their two years' national service, are making their contribution to the consolidation of the Reserve Army. The Regimental stream is flowing as strongly as ever as all of them, in their several ways, strive faithfully to uphold the Regiment's name and traditions. Long may their silver bugles blow!

APPENDIX

The Allied Regiments

The Regiment is proud to be affiliated with three Regiments in the nations of the Commonwealth, two in New Zealand and one in Canada. The Canterbury Regiment of New Zealand was the first to be shown in the Army List as allied to the Durham Light Infantry in 1913 and the Winnipeg Light Infantry of Canada followed suit in the following year.

It is only fitting that in this story of the Regiment's war their doings should be mentioned too ; and if New Zealand receives pride of place, this is not merely because the ties with them are slightly older but because the Winnipeg Light Infantry was a Reserve Regiment and has no distinctive war history which can be recorded.

I

THE CANTERBURY REGIMENT AND THE NELSON-MARLBOROUGH-WEST COAST REGIMENT

It is not possible to record the activities of each individual Regiment for there is little to tell. Both Regiments were Territorial Regiments, but on the outbreak of war the Canterbury Regiment had six battalions embodied for home service and the Nelson-Marlborough-West Coast Regiment three. None saw any fighting as such, for none left New Zealand; but the Canterbury Regiment provided 'A' Company and the Nelson-Marlborough-West Coast Regiment 'C' Company in each of the 20th, 23rd and 26th Battalions of the 2nd New Zealand Expeditionary Force. The story of the two Regiments must, therefore, inevitably be the story of these battalions of which each Regiment's men formed an integral part; and when the time comes for battle honours to be awarded each Regiment will take the honours awarded to the three battalions.

The 20th Battalion was formed on the 5th of October 1939 under the command of Lieutenant-Colonel, now Major-General, Sir Howard Kippenberger, and was sent to Egypt where it arrived in February of the following year as part of 4 New Zealand Brigade. There it settled down to some hard training until April 1941, when it crossed over to Greece and saw some fighting in the campaign against the Germans there during which Sergeant J. D. Hinton won the Victoria Cross for his conduct in the fighting at Kalamata. It was a severe campaign, but not more so than that of the following month when the Battalion was heavily engaged in the defence of Crete. It fought two tough actions at Maleme and at Galatas, and when it returned to Egypt was only just over three hundred strong: but it could boast the proud distinction of having, in Lieutenant Upham, a second member of the Battalion as the winner of the Victoria Cross within the space of barely two months.

It was in Greece and Crete that the 23rd Battalion also saw its first active service. This Battalion, too, was formed at the end of 1939 at Canterbury and it became part of 5 New Zealand Brigade. Its officers, nearly all ex-Territorials or Reservists, reported to camp in November, the N.C.O.s in December, and the men—all volunteers—in January 1940. After its initial training was completed, the Battalion set sail in May, under the command of Lieutenant-Colonel A. S. Falconer, as part of the second echelon of the 2nd New Zealand Expeditionary Force. Destined for Egypt, it was, however, diverted to England when France fell and formed part of the island garrison until January 1941. Then it sailed once more for Egypt, to arrive just in time to move to Katerini in northern Greece which it reached on the 29th of March.

During the Greek campaign the Battalion was engaged only at Mount Olympus where it beat off several German attacks and sustained some fifty casualties. But the main fighting was to come in Crete where, like the 20th Battalion, it found itself in positions defending Maleme aerodrome. After a week of air raids, the German airborne attack was launched on the 20th of May and on that very morning the Battalion killed and counted four hundred parachutists dropped in its area. However, the Germans managed at long last to secure the aerodrome and the Battalion, with the rest of 5 New Zealand Brigade, had to fall back first to Platanias and then to the Galatas line. Here it fought its finest action of the war when, on the night of the 25th, two companies, led by two old tanks of the 3rd Hussars, recaptured the village of Galatas after very fierce hand-to-hand fighting. The same night, however, the Galatas line was abandoned and the Battalion withdrew to Canea. Then followed a gruelling withdrawal across Crete to Sphakia where, after having fought several minor actions en route, the three hundred surviving members of the Battalion were evacuated by the Royal Navy to Alexandria on the night of the 31st. For his part in this short campaign Sergeant A. C. Hulme won the Battalion's only Victoria Cross.

The 26th Battalion was formed last of all—in April 1940—under Lieutenant-Colonel J. R. Page and, as part of 6 New Zealand Brigade, reached Greece like its comrades of the 20th and 23rd. But it did not see much action; indeed, it spent far more time moving about than actually fighting; and when the order to evacuate Greece was given, it returned direct to Egypt.

After a period of rest and reorganisation all three Battalions saw some very hard fighting in the second Libyan campaign of 1941. The 20th Battalion—still under Colonel Kippenberger—fought three actions at Menastir in two days and another at Bir Chleta in which it took seven hundred and fifty German prisoners. Then, with the 18th Battalion, it stormed Belhamed Hill without artillery support on the night of the 25th of November and took its objectives against most determined resistance but with heavy casualties. During the same period, between the 23rd and 30th of November, the 26th Battalion fought a series of very severe actions round Sidi Rezegh; but on the 30th, considerably depleted, it was overrun by the 15th Panzer Division, Colonel Page was badly wounded and only a hundred and six officers and men returned to Egypt. Next day the 20th Battalion, reduced by then to nine officers and one hundred and eighty-six men, was attacked by forty tanks and five hundred infantrymen and completely overwhelmed after a bitter struggle lasting two hours. Only one man from the rifle companies survived. In contrast, the 23rd Battalion was comparatively fortunate, for though it fought several sharp and successful engagements around Capuzzo and Gazala, it lost only just over one hundred men.

All three Battalions were re-formed in Egypt and then sent to Syria. The nucleus of the 20th Battalion consisted of one hundred and twenty men of 'B' Echelon, together with the transport officer and the Padre. Lieutenant-Colonel Burrows succeeded to command. In the 26th Battalion Colonel Page's place was taken by Lieutenant-Colonel J. N. Peart. By June 1942 all three Battalions found themselves back in the desert and were soon in the thick of the fighting once again.

The melancholy story of the Eighth Army's retreat from Gazala and the fall of Tobruk has already been told elsewhere in this chronicle: and the New Zealand Division had come from Syria to help to stop the swift advance of Rommel's troops. On the 26th of June the Germans broke through to the north of the Division's positions at Mingar Qami, some twenty miles south of Mersa Matruh, by-passed them and then encircled and attacked them from three sides. Desperate fighting continued all day on the 27th and it seemed that the Division was doomed. Instead, however, it was decided to break out and the 20th Battalion, with the rest of 4 New Zealand Brigade, fixed bayonets and shortly after midnight moved due east across country to carve a passage through the enemy for itself and the divisional transport. For 1,000 yards no enemy was met: then firing broke out, the whole Brigade charged in line and, beneath the light of the moon, routed the Germans in what was, for the Battalion at any rate, some of the fiercest and bloodiest hand-to-hand fighting in its history. The rest of the Division, in which were the 23rd and 26th Battalions, struck south by circuitous routes and reorganised in fine fettle near the Alamein position some eighty miles away.

For the first fortnight of July General Auchinleck pressed a series of counter-attacks against Rommel's forces before the Alamein position. On the 14th of July the 20th Battalion took part in the capture of Ruweisat ridge, which entailed an advance of 10,000 yards without artillery support and an assault which, though successful, resulted in fifty per cent casualties. The three rifle companies engaged were destroyed by a heavy counter-attack on the following afternoon—an action described by Padre Spence, in a superb piece of understatement, as " a certain amount of liveliness in our sector." In it Upham, now a Captain, won a bar to his Victoria Cross though he was badly wounded and taken prisoner. As a result of this action the remnants of the Battalion were withdrawn to a Base Camp and saw no further action for a year. They had in fact fought their last action as infantry; for they were now selected to retrain as an armoured regiment.

The 23rd Battalion, too, played its part at Ruweisat, suffering over three hundred casualties and losing its C.O., Colonel Watson, as a prisoner: and the 26th Battalion, several days later, on the 21st of July, was engaged in the attack by 6 New Zealand Brigade on the El Mreir Depression in which other units were virtually lost but in which the Battalion managed successfully to extricate itself. When, early in September, Rommel had his final fling and tried to break the Alamein position at Alam Halfa, the Battalion took a notable share in his defeat, though it lost one whole company which was cut off and surrounded—the twelve unwounded survivors only surrendered when their ammunition ran out—and its C.O., Colonel Peart, who was, unhappily, killed.

The 23rd and 26th Battalions now experienced the lull which coincided with the preparations for the Battle of Alamein in October. The arrival of Generals Montgomery and Alexander, as has been already described, wrought a remarkable change in the conduct of the desert war; and from the moment that the assault on the Germans at Alamein was launched, the Eighth Army never looked back. Both Battalions were heavily engaged in the initial attack on the 23rd, taking all their objectives, though not without loss; and when, on the 4th of November, the German line finally cracked, both joined in the pursuit westwards towards Tunisia. The 26th Battalion was halted at Matruh, but the 23rd went on to participate in the almost successful attempt to cut off the Axis columns at El Agheila on the 16th of December and, next day, was in action against a German rearguard at Nofilia. From there they forged ahead past Tripoli, to be lightly engaged at Medenine before taking part in the march through the Matmata Hills which dealt the final blow to the Germans in the Mareth line. By this time the 26th Battalion had moved up once more; and, indeed, it, too, joined the sweep round the Germans' right flank at Mareth and distinguished itself in the attack and capture of a feature known as Point 201 which was the key to the successful breaching of the Tebaga gap a few days later. From then until the final surrender of the Axis in Tunisia both Battalions had their full share of the arduous pursuit culminating in the battle of

Enfidaville; and on the 19th of April the 23rd Battalion participated in the attack on Takrouna, a village perched on a sheer rock three hundred feet above the plain. Thereafter their duty in Africa was virtually done.

Mid-May saw the end of the war in Tunis. There was in effect no enemy left in North Africa and the New Zealand Division had now to leap across the sea. But not at once; for it was not till November that the 23rd and 26th Battalions, joined again by the 20th in its new armoured role, were in action once again with the Eighth Army on the River Sangro in Italy. All Battalions saw really hard fighting. The 20th on one occasion, near Orsogna, lost nearly half its tanks and its C.O. wounded; and the 23rd lost its C.O., Colonel Romans, who died of wounds, as well as some two hundred killed and wounded. In March of 1944 in the battles for Cassino a squadron of the 20th Battalion under Major P. Barton nearly reached the monastery in an exceptionally thrusting attack; and the wrecks of its tanks still lie on the top of Monte Cassino where they were knocked out. The 23rd spent a week in Cassino itself where it suffered over two hundred casualties; while the 26th, under Lieutenant-Colonel Richards, took part on the 15th of March in a memorable and successful assault on the railway station and the "Hummocks", though at heavy cost.

All three Battalions ended the war in Italy. With the 2nd New Zealand Division they saw it through to the bitter end. The advance to Florence, the winter campaign of 1944 on the Adriatic Coast and the breaking of the Gothic line—in all these they played their part, as well as in the final advances which ended in the capture of Trieste and the surrender of the German Armies in Italy. Then, with the job done, they passed into peaceful retirement and each was quietly disbanded during the latter months of 1945.

2

THE WINNIPEG LIGHT INFANTRY

Just before the outbreak of war—on the 26th of August to be exact—the Winnipeg Light Infantry was called out for guard duty in its role of a reserve regiment. A reserve regiment it remained throughout the war and, though it sent some fifteen officers and four hundred men to the Canadian Active Service Force, many of whom went overseas, it has as such no war history. It is perhaps interesting to note that at one stage of the war, when the Regiment sent a large draft to the 100th Canadian Militia Training Centre, one of the officers was Major Critchley who had served for eighteen years with the Durham Light Infantry and seen service with them in India.

On Wednesday the 25th of March, 1942, the Winnipeg Light Infantry was ordered to be brought up to strength as a rifle regiment for service overseas and in due course Lieutenant-Colonel H. F. Cotton was placed in command. In June it was sent to Vernon, British Columbia, where it trained under 19 Brigade until January 1943: but when that Brigade was disbanded in the following autumn it went to the Combined Operations School at Courtenay, British Columbia. After further training at various stations in British Columbia, it returned to Winnipeg in December 1944 and sailed for the United Kingdom on the 3rd of January, 1945. Unfortunately, it did not even then see active service as a Regiment; for ten days after landing it was disbanded to provide reinforcements for infantry units of the First Canadian Army. That was the end of its war, but, happily, in 1946, it was reorganised again and now flourishes.

Index

Abbeville, 35, 41
Achicourt, 27
Aci S. Filippo, 131, 132
Agedabia, 105
Agheila, 54, 105, 106
Ahmednagar, 162, 163, 182, 183, 193
Ain el Assal, 59
Ainley, Lieutenant Jock, 188
Akranes, 76
Akyab, 163, 165, 166, 167, 168
Alam Halfa, 340
Albert Canal, 270, 309
Alexander, General, 98, 159, 340
Alexandria, 53, 61, 69, 74, 97, 118, 219, 338
Aleppo, 60
Algiers, 134
Allen, Major Robert, 171, 175, 186
Amiens, 7, 254
Amriya, 219
Anderson, Major Willie, 289
Andrews, Sergeant Charles, 191
Annand, Second-Lieutenant Dickie, 14, 15
Antimachia, 210, 211, 212, 213, 215
Antwerp, 270, 306, 307
Appleby, Lieutenant-Colonel "Ambrose", 313, 315
Apsa, River, 152
Aradura Spur, 194
Arakan, 165, 182, 183, 184, 185, 195
Ardennes Offensive, 287, 303, 309
Arderne, Lieutenant-Colonel (later Brigadier) Eustace, 50, 51, 52, 56, 60, 68, 73, 225
Argentan, 250, 253
Armitage, Captain Frank, 216, 217
Arnhem, 280, 281, 282, 309
Arras, 6, 9, 24, 25, 28, 35, 36, 40, 254
Arromanches, 238, 306
Ashton, Captain Tony, 289
Athens, 156, 157, 158, 159
Atkinson, Captain (later Major) Reggie, 129, 270, 273, 277
Auchinleck, General, 84, 339
Avola, 119, 122

Baal, 283
Bailey, Captain Bill, 293
Bakenhoven, 288
Baker, Lieutenant, 189
Baldy, 134
Ballance, Major George, 138, 149

Ballantyne, Second-Lieutenant Bruce, 68
Balzanino Canal, 155
Bandel, 207
Bannerman, Major David, 136
Bardell, Lieutenant Terry, 168, 180
Bardia, 53, 54, 85
Barearse Spur, 148, 149
Barnard Castle, 2, 326, 327, 335
Barnett, Private, 230
Barry, Captain Milner, 216
Barton, Major P. 341
Bassum, 297
Battiscombe, Major Sammy, 27, 33, 86, 97, 99
Bayeux, 238, 241, 244, 262
Beak, Major-General, 73
  Brigadier, 107, 119
Beattie, Captain (later Major) Chris, 111, 271
Beart, Major Tim, 6, 26, 27, 82, 86
Beaumetz, 37, 39, 41, 42
Beaurains, 26, 27
Beauvais, 254
Beeringen, 270, 279, 280, 309
Beja, 139
Belgaum, 183
Belhamed Hill, 338
Bell, Corporal, 109
Bell, Lieutenant "Ding", 175
Belsen, 310, 311
Bemmel, 283
Benghazi, 54, 85, 105, 106
Benina, 106, 107
Benson, Captain Norman, 235
Bergues Canal, 32
Berles, 41, 42
Berlin, 299
Béthune, 18
Bewick, Lieutenant Quartermaster Tommy, 179
Birchenough, Second-Lieutenant (later Captain) "Beagle", 53, 214
Bir Chleta, 338
Bir Hacheim, 85, 86, 88, 89, 91
Bir Thalata, 93
Bizerta, 134, 135, 139, 142, 143
Blackett, Captain Rupert, 12, 16
Blenkinsop, Sergeant, 68
Blida, 142
Bloiry, 6
Blondous, 76, 79, 80
Boisleux-au-Mont, 25
Bologna, 225, 232, 234

INDEX

Bombay, 162, 163, 182, 183
Bonham, Lieutenant Charles, 13, 17
Borganes, 76
Borgo, 152, 153
Borken, 292, 293, 294
Bou Araba, 140, 141
Bourth, 254
Bowman, Corporal "Big", 205
Boys-Stones, Major R. 321, 322
Bramwell, Colonel John, 38
Brancepeth, 134, 285, 313, 317, 324, 331
Brancepeth Castle, 329, 330
Brancepeth Experiment, 333, 335
Brannagan, Company Sergeant-Major Matthew, 112, 127
Braveley, Lance-Corporal, 178
Breden, Corporal Arthur, 189, 190
"Breconshire," S.S., 71, 72
Brewis, Major James, 260
Bridlington, 161
Broadhead, Sergeant-Major George 138
Brown, Lieutenant-Colonel Jack, 183, 189, 193
Brown, Private James, 102
Brown, Sergeant, 267
Browne, Captain (later Major) "Topper", 67, 74, 214, 216, 220
Brussels, 255, 269, 270, 279, 306, 307, 308
Bulciano, 222
Buq Buq, 58, 105
Burkmar, Lieutenant Jack, 194
Burma, 21, 168, 182, 183, 184
Burrows, Lieutenant-Colonel, 339
Bush, Regimental-Sergeant-Major (later Lieutenant Quartermaster) John, 47, 213, 214

Caen, 250, 258, 263, 264, 265
Cairo, 118, 151
Calabritto, 148
Calais, 28, 43
Calcutta, 183, 207
Calderbrook, Lance-Corporal, 142
Calonnes-sur-Lys, 18, 19
Cambligneul, 40
Cambrai, 28, 36
Camino Massif, 148, 151
Camphin, 30
Canal du Nord, 36
Canea, 338
Canova River, 228, 229
Canterbury Regiment, 336
Cape Phoca, 210
Capua, 147
Capuzzo, 55, 56, 57, 338

Carinola, 147
Carr, Sergeant-Major Wally, 213
Carvin, 30, 31
Casa Oppio, 233
Casale, 147
Cassino, 148, 341
Casone, 233
Castel del Rio, 232
Castelrosso, 217
Catania, 123, 125, 131
Cesena, 153, 154, 223, 224, 225
Chamberlain, Captain Tim, 105
Chambers, Private Frank, 141
Chambois, 253, 254
Chapman, Captain Jimmy, 123
Chapman, Private Percy, 38
Cherbourg, 5
Chindwin, The, 184, 185, 196, 197, 199, 200
Chittagong, 163, 164, 167, 182
Churchill, Brigadier Jackie, 5, 7, 31, 33, 82
Churchill, Rt. Hon. Winston S., 80, 142, 327
"Clan Campbell," S.S., 71, 72
Clark, General Mark, 143
Clapton, Major Tommy, 243
Clarke, Major (later Lieutenant-Colonel) Andrew, 89, 91, 99, 118, 130, 131
Cole, Sir Ralph, Bart., 2
Collins, Lieutenant Russell, 146
Conca, River, 152, 153
Condé-sur-Seulles, 241, 243
Condé-sur-Noireau, 250, 251, 253
Corap, General, 24
Cooke, Lieutenant Brian, 176
Corpo di Cava, 144, 145
Cos, Island of, 209, 213, 214, 215
Cosina, River, 155
Cotton, Lieutenant-Colonel H. F., 342
Courtenay, British Columbia, 342
Cousens, Major Johnny, 15, 17
Craig, Lieutenant John, 62
Cramsie, Major, 295
Crawford, Sergeant William, 113
Crawley, Private, 64
Cristot, 257, 258
Critchley, Major, 342
Croce, 223, 224
Croxdale Viaduct, 321
Curtis, General, 42
Cyprus, 83, 217, 218

Dabner, Private Thomas, 42
Dainville, 25, 26
Daly, Corporal, 109, 110
Darlington, Earl of, 2

INDEX

Delaney, Lieutenant, 256
Dempsey, General, 304
Dendre, River, 23
Dent, Corporal, 329
Dick, 149, 150
Diepholz, 297
Diest, 309
Dieteren, 287, 288, 289
Dilsen, 286
" Dilwara," S.S. 207
Dimapur, 183, 184, 185, 193
" D.I.S. Ridge," 192
Ditchburn, Lieutenant, 224
Dives, River, 265
Dixon, Captain, 7
Djebel Aboid, 139, 151
Djebel Romana, 118
Doenitz, Admiral, 299
Donbaik, 167, 168, 169, 170, 171, 172, 173, 176, 177, 178
Doornboom, 274, 275, 276
Douai, 9, 18, 24
Douglas, Corporal, 278
Dragone, 144
Dufton, Second-Lieutenant Ronald, 70
Duffy, Major Frank, 144
Duisans, 26, 27
Dunkirk, 31, 32, 34, 35, 42, 82, 161, 316, 330
Dunlop, Sergeant Bob, 189
Dunn, Sergeant Albert, 102
Dunn, Major Ted, 243
Durham City, 315, 333
Durham, Earl of, 2
Durham Light Infantry Training Centre, 329
Dyle, River, 10, 12, 23

Eardley-Wilmot, Captain Tony, 114
Easington, 307
Easingwold, 305
Eastwood, General, 315
Eden, Rt. Hon. Anthony, 142
Edinburgh, 313
E.D.E.S., 156
Edwards, Lance-Corporal, 267
Edwards, Private, 275
Eindhoven, 280
Eisenhower, General, 134, 143
E.L.A.S., 156, 157, 158, 159
El Adem, 66, 69, 85, 105
El Agheila, 85, 340
El Alamein, 94, 97, 98, 100, 106, 339, 340
Elbe, River, 292, 298
" Elbow, The," 174, 175
El Daba, 105
El Duda, 65, 66, 67

El Gobi, 85
El Hamma, 106, 108, 117
Ellison, Captain Robert, 261
Ellon, 244
El Mrassus, 92
El Mreir Depression, 340
Emieville, 264, 265
Ems, River, 295
Enfidaville, 118, 341
English, Captain (later Major) Ian, 104, 110, 111, 251
Escaut Canal, 18
Eski Kellek, 84
Etherington, Private, 90
Etherington, Sergeant-Major Miles, 138
Evans, Lieutenant Lloyd, 224
Exel, 309

Faenza, 155, 225, 228
Falaise, 250, 252, 253, 254, 270, 301, 302, 308
Falconer, Lieutenant-Colonel A. S., 337
Famagusta, 218
Fearon, Private George, 97
Feetham, Lieutenant-Colonel O. J., 307
Fenham Barracks, 329
Ferens, Major Mike, 90, 92, 93
Ferguson, Lieutenant, 222
Ferrara, 235
Ficheux, 38, 39, 41
Field, Captain Winston, 276, 280
Filey, 305
Fillingham, Lieutenant-Colonel George, 327, 328
Fisher, Corporal, 267
Fishwick, Sergeant, 216
Fiumicino, River, 153
Flanagan, Regimental-Sergeant-Major, 47, 67, 213, 218
Flamborough Head, 306
Flers, 253
Floridia, 123
Folkestone, 314
Fontenay, 258
Forli, 155, 225, 232
Forrest Farm, 325
Fort Maddalena, 55, 89, 92
Foul Point, 165, 166, 167, 168
Fox-Davies, Major Harley, 55, 57
Freeman, Lieutenant James, 175
Friedenberg, Admiral, 299
Fruer, Lieutenant Mike, 147
" F.S.D. Ridge," 192, 193
Fuka, 96, 97, 105

Gabes, 117
Gafor, 140
Gaines, Regimental-Quartermaster-Sergeant Larry, 135

Galatas, 337, 338
Gamelin, General, 24
Gardner, Captain (later Major) Brian, 131, 252
Garigliano River, 148, 150
" Garrison Hill," 186, 192, 193, 198
Gazala, 84, 85, 86, 89, 338, 339
Geilenkirchen, 287
Gela, 122
Gemen, 294
Gemmano, 152, 153, 155
Geneifa, 218
Gerry, Private Roy, 224
Gheel, 271, 273, 274, 275, 276, 277, 278, 279, 280, 309
Givenchy, 29
Goldschmidt, Colonel G. T., 47, 49, 50
Gondecourt, 41
Gort, Lord, 30
Gothic Line, 151, 152, 153, 221, 228, 341
Goulden, Captain Charlie, 109
Goubellat, 140, 142
Grave, 280
Gray, Captain Jim, 68, 213, 224, 229, 330
Greece, 155, 156
Green, Private, 27
Green, Lieutenant-Colonel Arthur, 239, 248, 270, 273, 274, 283
Green Hill, 134, 139
Green, Sergeant, 267
Greenwell, Lieutenant Francis, 175, 192, 194
Gregson, Lieutenant John, 19
Griffin, Lieutenant-Colonel E. H. L. Lysaght, 46, 47
Grundy, Lieutenant " Solomon," 231
Guisborough, 305
Gunnerton, 318

Haalderen, 283
Hachana Ridge, 118
Haldern, 310
Halfaya Pass, 48, 54, 55, 56
Halliday, Lieutenant Ted, 298
Hamburg, 298, 299, 300, 304
Hamilton, Lieutenant-Colonel Denis, 265
Hampson, Lieutenant Philip, 87
Hanmer, Major (later Lieutenant-Colonel) Michael, 161, 255, 258, 259, 265, 283
Hanover, 312
Harburg, 298
Harker, Lieutenant Chris, 224
Hasted, Lieutenant-Colonel J. O. C., 324, 329, 330, 332

Hauteville, 39
Haydon Bridge, 317
Hazelrigg, Major Arthur, 222
Heinsberg, 287
Henin, 27
Herenthals, 271
Hermaville, 39
Heslop, Lieutenant-Colonel E. T., 317, 318, 319
Hessle, 315
Higginson, Private William, 113
Hill 600, 144
Hill 414, 152
Hill 449, 152, 153
Hill 500, 170
Hill 823, 170
Hill 566, 171
Hingen, 289, 290, 291
Hinton, Sergeant J. D., 337
Hittfeldt, 298
Hodgson, Major Mike, 224, 231
Hoggard, Lieutenant Kenneth, 259
Hogg, Sergeant Walter, 194
Holmes, Private, 229
Holmes, Captain Graham, 176
Hobkinson, Private William, 224
Hong Kong, 46
Horden, 307
Hornsea, 314
Hottot, 245, 249
Houghton, Corporal William, 181
Houle, Private, 33
Howard, Lieutenant Wally, 221
Howe, Captain Marcus, 226, 235
Htizwe, 177
Huddersfield, 161
Hudson, Captain, 129, 130
Hudson, Major John, 246
Hulme, Sergeant A. C., 338
Hungate, Captain Denis, 171
Hunter, Lance-Corporal James, 271
Hunter, Sergeant-Major Joseph, 148
Hunter's Bay, 168
Hunt's Gap, 139
Hutton, Captain (later Major) Bill, 13, 14, 16, 161, 171, 175
Hutton-in-the-Forest, 318
Hyde-Thompson, Second-Lieutenant John, 12, 16

Ibbenburen, 296, 297
Iceland, 75
Imphal, 184, 185, 192, 195, 196, 197
India, 161
Indin, 177, 178, 179, 180
Ineson, Sergeant-Major John, 251
Ingleton, Lieutenant, 297
Insayria, 209

INDEX 347

Iraq, 84
Irrawaddy, 201, 202, 203, 204, 206
Irvine, Major Charles d'Arcy, 246
"Island, The" 282, 284, 286, 309.

Jackman, Lieutenant A. F., 127
Jackson, Lieutenant-Colonel "Jake" 86, 110
Jeffreys, Lieutenant-Colonel Peter, 34, 82, 326, 327
Jefna, 134, 135
Jenn, Private, 267
Jennings, Regimental-Sergeant-Major "Spike", 83, 96
Jodoigne, 307
Johnston, Major Robin, 53
Josephine, 277, 280
Jotsoma, 194
Juvigny, 245

Kabo Weir, 202
Kaduma, 202
Kaladan Valley, 166, 177
Kalewa, 184
Kalamata, 337
Kanzauk Pass, 177
Kargiou, 215
Karnaphuli, River, 165
Katerini, 337
Keith, Captain Adrian, 56, 57, 68, 69
Kelly, Captain Phil, 171, 172, 176
Kelly, Captain Sean, 171, 173, 189, 190, 191, 197, 201, 204
Kemp, Sergeant-Major James, 33
Kharakvasla, Lake, 163
Killem Linde, 44
King, Lieutenant, 44
"Kingston," H.M.S., 71
Kinsel, General, 299
Kipling, Captain John, 38
Kippenberger, Lieutenant-Colonel (later Major-General) Sir Howard, 336, 338
Kirby, Major (later Lieutenant-Colonel) John, 71, 74, 212
Kirby, Captain Maurice, 85, 86, 103, 241, 248
Kirkuk, 84
Kirkup, Brigadier Philip, 5, 36, 42, 255
Knightsbridge, 85
Kohima, 184, 185, 186, 192, 194, 195, 196, 198
Korea, 335
Krom Beek, 290
Ksiba Ouest, 108, 109, 110, 113, 116

"Kuki's Piquet," 187, 188, 190, 193
Kyaukpandu, 177, 178, 179, 180

La Bassée, 18, 23, 25, 30, 44
Lambaguna, 180, 181
Lambton, Colonel John, 2
Lamone Valley, 228
La Murata, 148
Langrune, 308
La Panne, 44
La Riviére, 238
La Tombe, 10, 12
Lattre, 37, 39, 40
Laungchaung, 167
Lax, Lieutenant Brian, 138
Leather, Captain Mark, 214
Lees, Captain Robin, 57
Leese, General Sir Oliver, 151
Le Hamel, 238
Lens, 41, 308
Lentini, 123, 124
Le Plessis-Grimault, 251
Leven, 315
Lewis, Captain Peter, 112
Leybourne, Lieutenant-Colonel Angus, 4
Liddle, Second-Lieutenant Ben, 59
Lidwill, Major Bob, 112, 118, 127, 130, 239, 242, 243, 248, 251
Lightfoot, Regimental-Quartermaster-Sergeant Thomas, 91
Lille, 6, 7, 43
Lingèvres, 245, 246, 247
Lion-sur-Mer, 308
Loftos Kostello, 157, 158
Louvain, 307
Low, Major, 260
Lowe, Lieutenant-Colonel Harry, 47
Lowe, Corporal, 78
Lugo, 23 4
Lyster-Todd, Second-Lieutenant Hugh 161
Lyster-Todd, Major George, 179

Maas, River, 280, 287
Macartney, Major Sam, 290
Macaulay, Major, 229
Madonna el Monte, Monastery, 154
Maier, Captain Gerald, 251
Maleme, 337
Malines, 308
Malone, Sergeant Joseph, 35
Malta, 71
Malton, 305
Mandalay, 200, 201, 204, 205
Manipur, State of, 184

348 INDEX

Mareth Line, 106, 107, 116, 117, 139
Marienbaum, 310
Marley, Lieutenant-Colonel David, 39, 40, 41, 42, 44, 76, 78, 80, 305
" Marley Force," 43
Maroeuil, 27
Martel, General Sir Gifford, 7, 31
Martin, Major Arthur, 141
Maschen, 298
Mason, Lieutenant, 229
Mason, Major Oliver, 267
Mataguchi, General, 184
Mateur, 134
Mather, Lieutenant-Colonel Bill, 307
Matthews, Private George, 190
Mattison, Captain, 175
Matmata Hills, 106, 117, 340
Maungdaw, 165, 166, 167, 168, 180, 181
May, Captain (later Lieutenant-Colonel) " Crackers," 54, 56, 57, 218, 221, 222, 223, 227, 231, 232, 236
Mayu Pensinsular, 165, 166, 169, 177
Mayu, River, 165, 167, 177, 181
McArthur, Corporal, 260
McBain, Major (later Lieutenant-Colonel) Hubert, 6, 324, 326, 328, 332
McCleary, Corporal John, 173, 181
McGary, Sergeant, 226
McKeown, Private Terence, 181
McLane, Sergeant-Major Martin, 175
McLaren, Major (later Lieutenant-Colonel) Ross, 26, 28, 34
McMichael, Captain Bill, 261, 262
McNally, Lieutenant, 294
Medenine, 106, 340
Meikle, Second-Lieutenants Jack and Robert, 57
Meiktila, 51, 52, 205, 206
Mena, 218, 220
Menastir, 338
Menzies, Major Roy 224
Mersa Matruh, 47, 49, 50, 53, 54, 93, 94
Messina, 132
Mesum, 295, 296
Metcalf, Sergeant John, 70
Metcalfe, Company-Sergeant-Major, 13, 14, 20
Metforth, Private Harry, 57
Meteren, 43, 44
Metherington, Sergeant, 44
Mezidon, 265, 266
Michael, Private " Mike," 113
Middleton, Sergeant Joe, 276
Middleton St. George, 325
Milburn, Private G. R., 321
Milestone 86, 198, 199
Miller, Lieutenant-Colonel Harry, 4, 34

Mingaladon, 207
Mingar Qami, 339
Mitchell, Captain, 221
Moascar, 47, 70
Mogg, Major (later Lieutenant, Colonel) John, 247, 252, 290, 294 295, 297
Monastery Hill, 148
Mondaino, 152
Monkey 16, 169
Monkey 24, 169
Monopoles, 136, 137
Monte Camino, 148
Monte Croce, 147
Mont de la Vigne, 266, 268
Monte di Amica, 144
Monte Farneto 223
Montefiore, 155
Monte Grande, 232
Monteleone, 224
Monte Spaccato, 223
Monte Spaduro, 232, 233
Montfort, 289
Montgomery, General (later Field-Marshal), 98, 99, 106, 117, 237, 268, 280, 299, 340
Montone River, 225, 227
Morant, Captain John, 146
Morkill, Lieutenant-Colonel H. B., 313, 316
Morley, Corporal, 257
Morrough-Bernard, Colonel, 133
Mortola, 148
Mountbatten, Lord Louis, 208
Mount Etna, 131
Mount Hermon, 59
Mount Olympus, 337
Mont Pinçon, 250
Murray, Colonel, 133
Myebon, 168
Myhinlut, 180
Myingyan, 207
Myttinge River, 205, 206

Naf River, 165, 168
Naples, 144, 145, 147, 151
Neder Rhine, River, 282, 309
Nelson-Marlborough-West Coast Regiment, 336
Neuville St. Vaast, 27
Newman, Captain Bert, 135
Ngatayaw, 203
Nicholson, Captain J. B., 261
Nijmegen, 280, 282 283, 284, 303, 309
Noble, Sergeant-Major Joseph, 206
Nofilia, 340

INDEX 349

Normandy, 237
"North Promontory", 174
Nuncq, 8, 35, 41

O'Conor, Captain Rory, 278
Odon, River, 308
Oldham, Lieutenant Quartermaster, 40
Oldman, Lieutenant-Colonel Hugh, 254
Orne, River, 238, 308
Ortona 220
Osnabruck, 310
Otley, 314, 315
Oued Zarga, 140
Ouerzi, 108, 111, 112, 113, 115
Ouerzi Est, 113, 114, 115
Ouerzi Ouest, 114, 115
Ourville, 250
Ovenden, Major Dick, 96, 116
Overyssche, 16, 17
Oxley, Lieutenant-Colonel C. W., 315

Paga, 201
Page, Regimental-Sergeant-Major Arthur, 96, 103
Page, Lieutenant-Colonel J. R., 338, 339
Paget, General, 327
Paignton, 314
Palazzola, 123
Pallister, Lieutenant Keith, 261
"Pampas" S.S., 71, 72
Parc de Boislande, 257, 258
Parker, Captain Dominic, 123
Parr, Padre George, 222, 231
Parry, Private J., 326
Paton Lieutenant-Colonel Duncan 332
Patras, 159
Peace, Captain Charles, 293
Pearson, Captain Oswald, 16, 161
Pearson, Platoon-Sergeant-Major, 20
Pearson, Lieutenant-Colonel Alastair, 126
Pearson, Captain Jack, 258
Peart, Lieutenant-Colonel J. N., 339, 340
Peckett, Private J., 157
Pegu, 207
Peking, 46
Penrith, 318
Penzance, 315, 316
Percy, Lieutenant-Colonel (later Brigadier) Jos, 34, 82, 92, 99, 100, 107
Pergola Ridge, 228
Péronne, 24

Perranporth, 306
Perugia, 220
Pesaro, 152
Pestridge, Lieutenant John, 327
Petit Vimy, 25, 28
Petre, General, 24
"Petreforce." 24, 40
Petriano, 152
Phaleron, 156, 157
Picquigny, 254
Pinkney, Platoon-Sergeant-Major George, 13
Pinyaing, 200
Piraeus, 157, 158
Pirie, Quartermaster-Sergeant Jock, 219
Pitt, Lieutenant (later Captain) Francis, 7, 95
Platanias, 337
Plemper, Sergeant-Major John, 137
"Plonk," 62, 65, 66, 70
Pluck, Sergeant Ernest, 224
Point 683, 149
Point 620, 149, 150
Point 430, 149, 150
Point 420, 149, 150
Point 251, 178, 179
Point 168, 229
Po Valley, 159, 160, 234
Pont du Fahs, 141
Poona, 182
Port Said, 119, 151
Posterholt, 291
Preston, Lieutenant-Colonel John, 139, 141, 145, 149, 150, 151, 328
Primosole Bridge, 123, 124
Pringle, Captain Bobby, 123
Prome, 207
Protano, Private, 243
Provin, 30

Qaderna, River, 235
Qartolo, 228
Qassassin, 53, 58, 70, 83
Quattara Depression, 99

Randall, Sergeant, 109, 110
Randall, Lieutenant, 112
Rangoon, 206, 207, 208
Rasmussen, Sergeant, 230
Rathedaung, 167, 177
Rauray, 257, 258, 259, 260, 262
Ravenna, 228
Reay, Lieutenant-Colonel, J. K., 305
Reed, Lieutenant John, 247

Reighton, 306
Reykjavik, 76, 79, 80
Reynolds, Lieutenant Tom, 141
Rhine, River, 280, 281, 292, 295, 297, 303, 304, 309
Rhodes, 209
Ridealgh, Captain Bill 274
Rice, Padre Dick, 161, 175, 195
Richards, Lieutenant-Colonel, 341
Richardson, Lieutenant, 111
Riley, Captain, 266
Rimini, 225
Ringsloot Canal, 32, 33, 34
Ritchie, General, 88
Robinson, Major Bill, 131
Robinson, Captain George, 38, 39
Robinson, Major (later Lieutenant Colonel) L. a B., 193, 199
Rochester, Company-Sergeant-Major, 260
Roer, River, 287, 291
Roermond, 287
Romans, Lieutenant Colonel, 341
Rome, 148, 151, 155, 220
Rome, Lieutenant Pat, 179, 189, 201
Rolland, Lieutenant John, 173
Rommel, Field-Marshal Erwin, 29, 54, 60, 85, 86, 87, 93, 97, 99, 105, 106, 339, 340
Roper, John, 70
Rose, Bandmaster Frank, 285
Rowe, Corporal, 262
Rubicon River, 222
Rudd, Second-Lieutenant J. W., 161
Rumble, Major, 288
Runstedt, General von, 28, 287, 303, 310
Ruweisat Ridge, 339, 340

St. Floris, 19
St. Joost, 289, 290, 291
St. Léger, 238, 242
St. Lô, 250, 265
St. Laurent, 238
St. Pierre, 242, 244
St. Pierre la Vieille, 251, 252, 256
St. Remy, 7
St. Venant, 18, 19, 20, 21
Salerno, 143, 144
San Clemente Ford, 233
Sandars, Lieutenant-Colonel "Jumbo" 255, 266
Sanderson, Major Keith, 266
San Giovanni, 221
Sangro, River 341
San Marino, Republic of 153
Savio, River, 154, 223, 225
Schilberg, 289, 291

School Aycliffe, 324
Scobie, General, 156
Scott, Sergeant, 176
Scott, Company-Sergeant-Major (later Regimental Sergeant-Major), 219,
Scorton, 325
Scriven, Corporal David, 128
Seaford, 315, 316
Seclin, 41
Sedgefield, 305
Sedjenane, 134, 135, 136, 137, 138, 139
Seggie, Lieutenant George, 278
Seine, River, 254, 265, 302, 303, 308
Selby, General, 51
Self, Sergeant George, 271, 274
Sell, Captain Harry, 29, 89, 90, 91
Senio, River, 228, 230
Senior, Brigadier Ronnie, 119, 242
Sensée, River, 25, 26
Serra Ridge, 152
Seulles, River, 244
Shanhaikwan, 46
Shepherd's Crook, 169, 173
Sherlaw, Lieutenant Ronnie, 144
Shipley, Captain Alan, 41, 44
Shorncliffe, 314
Shuttle, Captain Tony, 192
Shwebo, 202
Sicily, 119
Sidi Barani, 50, 51, 52, 69, 105
Sidi Rezegh, 66, 338
Sidi, Barka, 140, 141
Sievwright, Lieutenant George, 212
Sillaro Valley, 232
Sillaro, River, 234
Simeto River, 123
Simpson, Lieutenant-Colonel W. F., 4, 15, 17, 21, 34, 323
Simpson, Major Bobby, 6
Singleton, Lance-Corporal, 265
Sipadon Chaung, 201
Sittard, 286, 287
Skagastrond, 76, 78
Slight, Major Campbell, 92, 93
Slee, Lieutenant Bill, 289
Slim, General, 199
Sogliano, 222, 223, 225
Soignies, Forest of, 16, 17
Solarino, 123, 125
Somme, River, 254, 303
Sommervieu, 241
Sollum, 49, 54, 55, 85
Sortino, 123, 124
"South Promontory", 174
Southey, Lieutenant-Colonel C. A., 199, 202
Smythe, Brigadier H. E. F., 316
Spence, Padre, 339
Spencer, Lance-Corporal, 190
Sphakia, 338

INDEX 351

Stadtlohn, 294, 295
Stafford, Captain Jack, 64, 214
Stafford, Lieutenant-Colonel J. E., 321, 322
Steelen, 271, 274, 279
Steil, 289, 291
Stevenson, Lance-Sergeant, 176
Stewart, Sergeant Obadiah, 64
Stilwell, General, 184
Stobart, Major (later Lieutenant-Colonel) George, 161, 162, 163
Stock, Captain Roger, 176, 189
Stockton, Lieutenant Peter, 190
Stokell, Lance-Corporal, 190
Stokt, 274, 275
Storey, Major J., 301
Suddes, Sergeant-Major Robert, 173
Suez, 47
Sugar 4, 169, 171, 174, 175, 176
Sugar 5, 169, 171, 174, 175, 176
Sugarloaf, 134, 135
Sunderland, 333
" Supercharge," Operation, 100
Susteren, 288, 289
Swinburne, Lieutenant-Colonel, 38
Symes, Private John, 60
Syria, 58

Takrouna, 341
" Talma," S.S., 47
Taormina, 132
Taranto, 220
Tate, Lieutenant J., 326
Taylor, Major John, 221, 232
Taylor, Lieutenant, 296
Teano, River, 147
Tebaga Gap, 340
Temara, 139
Temple, Private Oswald, 64
" Terrace Hill," 186
Terrell, Major Stephen, 294, 298
Tessel-Bretteville, 242, 244
Thélus, 36, 39, 41
Theobalds, Major (later Lieutenant-Colonel) Jack, 162, 163, 175, 176, 179, 180, 183
Thetkegyin, 200
Thomas, Lieutenant Cliff, 266
Thomasson, Regimental-Sergeant-Major, 146
Thompson, Corporal, 13
Thomson, Captain, 283
Thornley, Lieutenant 229
Thornton Sergeant-Major Leslie, 147
Thorogood, Lance-Corporal Peter, 221
Thorpe, Captain John, 212, 213
Tiber Valley, 220
Tiddim, 185

Tientsin, 46
Tilly, 245, 248, 249, 257, 258, 262, 264
Tobruk, 49, 53, 54, 60, 61, 65, 69, 85, 86, 93, 105, 106, 339
Tournai, 17
Tow Law, 327, 328
Towns, Second-Lieutenant Harry, 65
Townsend, Private, 260
Tripoli, 105, 106
Trun, 252
Tubbs, Captain Frank, 13, 16
Tunis, 118, 134, 140, 142
Turnbull, Sergeant Thomas, 175, 176
" Twin Knobs," 173, 176

Upham, Lieutenant (later Captain), 337, 339
Uso, River, 153

Vaux, Major (later Lieutenant-Colonel) Hugh, 62, 212, 214, 217, 218, 219, 221
Veghel, 280
Venafro, 220
Vernon. British Columbia, 342
Verrières, 245, 246, 247, 248
Vienna, 160
Vietri Defile, 144, 145
Villa, 152
" Ville d'Oran," M.V., 159
Villers-Bocage, 242, 244, 250
Vimy Ridge, 25, 29
Vizard, Captain Arthur, 139
Vloed Beek, 288, 289
Volturno, 145, 146

Waal, 280, 282
Wadebridge, 315
Wadi Akarit, 117, 118
Wadi Zigzaou, 107, 108, 113, 114, 117
Wakenshaw, Private Adam, 94, 95
Wales, Sergeant-Major Wilson, 141
Walker, Platoon-Sergeant-Major Frank, 13
Walker, Lieutenant, 228
Wallbanks, Lance-Sergeant Stanley, 243
Wallis, Lieutenant Bernard, 223
Walton, Private George, 38, 39
Walton, Brigadier, 248
Wancourt, 37, 38, 39

Ware, Lieutenant-Colonel Richard, 76, 80, 133, 139
Ward, Private, 190, 267
Ward, Corporal, 329
Warlus, 26, 28
"Warspite" H.M.S., 249
Waterhouse, Major (later Lieutenant-Colonel) "Tank," 187, 188, 189, 202
Watson, Major (later Lieutenant-Colonel) Bill, 90, 99, 101, 104, 116, 118, 120, 122, 123, 189, 239
Watson, Corporal, 233
Watson, Sam, 328
Watson, Colonel, 340
Watts, Sergeant-Major, 115
Wavell, General, 51, 331
Weert, 291, 292
Wesel, 292
West Hartlepool 307, 317
Weygand, General, 24
White, "Scotty," 109, 110
Whittaker, Colour-Sergeant Richard, 181
Wiehe, Lieutenant-Colonel Ivar, 161, 162
Wildeshausen, 297
Wilson, Lance-Corporal Edward, 35
Wilson, General Maitland, 51
Wilson, Lieutenant Martin, 173, 177, 189
Wingate, General, 195
Winkelom, 274
Winnipeg Light Infantry, 342
Woking, 4

Wolz, General, 299
Wood, Captain (later Major) George, 33, 115, 239, 248, 273, 274, 276, 278
Wood, Colour-Sergeant George, 181
Wood, Private, 190
Wood, Major Ken, 273, 276
Woodhead, Corporal, 258
Woods, Lieutenant-Colonel Humphrey, 239, 247
Worrall, Major Dennis, 139, 145, 151, 154
Worrall, Major Teddy, 102, 109, 110, 111
Wright, Lance-Corporal, 65

Xanten, 304

Yate, Lieutenant-Colonel Victor, 6, 82, 86
Yeu, 202
Ypres, 30, 31

Zarat Sudest, 114, 115
Zollaro, 152

www.ingramcontent.com/pod-product-compliance
Lightning Source LLC
Chambersburg PA
CBHW021828220426
43663CB00005B/166